My *Italian*
Adventures

My *Italian* *Adventures*

AN ENGLISH GIRL AT WAR 1943-47

Lucy de Burgh

Front and back cover images: Author's collection.

First published 2013

The History Press
The Mill, Brimscombe Port
Stroud, Gloucestershire, GL5 2QG
www.thehistorypress.co.uk

British Library Cataloguing in Publication Data.
A catalogue record for this book is available from the British Library.

ISBN 978 0 7524 9965 9

Typesetting and origination by The History Press
Printed in Great Britain

Contents

The Monte San Martino Trust

*I*n September 1943, after Italy signed an armistice, tens of thousands of Allied prisoners of war sought to make good their opportunity to escape from captivity and recapture by the Germans.

The author of this book, Lucy de Burgh (*née* Addey), has donated her royalties to the Monte San Martino Trust, a charity established to commemorate the bravery of those Italians who assisted the fugitives.

Lucy Addey was the intelligence officer in the Allied Screening Commission, which investigated the fate of those fugitives after the Allied invasion of Italy. She later married its commanding officer, who had himself been helped following his own escape from Fontanellato Camp, near Parma. Their admiration for the Italians whom the Trust seeks to remember is recorded in this book.

The Monte San Martino Trust is named after a small village in the Marche region of Italy, as a tribute to the villagers, who were amongst the first to help the founder of the organisation, Keith Killby, and many others.

The Italians, many of them extremely poor farmers, shared what little food they had, provided clothing and shelter, and generally did what they could to help the escapers on their way. In doing so, they risked imprisonment and the loss of their property. Many even paid with their lives.

Every summer, the Trust brings twenty young Italians to England for a month to learn English, in Oxford and London, and to experience the British way of life. The students come from the regions of Italy where escaping prisoners found refuge, and many of them come from families who themselves sheltered prisoners – and possess Alexander Certificates to prove it.

The Trust links the escapers, and their descendants, with the Italian families by organising fundraising events and commemorative trails in Italy. The Trust also has an archive of 100 POW manuscript diaries and books, an important source for historians of the period, and a priceless memorial to some very brave Italians, and their kindness to strangers.

My own father was also in Fontanellato Camp, and owed his own eventual safe return to the many families who sheltered him and, in particular, to two Italian partisans who died helping him cross the final mountain range.

The Trust (registered charity No.1113897) relies entirely on donations to carry out its work. If you would like further information, or if you would like to make a donation, please visit our website www.msmtrust.org.uk

Sir Nicholas Young
Chairman, Monte San Martino Trust
Chief Executive, The Red Cross
London, August 2012

Foreword

*M*any twenty-first century people who are not Italian merely have a vague notion of Mussolini's Italy during the war as a Fascist state that was a bungling accessory to Hitler's tyranny. In truth, as historians know, the principal victims of Mussolini's grotesque political and imperialistic pretensions were his own people. If he had preserved Italian neutrality in 1940, instead of plunging into the war in hopes of a share of Nazi booty, I believe that he might have sustained his dictatorship for many years in the same fashion as General Franco of Spain, who presided over more mass murders than the Duce, yet was eventually welcomed into membership of NATO. It is unlikely that Hitler would have invaded Italy merely because Mussolini clung to non-belligerent status; the country had nothing Nazi Germany valued. As it was, however, between 1940 and 1945 the catastrophic consequences of adherence to the Axis were visited upon Italy. What I mostly want to do here is to offer a brief narrative of what ordinary Italian people suffered in the war, especially in its last two years.

Italy's surrender in 1943 precipitated a mass migration of British POWs, set free from camps in the north to undertake treks down the Apennines towards the Allied lines. A defining characteristic of such odysseys, many of which lasted months, was the succour such men received. Peasant kindness was prompted by an instinctive human sympathy, rather than by any great ideological enthusiasm for the Allied cause, and it deeply moved its beneficiaries. The Germans punished civilians who assisted escapers by the destruction of their homes, and often by death. Yet sanctions proved ineffectual: thousands of British soldiers were sheltered by tens of thousands of Italian country folk whose courage and charity represented, I suggest, the noblest aspect of Italy's unhappy role in the war. A young Canadian soldier, Farley Mowat, arrived in the country with a contempt for its people. But he changed his mind after living among them. Mowat wrote home from a foxhole below Monte Cassino:

> …it turns out they're the ones who are really the salt of the earth. The ordinary folk, that is. They have to work so hard to stay alive it's a wonder they aren't as sour as green lemons, but instead they're full of fun and laughter. They're also tough as hell… They ought to hate our guts as much as Jerry's but the only ones I wouldn't trust are the priests and lawyers.

For many months even before Marshal Badoglio's government surrendered to the Allies, his fellow-countrymen saw themselves not as belligerents, but instead as helpless victims. The American-born writer Iris Origo, living in a *castello* in Tuscany with her Italian husband, wrote in her diary:

> It is… necessary to… realize how widespread is the conviction among Italians that the war was a calamity imposed upon them by German forces – in no sense the will of the Italian people, and therefore something for which they cannot be held responsible.

The Italians' overthrow of Mussolini and declaration of war on Germany in October 1943, far from bringing a cessation of bloodshed and freeing their country to embrace the Allies, exposed it to devastation at the hands of both warring armies. The view of many Italians about their nation's change of allegiance, and about the Germans, was expressed in a letter one man wrote two days later: 'I won't fight on their side – nor against them, although I think them disgusting.' Iris Origo noted: 'The great mass of Italians "*tira a campare*" – just rub along.' Emanuele Artom, a member of a Torinese Jewish intellectual resistance group, wrote:

> Half Italy is German, half is English and there is no longer an Italian Italy. There are those who have taken off their uniforms to flee the Germans; there are those who are worried about how they will support themselves; and finally there are those who announce that now is the moment of choice, to go to war against a new enemy.

Artom himself was captured, tortured and executed in the following year.

Nazi repression and fear of being deported to Germany for forced labour provoked a dramatic growth of partisan activity, especially in the north of Italy. Young men took to the mountains and pursued lives of semi-banditry: by the war's end, at least 150,000 Italians were under arms as guerrillas. Political divisions caused factional warfare in many areas, notably between Royalists and Communists. Some Fascists continued to fight alongside the Germans, while the Allies raised their own Italian units to reinforce the overstretched Anglo-American armies. Italians were united only in their desperate desire for all the belligerents to quit their shores.

Instead, their agony persisted and deepened. In June 1944, amid the euphoria of the Allied armies' advance on Rome, the commander-in-chief General Sir Harold Alexander made a gravely ill-judged radio broadcast appeal to Italy's partisans, calling on them to rise in arms against the Germans. Many communities consequently suffered savage repression, when the Allied breakthrough proved inconclusive. After the war, Italians compared Anglo-American incitement to a partisan revolt, followed by the subsequent abandonment of the population to retribution, with the Russians' failure to succour Warsaw during its equally disastrous Warsaw Rising in the autumn of 1944. The lesson was indeed the same: Allied commanders who promoted guerrilla warfare behind the Axis lines accepted a heavy moral responsibility for the horrors that followed.

The Germans, having previously regarded the Italians merely as feeble allies, now viewed them as traitors. An Italian officer, Lieutenant Pedro Ferreira, wrote: 'We are poor wretches, poor beings left to the mercy of events, without homeland, without law or sense of honour.' He was serving in Yugoslavia, where many of his comrades were shot by the Germans after the armistice. The Nazi General Albert Kesselring ruled Italy with a ruthlessness vividly documented in his order of 17 June 1944:

> The fight against the partisans must be conducted with all means at our disposal and with utmost severity. I will protect any commander who exceeds our usual restraint in the choice and severity of the methods he adopts against partisans. In this connection the principle holds good that a mistake in the choice of methods in executing one's orders is better than failure or neglect to act.

He added on 1 July: 'Wherever there is evidence of considerable numbers of partisan groups a proportion of the male population will be shot.'

The most notorious massacre of innocents was carried out at Hitler's behest, with Kesselring's endorsement, under the direction of Rome's Gestapo chief. On 23 March 1944, partisans attacked a marching column of German troops in the Via Rasella. Gunfire and explosives killed thirty-three Germans and ten civilians. In reprisal, Hitler demanded the deaths of ten Italians for each German. Next afternoon, 335 prisoners were taken from the Regina Coeli prison to the Ardeatine Caves. They were a random miscellany of actors, lawyers, doctors, shopkeepers, cabinet-makers, an opera singer and a priest. Some were communists, and seventy-five were Jews. Two hundred of them had been seized in the streets near the Via Rasella following the partisan attack, though none was involved in it. In batches of five, they were led into the caves, executed, the bodies left where they fell; the Germans used explosives to close a shaft in a half-hearted attempt to conceal the massacre. Still, the caves became a place of pilgrimage and tears.

There were a handful of survivors of another massacre, in the churchyard at Marzabotto, a picturesque little town at the foot of the Apennines, where in September 1944 Waffen-SS troops exacted a terrible revenge on the civilian population for local partisan activity and assistance given to Allied prisoners: 'All the children were killed in their mothers' arms,' wrote a woman who miraculously lived. Though herself badly hit, she lay motionless under the dead:

> Above and beside me were the bodies of my cousins and of my mother. I lay motionless all that night, through next day and the night following, in rain and a sea of blood. I almost stopped breathing.

At dawn on the second day, she and four other wounded women crawled out from beneath the heaped corpses. Of her own family, five had been killed. In all, 147 people died at the church, including the priests who had been officiating when the SS arrived; twenty-eight families were wiped out. At nearby Casolari a further 282 victims perished, including thirty-eight children and two nuns. The final local civilian toll was 1,830, and moved Mussolini to make a vain protest to Hitler. This was the sort of price many Italian communities paid for resisting Nazism, and which contributed heavily to the country's wartime civilian death toll of 153,000, three times that of Britain. Three-quarters of that number perished after the Italian armistice.

If the Allied invaders never matched the sort of horrors the Nazis inflicted on Italians, they were parties to lesser crimes: French colonial troops, especially, committed large-scale atrocities. 'Whenever they take a town or a village, a wholesale rape of the population takes place,' wrote a British NCO, Norman Lewis:

Recently all females in the villages of Patricia, Pofi, Supino and Morolo were violated. In Lenola… fifty women were raped, but – as these were not enough to go round – children and even old men were violated. Today I went to Santa Maria a Vico to see a girl said to have been driven insane as the result of an attack by a large party of Moors… She was unable to walk… At last one had faced the flesh-and-blood reality of the kind of horror that drove the whole female population of Macedonian villages two centuries ago to throw themselves from the cliffs rather than fall into the hands of the advancing Turks.

Such Allied excesses, matched by the effects of air and artillery bombardment through the long struggle up the peninsula, ensured that few Italians gained much joy from their 'deliverance'. Two soldiers of 4th Indian Division were chasing a chicken around a farmyard when a window of the adjoining house was thrown open: 'A woman's head appeared, and a totally unexpected English voice called out "**** off, and leave my ****ing 'ens alone. We don't need no liberation 'ere."'

The wild Italian countryside and hospitable customs of its inhabitants prompted desertions from the Allied armies on a scale greater than in any other theatre. The rear areas teemed with military fugitives, men 'on the trot' – overwhelmingly infantry because they recognised their own poor prospects of survival at the Front. Thirty thousand British deserters were estimated by some informed senior officers to be at liberty in Italy in 1944–45 – the equivalent of two divisions – and around half that number of Americans.

Both the Germans and Allies distributed broadsheets to the population, making competing demands for their aid. Iris Origo wrote:

The peasants read these leaflets with bewildered anxiety as to their own fate, and complete indifference (in most cases) to the main issue: *Che sara di noi*? – What will become of us? All that they want is peace – to get back to their land – and to save their sons. They live in a state of chronic uncertainty about what to expect from the arrival of soldiers of any nationality. They might bring food or massacre, liberation or pillage.

On the afternoon of 12 June 1944, Origo was in the garden of her *castello* rehearsing *Sleeping Beauty* with her resident complement of refugee children, when a party of heavily armed German troops descended from a truck.

Full of terror, she asked what they wanted, to receive a wholly unexpected answer:

> 'Please – wouldn't the children sing for us?' The children sang 'O Tannenbaum' and 'Stille Nacht' (which they learned last Christmas) – and tears come into the men's eyes. '*Die heimat – it takes us back to die Heimat!*' So they climb into their lorry and drive away.

Less than two weeks later, the area was occupied by French colonial troops. Here were the alleged liberators, yet Origo wrote bitterly:

> The Goums have completed what the Germans begun. They regard loot and rape as the just reward for battle, and have indulged freely in both. Not only girls and young women, but even an old woman of eighty has been raped. Such has been Val d'Orcia's first introduction to Allied rule – so long and so eagerly awaited!

Allied forces sustained a sluggish advance up the peninsula, but from the summer of 1944 onwards, it was a source of dismay to Alexander's soldiers that Mediterranean operations and sacrifices commanded diminishing attention at home. 'We are the D-Day dodgers in sunny Italee', they sang, in irony, 'always on the vino, always on the spree…'. So they were regarded by some foolish people, who knew nothing of the reality of the mud, blood and misery in which the rival armies, and the Italian people, existed for most of the war years, the condition of the civilians being rendered far worse in the last years of the war by desperate hunger, indeed in some cases starvation.

For Italians, hunger was a persistent reality from the moment the country became a battlefield in 1943: 'My father had no steady income,' recalled the daughter of a rich Rome publisher:

Our savings were spent, we were many in the house, including two brothers in hiding. I went with my father to the [public] soup kitchen because my mother was ashamed to do so. We made our own soup from broad bean skins. We had no olive oil… A flask of oil cost 2,000 lire when our entire house had cost only 70,000. We bought whatever was available on the black market, bartering with silver, sheets, embroidered linen. Silver was worth less than flour; even our daughters' dowries were exchanged for meat or eggs. Then in November with the cold weather we had to exchange goods for coal: the longest queues formed at the coal merchants. We carried the sacks back on our own, because it was better that no man showed his face [lest he should be conscripted for forced labour].

The Allies who were supposedly liberating Italy treated the country with remarkable callousness. In December 1944, when there was hunger verging upon starvation in Italy, a British Embassy official in Washington visited Assistant Secretary of War John J. McCloy to protest against the policy of shipping extravagant quantities of supplies to US forces overseas, while Italian civilians were in desperate straits. 'In order to win the war,' he demanded of McCloy, 'were we not imperilling the political and social fabric of European civilization on which the future peace of the world depended?' This drew from Mr McCloy the immediate rejoinder that:

It was in British interests to remember that, as a result of the complete change in the economic and financial position of the British Commonwealth which the war had brought about, we, in the UK, depended at least as much upon the US as we did upon Europe. Was it wise to risk losing the support of the US in seeking the support of Western Europe? This was what was involved.

The shocked British official persisted in pressing the case for feeding Europe's civilians. McCloy stuck to his guns, asserting that it would be fatal for Britain 'to argue that the war in the Pacific should be retarded in order that the civilian population of Europe should be fed'. The Foreign Office in London professed acute dismay on receiving the minute of this meeting, but British impotence in the face of US dominance remained a towering reality. That only a relatively small number of Italians died of starvation between 1943 and 1945 was due first, to the illicit diversion of vast quantities of American rations to the black market, and thereafter to the people – much to the private enrichment of some US service personnel; and to the political influence of Italian-Americans at home, which belatedly persuaded Washington of the case for averting mass starvation.

So there it is – just a few vignettes which I hope help to illustrate the nature of the tragic experience that the Italian people endured in the Second World War. It is because, as a historian, I know more than most people about the story, and about the noble part played by some of its humblest people, that I am so happy to support the work of the Monte San Martino Trust. It strives to keep alive an understanding of what we, the British, owed to many fine Italians; to show our recognition of that old debt of our fathers and grandfathers; and to renew the bond. It is sometimes said that in Britain, we remain in the twenty-first century too preoccupied, even obsessed, with the Second World War. But there are some aspects of the legacy that richly deserve to be kept alive, and indeed to be renewed, in the fashion that the Trust aspires to do.

Sir Max Hastings

1

Joining Up

When the war broke out, I was at university studying French and German. Of course I wanted to rush off and join up, like everyone else, but my father persuaded me to stay on and finish my course, saying I would be more useful to the country fully trained than with no diploma or certificate at my fingertips. I hope subsequent events proved him right. In any case, my military career would undoubtedly have taken a different course had I not finished my studies and rounded them off with an arduous secretarial training course.

So it was eventually at Christmas 1941 that I had to make up my mind what form of war work to take up. I had an interview with my principal, who told me in no uncertain terms that she considered that I should join up. I was still attracted by the idea, but other forms of war work were gradually evolving for girls, and I had an interview for an interesting job, dealing with the foreign, in particular the enemy, press. If I had taken that, I would probably have stayed in the university town for the duration, but my principal was quite annoyed when I asked her for a reference for it, saying she had already told me it was my duty to join up. What finally decided me to join the ATS (Women's Auxiliary Territorial Service), which I shall continue to call them, as the WRAC (Women's Royal Army Corps) did not come into being until my service was over, was the fact that people in the provincial town where my home was, in our immediate circle, seemed to think it was shocking. In those days, the ATS were still a bit of a novelty and wild stories were in circulation about their supposed immorality, their undisciplined form of life, their rough ways and toughness and so on. The thought of joining this apparently ill-conditioned crowd of reprobate young women appealed to me tremendously, and within a short time I had applied at the local recruiting office. I was told that as I spoke German I must write to a certain branch of the War Office, which I did.

In due course, forms arrived for me to fill in and eventually I was called for interview in London. I went up for the day, dressed plainly, but I hoped not frumpily, in a check tweed costume and brown hat to tone in. The Board consisted of about five men and two women, one of whom later asked me questions in German. I don't remember being asked if I played cricket, but if I was, then the answer was in the affirmative. Fortunately, the interviewers would have no chance of measuring my utter lack of skill before taking me in or throwing me out. I was told that if accepted I would do a basic preliminary training followed by an officer's training, and then be posted to whatever work was in store for me. I had not wanted to become an officer, at least not so quickly, but as I was apparently being interviewed for the Intelligence Service, and at that time the only women allowed into it were officers, so I would have to be commissioned. As I knew absolutely nothing about army life, this information really made a very small impression on me. As long as I joined up, I really did not care what happened.

That interview was in April 1942. After being told in a letter that I had been accepted, I waited until June for instructions to proceed somewhere to start my training. It was a beautiful summer and it was my last at our home in the town where we had always lived. We did not have many raids, so the time passed pleasantly enough, but I was anxious to be off and on the job.

Finally, when the posting instructions did come, on 20 June, I discovered that I was not to go to a preliminary training centre, but straight to an OCTU (Officer Cadet Training Unit) in Edinburgh. I was not worried about going straight to the OCTU until I got there and found a most terrifying array of sergeant majors, CQMSs (company quartermaster sergeants), sergeants and corporals there for the same purpose as I, all bursting with military zeal and efficiency, and wondering who on earth this stray civilian was who had clocked in with them and appeared to be trying to get herself kitted out in second-hand khaki. Fortunately, I had two companions in distress, like myself under the Army Officers' Emergency Reserve arrangement. They were also in civvies, but by the end of the second day we were as well dressed as possible in new, part-worn uniforms, and fresh khaki stockings. We found the shoes agonising on parade. Luckily, I had come in an old pair of brogues, which I substituted as often as possible for the cruel new 'shoes leather lacing brown ATS' or whatever they were listed as. Needless to say, we three peculiarities were not sorry when our ultra-efficient companions all had to strip off their badges of rank. From then on we were all just officer-cadets.

Of course for us civilians, the new girls, life was all very strange and trying, to say the least, though even the 'old soldiers' who were with us did not find the OCTU course a party. During the first week I felt I should never survive it, and that I should soon become a raving lunatic. Lectures, parades, PT (physical training), kit inspections – all followed in a dizzy succession. And one *dare* not be late for anything. This last was particularly gruelling for me, not long from the gentler and more casual ways of a university town, but by the end of the first week I was resigned. If I were flung out, then that would be that. There was nothing humanly possible I could do about it, so it was better bow to the inevitable, and meanwhile do my best and enjoy what I could, the latter of which was was almost everything. With the aid of this philosophy of resignation, and the practical help and guidance of Tim, my room-mate, I was able to carry on, and even when large-scale sackings occurred round about the fourth week of the course, I remained unperturbed. The idea of becoming a private, possibly in 'Ack-Ack,'* was beginning to appeal to

* Anti-Aircraft Artillery.

me. After all, what did I want with a commission? I wanted to begin at the bottom and work my way up like the others. Only the thought of my father's disappointment if I failed to come through clouded my horizon – for his sake I would gladly sacrifice romantic dreams of a gun-site and the company of hearty and tough he-men of the Bombardiers.

Here a word about Tim. She was a real brick if ever there was one. She taught me how to make my shoes shine, how to polish my buttons all four at once, how to barrack my bed, how to lay my kit out for inspection, how to put on my cap (that most uninspiring portion of feminine attire), exactly how and whom to salute, and a hundred-and-one other useful bits of knowledge, without which I should have found the whole course far more trying than I actually did. She cheered me up when I was in despair, and she sympathised with me when nothing seemed right: my hair was too long and wouldn't stay in its net, my skirt was too long, or my pockets were undone, etc., etc. She was a real pal and we had great fun in our tiny little room. Of course at first she was astonished to find herself sharing a room with a queer bod like me, but she soon swallowed her amazement and set to work to mould me into at least a fairly presentable cadet, who very soon after the first week forgot she had just stepped into OCTU off a passing bus, as it were, whereas everyone else had been travelling towards it for some considerable time.

In our off-time we went off into Edinburgh and ate large sumptuous teas at one of the comfortable restaurants along Princes Street, or just walked up and down, studying the different uniforms, and getting quite a lot of fun out of saluting all officers, male and female, including the Poles, who were there in force at that time. The first time I attempted to salute a male officer, I nearly slipped and fell backwards, being so nervous about the correct procedure. After that I was more careful of my ground before I ventured on saluting when in town.

As I had an aunt in Edinburgh, I was sometimes able to get away from the military atmosphere and have a change. But I never minded going back. Timmy and I always had some spicy bit of gossip, mostly about our instructors, to entertain each other with. In the evenings sometimes, I studied King's Regulations and ATS Regulations with diligence, though how much I was really able to absorb in such a short time is doubtful. I managed to read the whole of the ATS Regulations, but fortunately perhaps there was no time to read any other army handbook in full.

When our passing-out parade took place, the Princess Royal took the salute. I was very impressed by her charm, and her wonderful complexion and hair. Thank goodness she did not speak to me, as I should have been frozen stiff with terror and am sure would not have been able to utter a word. As it was, a major misfortune befell me that day. While we were standing at ease before the parade really began, a bird dropped on me, and it was with the utmost difficulty that I surreptitiously cleaned away the mess from a shoe and my tunic. For years I looked upon that as a hideous and horrible occurrence, and a long time afterwards when I at last had the courage to confide in someone about it, they laughed and said that on the contrary it was a sign of good luck and nothing to worry about. Otherwise I thoroughly enjoyed the passing-out parade, as it was particularly inspiring to march to the band of the Dragoon Guards.

These parades meant extensive preparatory training and the sergeant major was busy for days drilling and grooming us all in readiness for the great events. She was of medium height, impeccably smart, and as peppery as one would ever wish a female sergeant major to be. 'Swing those arms,' she would roar, 'they won't come off,' as we trudged, or goose-stepped, up and down the parade ground. And we swung our arms shoulder high, so that nearly all the muscles of our backs and shoulders were stiff and aching, and one almost longed for one's arms to drop off, to prove the RSM (regimental sergeant major) false, if nothing else. Her eagle eyes picked out in a second any irregularity in the line, a hair out of place, or too generous an application of lipstick. This latter she would order to be removed with a handkerchief. To me she was on a pedestal of military perfection – a sort of Goddess Diana of the ATS. And I could never see her without thinking anxiously of how much I had put in my tunic pockets, or whether my shoes might be down-at-heel or my hairnet too low on my collar. She made us conscious of our appearance and bearing to the last.

As may be imagined, after these harrowing times, I went home on my end-of-leave course feeling quite an old hand after such a concentrated baptism of fire. I travelled down by train at night, spending most of the time in the corridor. The train was packed, and soldiers were lying along the floors, or on the racks, and even in the cloakrooms. Needless to say, sleep was impossible, but as long as one is going on leave one does not worry about sleep.

We had approximately ten days' leave, which I spent mostly in ordering and being fitted for my uniform by our tailor at home. It was expensive, but they made it well and to fit, and today one of my barathea uniforms has been transformed into quite a smart black costume, trimmed with black corduroy, which testifies to the quality of the material. I had my greatcoat lined with red, as that seemed to be the fashion at OCTU, even though my family was of the opinion that it was too flashy.

During this leave I received my posting orders, to an 'unknown destination', and was told that I would be met at a certain station. It all sounded terribly cloak and dagger, especially the mysterious letters denoting the name of my future unit. This was it. My military career was to start.

2

My First Posting

I have no very clear recollection of arriving at my first unit, as a second subaltern, ATS. I was appalled and overwhelmed by the preponderance of men over women in the mess – something I was to get far more used to later on. I felt gawky and quite speechless and was exceedingly glad when nobody took much notice of me, although everyone I was introduced to was extremely kind and friendly. But I felt very much at the bottom of the form. I had two companions in distress with me, however, and I found myself sharing a room with one of them, a girl of about 34, very attractive, who soon acquired the nickname of 'Birdsnest' on account of her hair-style, which was swept up and attached with combs at the crown.

We all started work in the general office, and to my chagrin I found my work consisted mainly of copy-typing, not even translating. For this, older and more experienced girls were employed, all of course holding officer rank. As for my work, mostly typing stencils in German and English, it did not seem worthwhile being commissioned for, but I consoled myself with the fact that it was at least 'TOP SECRET'.

I soon made a friend of Jacqueline, who had been in the original FANYs (First Aid Nursing Yeomanry), and when that corps was divided into the so-called Free FANYs and ATS, had elected to join the ATS. We used to go for walks after dinner in the evening, along the peaceful country lanes, and she would tell me of her ambition to go overseas and also of her many admirers of the opposite sex, though at times she seemed herself to have an innate contempt for the men we came into daily contact with. She told me I should not stay 'stuck in the mud' at this secret address, c/o the GPO, for all the war, but should also try to get abroad.

I had only just joined up, and frankly the idea of going overseas had not yet suggested itself to me, but I wrote to my father, whose advice I always sought, and to my surprise he said it would be an excellent idea and urged me to apply without delay. But I dallied a little longer, and meanwhile Jacqueline went off, wearing an engagement ring on the fourth finger of each hand, and I missed her exhilarating company and robust sense of humour. I heard some months afterwards that she had gone out to a corresponding unit in Cairo, affiliated to ours, and had been the only woman on a large troopship. In those days, the convoys made an enormous detour across the Atlantic, and Jacqueline landed in Brazil, or touched there, and finally put in at Cape Town and Durban, completing the rest of the journey by train from South Africa. She told me that on Christmas Day 1942 she had been invited for a drink by every man on board, but as she was completely teetotal, had herself only drunk lemonade, having been able to play skilfully with the glasses and, unobserved, leave them untasted on the bar, so that she offended no-one. Needless to say, her drinks were not wasted.

Jacqueline had worked in a different office from mine, which she shared with one other girl and two men officers, and her place was taken by another ATS subaltern. I had occasionally assisted Jacqueline with the typing of her long reports in English, as we in the office were not always at top pressure, and likewise were sometimes able to give her successor a hand. She was called Roberta, and she also had applied for overseas service. When she too went off, it was not really unnatural that I should be chosen to take her place. This pleased me greatly, the office was smaller and I was away from the madding crowd. I had some very interesting indexing to do, which would have made me happier had it been of more use, but so much effort seemed to be put into what was little used. The worst of war is that you must always prepare for any eventuality, and so much spadework was necessary, and so I worked away on the index; indeed, to my intense gratification and that of the other people working on it too, it was sometimes used for important reports.

My new boss was an intellectual captain, very keen on his job, so much so that he used to ascertain whether the CO (Commanding Officer) was free to grant him an interview by peering through the keyhole of the door leading directly from the colonel's office to the main corridor of the block. Captain Heath was large and burly and the portion of his anatomy thus protruding caused quite an obstacle in the traffic up and down the passageway.

Our other male member was a Captain Smithers, affection-ately known as 'Auntie'. His chief claim to eccentricity was that he ate no lunch. While we were all digesting whatever RASC (Royal Army Service Corps) had provided, his poor inside would be painfully rumbling between 2 p.m. and 3 p.m. At three o'clock he broke his fast and allowed himself his sand-wiches, neatly packed in a tin each morning by his wife, for he was billeted at home. Occasionally, when a general's inspection was in the offing, Auntie had to retire to the office cupboard and demolish his sandwiches in hiding. His main meal of the day was in the evening and he then made up for his missing lunch. Sometimes he would invite us all to dinner, where we fed like Epicureans. He and his wife were experts in food and wine, and even in 1943 they were able to produce caviar.

But an even more happy memory is that of the delight-ful evenings we spent in the Smithers' large and attractive flat, forgetting the war for a time and discussing many interest-ing things, such as art and foreign travel, which one tended to forget in those gloomy days. Captain Heath and his wife also entertained us very kindly, and these excursions away from the mess made a very pleasant change from the customary routine of dinner, coffee, chores and bed.

Hilary, the other ATS officer, was a junior commander, with three pips. She was a strange, quiet and modest person, but we got on well together, though she hated and shunned social life, whereas I enjoyed it. After my initial shyness had worn off, I was beginning to find interest in the huge crowd, constantly changing, in the large inter-service mess in which we lived. Once a week or so, I went to the Other Ranks' (ORs) dances, and began to realise what very good dancers the soldiers were.

We had a company of ATs attached to us, and they did all the cooking, batting for the women officers and administrative clerking. Later on, as manpower became tighter and tighter, they also did batting for the male officers, but only after very specific rules had been laid down for their observance – and that of their officers. They were not allowed in the officers' quarters before 8 a.m. or after 8 p.m., etc., etc. My batwoman was a twin, or rather the two twins batted for our wing. To me they both looked exactly alike and I never could tell the difference, although people told me that one of them had false teeth and was therefore distinguishable from her sister. Anyway, they looked after us splendidly and were always bright and cheerful.

As regards the food, it was not at all bad, though I have felt positive nausea ever since at the sight of a bread-and-butter pudding, so often did the spare bread get used up in this way. One thing in connection with the food was the tinned milk – we had mostly tinned milk, some sweet, which took a lot of getting used to. When the unit qualified for a full time ATS messing officer, the catering improved. Funnily enough, I became very friendly with the messing officer and found that I had known her husband, then serving overseas, since childhood.

I had a small electric ring stove, on which I used to boil cocoa at night (I think we scrounged a little left-over milk). This was most comforting last thing, although it was forbidden to use electrical appliances. We even made marmalade out of one or two oranges – or even just orange peel – later on, after everyone was given individual rations of sugar. The girls made excellent cakes for afternoon tea, which we had in the mess, going back to the office afterwards. We appreciated that tea, which was most refreshing after poring over reports and papers all afternoon, especially in the hot summer. Something which grew in abundance locally was mushrooms, which could be gathered in the fields around our stately home. I had a nice boyfriend, who picked them for me and gave them to an ATS waitress before breakfast. I can still see her look of conspiratorial glee as she served me with the token mushrooms.

During my work at this time I met many interesting people, who in civvy street had done all sorts of different jobs. Most of them had travelled, some very extensively. There were among us a famous pianist, a conductor, a well-known actor, an outstanding psychiatrist, people who had been in business or the consular service, teachers, lawyers and people of other professions. The psychiatrist was held in awe by some, in scorn by others, but in general was universally liked, and quite well aware of the effect that his designation, belonging to the 'Army Psychiatric Corps', had on the most hard-bitten of officers. I always remember him at breakfast, which he invariably attended bright and early; he was very alert at all times, perhaps in contrast to everyone else, especially first thing in the morning. With a charming smile he would bend towards his next-door neighbour, or the man opposite, and enquire quite innocently and apropos of nothing, 'And what do *you* think of Beethoven?' Some people maintained that he was writing secret psychological analyses of us all, while others quoted him as saying that the only sane person in the whole unit was the transport officer. I just remember him making me earrings of cherries at a dance in summer 1943, but doubtless he had forgotten psychology on that occasion.

Christmas 1942, my first in the army, was wonderful. The officers served the troops at midday and had their own party in the evening. I remember washing up and scouring some of the most enormous pots and pans I had ever seen. It was tremendous fun, as was also the Christmas dance. We had a very good band, for talent was not lacking. Most of the soldiers were not afraid to dance with one if one wore pips on one's shoulders, thank goodness, or we might have had a pretty thin time. Our office cleaner used to make a point of dancing with all the ladies – in fact sometimes more than convention permitted. Sometimes his swarthy Celtic face with its shock of unruly black hair would appear at our office windows at the most unexpected moments, with a naughty look in his black gleaming eyes. His nickname was Sambo. We missed him when he went off to more active service, as a lot of our other ranks did as time wore on.

The girls lived in a compound away from the main building, mostly in Nissen huts. They were probably not too comfortable, but complained very little. At least they had good food, and enough of it, and they could never have lacked boyfriends.

During 1943 our American invasion began, and we soon had a great many Americans of different ranks and services attached to us. Some of them were still 'unassimilated', as one might say, i.e., they were still more European, of different countries, than actually American, with their own particular accents and mannerisms. But somehow they already bore a stamp that unmistakably marked them out as from the US.

In our office also we had a change. Hilary went away for health reasons, and I took over from her and was given one assistant, and then another. The second wore her hair in a swept-up style like my room-mate and became known, likewise affectionately, as 'Bath-Cap'. She had a double-barrelled name that took one right back to Killarney, or some such place, and was, I would say, an Irish rebel. She eventually succeeded me in the office.

Meanwhile, I had put in my application for a transfer overseas after Christmas 1942. It was not viewed with much favour and, I suspect, was shelved for some months. I submitted it three times in all, either written or verbally. On one occasion, the colonel told me I was a 'naughty girl' to wish to go overseas, but that did not deter me. My father kept on pressing me to be more active about it, but I had a horror of senior ranks and interviews with them, and I hated making a nuisance of myself – my parents did not realise that the commanding officer and the second-in-command were like the gods in Valhalla to a young, inexperienced and nervous second subaltern. But finally the index got me down, and as I was becoming increasingly interested in the administrative side of ATS work, I decided to try for a transfer to that, and asked to be sent on the admin course at Egham. Needless to say, my request was refused, but I think the powers-that-be were tiring of my applications, because a short time afterwards the colonel's personal assistant sent for me and told me that I had just half a minute to make my mind up: did I want to go abroad, to an unknown destination, at any moment, or not? It did not take me half a minute to form my decision. It was the chance I had been waiting for and it would also get me out of an awkward predicament in my personal affairs, which was on my mind and had to be disposed of somehow. This was not the first time that I felt there is a hand guiding one's human destiny. I felt instinctively that this opportunity must be grasped, come what may.

3

Wheels Within Wheels

*A*fter the first thrilling moment of decision, there was a wait of about a month or six weeks. I was gripped in an agony of suspense, but meanwhile the battle for Naples had taken place and the Allies were moving up the Garigliano.

Two other girls were on the same venture with me – one a nice junior commander, with whom I had been associating at work during the last few months, and the other girl married to an officer who had been with our unit. She had been brought up and educated in Italy, and was hoping to join her husband, or be near him, somewhere in the Mediterranean, where we all *hoped* to be going, though we had not the slightest information on which to base our hopes.

While I was doing my secretarial course, I had started learning Italian with a German philosopher who had spent several years in Rome. We had begun the highly entertaining reading of Boccaccio, until my omniscient parent got wind of it. He then decreed that either I gave up Boccaccio or I gave up Italian. That was how we came to embark on Dante, but I am afraid *The Divine Comedy* is still more or less a closed book to me. During the evenings, however, I had been continuing my lessons with a charming Italian lady in London. It was rather an effort to get to her, but well worthwhile, for the lessons were entertaining. I thought that perhaps one day a slight knowledge of the language might come in useful – you never could tell.

After the interim period was up, I was sent for one day and told that together with the other two ATS officers I was to go on an ATS intelligence course – I believe the first of its kind, so we were very privileged. On 11 March 1944 we three joined the train at King's Cross en route for Leicester. From there, we were transported in a troop carrier to an enormous, bleak and rather forbidding barracks on the edge of the city. There was a contingent of ATS stationed there, and among other things, they looked after our messing and quarters. The former was excellent – in fact some of us went away with expanded waistlines – but the quarters were not so comfortable, as it was bitingly cold. We were in old-fashioned billets, which were extremely chilly and draughty and only heated by coal fires, which had to be lit after lecture hours and did not really warm the rooms, even by the time we went to bed. In our lecture room, which was a Nissen hut, we had a petrol stove contraption of some kind, which at times gave out a smoke-screen that made one cough and puff. At other times it radiated a fairly friendly warmth, which enabled one at least to concentrate, wrapped up in battledress, jerseys, scarves, and sometimes greatcoats.

But if we suffered a little from cold, all that was compensated for by the extreme interest of the course, to a large extent due to the excellence of our instructors, who did everything they could to make the subjects interesting, easily understandable and varied. Of course some of it was difficult for us to grasp, and when it came to an appreciation, most of us floundered at least a little (I did a lot), but in the ten days allotted to us, we acquired a very comprehensive panorama of intelligence in most of its branches, and came away feeling much better informed than when we arrived. Our instructors also brightened our classes with a host of amusing anecdotes and personal and practical experience in field security work, such as the attempted capture of Rommel in the desert. Anyway, a good time was had by all, and we regretfully parted from Leicester, our sorrow somewhat mitigated by relief at leaving the cold, draughty billets.

We returned to our units, but not for more than a month at most, as we then had three weeks' embarkation leave, a more than generous allowance. This I spent almost entirely at home, and was very busy collecting an enormous store of articles that I had heard were in short supply, such as cosmetics, toothpaste, kirby grips, sewing materials, notepaper, certain medicines and ointments and Keatings flea powder. In fact I had something like a small scale NAAFI (Navy, Army and Air Force Institutes) in my tin trunk, which I purchased in London while at the ATS holding unit in Bayswater.

We were posted to the holding unit about the middle of April, and there we were instructed on what kit we would need, told to buy some, and were issued with other. Some of the girls had managed to procure wonderful gabardine costumes in London, or were in the process of doing so, but as gabardine was difficult to come by and very expensive, I decided to make do with the issue of khaki drill, which included a tunic, into which brass buttons were fitted.

We naturally met other officers, and girls, like us posted overseas, and of course we were all speculating as to where we were going, especially as we were later listed in different drafts. In the transit mess there must have been about fifty of us at that time, and the CO of the holding unit decided it would be a good thing for the officers awaiting their posting to do drill every morning after breakfast. So drill we did, some of us feeling rather foolish, not having drilled for so long. But the sergeant major was very kindly, and took us quite gently, so that no too terrible *faux pas* were performed for the delectation of Other Ranks passing by.

After our drill we were usually free for the rest of the day to assemble our kit, buy our trunks and camp kit, say our goodbyes, or meet our boyfriends. My mother came up for two days and we went to two theatres, one where we saw Noel Coward's *Arc de Triomphe* and the other a magnificent play about the war in Greece, the title of which was *There Shall Be No Night*.

The holding unit was situated in a delightful modern patch of Bayswater, and I believe luxury flats now stand where our mess was. We were in a quiet corner, so that there was space for drill without being much overlooked, and altogether there was a little hive of ATS life concentrated in that one small area. There were four or five of us in one bedroom, which was large and airy, and there was a constant *va-et-vient* and an air of suppressed excitement.

We were of course all medically examined, and by the only woman MO (medical officer) I have ever come into professional contact with. Any inoculations we had not already had were brought up to date, including vaccination. I was still awaiting tetanus injections, but of that more later.

One morning we were issued with our khaki drill from the 'Q' stores. This was quite a ceremony. Each of us got three drill skirts, a drill tunic and brass buttons and rings to fit in, two bush shirts, three tropical Aertex shirts, cellular vests and pants for hot climates, a large tin mug, water bottle, haversack and kitbag. We were also given two mess tins and a small white coarse linen bag for haversack rations. In addition, those without camp kit were issued with it while we were at the holding unit. This consisted of a large canvas valise, which rolled up, containing a camp-bed, three army blankets, a small hard pillow, a ground sheet and a canvas bucket. I inherited my father's brown carpet-style kitbag from the 1914–1918 war. This included a nice camp chair, which folded up very conveniently in two pieces, a canvas bath that I never used, another bucket and a kapok mattress to go on the bed, which I got new.* I also bought a black tin uniform case from a shop in Praed Street, where we were recommended to go to buy containers for our luggage. The tin trunk was invaluable, and still is. We were otherwise allowed two cabin suitcases and a small hand-grip. The latter I had in brown leather with a zip. In addition, when we eventually left, we had to carry on our backs our haversacks holding the mess tins and sandwich bags with haversack rations in them, our gas masks, helmets, water bottles, with our tin mugs attached to the inside strap of our haversacks; this

---

*   These were donated to the Military Medical Museum in 2001.

latter contraption made a cheerful jingling sound as we moved in our harness. It must have been a fine peep-show for any Other Ranks about when we were paraded and drilled in full regalia of haversacks, gas masks, helmets, water-bottles and tin mugs, sweating in our battledresses one afternoon in a late and hot April. The hour chosen for the parade was needless to say 1400 hours sharp.

The quartermaster was very kind and helpful. She made sure that we were issued with all the kit that we would need, come what may, and gave us advice on fitting it, and so on. In one thing she failed us. She said that all khaki drill would shrink tremendously and we must buy it at least three sizes too big. Our discipline was good enough to ensure that we did this, but later results proved that the shrinkage was nothing like enough to warrant buying drill three sizes too large. If the New Look had come in a few years earlier, things might have been easier. The quartermaster told us to mark *all* our luggage with white paint, in large capital letters, with our name, rank, number, service and draft letters. I painted these symbols boldly, clearly, but without much artistry on my trunk, my two suitcases, my kitbag with camp kit, and my ordinary blue kitbag, also on my small handbag, my camera, and my mug, as I was taking no chances. As it was, I put one letter too many on my kitbag, so that my surname ensued with three 'As' on it. My room-mate Iris painted her letters on neatly and beautifully. She was ultra-efficient, and her inscribing was finished long before most of us had begun to clean our fingers that were glutinous with paint. We assisted a major of the Royal Army Medical Corps (RAMC) to paint her inscriptions on when we had done our own, so the job cannot have lacked interest. There was plenty of time for it, but what a job erasing it after service days were over! My camera is still embossed with my name, number, rank and service.

Eventually the notice was put up giving marching instructions for our draft. We were to leave by lorry at 2300 hours for an unknown destination. Haversack rations were to be collected from the mess, all cabin and hand kit would go in the troop carrier with us. Our 'hold' baggage would be taken off earlier and we would very probably not even see it until we arrived at our destination. We all had to be in the mess for our evening meal that night, but I managed to slip out afterwards to say some goodbyes. It was of course a strict secret that we were leaving that night. There was an air of suspense everywhere. The draft-conducting officers were getting very busy, for several drafts of ATS Other Ranks were due to depart soon after we had left, and everyone was wondering where we would be in another twenty-four hours' time, and what the journey would be like.

The moment finally came to drag our baggage downstairs, don our harness, sling our ATS handbags over our shoulders, and accept the welcome help of a cheerful soldier driver, who hoisted us up one-by-one into the troop carrier. Getting into a troop carrier is a most awkward and undignified affair for anyone in a skirt, but most of us were already in trousers, khaki or otherwise, which proved to be a wise move as the night was to be cold and none too comfortable. So there we sat, all thirteen of us who had done the course, somewhat breathless and overheated but as keen as mustard and thrilled to the marrow.

4

To an Unknown Destination

*W*e did not travel for long in the troop carrier, but soon came to King's Cross Station, which was very ill-lit on account of the blackout. There we became lost in a man's world, something that more or less pervaded the whole of our time overseas. Military police, smart and business-like, were directing the traffic and also the personnel. It was not long before we discovered the officer commanding the troop-train, and were ensconced in a coach set apart for women travellers, about four of us to a carriage, so we were lucky. Besides ourselves, there were some Queen Alexandra nurses, some physiotherapists and some Free FANYs on the train; the total female population amounted to about forty. The rest of the train was full of men of different ranks and representing many regiments and services. But that of course one could not tell at a glance; it was only later that one came to know who was there and what they were.

Fortunately there was no air raid, not even an alarm, and we finally moved gently out of the station at about 1 a.m. We seemed to advance very slowly and most of us were too excited to sleep, but sat up chatting or munching chocolates or biscuits. Towards morning I dozed a little and woke up to find the train meandering through what seemed miles of storage yards and railway sidings. It was about 7 a.m. and a grey drizzly morning. After studying every possible hoarding minutely, we decided that we must be moving into Liverpool. This slow progress lasted some time, and included a certain amount of shunting to and fro, but we eventually came to a halt, within sight of the looming funnels of waiting ships. Everywhere seemed grey and rather depressing, but a cup of tea brightened the outlook, and from then on we craned out of the windows, eager to miss nothing that might take place.

It was about 9 a.m. that we were de-trained and, lugging our cases and grips, we clambered up the gangway of what seemed to me, after my experience of small channel steamers, an enormous ship. We were given breakfast shortly afterwards, and very welcome it was too. We then set about unpacking our affairs, trying on our lifebelts, and finding our way about. I was sharing a cabin with our junior commander, Wilhelmina Boswell, commonly known as Willy. She was the most senior woman on board and was quite soon nominated CO of the female section, including ATs, nurses, masseuses and FANYs. The FANYs did not greatly fancy an AT CO, and did not pay much attention to any arrangements made, so perhaps it is just as well that there were so few of us in proportion to the enormous number of men that 'the eye missed much of what went on and therefore not much was grieved after'. There must have been several thousand on board altogether, as other trains besides ours disgorged their mostly khaki-clad passengers into the ship.

The first thing to be impressed on us was naturally the importance of always having one's lifebelt with one, and learning to distinguish the alarms, and being prepared to abandon ship if that should, in the event of an enemy submarine attack, prove necessary. After that there were few rules and regulations, apart from the times for meals, fire precautions and such obvious matters.

I spent the first evening on deck talking to a major in the Tank Corps. We had not weighed anchor when I went to my cabin, but when I awoke we were at sea and the ship was heaving gently on a slight swell. Next day, Iris was not very happy, being almost the only bad sailor amongst us. Apart from her, we all enjoyed a hearty breakfast, particularly savouring the first white bread for many months.

We came into the Firth of Clyde at about three o'clock that afternoon, having left the blue Mountains of Mourne in the distance on our port side. I would not personally have known where we were, but there were quite a few people about who knew the landscape from pre-war days.

The Clyde is a most magnificent sight and I was thrilled to see it. It is perhaps something like a fjord, with coves, promontories and islands, and all the land was so green and fresh. There we were evidently to join our convoy, for until then we had been solo. But it was comforting to think that we should soon have the escort of destroyers, and perhaps submarines, for it was a large convoy of which we were to form part. Of course none of this information was given to us. It was gleaned and passed on, probably exaggerated and perhaps falsified, but circulated it most certainly was. We had our first boat-drill and felt rather foolish parading with a great cushion in front and behind. We knew where to go and what to do should the alarm be given. And we were seriously warned of the dangers of *ever* being without one's lifebelt. Gas masks, the *bête-noire* of uniform, now assumed a very secondary role.

We got ourselves orientated and installed on the ship. Willy and I were moved into a state cabin – a great privilege and accorded to her as CO Women. But it was more convenient, as it was necessary for her cabin to assume a certain official aspect and some business naturally had to be transacted there. I was sharing with her, and as we were already friends and had worked together, I became her adjutant (of sorts) and thus was fortunate enough to come in for the privilege of the state cabin, which was a sort of glorified bed-sitting room. The beds, *not* bunks, were of white oak, and there was a nice writing desk against one wall. There was also a carpet and two easy chairs, as well as an upright chair. Thus we really were in the lap of luxury, and as we were both good sailors and as fit as fiddles on board, our trip was an extremely pleasant one, and we endured none of the hardships of troopships; there certainly are compensations for belonging to the weaker sex.

We must have left the Clyde in the early hours of the following morning, for the next day we were again on the open sea with not a sign of land anywhere and only the distant outlines of the sister ships in our convoy. We had an escort, but it was very unobtrusive and I never saw a submarine, except at the cinema!

For the first two or three days it was grey and cold, but one could take plenty of exercise promenading on the deck. I believe our route went out well west into the Atlantic, so that we completely avoided Brittany and the north coast of Spain. But presently we must have veered south or south-east, for the weather began to warm up and the sun shone radiantly. There was a marked contrast between the grey, cloud-ridden sky of the north and the bright southern blue, which all of a sudden seemed to replace it.

The moment the weather became a trifle warmer we started PT on deck. The assorted female crowd did it on an upper deck under the instruction of a male warrant officer. He did not make it too arduous, and it was enjoyable, the only thing marring it being the audience of men who would finish their own exercises and then come to see how we were getting on. For that reason, enthusiasm slacked off in our ranks, but unfortunately this did not seem to deter our supporters.

A far more pleasant feature of our daily life was the dancing that took place on deck. All the girls were encouraged to take part and most of us did. We danced in the afternoons with the soldiers and in the evenings with the officers. The music was provided by a Guards band, which the ship was lucky enough to be transporting overseas. They played marvellously, and as well as providing dance music, also gave open-air concerts in the evenings.

Once in the south, of course, we spent practically all our time on deck, and khaki drill became the order of the day. Here it must be related that the quartermaster's prognostics about shrinkage proved entirely misleading. In spite of leaving our skirts and shirts in seawater for days, they scarcely shrank at all, and as a result we were obliged to wear long and distinctly dowdy skirts until it was possible to alter them. They were too long and also too wide, and in most cases had to be completely remade later on. The bush shirts were the same. So we managed with barathea skirts and tropical shirts, i.e., ordinary shirts with epaulettes and open attached collars, until the necessary alterations had been done. We spent some time sewing pips on our epaulettes, for it was actually forbidden to go without. Sunglasses, also, were now generally worn. As the climate became hotter, people began to speculate yet again as to our destination, and some of them asked Iris, fluent in Italian, if she would give them lessons in the language.

There was a NAAFI shop on the boat and the allowance of sweets and cigarettes was most generous. The sweets we positively guzzled, having been short of sugar for so long. The only drinks obtainable were soft ginger beer, lemonade and other soft drinks. Perhaps just as well.

The RAF Gang Show were among the passengers, and one night they gave an excellent performance. I especially remember a prophetic sort of scene, where two men returned from war-service, one who had been a wing commander and the other an ordinary airman. In private life, however, the wing commander was a butler and the airman his employer. They found it somewhat difficult to settle down to their old ways again, and the employer's wife was not a little puzzled when her husband would jump up as the butler entered the room and address him as 'Sir'.

Somehow we learned that we were to pass through the Straits of Gibraltar, and so there was great excitement. The blackout unfortunately prevented us from seeing anything of the Rock, but we could see the lights of Tangier on our right, twinkling merrily for some time, and a distant light or so on the Spanish coast. Probably few of the passengers knew exactly when we passed through the Straits, although many stayed up late that night in the hope of seeing something; it was said to be about midnight when we actually passed through.

A day or so after this we had an alarm and had to go to 'action stations' in the early hours of the morning. There were sounds of distant thuds and gunfire. A destroyer nearby was dropping depth charges. But we were saved, and not one ship in the convoy was hit. Of course one never heard exactly what happened, at least not if one was in our humble station, but I did hear later that the convoy succeeding ours had had a pasting and several ships were hit, and quite a few people had to take to the boats.

A day or so later we passed the Italian island of Pantelleria, leaving it on our port side. It looked wonderful in the evening light, a sheer, grey rock jutting up out of the sea, suffused in the cochineal-coloured rays of the setting sun.

Meanwhile we girls had managed to make quite a few friends on board, and were getting used to the sun and thoroughly enjoying life. When the ship entered the Mediterranean zone, all passengers were introduced to the consumption of mepacrine. This was no magic potion, but a yellow substance in the form of small pills, about the size of a half-grain luminal, of which we were ordered to take three a day. This was supposed to guarantee one against malaria. Many people did not take these, scorning them and sceptical of their efficacy, or on account of the peculiar effect they had. They seemed to affect people differently. On some they had the effect of alcohol, and poor Iris was one of these, as she quite lost her balance and in the end gave up the struggle. Other people felt giddy and had headaches, and yet others felt the effect of a good purge. Others still said that mepacrine made them feel sick. I continued to take them, as I was very prone to insect bites and had perhaps a blind faith in them as they were prescribed by the 'authorities'. After all, surely the War Office would not pay for such immense quantities of mepacrine, if they were not considered at the highest level to be of considerable value?

Before any mainland came into sight again, we were each issued with a small yellow booklet, giving us some history and general information about the Mediterranean zone, health precautions to be taken (including the use of mepacrine) and the sort of attitude the British troops were expected to adopt towards the civilian population of an occupied country. This was certainly a great step forward – now it only remained to land, and the rumour went round that we were going to Algiers. The powers that be, however, decreed differently, and it was on the evening of our ninth day at sea that we came within sight of land, by now being separated from the rest of the convoy who had vanished into the blue distance. It was a real Mediterranean evening, calm, with an impression of blueness that one never sees in our northerly clime. The sun was slowly setting and forming into a vast red ball in the west, whose reflections lit up the little red-roofed houses and the red sandstone cliffs of a smallish port with the glow of a crimson lantern. I was leaning over the bows of the ship talking to one of the MOs, whom I had discovered to be a family friend and from the same part of England as myself. And as our ship slowly slipped into port and passed the jetty of the harbour, we watched the changing crimson of the paling light as it gradually and imperceptibly merged to mauve and then violet, later to complete the spectrum from ultramarine to indigo. But by the time the stars were twinkling we were having our evening meal, and the gossip, of course, was circulating as to where we were.

It was not long before everyone on board knew that we had docked at Oran, and furthermore that unlike the rest of our convoy we were not to unload at Algiers, but here, the very next day, and were to complete the journey by train. Stories of transcontinental troop-trains did not bear any resemblance to the reputation of the once famous Orient Express, and faces became a trifle dubious. But time marched on, and the next morning at about ten o'clock we females found ourselves travelling in troop-carriers up the road from dock to station, and shortly afterwards were installed in carriages in a long troop-train – half a mile long, it seemed to me. The officers were very favoured, for they at least had carriages to travel in, even though not very comfortable ones, whereas the men had only cattle trucks. The ATs and other girls were still more favoured in being given the only First Class coach. In this way, the Army always behaved very decently towards us, and on every single journey I took we were always taken marvellous care of by CO troops, train-conducting officers and transit camp officers. Which all goes to prove that the Englishman has lost none of his traditional gallantry.

We were scheduled to move off at twelve, but it must have been after one by the time all the long lines of soldiers were allotted their trucks and the mountains of kit were stowed away in the luggage vans. During this time, our train was a great source of interest to a number of rather ragged little urchins, who were mainly on the quest for titbits, especially sweets. At last, after several whistles had been blown, the officer i/c Oran station waved the train off, and then probably went back to his mess for a nice, cooling and most likely stiff drink. For it must have been a big responsibility and hot work getting us under way.

I would not have fancied being stationed in Oran, for there can be little to do there, and the cleavage between the French and Arab subjects must have made the situation rather tense and difficult at times. But to look at from the sea Oran was wonderful – it was only when you landed that the illusion of aethereal beauty was dispelled, and one saw the shabby tumbledown houses and the poorly-dressed, though cheerful, population. For the first time, we saw men wearing fezzes, which gave one a nice feeling of experiencing Oriental glamour, and made one wonder whether the wearers kept harems. Probably in reality they could not afford harems, but concentrated on the black market.

As we travelled at an average speed of about 15mph into the interior of Algeria, we were to see more of the dark-skinned and gleaming-eyed Arab people. We stopped at every village, sometimes for nearly an hour. At each such stop, a number of soldiers left the train and disappeared out of the station off to the village, which usually seemed situated a few hundred yards, or perhaps half a mile, from the railway. They would return carrying bottles of cheap local red wine or other bargains, some of them running as the train whistle blew repeatedly, each blast more urgent than the last, to warn malingerers that they would be left behind if they did not return to the fold immediately. Sometimes the train would even be moving out as latecomers came dashing up to the small, hut-like stations, catching up with the coaches and helped in by willing hands, or actually in several instances, jumping on to the roof of the end coaches and running along until they came to their own truck. Rations were issued to us in tins, and we were given enormous loaves to carve up ourselves. Tea was made from the engine two or three times during the journey, and the second time was at about 2 a.m. I queued up in a colossal crowd of very happy and cheery soldiery for some mugsful for our carriage. The tea was sweet, strong and very hot. It revived one's flagging spirits and made the dawn seem less dismal.

The first part of the journey was mainly across dry, rather barren plains, but towards evening we came to green patches, something perhaps on the lines of an oasis, and here were villages with attractive villas of the French type, and great trees with luxuriant foliage, and climbing roses. We went through one such village just before dark, and there were cyclists and cars busying up and down the main road, which was just beside the station. The officials of course were French, but there were plenty of Arabs to be seen, and the barefooted children would run to the train at every station, holding out grubby palms for anything edible that would be thrown or handed to them from the carriage windows, running after us, sometimes with scruffy dogs, as we moved slowly out of the stations on our way.

The night was rather trying, as several girls were not feeling well. It was hot and stuffy, the bully beef was not very appetising, we were none of us very skilled with tin-openers, and the insect population was commencing its activities. This last was my main ordeal. I seemed to attract mosquitoes and other unmentionables, in spite of Keatings and anti-insect cream. After the early tea we had a little sleep, and soon after eight Iris and I made sure of being among the first to visit the toilet and try to repair our ravaged and travel-weary faces and coiffures. Iris as usual emerged looking immaculate: I tried to pretend I did.

It must have been about two o'clock when we at last steamed into Algiers station, having passed many marshalling yards and railway sidings, and been soundly told off for scattering bully-beef tins to some of the hungry and appealing ragamuffins following our slow progress along the lines. It was difficult to refuse those dark eyes and urgent requests of '*plees, mees, shocola*', and soon our entire remaining stock of sweets was exhausted.

We were not sorry to arrive and emerge from the hot and dusty carriages. Willy, Iris and I found to our chagrin that we were obliged to part from our ten companions, and were soon in a PU (a small covered army van), being driven swiftly up the villa-lined slopes of the higher part of the town towards the country. Below us lay the harbour, dotted with troopships, grey like the naval vessels against the blue sky. The sun was brilliant and the white buildings looked clean and fresh. The trees were at their best and we felt glad to be on the shores of the Mediterranean.

5

Algerian Interlude

We drove on, past the attractive villas shaded by luxuriant palms and adorned by cactuses in pots, and creeping roses. The wisteria and lilac were still in bloom, and the air was perfumed, their scent blended with the nostalgic odour of oleanders. We were on the main road and there were tramlines on it too. Every now and then we would pass a typical French tram, the interior crammed and the gallery at the back overflowing with a motley crowd in rather variegated attire, many of them in Arab dress or just wearing a fez with their European clothes. An occasional British uniform appeared a little incongruous in the scrum. It was hot and the passengers looked sticky, but they seemed cheerful enough – and indeed there was a cheerful spirit prevailing everywhere, for Cassino had fallen to the Allied troops only a few days earlier. The war seemed to be nearing its end. No-one could have foreseen the long and bitter struggle that would take place in the twelve months to come.

Soon we were away from the outskirts of Algiers and, still climbing, in the open country. Always the air was hot and brilliant, and the trees were remarkable for their rich foliage. We passed through one or two Arab villages, where one could see some of the inhabitants sitting and sipping coffee, many cross-legged on the ground. It must have been the very black and sweet Turkish coffee, 'cafe arabe', as it is called. Others would be haggling over business deals, or driving long-suffering mules with enormous burdens, perhaps to market or returning from a fair. One would also see Arab women carrying bundles or pitchers on their heads – Europe seemed to wane as we advanced further into the country, for the oriental influence was strongest in these villages. It was therefore with quite a surprise that at the end of a long village street, we came upon a road lined with modern French villas, and soon passed through the gate of one of them, which seemed surrounded with barbed wire, and at whose entrance a sentry on duty came smartly to attention.

We were quickly introduced to the major in charge of administration, who scrutinised our papers and told us briefly that we would have to wait for a few days until our passages to Italy were arranged. We had not expected this, and in truth we were not very happy about it, for we had all three been promised a change from the type of work we had been doing until then, and had hoped to be employed in the big headquarters, where the other ten from our course were to work. Fate had decreed otherwise, and there was nothing for us to do but assent and obey orders. We meanwhile bided our time, but decided to ask for an interview with the chief AT and request a transfer.

Shortly after this, we were escorted to our billets by another ATS officer. Willy and I had two nice little rooms in a French villa, which was beautifully clean and cool and refreshing, with the French shutters tightly closed to keep out the sun during the heat of the day. We began to unpack, while trying to improve the appearance of our khaki drill, which was to be a problem for some little time yet. Iris meanwhile was quartered in another house, a little further up the road.

We had dinner in the mess that night, and were for the first time in a mess run by the Americans. The new unit was also inter-service, and this time the CO was an American, and his second-in-command was British. The food in the mess was mainly American, and the batmen, cook and other kitchen staff were either American, or Italian so-called 'co-operators'. These latter, to the best of my knowledge, were Italians who had laid down their arms at the time of the Armistice in 1943, some of them in Abyssinia, Libya, etc., and had volunteered to work for the British forces in a paramilitary capacity. There was an ex-sergeant major of the Bersaglieri in this mess, and very smart and capable he was too.

We felt a little strange that evening, for everyone else seemed so much at home and at ease in the country, in their clothes and with the mixed crowds in the mess, representing different nationalities and services. Some of the Americans had strange names – Polish, Italian, Russian and even German – and even more than when in the United Kingdom I began to understand why the United States has been called a 'melting-pot'. The food seemed strange at first, coffee at the beginning of the meal in a pot on the table, as much as you liked, and sweet and savoury things all mixed up. We retired early that night, and were woken at about eight the following morning by Madame, who brought us a small cup of black coffee. She told us that there was a danger of locusts, as one or two had been seen about, and this usually heralded the approach of a cloud of them.

One would see donkeys or mules patiently plodding along under their huge loads, driven slowly down the road by Arab women or children, most of them barefoot or wearing crude sandals. They would urge on their beasts with loud cries, slapping them with switches and jangling the bells on their harness. It was a ten-minute walk downhill for us to the mess, and that first morning Willy and I waited for Iris, and then we all strolled down together at about nine. As there was nothing for us to do, we had been told to take things easily, and by the time we reached our destination at the bottom of the road, near the junction of the village street, which was the main thoroughfare from Algiers, everyone else had finished their breakfast and gone up to the office. The sergeant major of the Bersaglieri served us on the veranda in front of the mess – coffee, fried eggs and pancakes, apricots and cherries. We discovered that the pancakes were an American fashion, and the Americans would happily eat pancakes, bacon and marmalade or jam all at once, which seemed strange to us, but we got used to it in time. Anyway, said pancakes were delicious, made with dehydrated egg, about a quarter of an inch thick, dryish, and very nourishing.

That afternoon we were taken into the headquarters in Algiers to see the Head AT in the command, which was at that time BNAF – British North African Forces. She was the first woman I saw in uniform wearing a kilt and looked very impressive, especially as she was tall and handsome. She heard our troubles with much sympathy, and while not holding out great hopes of a change, said she would see what could be done. I was very impressed by her personal assistant, or female ADC (Assistant Division Commander), who was the smartest girl in uniform I had then seen. She managed to look most attractive in her khaki drill, despite the short, tight skirt – and she was wearing more make-up than most. I noticed that quite a few women overseas did this, and it seemed to fit in with the brilliance of the climate. I believe the PA mentioned above, a junior commander, was a great personality and well-known in the command. Certainly a lot of people seemed to know her, and as she had great charm, that was not at all surprising.

The following day we decided to hitchhike into Algiers. This was the usual practice overseas and it was very easy, especially if you were a girl, to get a lift, as there was always plenty of military traffic on the roads, particularly in the earlier days. As it happened, there was a truck going in from our unit, taking some American GIs to the American ORs' club, so we got a lift with them. We were soon whizzing down into the town at great speed, passing the same villas that we had seen on our way up two days previously. By now we felt much more confident and not quite so 'green'. They dropped us at the Aletti, one of the biggest hotels in Algiers, which had been taken over as an Allied officers' club. It was dark and cool inside, but there was nothing doing, because the middle of the afternoon is always a dead hour in hot climates. We left the one or two slumberers to slumber on in their armchairs and walked back up the hill to where we had heard that the YWCA was situated. There we slaked our considerable thirst with large earthenware cups of boiling tea, and ate tiny sandwiches and dainty little cakes. The YWs were the greatest boon to service girls of all ranks overseas. There, one could always get a nice meal, a bath, a bed or just a comfortable chair to relax quietly in, and there were always beautiful flowers in every room. It was peaceful, and whoever requisitioned the buildings for the use of YWs always seemed to select just the right place, with a homely, comfortable and tranquil atmosphere. It was somewhere that one could really relax from the hurly-burly of roaring transport, a crowded mess, or after a long day trying to work hard when dripping with heat and beset with flies, or in winter frozen with cold when fuel was scarce or nonexistent.

The YW at Algiers was on the main road leading through the town, and it had a pleasantly cool atmosphere and a cleanliness and freshness. After puffing up from the lower town in the May heat, which was hotter than it ever is in England in August, one sank thankfully into a chair and was glad to turn over the pages of an English magazine, perhaps several months old, but news to us. One might be sitting next to an ATS corporal, a QA sister, a physiotherapist, a civilian girl perhaps employed by the Foreign Office, a 'Free Fanny'*, a Wren officer or a WAAF of other rank. During my time overseas, I must have met representatives from all the women's services in various YWs, and the personnel of the latter were invariably charming and helpful. Besides staffing the hotel itself and looking after the catering, the civilian workers, the accommodation and the stores, including the inventory (very important in a requisitioned hotel), they also provided a complete entertainment guide. They sometimes arranged excursions, effected introductions for lonely girls or for men and girls on leave who wanted company, but were too shy or lacked the opportunity to find it, organised dances, and last but not least, always had a small chapel where one had the opportunity to attend Holy Communion and other services. In addition to all this, they coped with any individual problems and welfare questions that might crop up. These places were a comfortable and homely place for a rendezvous, and probably a large

---

*   Free Fanny – Free FANY (First Aid Nursing Yeomanry)

percentage of the many service romances were fostered by the kindly helpers there. No doubt any of them interested in match-making must have had wedding bells constantly tinkling in their ears – they certainly could not lack scope for their inclinations.

Opposite the YW in Algiers was the office of Thomas Cook & Son, and it was placarded extensively with invitations to go on a tour of the Kasbah, the famous native quarter of Algiers, whence, it was rumoured, Allied soldiers had not infrequently disap-peared in search of adventure, never to return. Some of their bodies were found, and others were just never seen alive again. But, with Thomas Cook & Son, in broad daylight and accom-panied by experienced and accredited guides, one need have no fear, and so we booked to go on one such excursion, deciding to ignore the horrific stories we heard of a stench that took one's breath away. In actual fact, I did not find the smell unbearable, and the visit was so fascinating that I forgot any sordidness that there might have been.

We went along tiny narrow streets, where curtains of beads hung over the doors to keep out the heat and the flies. In some of these little house-fronts craftsmen were busy – cobblers, knife-grinders, tailors, bakers and others. Everywhere were Arabs selling fruit in huge baskets, or nuts, or peculiar sweets and cakes on trays, some still hot. There were rather straggly-looking stray dogs, and numbers of little barefooted, grinning children of all ages. We visited a mosque, and saw Moslems at prayer. It was all in white stone and gleamed in the bright sunshine. When you first stepped over the threshold, it was almost impossible to see after the glare outside. We also visited one or two Arab houses, and I particularly remember one that was all painted blue, with a magnificent courtyard in the middle, where a fountain splashed into a marble basin of water, and palms and grass were of a green never seen in the fields and gardens, so sheltered were they from the heat and dust. The balcony and roof were ornamented with the sculptured marble, which reminded me of fretwork, and the atmosphere was one of coolness and perfume. Only a stone's throw away, in the street alongside, was the scramble of busy urban life, and not far away the hoot of motor-horns and the rumble of heavy traffic. Centuries of time seemed to separate the seclusion of this Arab dwelling from the modernity of the mechanised thoroughfare so close at hand.

We also had the luck to see another such interior, not so old, but in a not dissimilar style, at a dance to which we were invited outside Algiers, in a house taken over as an officers' mess. There the floors and walls were covered in mosaics, and the hall, where the dance took place, was in the centre of the building and vaulted with pillars almost like a church. This ecclesiastical appearance did not detract from the gaiety of the evening nor lessen the urgent syncopation of the army band, playing for the dancers, and the frequent imbibing of bottled American beer added to the jollity, for it was a hot sultry evening.

We were experiencing for the first time the real joy of tropical uniform – open collar, sleeves rolled up, and for the women, ankle socks, except at night. For the evenings it was strictly laid down that we should wear stockings, and the men trousers. Everyone also had to roll down their sleeves, and for dinner or for official occasions it was the rule to wear a collar and tie. But it was delightful in the hot days to wear just the minimum and be free of stockings and the sticky agony of a 'roll-on', which in the midday heat was martyrdom. In this climate, however, the nights were warm and balmy. One evening a film was shown out on the veranda in front of the mess; overhead the stars twinkled and below us in the street half the population were gathered to listen.

One day we had a very pleasant bathe, not far from Algiers, up the coast to the west. It was extremely windy, although I do not know the name of the local winds, but it seemed a sort of *scirocco* – hot, dry and very gusty. Willy and I went with a WAAF (Women's Auxiliary Air Force) officer and two escorts, and were rather startled to find that one was supposed to undress on the open beach, where there was not much cover and on the edge of which were some small stone houses. As there seemed to be very few people about, we separated from our escorts and managed the undressing part fairly well. The bathe was lovely, and we enjoyed the big rollers and dashing surf, swept in all directions by the wind. Dressing was not so good, for sand seemed to cling to one everywhere. It whirled all round, into one's clothes and blinding one's sight, and the wind swept our towels up and away just at the wrong moment. But we managed to get on our clothes with a certain amount of bad language, and on my part fervid inward vows that I would never again be persuaded to undertake such a bathing excursion. We assumed that we had at least enjoyed some privacy, but as we collected our damp and sandy costumes and tried to make some order of our disarranged and sand-matted hair, we saw at a window of one of the houses above quite a crowd of dark grinning faces of different sizes watching us with evident amusement. An Arab family must have been the inhabitants of the house and were spending the stormy day indoors – doubtless we had provided them with quite an amusing pantomime to enliven their day.

During this time we had no actual work to do, so we spent our time looking over our kit, turning up the hems of our voluminous skirts, seeing what we could of Algiers, having our hair done, and in general getting ourselves acclimatised to the life. I went to a French hairdresser near the YW. He was very pro-Ally, and told me how bad things had been under the Germans, and how the loyal French had been in danger of arrest at any time, needing to tread very carefully if their sympathies were with de Gaulle. I had to take my own towel and shampoo, which latter I bought in the NAAFI, for the French were short of food, soap, wool and indeed every sort of necessity. I was able to arrange for my mother to send some knitting wool from England a little later for Madame, whose daughter was expecting a baby and was sorely lacking in materials for her layette. The shops were very bare and, except for exorbitantly expensive leather goods and equally dear but very attractive sweetmeats such as dates and walnuts stuffed with marzipan, there was very little one could buy. There was a forces gift shop, and I purchased there a very lovely pocket book for my father in red Moroccan leather, stamped in gold, and also a small earthenware ashtray. I sent home a box of marzipan-filled dates from a shop, which said they sent purchases home direct for the forces. Unfortunately, it never arrived, and was perhaps on a ship that sank or was pilfered. This was almost the only item that I ever lost in transit, which was a good record and good fortune.

The life of Algiers at that time, apart from the continuous military activity and the business it occasioned in the port and the streets, seemed almost at a standstill. Many buildings were requisitioned, and there was no theatre but opera, and that offered only a variety with some slightly 'shocking' acts to attract the forces. I never went, as the management did not intend ladies to be part of the audience. We did however manage to hear *Thaïs* at the Opera House. There were one or two cinemas, showing rather second-rate films, and there were of course the cafés, where the many enforced idlers could take black coffee (which was probably mostly ersatz) or drink an inferior aperitif. Trade and commerce seemed almost non-existent. The civilian population were engrossed in the day-to-day struggle for sufficient food to keep body and soul together, and the Allied soldiers did not generally have enough money to pay the high prices for what was offered in the way of luxury goods to send home to their families. We were not there long enough to make much personal acquaintance with the local inhabitants, and indeed I did not even have time to look up a lady to whom I was given an introduction by an American in England. I have since greatly regretted this, but living out in the country, within sight of the distant Atlas range as we did, our expeditions into Algiers were necessarily limited, and when we did go it was usually for a specific purpose, such as a visit to headquarters – the Allied Forces Headquarters, as it was then called.

We had another interview with the chief AT, and this time she told us kindly but firmly that we were needed in Italy and must go there. Iris meanwhile had heard from her husband that he was already there, not far from Naples, and so she was of course quite resigned to the prospective journey. I had already begun to think that perhaps it would be more fun to be nearer the war than Algiers, and was quite consoled by the joyful anticipation of yet another sea voyage. Willy was not so easily baulked in her desire for a change, but just then there was nothing one could do but acquiesce and obey orders with as good a grace as possible. This was made easy because everyone was so nice, and we heard of friends from the UK, who were already on the other side, so that everything conspired to ease the situation.

Meanwhile, I was suffering terribly from the insects. We counted about 500 bites, mostly on my arms, neck, legs and hands. I used anti-insect cream, smoked and did everything possible to discourage the creatures, but evidently I was too attractive to the brutes. This was the only fly in the ointment! Thank goodness the locusts did not bite too, for that would have been the last straw. Soon after we arrived, the threatened cloud appeared and lasted several days. Locusts are about two inches long, and the complete span of their wings must be about four to five inches. They are shaped like a grasshopper, but of course bigger, and are precisely the colour of Colman's mustard. Their eyes are like the old-fashioned black-topped pins, and are beady and knowing. The noise made by their defenceless bodies as you crunch them underfoot is like a cow chewing, but the knowledge of what is happening is nauseating. Of course one should destroy as many as possible, but I could not bring myself to crush many of them like this. Instead, I helped Madame as much as I could to scare them out of her garden into the next-door neighbour's, as that seemed to be the best method of ridding oneself of the plague. I beat on a mess tin with a pair of scissors, going round and round the garden with this pseudo tom-tom. Madame and her husband and maid were outdoors most of the day, scaring the locusts away with sticks, but nevertheless they stripped a lot of plants, currants and strawberries. Everywhere around us, the air was echoing with the wail of the Arabs trying to rid their land of this really devastating scourge. The family's food depended very much on fruit and vegetables from the garden and the small patch of home-grown wheat or barley. In the office garden, some of the officers helped the owners to fight the pests with squash rackets, quite an effective weapon for slaying them. The road was covered with their yellow bodies, and every car that passed made a scrunching sound as if driving over partly frozen snow. After four or five days they became less, and the crestfallen farmers and householders began to count their losses. I learned that nowadays modern science is usually able to destroy or deflect a locust swarm by spraying their breeding area with poisoned gas or liquid from aeroplanes, but owing to the disorganisation caused by the war that year, and probably over the previous few years, it had not been done, and hence the invasion. It was said that some of the nomadic tribes still ate locusts, after the manner of John the Baptist, but personally I would have to be at near starvation to consider it.

Arrangements meanwhile were going ahead for our transportation, and on the tenth day after our arrival, Iris and I were once again on board a troopship, waiting to sail, this time for Naples. I was sorry to leave Algiers, which has ever since held great fascination for me and which I long to visit again. It evokes such pictures for me: the white mosques, their interior walls covered with Byzantine mosaics, the cool palmy courtyards of Arab houses, the sunny beflowered villas of the French; then there are the wealthy Arab women with their beautiful silk gowns and yashmaks, below which step daintily the most exquisite silk stockings and the smartest style of Parisian shoe; the children of the Arabs, dirty, ill-fed and worse clad, often in rags, but grinning, impish, insouciant; the patient beasts of burden, the men in their fezzes, smoking and talking eternally in masculine conclaves; the blue sea, and inland the lush, green vegetation; the curious mixture, scarcely a fusion, of Eastern and Western culture, each existing alongside the other, sometimes jealous or overbearing, but always persisting; and the sun, brilliant, exhausting, but to me at least, invigorating and wonderful.

It was with sincere regret that we slid slowly out of port the following night, watching the thousand twinkling lights that defied the partial blackout, leaving Algiers to its night of scents, smells, anxieties, crime, hunger and all the other myriad threads that make up the life of this Western and yet Oriental city, so romantic to the outsider, and, who knows, perhaps to the inhabitants so unbearable, even tragic.

6

See Naples —
and Live!

*T*his time Iris and I were in a cabin for two, which was converted into a cabin for four, and as we were four ATs, none very small and one unusually large, there was not a lot of space to move. It would not have been so bad if Iris had not declared the first night that she had bedbugs. I was quite exhausted by the packing up, goodbyes, and by the enervating effect of mepacrine, and when she woke me at about 3 a.m., declaring that she was being bitten all over, I was not very enthusiastic, especially as despite an intensive search we could not locate one bedbug. Nearly all night she was tossing and turning, switching the light on and off, and every now and then getting down from her bunk, which was above mine, and altogether the night was a very restless affair. In the morning the steward could find no bedbugs at all, but each night it was the same; Iris was definitely bitten, but by what and how no-one knew. Looking back on it, I think perhaps she was just suffering from heat bumps. She also had to give up mepacrine, as it upset her too much. In between commiserating with Iris, I made the acquaintance of an officer who turned out to be Italian and was being repatriated to work with the Allied forces. There were only we four girls on board, and so we were even more hopelessly outnumbered than before, but there was no social life on this ship. Everyone was bent on getting down to the job without further delay, and the atmosphere was official and businesslike.

Altogether, we were four days on the journey, and we passed the coast of Sicily about the third day. Doubtless the ship was making long detours to avoid detection by enemy aircraft. Due to the war on the bedbugs, I overslept the morning we entered Naples harbour, and awoke to find the others up on deck, and looking through the porthole I saw the white houses on the waterfront. I dressed hurriedly, and rushed up on deck to find nearly everyone else leaning over the side. We were almost in by then, and certainly the approach to Naples by sea is worth seeing. Vesuvius, now smoking gently after its recent eruption, towered up on our right; in front were the city and port, surmounted by the ancient castle of the Kings of Naples, and to the left many houses, lining the cliffs as far as the end of the promontory. There was a slight heat-haze, and everything was bathed in the warm, pinkish sunshine of early morning, for it was only about eight o' clock. Above the houses, on the hillsides and the slopes of the volcano, were acres and acres of greenery, which we later discovered were the vines, from whence doubtless the famous local wine, Lacryma Christi or Tears of Christ, is vintaged.

But we had no thought that morning but to gather up our baggage and prepare ourselves for landing. There were other troopships in port, and all along the quay stood a large and varied collection of army vehicles, troop-carriers, 15cwts, PUs, jeeps, gun-carriers and a few tanks. Troops were unloading in long, buff-coloured columns, laden with heavy packs, slung about with haversacks and gas masks, with tin helmets on their heads, and pushing bulging kitbags down the gangways of the ships or dragging them along the quay to the waiting transport. They seemed cheerful enough despite their back-breaking loads, but it suddenly pulled me up with a jerk and reminded me that only 60 miles away to the north lay the Front, where our men were consolidating their positions, preparing for the advance on Rome. These soldiers were probably reinforcements or replacements – some of them would perhaps never sail the sea home again. It was a sobering thought, and perhaps fortunately the busy atmosphere of efficient organisation, the brilliant scene and the by now familiar sight of small boys holding out grubby hands begging for 'shooey ga' or 'shocolato' helped to dispel the sense of melancholy it engendered.

Iris and I waited on deck, according to instructions, and presently a captain in a Scottish bonnet, khaki shorts and bush shirt came and asked for our names. He said, 'That's right, you're to come with me', and he gave us a hand with our baggage and led us down the gangway on to the quay, where after walking two or three hundred yards, dragging our bags with his help, we found a PU waiting for us. He told us he was the adjutant, and before long we were out of the dock, which was closely guarded by British and American MPs, and bowling through the streets of Naples, which seemed untidy, dirty and tatty, and showed considerable signs of bomb damage, and perhaps of street fighting too, as many of the buildings were pockmarked by either bomb splinters or shrapnel. There seemed to be mountains of fruit everywhere for sale, and dark, plump women in black dresses, or olive-skinned swarthy men with flashing black eyes, were superintending the transactions. There were the same bead curtains as in Algiers, and similar small shops. And children seemed to be everywhere, ragged, bare-footed, scrounging and with naughty eyes.

We were soon leaving the outskirts of Naples and jogging along the Salerno high road, one of Mussolini's broad concrete autostradas, in the direction of Vesuvius. The small village streets we passed went under the autostrada, and I noticed the verdant fruit trees on either side of the road, and the umbrella pines dotted everywhere. The umbrella pine is one of the most characteristic features of southern Italy. It has a tall trunk, bare over halfway up, and then the branches spread out at right angles to the trunk, so that the effect is indeed that of a large capacious umbrella.

Presently, we turned off the main road down a narrow alley beside the entrance to a detention camp, which was well protected by barbed wire and huge lights; these latter, I later saw, illuminated the entire perimeter of the camp at night, so that it would be no easy job to escape. The alley soon joined a narrow side road with a cobbled surface, and we plugged our way uphill, very soon turning into the courtyard of a large villa. This was the mess, and we were taken in and allowed to tidy up, for it was nearly lunch-time.

The first thing I remarked was the water shortage – there was a large tank for refilling buckets, and any other containers, standing in the front garden. We soon learned that the drainage had been badly damaged, and for the time being there was practically no water laid on at all, but it was brought up every day, well chlorinated, for human consumption, cooking, washing-up, etc. We had our first taste of chlorinated drinking water for lunch that day, and did not greatly care for it.

At lunch-time we were introduced to the colonel, our future CO, who was very charming, and quite disarmed me by calling me by my Christian name at once. He gave us confidence and made us feel at home and part of the show, in spite of our newness.

Once again, we were tremendously outnumbered by the men, and I felt very insignificant and mouse-like, and am sure blushed deeply whenever spoken to. This was Saturday, but there was no half-day holiday; indeed, days off, we learned, were nonexistent, for the army was preparing its further advance, Rome was expected to fall in a few days' time, and our unit had its part to play, like every other military, air or naval establishment in the command. Willy, however, had the brilliant idea of insisting that we must have the following day off for our unpacking, which seemed reasonable enough. Iris had been given the day off, as her husband had been advised of her arrival and was coming to visit her.

So after lunch and the making of these arrangements, we were taken along to our billet. We returned the way we had come, past the detention camp and out on to the main road. We turned right here, towards the sea, which was actually some way from us, and passed a row of white stone houses, very dirty, bullet-marked and slummy-looking. A host of the familiar grubby and cheery children played on the waste ground in front of these houses. At the end of the terrace, we turned left into the village street of Bellavista, another cobbled, winding, narrow lane like the one where the mess was. We walked for a few yards along the street and then turned right down another narrow alley and came to a large villa on our right, with a spacious porch and two doors. Iris and I were shown our room, which was one of three adjoining rooms in a fairly large flat, complete with bathroom. One other girl had the middle room. Willy was accommodated in the end room. The remaining three AT officers of the unit were in another villa. We comprised the whole female personnel – seven in all. Now for the first time we realised how useful our camp kit was to be. In the bedroom was a cupboard and some shelves and one chair, nothing else. Iris and I set to work unpacking our beds and set them up with some pinching of fingers and tugging and pulling to fit the canvas on to the prongs of the framework. My tin trunk became a bedside table and dressing table combined. It took us most of the afternoon to get sorted out.

The view from our bedroom window was magnificent. We looked north-west over the Bay of Naples. Below us were the apricot groves and the scattered houses of Bellavista, or 'Beautiful View', as the translation of the name goes, and very apt it was. Here and there, the tall umbrella pines towered over the landscape. In the port below several troopships lay at anchor.

Our house was so constructed that whereas our front door was on the ground floor, the bedrooms were on the first floor. The portion beneath our windows was occupied by a Neapolitan family, a nice vivacious little black-haired woman, with two attractive daughters and two or three small children, all of whom went barefoot. Her daughters cleaned our rooms and brought us a meagre ration of hot water to wash with in the morning, except when there was not enough water even for this purpose. Fortunately, we usually managed to procure one small canful each, but the sanitary system certainly was a trial. Baths were unknown, but occasionally the shower in our bathroom had enough water to make it workable in slow motion. I had not thought it possible to go more than a day without a bath, but soon found that one could quite happily go several months without it and although one missed it at first, one became accustomed to washing thoroughly and keeping clean, even in the intensely hot Italian summer.

That night a party was being given by an RAF unit affiliated to us, and they had invited the colonel and second-in-command, and any of the women officers who would like to attend. The others did not want to go, and so Willy and I were asked if we would like to. It was an opportunity to meet some of our future colleagues, and not having dates like some of our seniors, we accepted. It was not without some trepidation that I envisaged this evening with our CO. It was quite the first time I had been out in such august company, and I was very conscious of my humble rank and total lack of knowledge of local custom and *savoir-faire*, for everything here seemed different from Algiers – the people, the mess, which was British, the billets, and army life in general.

After dinner in the mess, we were packed into the back of the colonel's car, and soon found ourselves once more on the road for Naples. It was nearly dark by the time we reached our destination, and so I did not have much opportunity of observing the city. In any case, I was far too busy concentrating on my Ps and Qs, and hoping that my tie was straight and not 'under one ear', as one of my previous COs had told me I usually wore it.

We arrived and were introduced to a naval commander, various RAF officers and two WAAFs. This inter-service business was certainly varied, and you never knew whom you would meet with next, what service, rank or even nationality. I soon found a flight lieutenant of my acquaintance from UK days by the name of Hugh Tredgold. He had a lovely tenor voice and had sung with Sadler's Wells Opera before the war. It was not surprising that he was asked to sing, and as everyone crowded out on to a tiny balcony overlooking the bay, he sang some of the Italian songs that became so famous during the Italian campaign, such as 'Torn' a Sorrento', 'O sole mio' and 'Santa Lucia'. He also sang some airs from Verdi's operas, and I remember 'La donna è mobile' from *Rigoletto*. His voice rang and echoed across the water and penetrated the mild serenity of the night. I was thrilled with the singing, and war and the Front seemed to fade out of the picture.

For a few moments of sheer enjoyment we must all have forgotten why we were there. But the singer tired, and then there were drinks all round, followed by community singing, and finally the well-known 'Green grow the rushes, O', which usually provided the grand finale to most of our parties. We arrived back home at about midnight, and I was soon sound asleep after the heat of the day, the excitement of arrival and the unaccustomed drinks.

Next morning Willy came and told me to hurry up and get ready. Surprised, I said, 'But there's no hurry, we have all day to do our unpacking.' 'Don't be silly,' she said, 'we aren't going to finish it now, we're off to see a bit of the country. I have asked for a transfer to Bari, where someone is needed for translations, and so I intend to see what I can while I'm still here.' I did not argue, seeing that she was determined, and anyway the idea was attractive, especially as there were apparently to be no days off. After all, we *were* tired after the journey, or was it the party of the night before?

We set off at about 9.45 a.m. with some sandwiches from the mess. We stood on the main Naples–Salerno road and were very soon picked up by a 15cwt and were driving comfortably along. On either side we gazed at the vineyards and apricot groves, rising on the slopes of Vesuvius, which came nearer every moment. The eruption had not long since ceased, and indeed our own unit had at one time had fears of having to move, as the village that suffered this time, San Sebastiano, was only one or two kilometres away. On each side of the main road, the whole way to Salerno, were huge piles of black lava, which looked like gravel, but black. It was very dusty and one's eyes itched with the combined heat and dust. Our lift only took us halfway, as he had to turn off, so we were on the roadside again but before long had hailed a captain of the Royal Signals in a PU. He was going to Salerno and then on to a small rest-camp for his men, near Amalfi. We wanted to go to Amalfi and Positano on the Sorrento peninsula, which we had heard were fantastically beautiful, so he promised to take us as far as he was going. As he had taken part in the Salerno landings, he was able to explain to us exactly how it had all happened. Salerno itself was a bay with a small seaside town in its curve.

We struck off right along a narrow, winding road along the top of the cliff, and after half-an-hour's drive the captain stopped at a small white house perched on the edge, and told us that this was his destination. We all went in and found the Italian family, the owners, on their veranda overlooking the sea, from which there was a sheer drop of several hundred feet. They were about to have some food, and offered us wine and spaghetti. We in turn made them taste our sandwiches, and we all made an *al fresco* meal together in the living room, which was plain and very clean, with a red-and-white checked tablecloth and straight-backed chairs with rush seats.

After this, our escort told us he had business to see to and must go, but would drive us a little further. In actual fact, he took us past Amalfi, on to Positano, and then dropped us off at the top of a narrow winding lane down to the sea. There we parted company, he having first taken our telephone number, as his unit was soon holding a dance and he wanted us to be there.

Amalfi was very attractive, with a lovely cathedral, but we had no time to stop that day and hurried on to Positano. This remains in my memory as one of the loveliest places in Italy, that land of every kind of beauty spot. The tiny alley down to the beach was overhung with trees, after the manner of a Devonshire lane. Here and there were houses, or covered gateways, cactuses in pots, and creeping pink and red geraniums. There was a tea pavilion at the bottom of the alley, and then you turned right to the beach, along which there were several cafés and some rows of changing cabins. There we had the best bathe I ever had in Italy. The beach is sandy, and shelves down only gently. Positano is in the hollow of a small bay, so that the water is sheltered for bathers, and that day there was no violent surf, only a gentle swell. We were easily able to swim out to the diving raft. There were not many bathers, and they were all members of the Allied Forces. We got into conversation with an officer at one of the cafés where we had some lemonade.

When I came out of my cabin after the bathe, I could not see Willy anywhere, and finally discovered her seated at a table in the pavilion, drinking tea with three or four Canadians. I did not feel much in the mood for pleasantries, but as I was at once invited to join them for tea, and indeed hailed by everyone by my Christian name in a most familiar fashion, I had no alternative but to comply as graciously as possible. The Canadians were very chatty and jolly, and it was not long before I discovered that it was more or less of a foregone conclusion that they would drive us back to Salerno to dinner in their mess that night, and afterwards return us to our billet. I was disappointed to go back the way we had come, instead of via Sorrento and Castellamare, but, as Willy said, they were willing to take us all the way, and they were very friendly. I thought she was getting on exceedingly well with them.

It was by now about six o'clock, so we had drinks all round, and at about seven o'clock we left the sun-bathed pavilion, and once more climbed the lane with its uneven paving stones to the main road. There we saw white villas, one above the other on the steep hillside, embowered in their gardens full of fruit trees and vegetables, with here and there pots of cactus and geranium.

The drive there had been gentle and agreeable; the drive back was rather terrifying. We travelled in a large shooting-brake, which took the corners on the winding coast road at never less than about 50 miles an hour. I tried to concentrate on the scenery, which was not so easy as it changed with the rapidity of a whirlwind. But we arrived safely in Salerno and were taken to the Canadian mess in the main street, which seemed a rather gloomy building. I remember we had a well-cooked meal, but my chief recollection of this evening was the pressing invitations we received to stay the night, as there was plenty of accommodation, or so they said. But we insisted absolutely that we must go back, as we had to start work early next morning, and so eventually our hosts agreed to drive us back to our unit. We positively raced along the autostrada at about 70mph. I have rarely felt so frightened, but we got back safely at about midnight. I finished my unpacking the following evening.

In this way we passed our first complete day in Italy, and I have nothing but happy memories of it: the sunshine, the vegetation, the flowers, the scenery, the bustle of the army base, the obvious interest taken in us by quite 70 per cent of the officers and soldiers we came into contact with, the cheerful though rather needy Italian peasants, and the knowledge that, insignificant as we were, we would work to the best of our ability in the great cause we were all defending. All these thoughts combined to banish homesickness and promote even further my enthusiasm and *joie de vivre*. But publicly I kept it hidden and appeared reserved, for I remembered still that I was the newest new girl, Willy being superior in rank and Iris knowing the country and speaking the language like a native. For a long time to come, shyness was to be my greatest problem. As for the saying 'See Naples and die', that seemed paradoxical. Surely it ought to be 'See Naples and *live* – to the full!'

7

Just the Job

*W*ork began officially at 8.30 a.m., but the really keen types were there by eight. Breakfast began at 7.30 a.m. and went on until about 8.30 a.m., but everyone had finished by then. I soon discovered that if I went to breakfast early I escaped the masculine horde that usually surged in at about eight o'clock, and therefore I would get up by 6.45 a.m. and away by 7.15 a.m., as it was a good quarter of an hour's walk from our billet to the mess. It was lovely at that hour when the dew was still glistening on the trees and plants, and in the spiders' webs, which looked like silken tracery in the early morning sun. The heat of the day was not yet upon us and it was the best time to be out, other than in the evening after sundown.

Willy went off to Bari at about this time, and her room was soon taken by a different junior commander, by the name of Cicely Fowkes-Clevedon. She was another Italian speaker, like Iris, having been brought up in Florence. She was a tall, very slender girl, with medium-fair wavy hair, and she seemed possessed of a boundless enthusiasm for life. Perhaps that was what attracted me in her; at all events I came to know her quite well, and sometimes we went for walks together, up through the vineyards and the apricot groves to the slopes of Vesuvius. She was keen on walks before breakfast, but this meant rising by 6 a.m. at the latest, and I found that rather too much, especially as the heat during the day was very exhausting, and at that time we worked right through until seven o'clock or even later. But Cicely was used to the heat and it never worried her. I preferred to spend the evening at the window of our bedroom, from where I could watch the changing colours of the setting sun and the pink glow that suffused the port and the white villas. As the glow faded to pale blue, night gradually fell and the evening star shone ever more brightly in the sky, the only clear object in a world of softly blurred outlines and changing pastels.

In a flat adjacent to ours, part of the same house, were two or three male officers, and I soon made the acquaintance of one, as he was also an early riser and we met on the way to breakfast. He was called Toby and we became firm friends. Going into breakfast with Toby I did not feel quite so self-conscious as I did on my own. Sometimes Cicely would come along early too, but generally she liked to put a walk in first, saying she must keep fit, or something of the sort. Meanwhile we were introduced to our new work and met our future colleagues at work as well as at play.

On the way to breakfast each morning, little Italian boys and girls would rush at us from the terrace and shriek excitedly, '*Shocolat, per favore, signori caramelle*', and sometimes '*Sigarette per Pappa*'. I always tried to have a few sweets with me to distribute to the throng of eager little *bambini*, but there were scarcely ever enough to go round. Each day at the camp cook-house a small crowd of civilians would collect our leftovers, stale bread, etc., and I heard the admin officer saying that he did not know how to sift out the scores of applications from Italians to be taken on as civilian personnel, i.e., cooks, batmen, cleaners, etc. There were two women employed as cooks in the officers' mess, and they did their best, even to the making of porridge for breakfast. They had only an open coal fire to cook on, and consequently the toast was like rubber and usually burnt. Everything was rather greasy, cooked *all' Italiano*. Nearly all the rations were tinned or preserved in some way – tinned milk, dehydrated meat and potatoes, dried peas, dried egg, tinned bacon. The bread was American, made with white American flour; there was no butter, but an unpleasant, strong-tasting fat, which one could hardly honour with the name of margarine, and it took some getting used to.

The army imported almost everything at this stage, as the civilian population was very nearly starving. The only fresh food we had was fruit and occasionally a little salad. I felt very hungry, as the rations, though probably adequate in calories, did not seem to satisfy one, and as we had been starved of fruit for so long we used to buy it whenever possible. A week or so after my arrival the apricots were ripe, and for the first time I learned to appreciate a fresh, rather than a dried apricot. After that I must have eaten at least half a pound a day. In the mess we also had *nespoli*, something like a medlar, and later cherries. The fruit was wonderful, juicy and fresh and in limitless quantities. It was probably the standby of the Italians, for even flour was in short supply and they were hard put to find their daily dish of pasta.

On 4 June, just a week after we had landed in Italy, Rome fell. There was great rejoicing, and as some of our people went into the city immediately after, or at the same time, as the forward troops, we soon had news of conditions there. Reports began to come in after three or four days, and drivers, or officers reporting back, had wonderful tales to tell of the magnificent reception accorded the liberating army by the civilian population. Prince Doria was made *sindaco*, or lord mayor; he was well known for his pro-British leanings and his wife was Scottish. There was a purge going on of Fascist elements in the city government and among civil servants. Spies still lingering to report to the Germans were being rounded up, and everywhere the girls were out in their best frocks, with smiling faces, greeting the soldiers and welcoming them to the Eternal City. The children soon learnt the trick of wheedling bonbons or biscuits out of the sternest ally, and for a while the Romans forgot the horrors of the Gestapo and the spectre that had haunted them for so long – hunger. In reality there was little food, and for some time to come the citizens would be on very short commons. But the notorious torture chamber in the Via Tasso had been expunged, and the gates of the Vatican were once more open. Caruso, the infamous police chief, had been executed. A Highland officer, attached to us, arranged a parade of Scottish Pipers in St Peter's Square, and they were greeted with great enthusiasm.

Quite a number of escaped British prisoners and civilians who had managed to flee the internment camps had taken refuge in Vatican City. It was a joyful day for them when the Stars and Stripes and the Union Jack were unfurled on the Piazza Venezia, opposite the old palazzo of the same name, where Mussolini had been wont to speak from his famous balcony to crowds well drilled in the art of automatic appreciation. Rome Allied Area Command was set up and, as for most other units in our district, plans were going forward for our move up to Rome. An advance party went off to contact our forward members, and the rest of us kept our baggage semi-packed, ready to move at a moment's notice. Meanwhile, we enjoyed what we could of Naples.

The second Sunday I spent in Bellavista, some of us went up to the Palace of Caserta in the afternoon, where the Advanced Headquarters, Allied Armies Italy (AAI), were then situated, to inspect one of the first Panther tanks captured from the Germans. We were sitting in the back of a 15cwt, very much bumped about on the road, which was rough and uneven from shell holes and the passage of many tanks, enemy and Allied, and other vehicles. After we got back I did not feel very well, and developed some sort of 'gippy tummy' that night. This was an internal upset, some kind of chill in the stomach, and everyone seemed to get their dose sooner or later, and at periodic intervals. I was in bed for about three days, during which a kindly Aberdeenshire batman brought me marmalade sandwiches and weak sweetened tea in a Thermos from the mess, as there was no possibility of procuring any food at our billet. How I looked forward to that tea, and also to the water that he or one of the girls brought me, the water in the taps being quite undrinkable.

After I had recovered, the MO prescribed a mosquito net for me – which the quartermaster at first said was un-procurable – as I was still continuously being bitten, and the flies were really cruel in the office, attacking one's arms and legs under the table.

I believe the proximity of the battlefields made them particularly venomous that summer. It was sensible to have a fly switch, but I am afraid I never got one; I remember one man saying later on that he had swatted a hundred flies a day. I don't know what other swatting he can have had time for.

With a net one was at least safeguarded at night. I was beginning to have a real fear of malaria, but perhaps it was due to my conscientious consumption of mepacrine that I did not get it. The MO also elected to inject me for tetanus, but for some reason known only to himself he injected the serum into my forearm, fortunately the left one, but I spent several uncomfortable days with it – the prick itself was like a wasp sting. After my attack of gippy tummy, however, I suffered very little from any ailment, so perhaps it was as good as an inoculation. Our MO was a little, thickset Scotsman from 'Glasgie', and he was always kind to me. I remember being slightly startled when he visited me the Monday after our expedition to Caserta, and asked me what the matter was, and then enquired what medicine I would like.

After my few days off sick, I was back at work again, in an office, with two other ATs, the walls covered with maps. It was interesting work, again of a secret nature, with a direct bearing on the fighting taking place daily within a hundred miles of our office, so that one did feel near the war, although the doodlebugs were now devastating London. That was something I missed, leaving England just before they started – I hardly know whether to regret missing them or not. There was one air over Naples shortly after our arrival, and a great firing of Ack-Ack, but nothing was hit. That was the last time.

We worked very hard, and the work was absorbing. In the evenings, however, we were free to do as we liked. I met Jacky again, and one evening she suggested that we should supplement the rather unsatisfying mess dinner with a meal at a sort of *ristorante*, halfway up Vesuvius. One could get fresh eggs, she said. The idea was tempting, and we had so little diversion that I welcomed it as a change. It was a beautiful, warm night, and we set off at about eight o'clock, having about three-quarters of an hour's walk before us. I stuck to the main path, the tiny short cuts being in uncertain sandy ground that might give way and cause us to slither down at any moment. For this reason, I was terrified when Jacky would insist on taking these short-cuts, and with her long legs would plunge into the undergrowth and leave me to join her, panting and puffing, some way up. I was alarmed at the idea of her spraining an ankle or breaking a leg, for I was sure it would be impossible to carry her a yard, and it was an isolated part of the countryside.

As it was, we arrived safely and sat at a bare wooden table on the terrace overlooking the harbour, with Vesuvius towering above us, its slightly smoking crater a rather forbidding sight in the dusk. The *padrona* brought us two fried eggs each and some small fried new potatoes. We washed this feast down with Vesuvius wine, which I found a little bitter. Afterwards we paid our bill, which with the exchange at 400 lire to the pound, cost us about 10s each, and set off down the mountainside again. This time Jacky kept me company, so I was spared the worry of seeing her glissading down the scrubby slopes, on which everything grew in old lava, in the half-light. Vesuvius looked rather eerie as darkness fell, and I was glad to be back near the busy high road again, in the village street. But it was an enjoyable evening. All pleasures have to be paid for, however, it seems, and that night I suffered miserably from indigestion and vowed never to taste the wine again. Later experience taught me that it must have been immature, and indeed there was very little good wine about then, the Germans having commandeered every litre they could lay their hands on. '*Tedeschi portano via tutto*' ('The Germans have taken away everything'), the Italians said constantly, in the elliptical language of infinitives they often used for the troops.

Sometimes our evenings would be spent in a short excursion into the vineyards to buy a few apricots from the peasants, and chat to them about the war, as far as we could. They spoke for the most part a sort of dialect, at least it was not pure Italian, and seemed even to have occasional words of French, or something similar, in it. For instance, after nearly every sentence they would say, '*Compris*?', to see if we had understood. I discovered also the irritating way they had of talking in infinitives. This was with the best of intentions, to make the language more easily understandable to us, but as my teacher in London had gone out of her way to make me learn the verbs, I found it easier to follow a normal conversation with the proper verbal forms.

Once or twice, I went to the San Carlo Officers' Club in Naples. It was next door to the Opera, and at that time a very lively affair. There were one or two ladies who sang there, Italian songs and some of the well-known wartime melodies, the most famous of all, of course, being 'Lili Marlene', sung by Dietrich herself. I noticed that in between songs she usually sat at a table with one or two officers. The tables were grouped around the dance floor, but there were always far more men than women; at that time only British or American service girls could go there.

The club often became very lively as the evening progressed, and I remember once seeing young officers on leave having a fine rag on the stairs, jumping up and down like jack-in-the-boxes. There was a wonderful atmosphere of camaraderie at that time, and if somebody wanted to paint the town red, they were welcome to get away with as much jollification as they could before the MPs stepped in and quietened things down. The troops had a magnificent NAAFI/EFI (Expeditionary Forces Institute) nearby, in the Royal Palace. In between was the San Carlo Opera House, but I only heard one opera there, as we could so rarely get away in time for an evening performance. That occasion was after I had met a signals major at some party, who invited me to go to the opera with him one afternoon. I explained to him that it was impossible to leave the office except for an official reason. He suggested I should try the officers' shop, and I managed to get permission to go to it. I had a glorious sense of liberation as I stood on the edge of the road after lunch, waiting for someone to pick me up. In a minute a 2-tonner came along, with several NCOs in it. It stopped, but was so high that I could hardly get in. A burly sergeant came to my rescue and lifted me in bodily by the armpits, and soon I was chatting to them and hearing all about their life in camp. They were then out of the line, resting, and everyone was so kind, unbelievably so, and so courteous, that often one felt quite unworthy of it all, but also felt proud to be wearing the same uniform as these men.

Needless to say, the opera was an unforgettable experience. It was *Rigoletto*, and the scenery, the voices and the orchestra were excellent, as only Italian opera production can be. I remember still the unearthly moonlight of the isolated cottage where poor Gilda came to her tragic end, and the agonising lament of her father, when he learnt that he had unwittingly killed his own child, his only treasure.

The Opera House was packed with soldiers, and it was always full in Naples. We had especially good seats, and nearly the whole place was reserved for troops; the civilians at that time were only allowed a certain space in the gallery. After all, they could go to the Opera any time, but for the majority of British it was a rarely indulged pleasure. How can it be said that the British do not appreciate music? The operas and the concerts held every Sunday night in the Opera House were always performed before packed audiences, silent, attentive, and all dressed in slightly varying shades of khaki drill. We attended the Sunday evening concerts, when possible, coming into Naples on a Liberty truck, which picked us up afterwards to go home again. Sometimes we would go into the club afterwards for a refresher. On one occasion an American soldier, a corporal, conducted the Opera Orchestra. His reception was just what he deserved – there was a tremendous applause.

Just opposite the Opera House was the Galleria, which had suffered badly from bomb damage, especially as it had a glass roof, many hundreds of panes of which were partly smashed or non-existent. The Galleria had four entrances and there were shops all along them. There were cafés there too, and it was a general meeting place for the Neapolitans, where they talked business and conducted black market transactions. One could see them haggling over currency and other scarce commodities, such as American and English cigarettes, spirits, especially whisky, or perhaps tea or coffee. The Neapolitans were developing to a fine art their age-old gift for pilfering, and a substantial amount of NAAFI supplies, not to speak of vehicle stores, found their way regularly to the *Mercato Nero*. Among the shops in the Galleria were several where one could buy coral necklaces, cameo rings, and other coral trinkets, also films, combs and perfumes – but they were all expensive.

One of the entrances to the Galleria was off the Via Roma, one of the best known thoroughfares of Naples, which gave its name to a famous Italian song of that time –'Catari', or, as it was called in the English translation 'Down the Via Roma'. The Via Roma was long and narrow, with shops on either side, and leading off it to the north side, long winding alleys, even narrower, most of which were off limits to the forces. They had a reputation somewhat similar to that of the Kasbah in Algiers. A pungent odour of stale and mouldering vegetables, garlic and hot, unwashed humans would sometimes pervade one's nostrils when crossing these side turnings, and sometimes there were worse odours still. But to be fair, the Neapolitans were short of water, just as we were, and no-one could wash much in the city; and due to the bombing and passage of many vehicles, there was a persistent surface of dust everywhere, which whirled up with the slightest puff of wind and was disturbed by the passage of motor transport, the feet of horses or mules, or even the weary trudging of the passers-by. It was hot and tiring in Naples and many people avoided it for that reason.

But it had its fascination, and due to a fortunate combination of circumstances it became my job to visit the Survey Unit along the waterfront, where I had to obtain the latest maps needed by our officers for their work, and take them back to the unit. Usually this meant at least one visit a week into Naples, and I enjoyed the drive, the conversation with the driver and the change from the office. We would drive along past the famous old Castel dell'Ovo, a grim fortress jutting out from the sea, the Aquarium, and the Naval Officers' billets, where one occasionally saw a Wren, jaunty in her white tropical uniform. The Map Centre, which was situated in a slightly damaged and now empty school building. We passed a sort of street market on the way, and after procuring the maps I would stop and buy some fruit for my co-workers from the peasant women at the stalls, who as one passed by would call urgently, '*Ecco qui, Signori* (pronounced Sinyoree), *belle arance*', etc. I bought some lemons, beautiful big clean ones, with stalks and leaves, and sent them home. For the girls I would buy a kilo of enormous dark cherries, the best we had ever tasted, or perhaps some peaches, which positively melted in one's mouth. These were a welcome addition to the rather dry NAAFI buns a soldier brought us every morning with our sweetened NAAFI tea in a tin mug. But how welcome that tea was, even though one lost it almost immediately in thin trickles of perspiration that drib-bled down one's neck and legs, or beads of sweet that stood out from one's forehead and disorganised one's hair as effectively as if one had had a bath. There was also a dried fruit shop in the Via Roma, at the end nearest the sea, where you could buy boxes of almonds, walnuts, figs and raisins for varying prices and have them sent directly home. I sent home some almonds and raisins and also some lemons. I heard from my godmother, to whom I had also sent a mixed box of fruit, that she had auctioned a packet of almonds for £20 at a charity bazaar.

Apart from Naples itself there were many other things to be seen, if one had the time. Capri was just over the water, a blue silhouette, coloured like love-in-the-mist on a fine day, but few of us, if any, could get there for the present. We had a bathe at Torre Annunziata one evening, and it was delicious after a hot day at work, especially in view of the water shortage. Torre is one of the first places, or *spiaggie*, as the Italians call them, after Naples, on the bay towards Sorrento. Soon after it comes Castellamare, literally 'Castle on the Sea', and there is a castle there, right out in the bay, grim and with solid stone bastions, built on to a rock, the fortress of the local duke where he took refuge during the turbulent Middle Ages.

There was an officers' club at Castellamare, where we spent an enjoyable evening. On this occasion I was invited by Jean, the girl who had the middle room in our flat, to make up a party of four with a signals officer she knew, and his friend. They took us to Castellamare, and we had dinner at the club and afterwards went to the dance held close by. For the first time I saw Italian girls with our men, and though some were pretty, I must confess to not being very impressed, at least by the type present. But we enjoyed the dance, even though there was some sort of incident, which I only hazily remember. I think Jean's friend was jealous because someone tried to take her away from him, but it was all smoothed over, and we had several pleasant dates with the signals officers later on.

It was about that time that I went down to Portici one evening, the next village to Bellavista in the Naples direction, but much larger and really a small town, to locate a hairdresser. I made an appointment and returned a day or so later, armed with soap and towel, for the soap problem seemed universal at that time. The hairdresser was a man, and as he was also a barber, it was not surprising that I encountered several British soldiers in his shop. I got into conversation with a sergeant and heard about his experiences in the Italian campaign and about the desert – there was always so much to talk about. Finally he went off to be shorn, and a little later I was ushered into a compartment to have my hair washed for the first time in Italy, with my head held back over a small metal basin on a stand, as in France. While I was all in curlers, with the drier on my head, the sergeant suddenly appeared to say goodbye. He did not at all seem to mind my strange appearance, but insisted on shaking hands, as he said, with the first English girl he had met for three years. I was more than a little flattered.

At last the date of our departure for Rome was fixed – 4 July – exactly one month after the city's capture by the Allies. A bombed-out cinema studio, formerly Cinecittà (Cinema City), had been requisitioned to house our unit, and tents would house most of the soldiers. It had been used as a German prisoner-of-war camp and was in a bit of a mess, but the advance admin staff were doing their best to clean it up before the main party arrived.

Meanwhile, when much of the packing had been done, we had a little time on our hands, and Cicely and I took the opportunity to hitch-hike to Pompeii, also on the way to Salerno, and look at some of the truly amazing Roman remains there. The House of the Vestal Virgins has some of the most wonderful mosaics, but perhaps the street, with its centuries-old paving stones, still bearing the rut marks of Roman wagons, was what appealed to me most. The grass grew green between the ruins, cypresses stood sentinel over the dismembered temples, shops and homes. Beyond, rose steeply the walls of the once deadly volcano.

There seemed to be plenty of guides, and we found ourselves in a large party of assorted soldiers and sailors, some American, some British. We noticed, however, that the guides seemed reluctant to include us in their parties, and we quickly realised that we might spoil the 'fun' that was evidently to be had in certain parts. We therefore managed to secure a guide to ourselves, who took us on a respectable tour, and omitted the places considered suitable for 'men only' and the risqué jokes usually passed at such times. We drove off in high style in a carriage drawn by a horse, a sort of buggy, and had some refreshments in the town before hitching another lift to Bellavista.

Our final excursion was officially sponsored and was an ascent of the volcano itself. About fifteen of us set off, including three ATs and some sergeants. We drove as far as possible in two 15cwts, and then parked the vehicles and started off on foot. It was about five o'clock when we left the mess, and the climb up to the summit took about three-quarters of an hour. Some people decided not to attempt it, but rested by the vehicles and enjoyed the view. Others started but gave up halfway, while a few were grimly determined to reach the top, come what may, and a very few even seemed to be making a race of it. I did not race, but took it quite moderately. It was not at all difficult, only hard work, as there was a lot of loose lava on the path and one was inclined to slip back into it. The air was hot and dusty, and the nearer we got to the crater the stronger it was imbued with the smell of sulphur, which irritated one's nostrils and made one cough. Cicely was to the fore, striding ahead with her stick. It was a close race between her and two or three men, but she was determined to make it first, and so she did, outstripping us all.

Once there, we had a breath of fresh air, for it was quite high. The view is of course magnificent, for the whole panorama of Naples, the Bay, Sorrento and Capri is spread before one's eyes, and to the south Salerno and beyond. To the north we could distinguish the distant line of hills, in the midst of which lay Cassino, and near to which we were so soon to pass. And at our feet was the crater, the mysterious, steamy, hissing and rumbling interior of the volcano, which called to mind the adventures of Jules Verne or the strange underworld of Greek mythology. But the light was fading as the sun sank, molten red, in the west, and so we hurried down, slipping and glissading in clouds of dust to join the others at the trucks. Hot and parched with thirst, we arrived back at the mess at about eight o'clock, in time to consume ravenously whatever we could find in the way of a meal at that late hour. Washing the grit and dust from our hair and clothes was no joke, with the water situation still acute, but the effort was worthwhile. After all, one cannot go up a volcano just any day for a stroll.

Only one other incident enlivened the routine of my life in Bellavista, and that was my acquaintance with the dressmaker. The aforesaid khaki drill was badly in need of alteration, and I was recommended by another AT to try a little Italian dressmaker who lived below her in a ground-floor flat. It was part of a large square villa with terraces upstairs and down, each opening on to a luxuriant garden planted with apricot trees and rich with many other sorts of fruit and vegetables. I duly sought out the Signora in question, who had a baby of one month and little boy of about 2 years old, to whom I was always introduced, and if possible I would present him with a packet of fruit gums or some other delicacy. His mother made an excellent job of the drill, and at last I felt inconspicuous, with average-sized skirts and neatly fitting bush shirts. I was also told that the Signora Renata would make underclothes, and she offered to make me a brassiere, to give me a really nice shape, she said, moving her hands about expressively. When she made it, to my horror, she had given it the very voluptuous shape that was then the fashion in Italy, and into which the Italian girls habitually squeezed themselves. The 'ladies' of the Via Roma of course carried it to extremes. But I really could not refuse it; she was so keen to improve my figure. I discovered that she had made a similar garment for one of the other ATs, who felt the same as I did about feminine curves *in extremis*. So she gave hers to me too, and I sent them both home to England to a friend who might find them useful, in view of the prevalent clothes-rationing there. I heard they were very gratefully received. Whether or not they were ever worn I never knew.

The Signora had become quite a friend of mine, and when I went to collect any of my clothes, or discuss or fit them, I would sit and chat with her in her hot little parlour, where flies buzzed incessantly in concert. Sometimes she offered me a glass of red wine, and on one occasion I met two swarthy young Neapolitans there, and we all had wine and biscuits together, and smoked English cigarettes. I usually managed to take a piece of soap along on these visits, which was ecstatically greeted, for soap was like currency.

The day I said goodbye to Signora and her little family, I was astonished to hear her offering me marriage to her brother. '*Mio fratello vuole sposare a lei, Signorina*', she said, in the curious diction in use for the benefit of the Allies. I was somewhat startled, and enquired where her brother was. 'He is in Asmara, interned,' she replied, 'but he will be coming back, and would so much like to marry you.' I thought quickly, and said I felt honoured and flattered by the offer, but unfortunately had a fiancé in England whom I had promised to marry after the war, and therefore must decline with regret. The Signora also expressed regret. And we parted the best of friends.

We packed our kit a few days before departure, and our heavy baggage was loaded on to baggage trucks. We only took one grip each with us. I had brought three civilian dresses with me but found they were no use as we could not wear them, uniform being universally the order, and I really never had any occasion to wear them, at least not in those early days. So I presented one of them, a white linen tennis dress, to Giovanna, one of the girls who did our rooms and our laundry. She was delighted, and it suited her beautifully, with her dark eyes and hair. We presented as much in the way of chocolates, biscuits and cigarettes, with a bit of soap here and there, as we could spare, to the good woman and her family who had looked after us so kindly, and with them all out waving us farewell, we set off at about 8 a.m. on the morning of 4 July for Rome.

8

All Roads
Lead to Rome

*T*he AT officers, except Mabel, who stayed behind to come up with part of the rear party, were privileged in travelling faster and more comfortably than the rest of the unit. The Colonel drove up in his car with Jacky, his PA (personal assistant), and her friend Pam, while Cicely, Jean, Iris and I followed in a PU. The main convoy was setting off at about 6 a.m., whereas we did not have to be on the move until two hours later.

We traversed Naples, skirting the end of the Via Roma, ascended the hill on the other side, and took the road to Capua and Caserta. Capua was one of the most depressing places I have ever seen. It was grey and dingy, suffering much from war damage. The people were so very poor that they had long been unable to afford fresh paint for their houses, or anything to relieve the unpleasant dreariness and squalor of the place. Life for the inhabitants of Capua was at that time grim in the extreme, and beneath the blue sky and beaming sun their poverty, stark, sordid and inescapable, seemed to be thrown into relief; like a bad odour it hit one in the face, as it were, and one almost shuddered to think that human beings could live in such surroundings. Perhaps since the war things are better for the Capuans – I sincerely hope so. At that time they had also to put up with the continuous passage of everything pertaining to an army in the field: guns, ammunition lorries, vehicles carrying stores of every kind, troop-carriers, breakdown gangs, bailey bridge transporters, aeroplane parts, and – worst of the lot for the damage they did to the already hard-pressed road surfaces – tanks and Bren carriers. It was a constant stream, and on 4 July we formed part of it, and our unit's convoy was one of many streaming up north, through Capua, on the road to Rome.

After Capua we came to Caserta. The country was still flat, as there is a plain north of Naples until you come to the Volscian Mountains, but to the right was a line of hills, low and clearly silhouetted against the horizon. Caserta was a little better than Capua, and the move of AFHQ (Allied Forces Headquarters) from Algiers (which was in process of taking place, the advance party having arrived) was giving the inhabitants work, for the Army employed a large number of civilians everywhere in many menial capacities. This work and just the Army's existence in the place meant a great increase in food. Swill as we know it hardly existed in those days – the local population were only too glad to utilise the leftovers and to them every crumb had its value. Very few people in this country have ever been so near starvation as the Italians were that summer, after the long drawn-out and disastrous war into which Mussolini had launched them, against the desire of more than half the population, to satisfy his own crazy ambition.

On top of the losses in Africa, the Allied blockade, the ai raids in the north, the thousands of young men killed, wounded or imprisoned, the latter sent to forced labour camps by the Germans, and the consequent semi-paralysis of trade, business and agriculture, came the Armistice, and a species of civil war in Italy, when some sided with Badoglio and others with the Germans. The Germans had nothing but scorn for their late Allies, and did not scruple to wreak horrible vengeance on them whenever the occasion offered. Worse was still to come – many Italians had believed that the Armistice would bring them peace, that they would now be treated as a friend by the Allies and that the Germans would withdraw from Italy. But instead they were between two stools – both sides hated them – and each was determined to drive the other out of the country. Italy became a cruel and bloody battleground, in which many innocent men, women and children perished, numerous beautiful works of art were damaged or destroyed, and the once verdant countryside was frequently scarred by shelling and made uninhabitable by mines. The people were downcast in the extreme, and under a bitter disillusionment. They had not wanted the war, and when at last it was possible to shake off Mussolini's yoke and offer friendship to the Allies, the latter had spurned their friendship and but grudgingly accepted their allegiance, not letting it be forgotten that Mussolini had stabbed France in the back in 1940, and making it plain that the Italians would have to work hard to get back into the good books of the world again.

In 1944, despite the gaiety of Rome and the joys of being liberated, Italians everywhere were experiencing a kind of hopeless despair and a paralytic lassitude, as the Allies pressed on and the battle waged ever fiercer. They could do nothing, for the fate of Italy was not in their hands; they had to stand by and watch the land they loved ruined and trampled on by the conglomerate armies of both sides. '*Che miseria*', they would say, as they sat mournfully at their cafés, gloomily surveying piles of rubble, or scrabbling in it for some remnant of household property, or waiting in queues at the Allied labour offices, trying to get some sort of job, with local government or road cleaning or driving, something to tide them over until the war was over and they could resume their lives again. '*O Dio, speriamo che finirà presto la guerra,*' one heard the women say so often, '*non si può più – ormai l'Italia è finite asiamo – c'e tutto rovinato, tutto destrutto. I tedeschi ci hanno preso tutto.*' ('We can't go on any more – the Italians are finished – everything is ruined and destroyed. The Germans have taken everything away from us.')

As we drove on up north that day, only some of these facts were known to us, and although we noticed the destruction and ruination everywhere, we were partly distracted by the interest of the journey and the delight we all felt to be going to Rome. The Allied armies were advancing north of Rome and regrouping for the assault on Florence; meanwhile the Allied government in Rome was thoroughly established, and the Naples–Rome railway was already in the early stages of a long and laborious reconstruction. Outside the Italian theatre of war, the invasion of southern France was making steady progress, and the invasion of Normandy was achieving startling success, so morale was high and some optimists even expected an early surrender.

We had got down to the famous Pontine Marshes, not so very far from Anzio, when we halted for a picnic lunch in a field of Indian corn. Mussolini had made a good job of land recovery here, and it was a crying shame that the Germans, in order to bog the Allied transport, had re-flooded much of the recovered area, which was still underwater. The roads, being raised, were more or less dry, but there were long stretches of water, with trees and bushes protruding above the surface. To our right we had passed by the rather gloomy mountains, which on the Roman side are called the Alban Hills, and on our left we had branched away from the blue coastline, for our road, Route 7 as it is called, turns inland before Anzio. We had passed through Formia and Terracina, both badly battered, but lovely nevertheless, beside the brilliant cobalt-blue sea, bluer than I had ever seen it, even in Naples. We had passed the rock that is supposed to be the ancient seat of Circe, when she tried to beguile Odysseus from the path of duty, and we had left the sandy beaches, where no-one could bathe and no children could play in the warm inviting sand, because it was raked with jagged barbed wire, broken pill-boxes and crumpled gun emplacements. And now we were leaving the Pontine Marshes behind and rising into the Roman Campagna, that flat plain surrounding Rome, where the pines grow and from all parts of which you can see the dome of St Peter's, a distant landmark rising above the spires and roofs of the Eternal City.

We passed Velletri on the crest of the hill overlooking the plain, and saw fresh piles of rubble and crumbling homes, the result of the recent fighting, where crowds of townspeople seemed to have nothing to do but stand despairingly in groups discussing the depressing scene. Genzano, a little further on, was also in a bad way, and we saw the same dejected groups of inhabitants. We skirted Albano and saw the white towers of the Pope's summer residence at Castel Gandolfo; and then we sped on downhill, and left the main road near Ciampino airfield, where the wrecks of several planes and buildings razed to the ground gave one the impression of a sort of no-man's-land. Finally, we passed a Roman ruin on our right – it seemed strange to see a Roman ruin after all the contemporary ones, but it would doubtless outlive many of the latter, so firmly were the great blocks of stone placed one on another. We then turned in and struck another road, on each side of which were large buildings, all showing signs of damage. They were modern and must once have been very attractive, but now they had been ripped and gashed; in some places the whole construction was showing, the shoddy flooring and plaster walls revealing bad materials concealed by an ornamental veneer. Nevertheless, there were plenty still standing, even though a good many windows had been smashed, and we were to live in one of these erections, which had originally been cinema studios. Ours, as previously related, had been used by the Germans to house Allied prisoners, and we were told that the great hall, where they had lived, had been left full of foul straw, abounding with lice and fleas. All that had, however, been cleared away, and the place was as clean and free from pests as possible – certainly the admin staff had made a good job of it. But they had not been able to rid it of all its insect population, as I found later to my cost. The hall became our unit garage, and for some time to come one could not cross it without some encounter with the flea population.

We arrived at about three o'clock, and were soon drinking the inevitable cup of chow. Afterwards we ATs were shown our quarters, which were very nice. They had been dressing rooms, or perhaps wardrobe rooms, and were in the basement, but quite light and airy. We had four rooms, two large and two smaller, to house us seven ATs and two WAAFs who were to join us shortly. At the end of the corridor near the stairs were the washrooms, with four basins and about six showers, and WCs. It was quite private, the only problem being that the sentry on duty would be able to see in through the windows, especially at night when the lights were on, but rectified that a few days later by hanging net curtains across them.

Our rooms had been cleaned, but rather superficially, we felt, and so we set to work to give them an extra scour and to dust out the cupboards. The end room was destined for the WAAFs, so it had not been cleaned, as they were not expected for at least a week, but Cicely decided that she would like it; and although I pointed out that blood had been spilt on the floor, she would not be dissuaded from cleaning it out, blood and all, and installing herself there. I had gone up to the mess to borrow a broom from one of the batmen, and he had come down with me to see if he could help us. We were wandering from room to room, discussing the layout, when we got to the end room, which Cicely was busy putting in order. We all three had quite a long conversation, I standing in the middle. All of a sudden I noticed that Cicely was wearing no bush shirt and that the top half of her torso was covered only with a very flimsy vest. I looked quickly at the batman, but he was talking, staring straight ahead, as if J/Cdr Fowkes-Clevedon was, in Army language, perfectly 'properly dressed'. In fact, neither of them betrayed any emotion of any sort, except interest in domestic arrangements; but I suggested that Sims and I should have a look at one of the other rooms, which we did.

Once our rooms were more or less in order and we had set up our beds, we explored the building, commandeering for our own use any of the numerous pieces of furniture lying about that took our fancy, including some old bits of cinema sets. Most of these eventually, I am afraid, were broken up for firewood. There were dressing tables in the rooms, and we found some nice low stools to go with them and some attractive small tables. There being nothing left to do, I went for a stroll up the road with Toby and another man, the main convoy having by now clocked in, and we inspected two burnt-out tanks and various other pieces of wreckage, including helmets of varying types, shell-cases, etc., which were lying everywhere on the edges of the road and in ditches.

Ahead of us, orange and peach in the evening glow, were the Alban Hills, dotted with white houses in their lower reaches, and on their eastern flank a small white town, which I later learned was the renowned Frascati. To the east of us lay more hills, and to the north Rome itself. From the mound of the Roman ruin one could see the far-off dome of St Peter's, and the red roofs of the houses, golden in the sun. We were 9km, about 4½ miles, from Rome, and we wondered how often we could get in. There was a fair amount of Allied transport on our road, so we thought it should not be too difficult to make the journey once we had started.

It was hot and arid, and we were thirsty, and the dust parched our throats and powdered our shoes, which were supposed to always look as if they had just been rubbed up with spit and polish. I missed the freshness of Naples, and the apricot groves. It seemed flat and very isolated here after the glorious scenery we had just left. To the west of us was a magnificent avenue of towering umbrella pines, beyond which ran the old Roman aqueduct, through whose arches the sky showed the colour of tangerines until the sun dropped behind the horizon. A pink afterglow succeeded it, which in turn gradually diffused into shadow, so that only the outline of the hills to the south could be faintly discerned. Night falls quickly on the Campagna, and we hurried back to the enormous hall, which for the time being was used for our anteroom, or lounge, but I was tired after the journey and it was not long before turning in. I found Jean already installed, her curlers in, reading a book, and asking why ever I had wanted to go out souvenir-hunting, for we had brought back one or two old helmets and other such junk. 'You'll have plenty of time for that muck,' she said. She proved to be perfectly right. The helmets made good wastepaper baskets.

9

On the Fringe of the Eternal City

*T*he first night we spent in our new quarters was close and sultry, and indeed it was some time before we became accustomed to sleeping in the torrid atmosphere that prevailed that summer in the Campagna; those who had been in Cairo said that the Roman heat was as bad, perhaps worse.

I was to move and work in a different office, with a captain, who had not yet arrived from Algiers. According to all reports he was a good type and very enthusiastic about work, so it sounded all right, though I was sorry to leave female company again. But there was no choice, so why worry? It certainly was nice to have important decisions made for one. All one needed was resignation – or fortitude, if the decision was an unpleasant one.

The first morning there was not much to do, as the rear party had not yet arrived with all the files and office equipment. I spent most of the time cleaning out my new office and arranging the furniture as suitably as possible; also surreptitiously commandeering any items that I thought might be handy, including some spare Italian file covers and odds and ends of stationery, left since the cinema days in forgotten cupboards or out-of-the-way corners, doubtless undiscovered by the Germans who had preceded us.

In the afternoon, as there was no work to be done for the moment, Eileen and I decided to go into Rome. Eileen was Jacky's friend, but Jacky, being the colonel's PA, was of course busy, so we decided to take the opportunity of a breathing-space in our labours to get our first glimpse of the city whose name had been on everyone's lips now for several months past.

At two o'clock we were standing on the edge of the road, which was dry and dusty where the grass was withered and exhausted for want of rain, watching the traffic go by – Army vehicles, civilian carts with peasants taking a few wares in for sale or vats of wine; civilian cars, filled to overflowing, often with mattresses and luggage piled high on top; and pedestrians, footsore and weary, for there were no trams or buses. The trams just could not function for lack of electricity, and the buses for lack of petrol.

We hailed an open American truck and clambered into the back. Soon we were travelling rapidly along our road, at first past dried-up grassy fields, and then through a very dirty, shell-pocked village, where once more people lingered, conversing at length in whatever shade was to be found, and grubby children chased alongside us shouting, '*Caramelle, signorina, caramelle*'. Here the word '*signorina*' was used in full, and we very soon became aware that the Italian spoken in and around Rome was quite different from Neapolitan, to which we had hitherto been accustomed. I realised later that quite a few of us were practising our limited Italian with Neapolitan accents, but a few months' sojourn near Rome fortunately rectified that, for Neapolitan is looked down on by the rest of Italy, and the dialect is far from pure. Tuscan, especially as it is spoken in Siena, is reputed to be the purest form of Italian. Rome, of course, has its own dialect – in fact most parts of the country have. Needless to say, the Allied armies developed their own 'dialects' and adapted Italian terms and expressions for their own use.

We passed the length of the rather sordid looking village, and having crossed over a railway bridge, we continued under an aqueduct. After that came more houses, some rather shoddy looking, and we then came to a corner on which was a school, a fine building in the modern style. We turned left and passed some blocks of working-class flats, similar to those seen in the film *Open City*, and in a minute were on the main road, Route 7, which runs parallel to the ancient Roman Via Appia, which was the old-time thoroughfare. We joined the tramlines, disused, and a stream of military traffic, which was proceeding speedily down a long boulevard, with shops and flats on either side. We saw the names over the shops, designating their function, such fascinating names as '*Rosticerria*', '*Pasticceria*', '*Cartoleria*'. They mostly seemed to end in '-eria' ('*Rosticerria*', when literally translated, means 'Roastery'), but for cake shops and cafés, there was no 'cafeteria', so perhaps that was just an American invention.

Presently we came to an antique gateway, set in the old city walls. There were three entrances to the gateway: one said '*veicoli*', and all traffic entering the city went through this one. Our Americans dropped us on the other side, as they had to branch off, and we stood at the side of the road looking out for another lift. There was considerable civilian traffic here, and it seemed to be a general rendezvous. There were some small trucks, used as converted buses, and we saw some of these loaded up to their fullest capacity, waiting to start. The people inside were wedged in like sardines, and some were sitting on the edges protruding over the side, so great was the pressure from within. Ladders were propped against them from the ground, and when they were full, or rather when every square centimetre of space was utilised to the full, the ladderette would be taken off. And amid shouts of '*Ciao*' (so-long) and '*Arrivederci*' (goodbye) the *camionetta*, for so we soon learnt they were called, would move jerkily off, bursting at the seams with its human cargo, and start its creaky journey into the country. As we watched, people were arriving with bags, parcels and bundles of all shapes and sizes, some with worn old suitcases tied up with string, and were preparing to get into one or other of the waiting conveyances, *not* queuing up. There were priests and nuns, peasant women in black calico dresses, children, young men who might be returning home from the war, or evading their service, everyone rather hot and dusty, and here and there was the inevitable Italian policeman, or *Carabiniere*, in shabby, grubby and faded green uniform and a rather crumpled-looking peak cap. It was not until later that the *Carabinieri* were given new uniforms and achieved considerable smartness and discipline. For the time being, through no fault of their own, they were ill-paid and shabby and they did not quite know whom they were serving, for it goes without saying that they were under the strictest supervision from the Allied Control Commission.

Just back from this scene of ant-like activity, stood the Basilica of San Giovanni Laterano, a magnificent Renaissance church, with marble colonnades inside, and statues of the saints on the pinnacles of the facade. Ahead of us was a flight of steps leading up to a mosaic, a picture of Christ and the Apostles. The steps were very worn and rounded, as if they had been much used. I learnt later that they were the famous Passi Santi, or Sacred Steps, and that on a certain day each year the faithful mount them, kneeling, to supplicate for forgiveness of their sins.

There was so much to take in that one could not immediately form more than a fleeting impression of the scene, and it was not long before we had hailed a jeep and were hurrying on, deeper into the city, which was already beginning to fascinate us with its pulsating hidden life. We drove along a narrow and rather slummy street and then came out into an open once more; to the right of us were gardens on a slope and to our left the Coliseum. We did not need to have the Coliseum pointed out to us. It was there, just as one had always imagined it, only bigger and more massive, with its truly colossal blocks of stone and solid archways. We drove on, and another arch appeared to the left, and next to it more Roman ruins, which we learned afterwards were the Forum. To the right were yet more ruins and then a hill, with ancient houses and towers on it – the Aventine, as we later learned. It was then we caught sight of an amazing thing: in the midst of all this grey, pinky or rose-coloured stone, simmered something white as snow and dazzling in the sunshine. 'We call that the wedding cake,' said our driver casually. It was the Vittorio Emanuele Monument. I have heard many heated arguments about it, both for and against; it does not tone in with the rest of Rome, but because the city reflects the architecture and designs of so many periods and cults, there seems no reason why even the pre-1914 era should not have its monument. It is glaring, brutal and magnificently constructed, with some very fine sculpture. It can be seen from all the main parts of the city, its white roof towering nakedly above the rest, Roman, Romanesque, Gothic and Baroque. It is an integral part of modern Rome, just as much as Mussolini's famous stadium and the gorgeous modern railway station both fit in with the city's galaxy of architectural styles, worthy representatives of the Fascist régime, probably the best things that remain of that singularly undistinguished period of Italian history.

The Vittorio Emanuele Monument fills one side of the Piazza Venezia, the square already mentioned, where Mussolini made his speeches from a balcony on the first floor of the Palazzo Venezia. Opposite was another huge palazzo, and this building was taken over by the Allies as the seat of their government in Rome: the Rome Area Allied Command. Here the Union Jack and the Stars and Stripes hung side by side, and a mixed staff of British and Americans worked together to ensure the smooth functioning of the civil administration of the city, as well as the complicated maintenance of the Rome Garrison, the many 'leave' hotels, and the numerous and varied units situated in or around the city, such as Field Security, which checked on all undesirable or suspicious persons. It also included the staff of our own unit, doing special work, for we were under the War Office for our Intelligence directives, but under Rome Command for our administration. In that building many battles were later to be fought on the subjects of unit transport, fuel and stores of all kinds, as each unit tried to secure the best available for its own personnel, especially when the grimness of winter came upon us, and we discovered that Italy was not all sun, fruit, wine and song. But that was yet to come, and we were now sweltering in the heat of an almost tropical midsummer.

We skirted the piazza, whose centre was converted into a military car park, and took a long street leading out of it, opposite the 'Wedding Cake', and found it was called the 'Corso Umberto', '*corso*' being Italian for boulevard. There were stone buildings on either side, mostly in Renaissance style, with tall windows covered with iron grills, and sturdy oak doors studded with nails. We soon came to a square with a minaret in its centre. This was to the left of the Corso, and here on the right another wide boulevard turned up. We ascended this, noting with surprise how devoid the streets were of all civilian activity. By contrast there were numbers of troops, both English and American, strolling about, looking into the closed windows of the shops, or some of them talking to a few girls, who wore their hair very long and flowing, and most of them sporting the fashionable wedge-heeled shoe, which had not yet appeared in England. War and Occupation did not seem to put the Italian women out of fashion, or cause them to lose any of their dress sense.

We presently arrived at the Piazza Barberini, where several roads converged and where a fountain with stone figures stood in the middle. But it was dry and only a shallow layer of dirty water covered the bottom of the basin. Here the Hotel Bristol-Bernini had been taken over by the American forces for their Red Cross Club and PX. I never discovered what the magic letters 'PX' stood for, but the most wonderful things came from there. To the Italians it must have been symbolic of Santa Claus. Here then our friendly jeep driver left us and we turned left, up a long hill called the Via Vittoria Veneto, with lime trees on each side, whose shade we were only too glad to enjoy, for it was about three o'clock, zero hour in the summer heat. We wandered along and gazed in the shop windows, but found nothing to buy as all were closed, and everything was too expensive in any case. We did discover a hairdresser, and I made a mental note of its whereabouts, for we had no hot water and washing one's own hair was going to be somewhat of a bind. Hairdressers at least were not expensive, as yet.

We arrived at the top of the hill and came to another ancient gateway, very similar to the one by which we had entered the city. This turned out to be the Porta Pinciana. We went through it and into a beautiful park with tall pine trees. We did not venture far, but noticed several vendors of what must be black market cigarettes.

We also heard the already familiar, 'Mees, sell cigarette', whispered after us as we passed. We were in search of somewhere to have tea, but the one or two requisitioned hotels we came across were American, and Americans, it seemed, did not go in for afternoon tea. In the end, we entered an Italian café, which we learnt later was forbidden at that time, and there the proprietor was most obliging and gave us tea with water ices. He had no milk or cakes of any sort. There were hardly any customers, for trade had not recommenced, and many Romans were still out in the country, on their farms or at their seaside villas (if these were still inhabitable) or with relations. A great exodus had taken place, as although Rome had been declared an 'open city', many had feared the retribution of the Germans and had fled with a few belongings in case there should be widespread destruction. But the trek home had already begun, as had the enormous influx of refugees of many nationalities, which has been one of the city's greatest administrative problems ever since.

The population is said to have gone up 2 million since the war, and not much building has taken place since, owing to lack of materials. Small wonder that there are actually people living in caves, in Roman ruins or even out in the open. After we had rested for a time in the pleasant cool of the café, we strolled down the hill once more, waving at Toby, whom we caught sight of coming in an open truck with an assorted collection of soldiers. He must have hitched in too. Some of the passers-by looked at us rather curiously, and we realised that we must be amongst the first of the women's services to come to Rome. We found a lovely shop that sold combs, powders and perfumes. It was wonderful to buy a real tortoiseshell comb, and quite cheaply compared with English prices.

The shadows were lengthening, and the city was beginning to wake up from its afternoon siesta, but it was time for us to think of getting a lift back. We discovered that just in front of the Vittorio Emanuele building was the best place to pick up a vehicle going our way, and without difficulty we found transport and were soon on our return journey. I felt dazed and astonished, to think that I had actually at last visited Rome, of which I had heard so much, which my parents had visited ten years earlier, and of which I had read in history lessons. It gave one a sort of exhilarated feeling, but we knew that we were indeed in every sense on the fringe. We had lifted the cup to our lips – and to experience Rome is like drinking from the magic cup that had no dregs, and from which one could never drink too much.

10

Mädchen in Uniform

*T*he next day we unpacked all our files, typewriters, stationery, index cards and a host of other equipment necessary to the running of the office. My new boss arrived, and seemed quite pleasant and very businesslike. He set about a complete reorganisation of the work he had been given, and in view of the fighting then taking place, his work was of great value. He had an enormous large-scale map on the wall, showing the daily, almost hourly, progress of the battle, which Tony adjusted as each fresh report came in. Among my jobs was that of map curator, and this I found most interesting, and incidentally it taught me quite a lot of geography of which I had not even dreamt before. Some of the maps were illustrated in such beautiful colours, translucent blues and bright greens, that it was a real pleasure to handle them, and I became very proud of our collection, which grew progressively larger as time went on and was quite a library by the time I had to hand it over to someone else.

Shortly after Tony's arrival, we went off to the new Map Centre, which was right on the other side of the city. We drove in a Morris truck with a closed cabin, as there was nothing else available, and we two sat in front with the driver, it being so bumpy and dusty behind. It was an intensely hot day and we started off at about two o'clock. We went through the city to the Corso Umberto, and instead of turning right towards the PX we kept on to the end of the Corso, where it entered a large round piazza. On each side were sister churches, with shields over their doors, depicting the dove of peace with a leaf in its mouth, green and white on a blue background. To the right was a tree-covered slope leading up to the Borghese Gardens and, steeply rising from this, was a white stone terrace and balustrade. Ahead of us was yet another massive gateway in the walls. This was the Porta Flaminia, opening on to the Via Flaminia, and beside the gate was a very old stone church, Santa Maria del Popolo. There was not much traffic, and we bounded over the cobbles of the piazza and through the ancient arches, with now partially effaced Fascist slogans on the walls – ''*Viva il Duce. Morteagli Alleati!*' ('Long live the leader. Death to the Allies!')

The Via Flaminia is a great broad highway, which crosses one of the newest quarters of Rome, where there are some beautiful modern flats, cream, peach, pink and even blue, with window boxes, and small balconies or terraces, each with its little collection of flowerpots and cactuses. Finally we came to the Tiber, a green, muddy-looking river in the hot weather, wending its way sluggishly seawards; we turned right along its bank to the Ponte Milvio, the oldest bridge in Rome, very long and narrow, and for one-way traffic only. We crossed over and saw in front of us a rather modern-looking and not very impressive church. Now it was necessary to ask the way of some local inhabitants, and I being the only Italian speaker (if I could claim that qualification) was told to get out and make enquiries. After several minutes of inconclusive talking, shouting and gesticulating, we went on and questioned an old man tending large sunflowers in a small, dusty garden. We were getting our first experience of that almost universal response when one asks an Italian the way – '*sempre Diritto*', straight on.

A little further on, we turned left, up a steep and bumpy path, with no normal surface of any kind, and came to a large modern building with the usual signs of damage. In front, a neat, freshly painted notice stated, 'No. 2 Field Survey Unit'. We went in, and found that the Survey people were in the process of unpacking and organising themselves. We managed to obtain some of the maps we wanted, and set off once more inside the by now stiflingly hot cab, and were soon out on the main road by the church, and driving along the north bank of the Tiber towards a wide, modern bridge. This we crossed and, for a change, drove right along the bank of the river. What a magnificent sight! First, we passed the clean-looking modern flats mentioned before, and then came to older houses, all with green window-boxes and sometimes grey-striped sun-blinds. To the right of us unfolded the panorama of the bridges, one by one, in the immediate background of which was Monte Mario, its greenery showing up the white houses and the gleaming white dome of the wireless station. Nearby, we could see the famous Castel Sant'Angelo, where Benvenuto Cellini was imprisoned, and from where Tosca hurled herself to her death, the Palazzo di Giustizia, with its tall ornate pinnacles, and then the dome of St Peter's, rising majestically from the parchment walls of the Vatican City. Behind St Peter's was the green hill of the Janiculum. Along the river banks on either side were the cool lime trees, whose shade made the road at least bearable, despite the reflection of the burning sun, whose scorching rays were deflected from the pavements, thus doubling the intensity of the atmosphere. The colouring was something never to be forgotten, a scene of vivid contrasts, the dark green of the trees and grass enhanced by the vivid brightness of delicate pink or peach of the sunlit buildings, the brilliant, untrammelled blue of the sky, in which not a wisp of cloud was to be seen, and the grey-green of the river.

Here and there on the hills stood the black outline of a cypress tree, like a sentinel pointing up to the sky. We came to a fascinating little island in the river, crammed with houses of all shapes and sizes. Passing some Doric columns and other Roman remains, we skirted another amphitheatre, similar to the Coliseum, but which had been put to practical use – the upper part had been filled in and converted into flats. We then descended, past the Capitoline Hill, to the Piazza Venezia, and thence past the Coliseum to San Giovanni. By that time I was parched with thirst, and everything

I had on seemed to be glued to my body. I was very relieved when Tony said we would stop for a refresher. We sat outside a café on the Piazza San Giovanni and drank lemonade, made with fresh lemons, and for a wonder with plenty of sugar. After that we felt better and continued on our way, but by now the cream houses and the grey aqueduct were once more bathed in the sunset rays, and the houses on the Alban Hills seemed almost to wear haloes as they reflected the warm glow of the afternoon, offset by the dark green of the woods and fields.

Our office was soon enlivened by the arrival of a young captain, also from Algiers, called Jimmy. He was very cheerful, talked a lot, and seemed slightly bohemian to my mind. He was the most untidy person I had ever met, and as I was responsible for tidying up the office my job became twenty times more complicated after the arrival of Jimmy, who could not tolerate that anything he was working on should be touched, or, as he put it, 'tampered with'. One day I could stand it no longer, and I had one gorgeous tidy-up while Jimmy was out searching for Roman pottery, his favourite hobby outside his work. When he came in, he had one look round and then let go a flow of expletives liberally sprinkled with good strong language. It was as if a hailstorm had come down in the heat of the Roman afternoon. For once I was nettled, and before I knew what had occurred, I was soundly berating Jimmy for speaking to me in such a fashion, and then unknown to both of us, the colonel walked in, and I suddenly turned round and saw him, looking more than a little amused, and stopped as suddenly as I had begun, feeling rather foolish. But the colonel was both just and gallant, and as Jimmy was already known, in fact notorious, for his difficult ways, he was soon put in his place and in fact took it very well. The funny thing was that I really rather liked him, though at other times I detested him, for his sarcasm in particular. He was often trying to persuade me to go out hunting for Roman pottery with him in the evenings after

dinner, but it was intensely hot, and I did not fancy the gravel pit
next to the even dustier main road, where most of his best finds
were discovered, though to my mind none of them were much
catch. Still, Jimmy wanted to take up archaeology seriously after
the war. He also collected old enemy weapons, and presented me,
in addition to pieces of pottery, with a number of martial souvenirs, helmets, an old bayonet, which later became very useful
for hacking up firewood, some machine-gun bullets, and most
important, a Teller mine, which he promised he had freed from
all important fuses. Heaven knows why I believed so naively that
he had really done all that was necessary to make the landmine
harmless, but I did, perhaps because Tony seemed quite unperturbed by it. It was grand to possess a landmine as a souvenir,
although it became somewhat of an embarrassment later on and
nearly got me into serious trouble, by which time, of course,
Jimmy had returned to Algiers.

Meanwhile we had acquired a sergeant, Entwhistle, in the
office. He was a good type, though he was a little suspicious of
women officers, but we got on very well and he really was an
excellent worker. He had worked with Tony in Cairo and so they
were already a team. Jimmy eventually departed, as neither Tony
not Sgt Entwhistle could get on with him, they both being such
tidy beings. Although I was sorry to see him go, there was more
order and harmony in the office after he had left. The Teller mine
was meanwhile relegated to a cupboard, and luckily it was on my
afternoon off that the machine-gun bullets blew up in the secret
waste incinerator! Entwhistle, profiting by my absence, had had a
field-day, tidying up, and though no-one knew how the things got
among the secret waste, I had my suspicions. Fortunately, despite
the spray of bullets that emanated from the furnace, no-one was
even grazed – luckily, as an enquiry would have been awkward,
to say the least.

Our temporary home had a magnificent exterior, being a large
modern building with steps leading up to an impressive entrance,
from which more steps led up left and right to a courtyard, with
flowers and crazy paving. The flowers, needless to say, were

dried-up and ragged, as the sun beat hotly down on to the white concrete paving and steps round the edge of the cloister. Glass doors opened into it, but many of the panes were broken. Various rooms led off from this courtyard, and in front, over the steps, was the large room, already referred to, which we used as an anteroom. A bar at one end, and various armchairs, covered with rather dusty but comfortable woollen material that once might have been a sort of brick colour, plus upright chairs and small round tables, were produced from somewhere in the building.

A passage with rooms on either side led from the first court-yard into the second, and much the same layout occurred here. Beyond this was the other great hall, where the British prison-ers had lain in the straw, and further on still other rooms, rather small, but close together and convenient. These became the admin offices, and housed the camp commandant, the adju-tant, the guard commander, the MO and the MI room (Medical Inspection room) and the MT office (Motor Transport). Outbuildings accommodated the RSM and his tame blackbird, the Q stores and the ration store. The Other Ranks had a field cookhouse and slept in tents in the field beyond.

The rooms around the cloisters, mostly in the basement, were the officers' sleeping quarters, over three wings. The fourth base-ment wing housed a theatre with small rooms branching off it. Later on, during the winter, this was used for amateur dramatics. For the present it was disused, having no access to the outside for light, and electric current being extremely precious.

On either side of the building was a terrace, and it was won-derful to sit on the edge of the flat roof and from the north side gaze towards Rome, or on the south watch the sun on the near-est peak, Rocca di Papa, and the evening glow on the Alban Hills, of which Rocca di Papa is the highest. During our lunch-hour we would often have a little siesta on one of these terraces, although in August the sun was usually too hot to stay there for more than a few minutes. There was a garden of sorts outside, but it had been neglected for so long, or trampled over by a succession of troops, that there was not much left, except for a few straggling vegetables.

On the other side, towards Rome, was a small cottage, divided in two, where the former *custode* or caretaker lived, and in the other half some official connected with the former studio. These people and their families were allowed to stay on, and they had an unending source of interest in watching the doings of the English, whom doubtless they considered quite mad. One of the cottages I occasionally used to visit, and was invited to go one day when the eldest daughter, aged about eight, had a birthday. There were two little girls, and they were both spotlessly clean and had charming manners. I was even given eggs once or twice, which I hated to take for I knew that they had very little food, but they would brook no refusal. I was afraid to offend them, and so tried to make some return by taking them chocolate and soap, both rare and welcome commodities. They were also able to get some of the leftovers from the camp and were thus better placed than most civilians, although it was actually forbidden to give food to the population, or buy their food, or eat in their restaurants. Most of the civilian restaurants in Rome had the famous 'out of bounds' sign over their doors, although few of them were open at first. Some, however, were taken over by the Occupation authorities for the use of the Army and other services, for the RAF and Navy were also in Rome, as well as a Russian mission (a military mission to the Italian Army), quantities of Americans of all services, and some French, Polish and other liaison officers.

All round us in the fields were caches of bullets or forgotten shell cases, and for a month or so after our arrival there was a series of explosions as the sun touched them off, and sometimes a cloud of sparks would flash to and fro, accompanied by a rapid 'rat-a-tat-tat', as a pile of abandoned machine-gun ammunition exploded. Animals, or even people, occasionally set off concealed landmines, but I am thankful not to have witnessed such an accident, and in our area there were few. Further north they were far more common, and at that time the German shoe-mine, which was almost invisible, was disabling many of our soldiers. I often wondered how many of these perilous objects would remain in the soil and kill or maim some innocent peasant in later years.

One evening, immediately after high tea, Jacky took me for a walk in the fields, and then suggested we might try to obtain a glass of milk from a farm where milk could occasionally be found. I had not tasted fresh milk for several months and she had not done so for more than a year, so we set off for the farmhouse. This turned out to be a rough stone cottage, rather battered and dilapidated looking, surrounded by grey dry mud that had been moulded into ridges by caked-up cart tracks. We went round to the back past some loosely built stacks, ignoring the closed shutters at the front, and found the farmer and his family in the bare, stone-flagged kitchen. Chickens, cats and dogs were mingling happily in front of the door, and we heard cows lowing from neighbouring stalls. We explained haltingly what we were in search of, and they produced it at once and very willingly. We expressed appreciation to the best of our ability and they gave us to understand that we would always be welcome. On a subsequent visit they produced two eggs. But after that, our little adventure reached the ears of the MO, who scolded us roundly and told us frankly that we could carry on, but that he would not sympathise with us if we contracted TB. I was horrified, having then no idea of the high rate of tuberculosis prevalent in Italy. We did not drink any more milk, but continued to wander among the farms, sometimes along cart-tracks and lanes, sometimes on small footpaths. Here, depending upon the hours, one might meet children driving the cows home, perhaps urging on a dreamy-eyed beast with a small switch, uttering shrill cries of abuse, or a yoke of oxen, patiently drawing a simple wooden plough, for in the Campagna agricultural methods were still largely traditional. Or at other times, often in the midday break, we would climb the Roman ruins, and bask on a grassy spot, the now overgrown floor of some antique salon, the plain spread out beneath and around us, behind us the Alban Hills, and in front Rome with its distant spires and domes. Even at midday it was very quiet, except for the buzzing of insects and the occasional zooming of a bumblebee, doing the round of any small wild flowers growing between the sundered boulders; and always above us was the blue sky, to us Northerners, a constant source of wonderment and delight.

Tony, Entwhistle and I had a nice large, airy office looking towards Rome, with two big windows, actually with all their panes. The ATs' sleeping quarters were in the basement wing below the corridor outside our office, and so everything was very convenient, and it was easy to contact the housekeeper if one wanted anything done quickly. Some stairs led up from where the neck of the passage joined the two cloisters, and on the top here was a lovely spacious room, which became the officers' mess. It had windows all round, and in winter we could see the snow on the Umbrian Hills to the east, as we sat at table. A kitchen and small larder were attached to this room, and on the same floor a little room where the two cooks slept. The kitchen had an external ladder, so that stores, vegetables, etc. could be brought up from outside.

The stoves were coal ranges, but modern ones, and quite adequate for the numbers they had to cook for, which varied from fifty to a hundred, as the strength was constantly changing, through postings, attachments and the departure or return of officers and men on section duty or mobile duty. In that case they either lived in a requisitioned house nearer the line of fire, or were attached to a division, brigade or other formation, when they messed with whomever they were with and only took a vehicle and driver from us, the parent unit. When the hostilities ceased, the situation was much the same but they became more stationary, and mostly worked in groups, rather than in the isolated detachments operating when the fighting was still on.

We ATs were responsible for much of the clerical work and what would be called the 'stooging'. It was galling sometimes to feel that one was just a stooge, but then someone had to do the groundwork; it certainly could be done by women, and of course so much depended on whom one was stooging for. Even if sometimes we did wonder if we were worth our pips, we had the consolation of knowing that the work was important and had direct bearing on the action in our immediate theatre of war, and even in more remote theatres. Also, because it was highly confidential, we knew that we were useful and trusted. As officers, we were not much more trouble than the men, as we looked after ourselves entirely, the only difference being that we had to have separate quarters. Some people thought that we were a nuisance, but no-one can deny that women can undertake clerical work just as well, if not better, than men, and every woman employed in that way freed a man either for fighting or other more active service. We might not be able to go right forward like the male IOs (intelligence Officers), but we could do the research and typing in the background, which was essential for their job to be done thoroughly. We could assist in the running of the mess and take a part in the organisation of unit welfare. So all-in-all, disregarding the controversy for or against women officers, I feel that our presence fulfilled a need and achieved a purpose. That we fell in and out of love and got homesick occasionally seems to me only a side-issue. As long as it was remembered that, first and foremost, we were there to do a job, and not as playthings, then all was well. The Italians, for the most part, considered us to be morale-raisers for the troops, but then they did not have much experience of '*Mädchen* in uniform'.*

---

*   *Mädchen in Uniform* was a pre-war (1931) German film about Prussian military discipline in a girls' school.

11

Do in Rome as Rome Does

Not long after our arrival, Pam's boyfriend turned up in Rome and took her out. In those early days there were hardly any clubs or hotels yet properly taken over where one could go for a meal or entertainment, and so they went to a civilian place. Pam returned with the most glowing account of a fantastic restaurant, with shaded lights, curtained alcoves where couples could dine in romantic seclusion; soft, nostalgic airs played on melodious strings, exquisite food, including iced cakes and cream (only a memory to us), ancient floors and walls lined with bottles – and last, but not least, waiters attentive and only too anxious to please the victorious Allies. This positively fired one's imagination, and after a lunch of frittered bully-beef, dehydrated potato purée, dried peas and a good solid steam pudding, which sat like a leaden ball in the stomach on a hot July day, one's mouth just watered with gustatory envy. But the enchanted place was soon put out of bounds, and it was some time before it was reorganised and reopened as an officers' club. It was later called the 'Orso' and I often went there to dine and dance. But this was to come.

Meanwhile, another place opened for us, the Nirvanetta, a delightful garden with a dance floor in the middle and trees all round. Fairy lights hung in the trees, and an excellent orchestra, complete with accordion and guitar, played on a dais beside the floor. There we practised the tango and the rumba, swing steps and quick waltzes, for Italians never much played the unending foxtrot that prevails in England. There was a rhythm and a zest to their dance-music, not to mention the tuneful tangos and slow foxes, which you rarely find in a northern dance orchestra. Perhaps it was the moon and the stars overhead, perhaps partly also the relief that no Nazi spy might be among the guests, nor Fascist informer sitting nearby, sipping a glass of wine, his eyes open for an escaped Allied prisoner or anti-Fascist, but the orchestra played with real fervour and gaiety, and three young Italian girls, recruited to sing and partner unattached officers (who far outnumbered them), sang with great charm and much spirit. There was one little girl who only looked about eighteen, with a true, though not very loud, soprano voice, but her personality carried anything she sang right through to the hearts of the audience. She seemed fired with *joie de vivre*, whatever her private trouble may have been. Over and over again she was encored as her eyes sparkled, her active hands moved expressively, and she sang '*Chirribirri bee*' or perhaps '*Ho un sassolino nella scarpa, ai!*' ('There's a little pebble in my shoe – aha!'), or even 'Lili Marlene', the most popular song of all.

There was a bar inside as well as tables outside, where most of the men without partners would gather, and one used to see a great variety of unit flashes and uniforms. All sorts of people on leave would be meeting each other, some wearing long silk scarves and with long bristling moustaches. One would frequently watch friends slapping each other on the back, exchanging drinks and news, their conversation frequently punctuated with the universal 'old boy'. It was a great meeting place. I have never seen men pay so much attention to current fashion as some of them did overseas. Many grew enormous moustaches, competing as to its length with their friends; and gaily coloured scarves or handkerchiefs worn at the neck of their bush shirts, to keep them free from perspiration, were the vogue. Corduroy trousers and suede shoes were another desert mode that persevered throughout the Italian Campaign, and these fancies were much caricatured by the famous cartoonist 'Jon' in his sketches published in the Army-sponsored CMF (Central Mediterranean Forces) newspaper, the *Union Jack*, read eagerly every day. Our other source of news was the American *Stars & Stripes*, but home journals were usually several weeks, or even months, old before they reached us.

Most people of course drank wine, for we were already acquiring new tastes, but there was usually some whisky or gin available. It was here that I first drank Spumante, the Italian version of champagne, which is really more like our cider and which became such a favourite with the forces. A brand of it was manufactured near Rome, and so there was always plenty to be had, and it certainly made a party go and left no after-effects.

At about ten o'clock there was generally a cabaret, some dance-turn, which invariably included a scantily clad and glamorously made-up *danseuse*. Being a woman, I never took a great deal of interest in how much or how little the lady was wearing; as long as she danced well, I liked her. I suppose women never do understand the almost professional and certainly rapt interest that men invariably take in a female cabaret turn. There would be a hush, the buzz of animated conversation would momentarily cease, and all eyes would be turned towards the floor. One felt quite a cad if one asked for a cigarette, or blocked a male view by electing to 'disappear', at such a moment. There were male dancers too, some of them good, but mainly just partnering the girls and putting them through their paces.

Our recreational truck started on the return journey from the Piazza Venezia at eleven o'clock, and so we had a rush to get back there in time. But the evening was well worth the rush. Like many English girls, I had until that time never been to anything approaching a night club, and the Nirvanetta, with its music and lamps, the warm star-lit evenings and the scented atmosphere of the Mediterranean nights enthralled me and showed me something I had never even dreamt of. I had never danced out of doors, only once in a marquee, and it is a joy few people can experience in this uncertain, chilly, damp climate of ours.

And there was the atmosphere of the Army overseas, the comradeship and friendliness, because everyone was far from home, and you did not need to be introduced to become acquainted. Your uniform, whatever it was, provided sufficient introduction. Who and what you were in civilian life mattered not at all – people took you as they found you and judged you for what you were. In that sense life in the forces seemed to me truly democratic.

I startled some of our people by turning up at the Nirvanetta in the company of an American officer, who had given me a lift one day and we had become friendly. He was very nice, of Czech origin, but like so many of one's friends overseas, with the progress of the campaign he moved on, and we did not keep up a correspondence. Like all Americans, he was generous to the point of extravagance, and gave me long, fat, perfumed American cigarettes whenever we met, and on his last visit presented me with a beautiful painted scarf, a souvenir of Rome.

About ten days after our arrival, a staff captain from the RAAC (Royal Australian Armoured Corps) phoned up Jacky. He had met her on duty one day when she went down to HQ on an errand for the colonel, and asked her to dine in his mess and bring as many of the ATs and WAAFs as were free or cared to go – he would provide a sufficient number of escorts. Five of us accepted the invitation – Jacky, Jean, Pam, Phyllis (one of our WAAFs who had recently come up from Naples) and myself.

We all dressed up as smartly as we could, Pam of course far outstripping everyone else in her perfectly cut, cream silk gabardine tunic and skirt. Her face was tanned with the sun, and her hair naturally wavy, and worn rather long. With bright lipstick and coloured nail-varnish, and a perfect pair of silk stockings on her legs, she certainly showed how smart and attractive it was possible to look in uniform. Sophistication was reflected in every perfectly polished button and rang the keynote of her low, measured speech. All five of us collected in the anteroom and were offered drinks to warm us up. Presently the self-appointed lookout announced that unknown transport was arriving, presumably to fetch us. We were collected and driven off, half our male colleagues watching us depart with quizzical grins from the windows. It was always known when, and with whom, we went out, and in fact it seemed to be the before-dinner amusement of some members of the mess to watch the comings and goings from the windows of the anteroom. The ATs were particularly noticed, perhaps because there were so few of them. It was always remarked on if any of us appeared with a new boyfriend, but in time we got used to the banter and leg-pulling and rather enjoyed it.

So on this occasion we drove off pretending not to notice the audience, and were taken into Rome, to the winding boulevard with the lime trees on either side. We stopped at one of the largest hotels, Les Ambassadeurs, or Gli Ambasciatori as the Italians call it. There was an American as well as a British MP on duty outside. We left our hats (which in the hot weather were the only extra piece of uniform we wore) with an American corporal, and went down into the basement, into a long low room with a little platform at one end. It was illuminated by modern tube lighting, and always gave me the impression of the pink and green with which one coloured homemade marzipan before the war. At the far end was a small cocktail bar, and to one side, in the middle, was another dais for the orchestra. Comfortable plush seats lined the walls, and small tables and chairs were scattered here and there. We were very soon introduced to the rest of the party and sipped Gin Fizzes before going into dinner. This was where the inter-Allied staff of the RAAC messed, and very fine it was too – just the job, in fact. The dining room was enormous and very ornate, with chandeliers and gilt panelling, and steps led down into the body of the room, so that everyone could see who was coming in – and with whom! The messing was once more American, and so we had coffee with every course, and – most delicious – sweetcorn as a vegetable, in a creamy sauce. It was my first experience of corn on the cob, and I enjoyed it. On a subsequent occasion, however, when it was served *au naturel*, I found the eating of it less easy and it was somewhat of a task to try and make bright conversation while preserving some of one's lipstick and all of one's face powder. An orchestra played in one corner, and very obligingly performed arias from opera, or other favourites, on request. After dinner, we returned to the bar-cum-ballroom, and the rest of the evening passed pleasantly, dancing and chatting.

We went there on numerous occasions, and my particular escort used to beguile me with fascinating stories of the strange happenings at the Grand Hotel, one floor of which was taken over for very senior officers, the real high-ups of the RAAC and the Allied Commission; and where on other floors persisted the weird intrigues of beautiful titled ladies and notorious noblemen who had closed an eye to the iniquities of the Fascist régime, or had openly supported it, and others who had secretly fought it. Many of these people, some of them of foreign nobility, were scheming to reassert themselves and present the Allies with a clean sheet. The intrigues sounded like a novel, and made me think of the story of the Athene Palace, Bucharest.

The Grand was where my parents had stayed in 1934, when there was a waiter's strike and the heir to the Spanish throne had helped to serve the guests. I longed to visit this mysterious place and savour the exciting happenings, which were every day occurring within its luxurious walls. Perhaps my staff captain exaggerated, but if he did then it was pardonable, for the stories would not have been so enjoyable had they not been so fantastic.

As the weather got hotter, Jean and I began to take a short siesta on our beds after lunch, Italian-fashion, and it was necessary to have a shower or a cold sponge and change everything before going out in the evening. Sometimes the evenings were unbearably hot, and when tidying up in the office, or writing home, my clothes stuck to my body, and trickles of perspiration literally poured down my face. It made my hair so damp and clammy that it stuck to my scalp and I had to dry it with a towel. We often sat up late to enjoy the cooler moments towards eleven o'clock or midnight, and if we went out we did not care to hurry back. In our rooms it was stifling and airless, and sometimes we could hardly sleep for the heaviness of the atmosphere. The mosquito nets over our beds did not help, but they were necessary. Even so, I was steadily more and more bitten, and became quite ashamed of my arms and legs.

If I felt energetic enough to get up and go out for a while before breakfast, the best of the day was then to be enjoyed. Everything was fresh and the sun was warm, but not scorching. Sometimes we went for strolls after dark towards the old aqueduct, and past a farm, where we used to hear the chatter of the farmer and his family as they sat at their evening meal – '*la cena*', as it is known in Italy – probably just the same as when Caesar was a master of Rome and Rome ruled the world. Occasionally a shot would fire out – the Italians seem to be very trigger-happy, and once or twice some of us appeared to be the target, for shots whistled overhead. No-one came to harm, however, so it was probably just for sport. All Italians in the country seemed to carry weapons, and I suspected them of firing them into the air on occasions of excitement or perhaps despair. To let off a firearm seemed to relieve their pent-up feelings. They must often have felt like shooting someone in those difficult days.

Pope Pius XII started his daily audiences for the Allied Troops immediately upon their entry into Rome. I was privileged to attend one of these, one hot day towards the end of July. I went with Cicely, who was a Roman Catholic and could instruct me on the correct behaviour. We waited in an immense crowd at the door of the Vatican in one corner of St Peter's Square. There were officers and soldiers of many ranks, and from all the different forces and nationalities that made up the Allied Army in Italy. All were in khaki drill of slightly varying shades, or in white naval drill, the only relief being the coloured unit badges and flashes, or an occasional coloured scarf, strictly forbidden, but frequently worn nonetheless.

This motley throng waited outside the great doors until, just before midday, the portals opened and we were ushered down several long corridors. We crowded in, talking softly, for a subdued hush had come upon us, and entered the Audience Chamber, a long room with a stage at one end, the walls hung with unobtrusive, yet beautifully executed tapestries. There were windows along one side, and shafts of sunlight lit up the dark skin of an Indian soldier or the bleached hair of an Englishman. There were only a handful of girls, and Cicely and I were the only ATs; some of the girls were French, American or Polish. We all had our heads covered with veils, handed to us in advance, and were taken up to the front, for the rule was 'ladies and officers in front'. This was all organised by the Swiss Guards, magnificent in their huge mediaeval helmets, their striped breeches and doublets, and grasping their stout halberds.

On the stroke of noon there was a sudden silence, and the Holy Father, dressed in cream brocade, a tiny white skullcap on his head, was borne in by his attendant priests on a chair. Immediately a sort of tremor went through the mixed audience, and all, man and woman, officer and soldier, sank to their knees. The Pope then gave his blessing to us, afterwards addressing the gathering. He spoke for a while, first in English, and then in French. He then descended from the chair and circulated among the troops, chatting to first one and then another, blessing the objects, rosaries, prayer books, etc., which many held out to him. He spoke to us, mostly in French, and asked us kindly where we came from, and how we liked Italy and our work. Then he passed, a dignified, gracious, kindly presence, perfectly natural, and yet infinitely spiritual. After some twenty minutes, he ascended his chair again, gave us his blessing once more, and was then carried away, doubtless exhausted by his interview and the effort it must cost to give audiences day after day to several hundred men and women of different nationalities, sects and races. We were very impressed by the Holy Father himself and by the very real reverence of his audience, and also by the genuine comfort and inspiration that seemed to radiate from him. He did indeed behave like the Father of his People, and these audiences will be treasured memories for all who took part in them.

St Peter's itself has a wonderful exterior and a too magnificent interior. I loved its outside, but its inside is too vast and princely for me. Four or five of us escaped from the office and went down one hot morning in August. We left at about 8.30 a.m. and reached Vatican City at about nine o'clock, when the sun was just beginning to heat up the flagstones of the streets and the asphalt of St Peter's Square, as if it were warming the stones of a gigantic oven. This time we ventured through the gates of Vatican City, and had to hand over our identity cards at the passport office on the right of the gates. We passed into a square, enclosed by high, cream-coloured stone buildings, and in whose centre grew fresh green grass and tall palms.

It is quite impossible to describe all that we saw of the Vatican galleries, but we passed through numerous halls of magnificent tapestries, many of them created by the renowned Gobelin. Then there were further halls of paintings, and yet more of sculpture, including a copy of the famous Laocoön, the snake entwining in their death throes a father and his two sons. Then we visited the library currently in use, as well as the old library, a floor higher. Both old and new libraries have Gothic vaulted ceilings, decorated with brilliant painted frescoes of many designs. The upper library is particularly vivid, and its vaulted roof was 'piped', as it were, with aquamarine, bordered with multicoloured patterns. The whole roof was coloured, and on tables here and there were priceless works of art, such as an antique Chinese pot-pourri jar, 2ft high and of elaborate style. We saw priceless manuscripts and volumes illuminated by the monks in the Middle Ages, some of them with highly decorated covers. In a long gallery, which apart from a narrow path down one side was full of alcoves of bookshelves, we were shown the modern extension of the library proper. I asked how many books there were, but the librarian could not tell me – countless, he said, and almost all the books ever printed anywhere could be found in these galleries.

We regretfully dragged ourselves away from so much of immeasurable interest, for I was almost fainting with hunger and exhaustion from the heat. Tony, Nicky and I separated from the rest of our party and went up to the Pincio for lunch. The Pincio is at the far end of the Borghese Gardens, overlooking Rome from a height of 200 or 300ft above the Piazza del Popolo, the large round piazza with the twin churches from which one passes under the walls to pursue the Via Flaminia. From the great bal-ustraded terrace overlooking the piazza, if you walk back a little towards the south, you come to the Casina Valadier. The Valadier was simply a very attractive restaurant with a terrace overlooking the same magnificent view, including St Peter's and Monte Mario, but from a slightly different angle. There were striped shades and parasols up at lunch-time, for it was far too hot to linger long in the sun, and one had wear dark glasses as it was. This delightful spot was, needless to say, requisitioned by the Allied authorities as an officers' club, and it was a top favourite place for anyone visiting Rome. Here one could gaze at the breathtaking pano-rama, which was especially wonderful at night, as the sun sank and the changing light was reflected on the dome of St Peter's, the centuries-old stone of the Castel Sant'Angelo and the faded brick tiles of the roofs that lay below. Nearly all Roman houses seemed to have roof gardens, small verandas, terraces or just balconies, all filled with plants, cactuses, aspidistras and creepers, zealously tended and watered. From the Pincio, hundreds of tiny patches of green could be seen, sometimes brightened with a parasol or coloured deck chairs. As evening fell, the green became darker and darker, until it finally fused into the darkness of the night sky. Sometimes one would see a woman sitting at her window, embroidering or sewing, or just with her hands folded, resting awhile in the cool of the evening, and as all good Romans do, contemplating the changing colours of the sky, the deepening shadows, and last but not least, the passers-by and the bustle of evening activity.

To return to our story, we had a very pleasant lunch, which consisted of Army rations prepared by an expert Italian chef (it was amazing what the Italians could do with bully-beef, Spam or even that pet aversio, meat and veg). After that we strolled off into the Borghese Gardens, and came across several small don-keys, some saddled and one harnessed to a little cart. These were apparently for the children, but at that hour, about three o'clock, all Italian children were 'siestering', and so we took their place.

I rode in the tiny cart, and Tony and Nicky took a donkey each and rode on either side of me. My beast was very well-behaved, but Tony's soon got tired of the unwonted weight, and made a supreme effort, spurted forward, and finally forced his unwelcome rider to dismount. At that my steed also broke into a canter and soon brought me back to where we started from, where his master was watching us all in complete astonishment. He did not have to say, 'The English are mad'; he just looked it. We had not finished our adventures yet, and walked on until we found a row of small cars, also for the absent children. These proved easier to manage than the donkeys, and we had quite a lot of fun with them. We eventually returned them to their parking place and their protesting owner, and went on through the gardens, over a bridge and passed a field for horse-jumping, with a sort of sandy 'Rotten Row' going round it. At this hour of the day, there were naturally no equestrians, but later on, in the morning and the evening they were often to be seen – men, women, and children, and during the Occupation various assorted Allies.

We soon crossed the main road, which is a short-cut down to the Via Flaminia, avoiding the heavy traffic of the Corso Umberto. It is a much more enjoyable drive than through the streets, as the gardens are full of trees, and the descent down to the gates just outside the Flaminian Gate is lined and roofed with an immense avenue of umbrella pines. But walking straight up from the Casina Valadier, you pass over the upper reaches of this route and come to a walled garden on the left – 'Giardino del Lago', it is called. Here there are many plants – geraniums, begonias, heliotropes, amongst others, carefully tended – as well as rare trees and shrubs. At the far end is a small lake with water lilies floating on its surface, and a few little dinghies for hire; here and there are secluded seats, and there is a tiny loggia of sorts abutting on the lake. Perhaps on account of the water, or perhaps of the extra care given them, the trees and plants and the grass of this botanical garden are the greenest and freshest in Rome. The grass was a real sward, and did not show the burnt-up dryness prevalent everywhere else. Out of the garden once more, we wandered on among the pines, and came to the stadium, where nearly three years later the International Horse Show was held. For the present it was an immense MT park, and Indian troops were quartered in tents in a section of the Borghese Gardens. The ground everywhere was gently undulating, with small hollows and transversal paths, shaded by evergreen bushes or by the ubiquitous pines, which grew all around and to a great height. There was a smell of pine needles and resin, and it was quiet except for the intermittent chirping of an occasional cricket.

But it was time to return, and so we wended our way back to the Porta Pinciana, where a few Italians were selling nuts and fruit or trading in black market cigarettes, while the Allied transport was rapidly passing in and out – a ceaseless flow of men, stores and ammunition. Through the weather-beaten gateway as we looked back, we saw the stately pines, now black against the orange sky of late afternoon. I looked down, for someone was talking to me in very poor English; it was a small grubby boy, with dirty bare feet, and he was saying, '*Mees, geev caramelle, me fame*' (I'm hungry). Fortunately I had managed to obtain a few sweets from the Casina, so I could give him one or two. But we hurried on, for the children were like sparrows, and if one of them got something, they would multiply to a small crowd in a few moments and it was impossible to satisfy them, much as we hated to disappoint them. There were little boys also doing shoe-cleaning at stands in the streets, and it was sometimes very handy, after trudging through the heat and dust, to have one's shoes refurbished, and very efficiently they did it too. 'Shoe-shine', pronounced 'shoosha', they used to call as the soldiers passed, '*Maggiore, shoosha, sergente, shoosha, mees av shoosha…*'. These little shoe-blacks were the origin of the Italian film, *Sciuscià* (*Shoeshine*), pronounced in the same way.

Not far from the Casina Valadier, but along the escarpment overlooking the streets, instead of back into the gardens, is the Villa Medici. This is a magnificent Renaissance mansion, with tiled roof, a tower after the Tuscan style and wide overhanging eaves. It belongs to, or is leased by, the French government, and

I believe housed their Red Cross detachment in those days. Only a few steps further along is the church, Trinità dei Monti, and in front of it a small piazza and another balustrade, where is yet another good viewpoint, and down on each side go the famous Spanish Steps, down to Piazza di Spagna, with its cool fountain and its quaint old houses, among them the house where Keats lived and died, and where you may still see his furniture, and many of his books and letters, and those of Shelley.

One can walk along Via Sistina, on to the piazza in front of the church, and then to a fountain (painted by Corot) and another arbour where one can lean on a stone wall and gaze at the roofs, the verandas, St Peter's and the sunset (or sunrise, if one is up early enough). Walking further on, past the Casina Valadier, through the shady gardens to the grand *terrazza*, one comes to the best view of all. That is a favourite promenade for the Romans on summer evenings and on Sundays before lunch. You can see them, families together, and in the mornings and late afternoons, you often see nursemaids and mothers with the babies. But in the early days the civilian population was not so much in evidence, except for the girls who used to linger past the Casina, hoping to find an officer to take them in for a meal. So many girls were taken in at first that it was necessary to close the restaurant to civilians for at least a year.

Afterwards, as the Allied troops became fewer, this rule was relaxed and civilian girls were admitted with escorts. I well remember seeing some of them waiting outside before the ban was imposed, all beautifully dressed, well made-up, most attractive, but very thin. They wore a lot of white and pastel shades, and no doubt they made the ATs look like sacks with strings round them. But if one occasionally felt a twinge of jealousy for their attractiveness and feminine attire, one could not but pity them. We knew they would probably get the square meal a day they were hoping for, even if they had to pay for it in ways we would find hard to accept. Perhaps in their place we would have done the same, and slipped any titbits into our handbags for our small brothers and sisters at home.

It was around this time that I had the good fortune to meet a very charming Italian family, who lived in a lovely part of Rome near the Villa Torlonia, formerly Mussolini's summer residence, but taken over by the Allies for the RAF. I went several times to call on this family and sipped vermouth and discussed the war. As well as the father, an engineer (the '*ingeniere*'), who had given valuable technical information to the Allies since the Armistice, there was his wife, from the Trento in the north, with the blonde hair and fair skin that surprises the English, who expect all Italians to be dark and swarthy, and three lovely daughters, all in their teens. La Signora wanted me to do an exchange of conversation with her girls, but through lack of time and transport I could hardly ever get to see them and so to my great regret the scheme unfortunately failed. But it was a joy to sit in a normal household again, and relax on a comfortable sofa, looking at nicely polished furniture, a rug on the floor and a bookcase against the wall. I never realised until then how used I was getting to bare, sparsely furnished rooms, rough and ready serving of meals, and in fact a sort of semi-camp life, bereft of the trappings, finesses, luxuries and comforts of civilisation, or whatever one likes to call them.

For the first time I began to like the Italians. I had gone to Italy, and while keen to learn about the wonderful works of art and scenery that are so renowned, nevertheless sharing a prejudice against the 'Eyeties', which was almost universal in England and certainly in the British forces at that time. The father of these girls had taken grave risks to help the Allies. The girls were not only beautiful, they were intelligent and charming. Their mother, racked with worry about her relations in the north and suffering from bombing and lack of food, was just as kind and polite to me as though the Americans and British had never casually or mistakenly devastated complete residential quarters of some of the Italian cities. Among the poor people, too, I began to see not only resignation, but also courage and a philosophy that allowed them to enjoy the little that their life had to offer, and to laugh and joke, even though their country was ravaged, occupied and in the throes of being progressively and methodically destroyed by hostile armies. The Italians might not have distinguished themselves in Libya, but I began to realise that there were other kinds of courage besides that which we all so much admired, the latter partly the outcome of intensive training and rigidly enforced discipline. As a people, perhaps the Italians had failed, but individually they began to appear far less timorous, flippant and superficial than I had been given to understand and were generally represented. And so I was glad to know the *ingeniere* and his family. And in a way it felt homely to visit them – my only regret was that they lived so far away, right down the great Via Nomentana.

12

Excursions

We were still working at great pressure, which did not ease up after the fall of Florence on 14 August, for there seemed at that time nothing to stop our troops pushing on to Bologna. Already plans were being made for the Occupation of that city, and buildings earmarked for requisition. The Bolognesi would not perhaps have viewed with so much favour the coming of the liberators, had they realised what it would generally mean for them – the transition from one Occupation force to another. Meanwhile, bitter fighting was taking place in the mountains in the area of the rocky and barren Futa Pass, and again on the Adriatic coast. Our troops were delivering a fierce assault on the Gothic Line, the enemy's last line of fortification in Northern Italy.

All the time, there was a mass of transport moving north, and so it was not difficult to get a lift if one was going in the right direction; coming back, there was always a certain amount of traffic returning to base, or men going on leave. So one day Cicely and I managed to scrounge a day off and decided to hitchhike to Civitavecchia, on the coast north-west of Rome, about 35 miles away. This would be quite an adventure, we felt, as it had not so very long ago fallen to the British, and would be something new in the way of occupied towns for us to see. So we got a lift on unit transport into Rome, and then managed to get another lift to the other side of the Tiber. We walked on to a long wide railway bridge and up a hill, and then posted ourselves at the top, waiting for transport going north, up the coast road, Route 1, or the Via Aurelia, as it was called, for the main thoroughfares out of Rome still cling to the names allotted to them by the ancient Romans 2,000 years ago.

We stopped a very large open lorry with just the driver in front, and he agreed to take us to Civitavecchia. With some difficulty we mounted and sat in the back, on a pile of sacking. We had a lovely drive – one hour. We asked our driver to take us to just outside the town on the north side, as he was going further. Indeed, he offered to take us to Florence, and we would have accepted, had we been sure of getting back in time for duty the next morning.

So he dropped us at the edge of a sandy heath, within half a mile of the sea, and we set off on foot to find our way down to the water, as Cicely said that we must bathe. We stopped at a small shack and asked the way, and a farmer told us to be careful about mines. Apparently, the Germans had fairly sown the beaches with them in this area, and it was not certain that all had been cleared. We found a secluded portion of beach and managed a rather meagre bathe, being afraid to go in far because of the notices everywhere, saying, '*Pericolo di morte – mine*'. We ate our sandwiches on the pebbled beach, on the edge of the gently sloping warm waves, gazing out on a sea so blue that it seemed to fulfil all one's dreams of what the Mediterranean was really like. Overhead an occasional plover could be heard calling to its mate, and crickets chirruped off and on in the scrub and gorse behind us. We had bought some red wine from the farmer and put it in our water bottles, and this contributed to make one luxuriously sleepy and lazy. No wonder the Italians liked a siesta – I began to see the point of it. But the sun was shining relentlessly down on us, and eventually we had to move, for the danger of sunstroke is very real, and so we scrambled through the bushes and under a small railway line back to the main road. Here some very surprised Americans gave us a lift back into Civitavecchia itself.

We had seen from the beach outside the town just how badly smashed up the port was, and now we saw that the town also, including the railway, had undergone some very serious bombing. Many houses near the seafront were empty, and windows were broken, doors forced open, and everywhere there was dust and rubble. The sun shone and the sky was magnificently clear, but beneath the brilliant firmament was havoc caused by human beings. It all seemed such a ghastly waste. The town was deserted, with only a few small groups of people here and there, and the usual sprinkling of Occupation troops and neat sign-boards, directing one to the nearest REME (Royal Electrical and Mechanical Engineers) or MP (Military Police) post or other Occupation units.

As there was nothing to see except ruins, we did not stay long, but were soon out on the road again and hailed a passing truck. It was pleasanter to watch the white foam breaking on the beach – for at this point the road passes right along the water's edge – and to study the distant line of hills inland, than to gaze upon interminable heaps of rubble. As we glanced back, Civitavecchia looked romantic with its battlemented harbour walls and castle, and its houses silhouetted against the golden sunshine of late afternoon. In the distance one would not have realised that it was so destroyed – before the war it must have been a most attractive place, but how much reconstruction there was to be done before it even resembled its former self! Small wonder that the inhabitants looked despairing and hopeless. As for looking for the house in which Stendhal was reported to have lived, we did not have the face to enquire about it.

We passed along the waterfront of Santa Marinella, a mass of broken and twisted barbed wire and crumbling pill-boxes. Many villas here also were damaged or in ruins. Only the hydrangeas and oleanders were still blooming, untended in the abandoned gardens. We went on and crossed a ruined railway, with an entire train standing on it, completely burnt out and blackened; and all the time here and there one saw debris thrown up by the surge of battle that had passed over it. There were burnt-out tanks, bullets, helmets, all the usual relics, blackened and hideous, scarring the grassy hinterland. We passed a magnificent avenue of towering umbrella pines, which led, I learnt, to Fregene, which we hoped to visit later on.

At the little level crossings one would sometimes see a woman with her children watching the traffic pass. There were very few domestic animals. For the main part the country seemed absolutely deserted – a sort of no-man's-land. Then we passed on and once more came within sight of Rome – the dome of St Peter's lifted itself above the pinky roofs of the houses, and beyond rose the distant peaks of the Alban Hills. It was evening as we bumped down the cobbles back into the heart of Rome. The children were playing in the streets and there were the flowers and fruit for sale. As usual we had no difficulty in finding another truck to take us back from the Piazza Venezia.

Soon after it was known that a large unit had settled in the old Cine building, a stream of civilian applicants came begging for work. There was no way of restricting their entry until a barbed-wire perimeter had been completed round the entire building, outhouses and garden. Only the *custode*'s cottage remained outside. For the present, on account of the secret nature of the work, no civilians were to be employed except for a woman to look after the ATs. A large lady, by name Signora Pinto, was taken on, after due screening by the nearest Field Security Section. This established that she had not had contact with the enemy and, as far as could be ascertained, had in no way actively associated with the Fascists. She brought us lovely wide flat rush brooms and a few *stracci* or dusters. With these she kept our rooms spotless and did our washing to perfection, though I do not to this day know how she managed, for there was only cold water and we were strictly rationed for soap. I had a flat-iron and this she used, for electricity was also extremely scarce, at times non-existent. Signora Pinto then became part of our lives, and it was in affection and not disdain that she was nicknamed the 'Old Hag', commonly abbreviated to OH. Sometimes she would bring us delicacies, such as a form of cold pancake, which she made at home. She even sewed or knitted small things for us, and I still have some of her handiwork. She was devoted to 'her Signorine' as she considered us, and we were certainly lucky to get her.

On another occasion I managed to make an excursion to Ostia, which presented an even more desolate scene than Civitavecchia, its long sandy beaches a mass of barbed-wire entanglement and broken-up fortifications. The houses along the front had been badly knocked about and the town was practically deserted. Ostia Antica, the old Roman city, which we so much wanted to visit, was a minefield, and I was never able to go there; in fact, it was a long time before it could be visited with safety. A month later II District had been installed there, and one or two of us went over. I was surprised to find all the ATs glamorously got up in mufti, but with everyone in uniform you do at least know who and what everyone is, and do not commit the gaffe of slapping a lady major on the back or failing to call a female colonel 'Sir'.

Another ruined city was Tivoli, where I went one afternoon in late August with Jonathan, who was about to depart up north on attachment to an Indian division. He had made all his preparations, and was to start next day at crack of dawn, so we spent his last afternoon sightseeing. It was no conventional sightseeing, for the sights were mostly destroyed, or in the process of being repaired and put in order. The world-renowned Villa d'Este at Tivoli had been hit and was closed for repairs – there was no water for the famous fountains, and the gardens of the villas were closed. We drove on to what had been the main street, but was now piles of ruins with here and there a house left standing, but not spared from bullet marks or broken panes. A few people were to be seen, poorly dressed, some of them doing a little trade, inside stone doors hung with the inevitable bead curtains. There was an occasional mule, eating out of a moth-eaten nosebag, switching its tail to keep away a cloud of vicious flies. There was also a crowd of small children, who clustered round the truck as we stopped for a few minutes and demanded *caramelle*, holding out grubby brown hands and looking at us beseechingly. We had not many *caramelle* with us, but what we had they got. We bought some sweet white grapes to slake our thirst, for it was intensely hot and the sun seemed to focus on the rubble like a magnet, which threw back the heat in dusty, burning rays, parching one's throat and irritating one's eyes.

There was nothing more to do in Tivoli, so I lit a cigarette and gave a few to the crowd of children, who would doubtless do black market trade with them. They waved goodbye to us as we bumped up the street once more, out on the uneven high road, down through the silvery olive groves back to Rome, past the sulphur baths, which had also had their share of damage and were out of use for the time-being, though in any case there were no clients at present. Then back we went along the Via Tirbutina, into Rome, for dinner at the Pincio, and then a walk through the darkened streets, for a dance and a drink at the Nirvanetta; and after that the usual rush back to Piazza Venezia to pick up the recreation truck and go 'home'. On this occasion we missed the truck, and got a lift in a small Italian lorry, something like a *camionetta*, though fortunately it was empty. It took us most of the way and we walked the remainder, under the aqueduct in the moonlight, through the sleeping villages, which seemed almost desolate without their crowd of eager fruit-vendors, hoards of ragged children, and groups of grave-faced elders; then past the sand-pit where Jimmy used to dig for pieces of antique pottery, back to the barbed-wire perimeter, mosquito nets, and in my case, a sleepy Jean, who asked me where I had been, what I had been doing, with whom, and why. I was too tired to give her all the answers, so I just flopped into bed, and drowsy with sun, wine and the walk home, slept solidly until the batman knocked us up the next morning.

Not long after this, we did one or two evening excursions and this was very pleasant, for it was cool enough to move about without dripping with perspiration, provided one went a few miles out into the country. Our corner of the Campagna seemed to remain as equably sweltering as ever, and one was forced to wear the absolute minimum of clothing, which during the night usually meant nothing, as our ATS pyjamas were far too warm for that climate. One could not expect to be issued with summer pyjamas, but all the same, it seemed a little incongruous that the same pyjamas should be available in the semi-tropical heat of the Italian summer as were provided for the English winter.

One of our evening trips was to Fregene, where we bathed in the moonlight and had a picnic supper on the beach, the sea glistening blue and silver in front of us, and behind us a great wood of umbrella pines, its mysterious depths unveiled here and there by shafts of moonlight, which lit up the boles of the trees, thereby enhancing the obscurity and gloom of the rest. There was no sound but the eternal lapping of the swell on the shingle and the occasional cry of a night bird in the wood behind, for all the world like the enchanted forest of *Where the Rainbow Ends.* * One could imagine magic castles hidden there and dangerous monsters, but solid haversack sandwiches and a good tot of gin and lemon soon dispelled any morbid imaginings. The sea air was exhilarating, and as the darkness acted like a cloak, I could not resist performing to myself some amateur acrobatics and doing handstands and turning cartwheels on the beach. It gave one a wonderfully healthy feeling, even if the rest of the party did seem mildly surprised that Fregene could affect one that way. As the evening wore on, however, the wind began to rise, and so we packed up our rugs, haversacks and bathing clothes, loaded up our 15cwt, and traversed the pine wood, which looked more friendly when lit up by our headlamps – and so back to Rome.

Another evening such as this was spent beside Lake Albano. This time the drive was not so pleasant. We turned south down our road, towards Rocca di Papa, and then bumped for several miles over execrable road surfaces, and finally got lost. Then followed long and complicated discussions with local *contadini* (country people), and finally we seemed to be descending very steeply a narrow defile, apparently to the edge of the lake. I was

* The title of a children's play, popular at this time.

sitting in the back so I could only guess what was happening, as it was rather dark and we had wasted so much time getting lost and asking the way. We pulled up with a jerk, and there we really were, on the narrow edge of a small black lake, reflecting in its passive waters the millions of twinkling stars, which made the blue-black sky look like silk spotted with polka dots. We were ravenously hungry and made short work of the sandwiches.

Only about one of our party bathed, for the water did not seem very inviting. When somebody discovered some bones at the lake's edge, and finally the carcase of a dead dog, fortunately a fair way off, I was more than relieved that I had refused to be persuaded into it. Still, it was pleasant by the lakeside, and to the south, rising steeply, one could discern the shadowy line of Rocca di Papa, for we were just beneath it here. To the north-west were the roofs and turrets of the Pope's summer residence, Castel Gandolfo. All round the lake, the sides rose steeply and rockily, and immediately above us was a village.

We got lost again on the way back to camp, and this time things almost took a tragic turn. We were going down what seemed to be a perfectly good main road, when all of a sudden the 15cwt stopped with a violent jolt. We in the back jumped out to see what was wrong, and discovered the truck on the verge of a steep drop of at least 100ft. What had appeared to be a bridge was no more, and a railway line lay in shambles below us; the bridge was truncated at each end, but there was no sign of warning to tell the unwary motorist that all was not well. I breathed an inward prayer of gratitude to the Almighty.

We turned back and knocked at an Italian house for another direction. A man sleepily answered us through a window. All the inhabitants had retired, the doors were barred and bolted and there was not a light to be seen. The atmosphere was almost eerie, so utterly silent were the deserted village streets and the tightly shuttered houses. Not even a baby's cry broke the stillness, only the chugging of the engine and the clicking of loose stones on the uneven surface of the cobbled streets. It was late when we got back, and at the camp all was quiet, except for the sentry at the gate. Cyril and his friends dropped the three of us at the entrance, and drove back to their unit in the city, leaving the South African girl who had accompanied us at her billet on the way. After that I did not try any evening excursions for some time. Enjoyable as they were, after being bumped about for several hours over cobbled streets and roads gored by tank-tracks and shells, one felt like a wet rag the following morning, and to work in such a condition was, as the Italians used to say, '*niente di Buono*'.

There was, however, much to be seen in Rome and in our very limited spare time we saw as much as possible. Cicely and I visited the famous Sistine Chapel together, and saw Michelangelo's magnificent paintings there. The roof is completely painted over, and one gets a crick in the neck gazing up at it. I saw an American GI lying on a seat, face upwards, but he was quickly made to stand up by one of the vigilant curators. It took Michelangelo seventeen years to paint the roof of the Sistine Chapel.

On another afternoon Cicely and I visited the Castel Sant' Angelo, the great round tower on the edge of the Tiber, between the Vatican and the Palazzo di Giustizia. This colossal and massive edifice was originally early Roman, but was improved and enlarged upon by various governments up to the Renaissance period at least. There is a covered way, like an aqueduct to look at, connecting it with the interior of Vatican City, and it was along here that Pope Clement VII escaped to safety during the sack of the city by the French in 1527.

We crossed over a drawbridge just inside the main gate, and then visited a terrifying collection of dungeons and cells and saw some manholes where, our guide cheerfully explained, people used to disappear for good. He seemed to take particular pleasure in emphasising the gruesome parts of the castle, probably to give us an extra thrill and to see us shudder with horror. We saw the parapet over which La Tosca hurled herself to her death, we saw ancient cannon balls 2ft in diameter, we saw the famous statue of the mounted angel, so prominent in the view of Rome from the Pincio, and we saw the little tiled bath of the Popes, decorated in Pompeian style, but of the fifteenth century.

Yet most magnificent was the view from the top, the grey-green Tiber winding sluggishly below us, bordered with trees; to the west the Janiculum Hill, and in the immediate foreground St Peter's at its most magnificent. The people crossing the square in front of it and going up its steps looked no more than ants from the height of the castle, and to our left and all around, the city lay spread out before us, as on a pocket handkerchief. To the south we looked towards Castel Gandolfo. Everything was so beautifully framed in the rarefied blue, which seems to accentuate every outline, whether of buildings, hills or foliage, and which throws each object into sharp relief, so that not a thing appears out of place, and the whole presents a picture that one tries to memorise for life. I am sure that anyone who has not been in Italy can believe that the sky is as blue and the colours as vivid as they appear in the great masterpieces, for example, of Titian and Leonardo. Yet when you actually see and experience the Italian country and climate, then you realise that the Old Masters in no way exaggerated – for them beauty and truth were indeed synonymous.

13

Live and Learn

*A*s the weeks passed by, new officers and men joined us – we heard that the stupendous move of AFHQ had been completed and the great headquarters was now housed in the vast palace of Caserta, and in the surrounding maze of Army huts and other outbuildings and a forest of tents, American and British. It was said that a great many files had been lost in transit from Algiers, but one never knew the truth – rumours were rampant. Meanwhile our unit was growing apace, with additions from North Africa, the permanent attachment of an RAF Section, and others posted in from the Middle East and Greece, as well as a few additions from the United Kingdom. Mail from home was extremely erratic, and took a fortnight at least by airmail; parcels took anything from one to four months. We had a wireless, a requisitioned one, I think, and used to tune in to the news at home, but even that was made difficult by the efficient German jamming system. And so, more or less cut off from home, and still set apart from Italian civilisation sufficiently to make fraternisation fairly rare, units in CMF naturally created their own amusements. So it was that the Army welfare organisation expanded rapidly, providing facilities for the ever-increasing numbers of men and women with free time on their hands and long empty evenings in which there was at first nothing much to do, and resources, when letters had been written and a stroll in the neighbourhood taken, were extremely limited.

The first thing to be organised in our particular show, within a few days of our arrival, was a canteen for men, where they could sit in the evenings, buy their NAAFI goods, including cigarettes and sweets, and obtain something alcoholic, mainly vermouth. There was practically no beer to be had, except some American canned stuff. Later on, a brewery on the outskirts of Rome was repaired and reopened, and produced a rather thin light brew, which I gathered was not up to British standards.

On the opposite side of the road from our camp, and a little further out towards the mountains, was another requisitioned cinema studio, with all its various buildings. This had been taken over as a refugee camp – a temporary asylum for many hundreds, later thousands, of displaced persons of many nationalities, who seemed to be converging on Rome in a steady, if apparently inconsiderable, trickle. There were three British people running it, and how they coped with their heterogeneous collection of charges I could never understand. Apart from the language difficulties, there were all sorts of problems: people with missing relatives, those who were diseased or suffering from malnutrition, orphans, a shortage of clothes and a chronic lack of money. Some of the inmates had travelled surreptitiously for hundreds of miles across Occupied Europe, carrying only a small bag, and constantly on the run for fear of being caught by the ever-vigilant Gestapo. It was natural that members of our camp should before long become acquainted with their international neighbours, and soon various people were finding their way over the road to the dances run by the refugee authorities, or 'fratting' with the inmates.

I only went to one such dance, and it was at the end of a dinner-party at the Pincio. We got back, six of us, at approximately 10.30 p.m., and heard that there was a dance on over the way. A Scotsman with a trailing and belligerent moustache announced that he was going over in his jeep and would give us a lift. Within two minutes the jeep, much overcrowded, was off and under way. We drove straight into the camp, but it was dark and we could not find the dance-hall or where to get into it, and we soon got lost in a maze of buildings and barbed-wire fences. At last we spotted lights and heard music, but could not get to it for a 7ft barbed wire erection stood in the way – goodness knows what it was doing there! Someone suggested scaling this obstacle, and the idea was hailed with enthusiasm. Two or three of the men started up, and before I was aware of what I was doing I found myself automatically following them and at the top of the fence, looking down on some startled Italians underneath, who were wringing their hands and crying, '*Mamma mia, la Signorina, come si fa!*' Jonathan, however, was waiting with them, encouraging me and ready to catch me if I were to fall, so I descended a little gingerly, glad my skirt was of good strong drill, and that I was wearing respectable khaki underwear beneath it, and was soon on terra firma once more.

We quickly made our way to the dance-hall, and found a strangely mixed party in progress, but everyone seemed to be enjoying themselves. We at once espied our CO, who had looked in for a short time, and was dancing with a lady, of whom I had heard, known as the 'Baroness'. I was introduced to her, and she told me, in German, her story, how she had left her husband in Berlin (I think he was the Baron), and had fled, in danger of persecution, finally ending up in Rome. The story was long and garbled, and I did not make it all out against the blare of the accordions and saxophones, but it sounded genuine enough. In any case, one could not help liking the Baroness with her bland smile and permanent cheerfulness. I found myself dancing with foreigners during a Paul Jones, and though I could not really say what nationality they were, one or two were definitely Italian, going by their rather jiggly style of dancing, which seems to be the custom among many Italians. It seemed very strange to be dancing with dark-haired civilians, in rubber-soled shoes and open-necked shirts, having been partnered by khaki for so long. I think the boys in mufti thought I was a bit of a 'wow', dressed up as an officer wearing a shirt.

The evening, a Saturday, was rounded off with a party in the mess, but I retired halfway through, in accordance with tradition. It was not looked on with favour that lady members should see mess parties through to the bitter end. About eleven o'clock things usually became a little rowdy and songs became less polite. Generally speaking, I took the singing of a fairly decent version of 'Alouette' as the signal for my departure. Mess parties in this particular place very often finished up with a performance known as the '*Carabinieri Reali*' (literally, 'Royal Carabinieri', or 'guards'). Now that Italy is a Republic the Carabineers are not 'royal' any longer, but just pure and simple *Carabinieri*, and act as policeman for the maintenance of law and order. The *Carabinieri Reali* consisted in sailing down one of the two flights of steps outside the ante-room doors to the ground floor and front entrance on a tea-tray. Who initiated this practice and christened it was a mystery to me. Sometimes after we had gone to bed we used to hear distant singing and racketing and crashing, which we knew meant that a party was in process, and the *Carabinieri* in full swing. On one momentous occasion, however, I was allowed to take part in the ritual and made the descent on a tray covered with a cushion and escorted by a captain, so that it was like riding on the back of a motor-bike, or going down a toboggan run. I repeated it once, and then decided I had to be fit to sit at a typewriter the following day.

Jean was a great worry to me around this time. She was suffering from severe migraines, and to counter this Doc was giving her pills, some of which contained opium. She was taking more than she ought, or so I thought, and sometimes in the morning she lay absolutely doggo and I would take a sponge to wake her up. This of course infuriated her, but I obstinately insisted on rousing her, and completely ignored her angry protests. I just lifted up the mosquito net and applied a cold sponge to her face. I was very anxious about her, as she was unhappy and depressed. She had been in Cairo, and had really done too much time overseas for one of her temperament. She got a transfer some months after we had been in Italy, and I think the change at least helped her. The trouble was that if you did get down there was not much outside relief, at least at that time, to counter your depression and take your mind off it. When I got at all melancholic, I usually tried to get to an OR's dance or some such function, finding the best antidote was to mix with other people, and perhaps share their troubles. Jean had other worries too – she had an unhappy love affair – who didn't if it came to that – but it gave her a sort of melancholia. Here again, I think the transfer helped her; she got away from the scene of it, at least.

Round about this time Cicely took me one day to visit some friends of hers in Rome. They had a lovely flat in a beautiful old palazzo behind the Piazza Venezia. The husband was a partisan, although I did not know it until over two years later, and as he had two or three small children he must have taken great risks, for there was always the danger of reprisals being taken against the family if a partisan was caught or blacklisted. His wife was English, and for the first time in an Italian house I ate a more or less English tea, with thin bread and butter and a jug of hot water for replenishing the teapot. A lot of Italian was spoken, but I did not understand a great deal. It seemed strange and faintly nostalgic to be in an English home once more, for the atmosphere was indefinably and yet unmistakably English.

Meeting the *ingeniere* and his wife and now meeting this family, friends of Cicely's since long before the war, brought home to me very clearly that I must do something about improving and enlarging my knowledge of Italian. As it was, my scope for practice was limited – just Signora Pinto, asking a civilian the way in Rome, the cloakroom girls at the officers' clubs, and my hairdresser. My hairdresser was a young man called Nino, short, dark and alert. His manners did not seem quite the same as those of a British hairdresser – he was much more gallant, and rather too caressing, it seemed to me. Then one day he enquired what I did on my days off, and asked me whether I would meet him. Then we would go for a walk together, he said. I protested that I hardly ever had a day off, and that in any case I would be very busy when I did. He would not take no for an answer, and insisted on my taking his telephone number, and besought me to ring him up and make an assignation at the first possible moment. If he were out, then his sister would be delighted to speak to me and arrange matters, he said. I had my doubts about this, but in order to pacify him I took the card with his name and telephone number on it. Nino did my hair well, and the shop where he worked was in a convenient place, but there was nothing for it but to change my *parrucchiere* and so I got Iris to recommend me to her hairdresser, the one she had known before the war. I went there, in the Via Sicilia, but the assistants were always very booked up, and finally passed me on to their sister shop. It was in a part of Rome I did not know very well, and rather inaccessible, but a young man called Pietro took me on there. This shop was not so élite as the other two had been, especially Nino's, and when one's hair was being dried, one got ejected from the cubicle and sat down among assorted chairs in the entrance hall, where other customers were perched under driers, husbands were waiting and children were running round playing 'catch me if you can' in and out of the chairs. The telephone at the desk near the door rang continually, the assistants shouted at each other across the room over the hum of the driers, the shrill voices of the toddlers and the angry commands of exasperated mamas, overheated under their machines – altogether there was a general pandemonium, but tempered with friendliness and good humour.

I often chatted with other customers, while waiting for Pietro to begin on me, for I discovered that Italian hairdressers were not always ready to do one's coiffeur on time, although they were much more punctual than one would suppose from the reputation Latins generally have in time-conscious Britain.

It was a pity one had to put such a dreadful ATS hat on the top of one's coiffure, and all the hairdressers bewailed it, for it spoilt their work of which they were conscious and justly proud. When we were allowed to wear berets it was better. How much more comfortable the berets were, and what a pity that they are not the universal headgear of the women's services!

My rare days off usually included a visit to Pietro and also to the officers' shop, which was a large requisitioned store, not far from the Piazza Venezia and near another ruined Roman forum. Nearby, in front of one of the many baroque churches of Rome, were two or three flower-stalls. The flower-stalls of Rome are one of the greatest ornaments of the city. They are usually shielded by large faded parasols, for the sun is so strong that no dye will last long in it. Underneath one sees a multicoloured array of vivid, fresh and varied blooms, giving out a delicious fragrance, the nostalgic blend of exotic perfumes. On the Piazza di Spagna, at the foot of the Spanish Steps, previously mentioned, there are several flower-stalls, displaying gladioli, marguerites, lilies, roses, tulips, lilies of the valley, cornflowers, violets, forget-me-nots, narcissi and many more, according to the season, and usually there are just a few cactuses for sale as well. The flower-sellers are sturdy independent folk, and as keen as mustard to sell their wares. But flowers were an expensive luxury and could not often be indulged in, although in keeping with Italian custom one usually took a small bouquet to one's hostess when invited out, or when calling.

There were Italian women employed in the officers' shop and mostly they spoke all the necessary English, although I had the impression that they had not known the language for long, and were in the throes of mastering it. There was at least one warrant officer in charge, and an officer supervising everything. In the early days of these shops, one could buy more or less what one wanted, but then rationing started, mainly, I think, on account of a suspected black market. Certainly it would have been very easy to dispose of one's uniform if so desired, for eager buyers were to be found everywhere and sometimes followed one in the street. From that time on, khaki clothing amongst the civilian population became more and more general, and by the end of the ensuing winter of 1944–45, one hardly saw a child not wearing some portion of military attire – a balaclava helmet, scarf, gloves, wind-jacket, a beret or little shorts or trousers made from American blankets. Battledress on adults was quite frequent, not to speak of coats and even trousers made from American blankets. Thefts from stores must have totalled enormous sums, and in spite of rigid supervision it was impossible to stop them. It was positively fashionable for the civilian population to sport khaki, and certainly in some cases it must have represented a triumph over the Occupation forces. I heard that the Poles were particularly good black marketeers, and that Polish officers would come out of the shop with a pair of shoes under their arms and sell them round the corner to a waiting dealer, but I never saw this happen. In fact, I never saw anyone in uniform concluding a deal. I confess myself to once purchasing a pair of bedroom slippers with seventy 'tenners' – tipping with cigarettes was of course the rule. Cigarettes in particular and other NAAFI goods in general, constituted a valuable currency, worth more than paper lire, of which there were plenty, printed freshly by the Occupation authorities, and nice and clean compared with the ragged old notes of the Italian administration. The new notes, however, were easy to forge and every so often an order went round that all notes were to be carefully scrutinised and signed on the back when purchasing with 500 or 1,000 lira notes.

All British uniforms and nationalities could be seen at the shop, and these included Sikhs and Gurkhas. Rome was beginning to develop into a busy centre for leave, hospitals, base-troops of all descriptions, and all in all it was becoming a sort of second Cairo.

More members of the Women's Forces were arriving, including a batch of South African sergeants, whom we called 'wozzies'. There was an ATS company at Caserta, and rumours that there would soon be one in Rome. We heard that some of our own girls were to be shipped over from Cairo, but before that we had a visit from the acting chief of the ATS. It was no longer the Scottish CO, but a general's daughter, and very smart and correct withal. The AT officers had a polite drink with her in the anteroom and then went up to lunch rather late, and sat at a table specially reserved for us on this auspicious occasion. The room was full of men and hushed expectantly as we all trooped into the mess. Glancing over my shoulder before sitting down, I caught one or two surreptitious winks. But the buzz of conversation was soon resumed, except at our table, where it was rather forced. It would have been very dreary if the colonel had not stimulated it with jovial and hearty quips, which raised a frequent laugh. It is a pity that a senior woman officer's visit seems to leave one tongue-tied, like a Victorian miss at her first dance, except for a few bold and fearless spirits. Personally I was always one of the tongue-tied ones, and even later I never completely managed to untie my tongue, despite having had much more experience of senior ATs. As they are all, almost without exception, charming persons, it is to be deplored, but there it is.

With the influx of service girls, the Albergo Vittoria, near the Pincio Gardens, was taken over and opened as the Rome YWCA, and became quite a famous meeting-place for service women, and often men, from all over Italy. We went there on our days off, for tea in the comfortable lounge or for lunch in the cool, spotless dining-room. When there was sleeping accommodation available, we would stay the night in order to enjoy the luxury of a bath. Hot water was usually available there once the water system in Rome had begun operating again, even though electricity was still very precarious. It was heaven to luxuriate in a bath after three months without, but the luxury was at first not often obtainable. This made it the more appreciated, and it was well worth the effort sometimes to go there for dinner after work and to stay the night, getting up early next morning to catch the truck that took one or two officers up to our camp each day.

Iris was amongst these people, as she and her husband had managed to obtain permission to occupy her parents' former flat in the Via Venti Settembre, and she came out to work each day, while her husband was at an office in Rome. Occasionally he had to go north on detachment and then she would come back to camp, slightly disgruntled I suspect, but it was fun to have her with us again, with her Italian accent and very English sense of humour. She now went armed and invariably slept with a tiny revolver on her bedside table. She explained that sometimes when her husband had to go off suddenly, she was left alone in the flat and, with things as they were then, it was safer to have this protection. I agreed, though it hardly seemed necessary to continue the practice in our well-guarded camp, inside a six-foot barbed-wire perimeter. Still, it was exciting to have someone sleeping in the next bed with a revolver under her pillow. It was perhaps the nearest I would ever get to firearms, apart from Jimmy's ramshackle trophies. If at that time I had read *Private Angelo** I should have felt a fellow-feeling for him!

---

*   Erik Linklater's 1946 novel about an Italian soldier in the Second World War.

14

Roman Winter I

*B*y the beginning of October, the days were growing palpably shorter, and were cooler and fresher, but at midday it seemed almost as hot as ever, and one could still have lunch on the terrace at the Pincio on a day off and sit in one's shirt-sleeves in perfect comfort. By the middle of the month, the order had been issued for all ranks to change from khaki drill to winter uniform, and we were certainly glad of the extra warmth in the evenings. The air was purer and rarer than ever, and the line of the Sabine Hills to the east was more clear-cut now that the summer haze had gone. The trees were shedding dried-up brown leaves, but one did not notice this aspect of autumn nearly as much as in England, for there were so many pines, cypresses and other evergreens in proportion to the comparatively small number of deciduous trees that the general impression of the foliage did not alter greatly. The corn had mostly been cut before we left Naples, but the stubble was not yet all ploughed in, and had gone a muddy brown with the constant wear of sun and drought. Still the freshness of the atmosphere and cool breeze from the mountains gave us a new energy, and life seemed to wake up after the long enervating heat of the summer.

By this time we were for the most part adequately familiar with our way about Rome. A very good brief guide was published in English for the forces, and vendors of town plans were to be seen at every corner, pressing khaki-clad passers-by to buy a '*Pianta di Roma*'. Guides were also becoming numerous, and you had to be careful not to get into the clutches of any such person, for you never knew how far you would be taken, or at what price. But mostly we did not have time for such tours.

Some of the shops were reopening, and I discovered one offering the most fascinating tiny china or pottery souvenirs, with flowers painted on them, and 'Assisi', 'Roma' and other place names painted in gay colours. There were minute baskets, and other small, similarly ornamented, but unmentionable objects. There were ashtrays, brightly decorated, with traditional proverbs and sayings on them, some of them in dialect. And then there were the characteristic ornaments and useful articles, such as egg-cups, spoons, paper-knives, and various beaten silver wares, embossed with crests and patterns. Lace-work was beginning to appear, and Venetian silk. Leather of all kinds, exquisitely worked, filled other windows.

Even the food situation was easing up a little. Some small cake-shops sold rich delicacies, cream buns, meringues and all sorts of sweets and chocolates. Everything was extremely expensive, and for the most part the Italian population could not afford such luxuries – I often wondered who could. On one or two occasions, Jacky and I defied the regulations and went into a tiny little cake-shop in the Via Sistina to eat brandy-snaps filled with cream – a risk both from the health and the discipline points of view, but Army rations, although excellent and generally sufficient, did not allow for many delicacies, and hardly satisfied a sweet tooth. Our chocolate ration was rather dull, and sometimes one just longed for something really luscious. The brandy snaps fulfilled this physical need, and gave one the gratuitous thrill of disobedience at the same time. One could eat cream buns with so much more enjoyment if one knew that at any moment the military police might appear and take one's names – it was definitely a case of 'forbidden fruits tasting sweetest'.

By now of course we had mastered the rudiments of colloquial Italian. The mysterious repetition of the word '*prego*' had been explained to us, but for a long time it was puzzling. Each time you thanked an Italian for anything, when you made a purchase, if you were served in a restaurant or whenever you asked the way somewhere, the person you were talking to said '*prego*'. If he was a man, and, wearing a hat, he raised it very politely as well. Having discovered that '*prego*' meant the equivalent of 'please don't mention it', but was much more concise, we used it too, and were quite surprised when it was taken as a matter of course by the Italians – they did not even raise their eyebrows when we said 'pray-go'. '*Ancora*' became a favourite word, and was used when one wanted a second helping at meal times, although a literal translation of it is not 'more', but 'still'. Some people amused themselves by translating English slang into literal Italian, which needless to say would have meant very little to the natives of Italy. Thus 'nothing doing' became '*niente facente*' and 'hangover' became '*sopra-pendente*'. There was quite a vocabulary of this kind, but unfortunately my memory has kept no record of the rest. As we had expert Italian speakers amongst our personnel, one could always pick up something useful in the language line; and meal-times became quite an opportunity for practising at least one's culinary Italian, as well as playing with the language.

My expanding vocabulary came in useful one day when Jacky suggested that I should join her for tea at the Grand on our day off. I did not know whether it was out of bounds, but we did not stop to ask. We entered the lofty vestibule and took our seats in the great lounge, with its steps and dais opposite the entrance. Ensconced in chintz-covered armchairs, we ate minute sandwiches and the most exquisite and daintiest little cakes imaginable; they were not quite small enough for *petits fours*, but had all their delicacy. There were only a few people taking tea that day, grand-looking elderly ladies for the most part. For the pleasure of tea drinking in that exalted company and enjoying the comfort of those so very English faded chintz armchairs, we had to pay through the nose. Even the ladies' cloakroom at the Grand was a magnificent affair, reminiscent of the Medici Chapel in Florence. The washbasins are built into marble frames, and the walls bear a sombre green parchment.

Before the summer was over, we had a visit from our 'Queen Bee', the Chief Commander (Lt Colonel) ATS, who had taken the place of the general's daughter. The new chief was in private life a wife, mother and grandmother, and in CMF she was immensely popular with everyone, not least the ATs. Needless to say, we were all on our best behaviour for her first visit, coloured nail varnish was removed, lipstick was modified, and one or two hair-nets appeared to hide hair growing well below the regulation 'inch above the collar' length. Everyone was in lisle stockings for once, for we could buy silk in Rome, and fortunately they soon became permitted, at least in the evenings. The visit went off very amicably, and indeed 'Ma Turner', as she was called, proved a good friend to us all, and I do not think there can be any member of the service who knew her and does not remember her with respect and affection.

By mid-October it was well known that a detachment of ATs from our affiliated unit in MEF (Middle East Forces) would be with us sometime in November. This influx occasioned a great deal of reorganisation, for whereas ATS officers 'muck in' in every sense except for actual sleeping quarters, ATS ORs have a whole host of regulations governing their treatment, discipline, welfare and so on, which are difficult to accommodate to the routine of a male personnel unit, run entirely by and for men. The AT staff officers were most affected, for we had to vacate our nice quiet secluded quarters and occupy various rooms around the cloisters, in the neighbourhood of the CO's bathroom and office, and near the office I worked in. This meant that we lost much of our privacy, and that when wandering down to wash in the morning (or along to the CO's bathroom, which we were permitted to use, provided we went early) one was liable to meet all sorts of people, from the CO himself to the duty officer or the duty NCO, doing their tour of inspection first thing in the morning. According to my former practice, I got up very early and completed my toilet before there was anyone much about, especially as the bathroom door had no lock, like most of our doors. On one occasion I did meet the company sergeant major, who gave me a smashing salute. I heard afterwards that he had maintained that one must salute an officer, however he or she was attired. I was glad I was wearing my long winter dressing gown. I was, however, determined to offset our losses with some advantage at least, and so I managed to arrange that the batman who called us each morning also brought us early morning tea, if we wanted it. The batmen had not formerly been allowed in our quarters, but had rung a bell at the end of the corridor. It was worth the loss of privacy to have a cup of hot strong 'chow' on a cold winter's morning.

For the winter was now coming upon us. The clear fresh days were still there, but now there was the tang of frost in the air, and the wind was unpleasantly biting in the cloisters and shooting at all angles through the broken panes. Fuel was already becoming a problem. It was the same throughout Italy that winter. Italy never has much coal, and almost all of it is imported. Imports had stopped during the war and the stocks were almost exhausted. The Allies were already importing a certain amount, but Bari, Taranto and Naples were the only possible ports, all the other big ports either being in German hands or out of commission through war damage. Fuel was therefore extremely scarce. There was a small allocation of coal for cooking, and that was all. Of course our building had radiators, but there was no fuel to work the system, which would have been extravagant in any case, as it would have burned up more than was actually needed. So there was just no heating at all, and as October drew to a close and the evenings became really chilly, we sat in the mess in jerseys, jerkins, wind-jackets and various other garments, and nothing seemed to warm the rooms, with their thin walls and many windows. C/Commander Turner said that the ATS regulations stated that there must be a fire in every room where an AT OR worked, and as the time drew near for the arrival of our detachment of girls, she paid us another visit and then personally went down to Rome Area Command to see the officer i/c fuel and state the case. Our commandant had only been able to obtain the minimum of old petrol drums, which were converted into stoves burning sawdust, and with regard to the ATS he was told there was no extra to be had. It was the same in every unit, and the scrounge for wood was beginning, in the course of which every available remnant of the cinema-set which the Italians had left behind was ruthlessly chopped up and burnt for firewood.

But Ma Turner must have waved her wand to some effect, for she did achieve what she had set out to do, and stoves were provided for the girls' sleeping quarters and their offices. After that there was some competition to work in an office where there was a girl. Where there was no girl, there would be no fire. Except in our office. Tony was not easily daunted, and he decided that we would construct a fireplace. We went over to another damaged and disused studio on the opposite side of the road and carried out a recce, and as a result we obtained various 'parts', such as lead piping, an old grate and loose bricks. Best of all, we discovered a dump of artificial peat, which must have escaped the notice of the local Italians who were fuel hunting, just as we were. There were one or two masons and builders among the troops and Tony got in touch with them, and between himself and Sgt Entwhistle, who was also a thoroughly practical person, a brick stove was constructed, with a pipe going out through the window, and a gap in the top where we put the fuel in. We burned peat, and the smell penetrated almost to the furthest corners of the sprawling buildings. We collected the peat in a jeep (I was able to help with this) and stored it in a cellar. At first the stove smoked horribly and many adjustments were performed on the pipe, necessitating repeated anxious conferences as to the best angle for placing the tubing, exactly where the bend in it should occur, whether it should have a cowl on top, and how long it should be. Our fire was the first one anywhere, even before the installation of the famous sawdust drums. After a few months the stove really settled down and worked quite well, though the smell of peat persisted and our clothes and hair all reeked with it. All sorts of people visited our office, ostensibly to look at maps or reports, but we knew the main attraction was the Heath Robinson erection in the corner, around which we had placed a few chairs, and where one could very satisfactorily warm one's numb toes and hands.

Washing water was another problem, for hot water did not exist, but we obtained some empty 7lb margarine tins from the cookhouse, and heated water fairly well on the top of the stove, though not quite to boiling point. If there were a few black specks in it, who cared? As regards hot-water bottles, which almost every English girl considers a necessity in winter, the ATs solved that problem by taking their bottles to the mess kitchen at about nine o'clock and filling them from a hot-water dixie. After that, the fire was allowed to go out until the following morning, when one of the cooks would get up early to light it. Unless it was lit early it would not be hot enough in time for breakfast, which still began at 7.50 a.m., even though the advent of winter weather meant that not many people were up as bright and early as in summer.

A week or two previously I had been in trouble with the camp commandant on account of my landmine. It was still in the office cupboard where we had stowed it after Jimmy's departure, and I had just about forgotten its existence. Then one evening, after I had been to Rome for the afternoon, the commandant called me over in the anteroom and asked me what the mine was doing in our office. He said it might blow the whole camp up, and as he was responsible, he would have to 'carry the can', and I must get rid of it forthwith. I protested that I had been promised that it was harmless, but he said with great scepticism that it must go. So I assured him that I would get rid of it, come what may. But it was not so easy. I approached various people who were going up north and asked them if they would take the mine to a scrap heap or a bomb disposal unit for me. After repeated efforts of this kind, explaining that I was under orders to dispose of it, I realised that no-one was going to take the risk of loading it on to their vehicle in case it exploded, and so I decided to get rid of it myself. Meanwhile I had taken it down to my room and was using it as a sort of footstool. I had not been nervous about it before, but now I began to wonder whether Jimmy was quite as reliable about bomb fuses as he said he was. Supposing he had only partially defused the mine? The thought was not pleasant, and with the approaching arrival of our ATS girls I decided that at all costs I must get rid of the menace before they came.

So, the evening before they were due to arrive I asked Cicely if she would like to take an early morning stroll with me next day. She accepted with pleasure and at seven o'clock I knocked on her door, carrying my Army kitbag and in it the mine. We started out, through the cloister, down the steps at the entrance, and out at the gates, past a sentry who looked a trifle surprised to see me carrying such a load at that hour of the morning. We walked down the road towards Rome, and if I had not been so concerned with the business in hand, I should have appreciated the dazzling light of the early morning and the clear sky and fresh air, against which the white buildings stood out like the ice of a glacier. After we had gone a few hundred yards, Cicely said, 'What's that you're carrying? It seems rather heavy.' 'It's a land-mine,' I said, somewhat fearful of her reaction. But she simply said, 'Oh really, do let me help you with it,' and without more ado she gave me one end of her stick, hoisted the bulky kitbag on to it, grasped the other end firmly, and with the fateful load between us, we proceeded down the road, eventually turning off to find a suitable dumping spot. I was very anxious to dump it where it could do no-one any harm, and so we eventually flung it into a running stream, where on account of the current it was unlikely that anyone would put animals to drink or allow children to paddle. The mine itself was sufficiently heavy not to be swept away, and should have sunk deep into the mud of the stream-bed. I sincerely hope it did.

That morning I ate my breakfast with a good appetite and a much-lightened conscience. I was now rid of the last of Jimmy's embarrassing gifts. The rest of his souvenirs Tony threw away, only keeping my bayonet, which was handy for hacking wood. Unfortunately, I eventually lost that, which was a pity, for it made a useful little chopper.

It was about the middle of November when our detachment arrived – about twelve girls, with one AT officer and an Army captain. Everyone got the latter two mixed up at once, and she was known as Captain Jones and he as Junior Commander Percy for almost the whole time that they were with us. The party looked tired and I was very struck by the girls' almost abnormal

pallor and thin figures, but of course most of them had been in
the Middle East for at least a year – some considerably more –
and they certainly looked as if they could do with some fresh air.
I doubt if they thought highly of their new quarters, although
everything had been done to make them as comfortable as possible, but in spite of the stoves it was by now really cold, and to
make matters worse, some parts of the building were damp and
the roof needed repairing.

I shared a small room with J/Cmdr Percy and one wall was
perpetually damp. We did try to dry it out a little by means of a
small electric ring, which I bought in Rome. This was contrary
to regulations, but the cold became so intense that we developed
conveniently short memories. Most of the broken panes had
been filled in, and so the wind did not whistle quite so fiercely
through the corridors, but the two cloisters were draughty
enough. The girls soon settled down, and as there were so few of
them, they had their meals in what had formerly been the cook's
bedroom, off the officers' mess. They were given the same food
as the officers, and there rarely seemed to be complaints about
their food. Jacky was responsible for them, and to the company
commander in Ostia, later Rome, but most of their administration was done by the camp staff. The regimental quartermaster,
with an AT officer as his assistant, looked after their clothing,
and the Pay Office worked out their wages, paid to them by Jacky.
Their catering was done by the messing officer (also Jacky at that
time), and their wash-place and corridor were cleaned by Signora
Pinto. Their work was fitted in with the rest in different offices,
and in this way they were very soon completely integrated into
the existing administration. Jacky listened to their personal problems, arranged their leave in conjunction with the officers they
worked under, and dealt with disciplinary matters. The rest of
us did 'duty office' about once a week, doing PT with the girls if
we liked, or playing games with them. As we were all staff officers, we were not given much in the way of disciplinary powers,
and there was some acrimonious comment when an orderly
room had to be held on a girl who came in late, worse the wear

for drink, and two external AT officers from a distant company came to take our orderly room. As it was, the whole thing was rather a farce, because the girl was awarded one week's CB [confined to barracks], in the middle of which her husband came over from Greece, posted to CMF, and was given a week's leave to see his wife in Rome. Much arguing to and fro took place, but her CB was eventually suspended. In any case, it was said that a captain had taken her out and plied her too generously with Italian wine, so surely the poor girl was not to blame, for how could she be acquainted with the potency of local beverages? With the approach of Christmas, Pte Fielding's behaviour was soon forgotten, and proved only to be a seven-day wonder after all. As it happened, she was a trained PT instructor, and took the PT sessions, which she did far more efficiently than the rest of her work.

A week or so before the girls arrived, Jacky and I were put on a Welfare Committee to help organise some entertainments in the camp and improve the rather depressing condition in which the men were obliged to pass their evenings. At that time they only had one late pass a week, and it was not always possible for them to get transport into Rome. In the unit, facilities were limited in the extreme. But the committee chairman, who was a young captain of the Middlesex Regiment, had invited on to it representatives of all ranks; and putting our heads together, we soon devised quite a revolutionary programme, which promised to make the winter a much gayer period than the autumn had been. First the situation for late passes was generally improved, and canteen facilities bettered. Whist drives were organised for one night each week, there was to be an almost weekly dance, held in the nearby village hall, and mobile cinemas were arranged for two or three evenings a week. On other nights we had gramophone recitals, which were quite popular, but naturally attracted a more restricted audience. There were occasional lectures by visiting officers, such as members of the Army Education Corps, and an amateur dramatic society was also formed. Books were collected for the unit's library, and a freer interchange of books with the central library at RAAC was arranged. Housey-housey parties were arranged every so often in the men's canteen, and prizes for the various competitive affairs were provided out of FRI. A photo club was initiated and became very popular. We procured a ping-pong table or two, and football was made possible by the loan of a field opposite. There was mixed netball for the very hardy, but I only tried it once – never again! At least every Saturday, there was a football match and our team became very good and played a lot of outside matches. A unit band emerged about this time, and that was so encouraged and assisted that it grew and developed into an excellent dance orchestra, and was soon in demand to play at dances other than our own.

In this way, what might have been a winter that was gruelling in the extreme – for it was only seldom that one could journey to Rome and make a 'break-out' – became reasonably full of interest.

The dances were great fun; naturally there was a considerable preponderance of men, but a certain number of local girls were admitted, and quite a few soldiers brought their own girlfriends. Some of these in turn brought their parents as chaperones, and their younger sisters and brothers too, so that the atmosphere was quite a domestic one, and it was not unusual to see small children scrambling for the refreshments during the interval. On one occasion I even saw a baby being suckled – but only once – I believe admission was not granted to infants in arms after that. Italians seem to have a knack of making themselves at home anywhere, and they were certainly at home at these dances. When the food was produced there was a wild rush; and one saw women surreptitiously, or quite openly, shovelling sandwiches, cakes or what-have-you into capacious shopping bags obviously brought for the purpose. Food was still terribly scarce, and there was no doubt that the civilian population was genuinely hungry; and it was not only the poorer people who filled their bags at the dances. At Christmas I went to an officers' mess party held in a beautiful requisitioned villa on the north side of the city, where some very 'élite' ladies were present. On this occasion, the refreshments really were a dream, but the reality of smart women quickly stowing goodies way in their exquisite leather handbags was unforgettable.

I personally never failed to enjoy myself at the unit dances. Some of the warrant officers, sergeants and other men there were really first-class dancers, and I usually danced each time with certain 'steadies'. I also had the satisfaction of teaching, or at least encouraging, a few people to dance. Notably proficient among my pupils was Sgt Bean from the General Office. I persuaded him to take to the floor one evening for a short time. He was very hesitant at first, but after trying a slow foxtrot at a few weekly or fortnightly dances, he soon gained confidence and finally became a confident and enthusiastic dancer.

Often, at the dances, the ATS girls were not happy with their Italian opposites and rivals. The green-eyed goddess was noticeable on several occasions, and what the women officers sometimes felt but took pains to hide, the girls showed quite openly. They did not think much of the men who went with 'Eyetie' girls, and said so. But the men retorted that they could not go out with English girls, because they only looked at officers, and so the battle royal was waged to and fro. However, it was not taken too seriously, and feelings were generally very cordial.

Sometime towards the end of November, Pamela Frankau, then a senior commander (major) in the ATS came to Rome. She gave a lecture in the Eden Hotel, and was entertained to a cocktail party there, arranged by the ATS staff from AFHQ. We were 'invited' and of course 'accepted'. But although this was one of the occasions when 'officers will be present' was implied, I do not remember any of our bunch other than Jacky and myself being at the Eden that night. Jacky had a half-day and, as was her wont, was taking tea in the Grand Hotel. The CO was going and offered me a lift down. We were to pick Jacky up on the way. When we reached the hotel it was dark and I went in to find her, but to my surprise there was complete darkness inside the hotel, except for a dim light in the vestibule. This did not seem normal; and then I heard something that was also not normal: the whole place seemed still and expectant, but suddenly the hush was broken by the soft chords of a piano playing the opening bars of a Verdi aria, and then the stillness was rent by the most perfect tones of a tenor – you could have indeed heard a pin drop. Everyone seemed in the grip of that magic – a sort of magnetic impulse that went from the singer in clear, ringing, pure, forceful tones straight to the hearts of his listeners. It *could* only be one man, but he had been interned by the Allies. Then a woman's voice chimed in, a soprano, also clear and true as a bell. The duo finished with a flourish, and the lights went up in a blaze of applause and cheering. I had been spellbound until that moment, but now I remembered the CO waiting in the car outside and decided that I must find Jacky, come what may. Time seemed to have stood still while the singing lasted, and it was with a wrench that I remembered that I was in uniform with two pips on my shoulder, looking for a captain with whom I was going to listen to a lecture by S/Cmdr Frankau, and that by this time a probably irate colonel in a staff car outside was waiting for us to join him. I pushed open the door of the spacious lounge, and saw Gigli himself on the dais, taking the bows, with his daughter, who was dressed in a black net evening gown with a wide skirt. I learnt from a porter that it was Gigli's first performance since his release from internment, and an unofficial affair at that. I glanced round at the audience – the élite of Rome, no doubt. I longed to stay and hear more and study the physiognomies of the collected notabilities, but time was short and I could see Jacky in the distance, wending her way towards me. We dared not wait a moment longer, and hurried out into the night.

In a few seconds we were hastening off in the staff car to the Eden Hotel, and if the CO thought it had taken me a long time to find Jacky, he said nothing – I could only imagine what he was thinking. It was not long before we were all drinking Martini cocktails in a small lounge at the Eden. The atmosphere was intimate and friendly, and there was not much standing on ceremony. For the life of me, I cannot remember the subject of the lecture, but I do recall very clearly that we were disappointed. Perhaps we had expected too much. But it was interesting to have heard Pamela Frankau, and she seemed a very nice person, though I thought she looked very masculine.

I do not remember exactly when the first officers' mess dance was held in our capacious anteroom, but it must have been at about this time, when the Other Ranks' Welfare Committee was thoroughly up-and-running. The mess decided they wanted a dance, and so Tony and one or two other enthusiasts worked hard in the evenings preparing decorations. A committee was formed for sending out invitations and making all the other arrangements – for the band, the bar, the 'eats', prizes and cloakroom arrangements. It was arranged that a general invitation should be sent to the hospital and to one or two 'female' institutions, inviting a crowd of girls along to partner the large number of men we anticipated. The first dance was a success and so the experiment was repeated fairly regularly.

It was on one of the first of such evenings, when we had a civilian orchestra, our own band not yet being quite in trim, that Doc became extremely happy and enjoyed himself a trifle excessively, so that his loud 'Glasgie' accents could be heard clearly in any lull in the music, and during the intervals. After 'God Save the King' I was astonished to hear loud raucous noises, something like pigs grunting, proceeding from the platform, and saw that Doc was up there, playing for dear life at the double bass, while the Italian musician stood beside him, wringing his hands in despair. Eventually there was a rending crack, and it was quite apparent that something had gone seriously wrong with the instrument. By now people had woken up to the fact that Doc had become somewhat of a menace that evening, and he was forcibly removed from the platform. The next morning the CO sent for him and asked him what explanation he had to offer for breaking the double bass, for which £6 damage must be paid. Doc appeared to have absolutely no recollection of the incident, but he had to pay up just the same – the witnesses against him were too numerous. 'If tha said a broke the wee thing, then a must ha' broken it, but a's certain a never did no such,' he explained in the mess.

On another occasion, when the hall was beautifully decorated and lit with shaded lamps, over which coloured tissue paper had been secured, a number of Queen Alexandra's nurses came from the hospital, and this time their matron, ranking as a lieutenant colonel, came too. Our CO, always gallant, invited the matron, a very correct lady, to dance and he was heard to say, as they floated by, 'This is a great occasion, ma'am, the first time in the history of my unit that two colonels have been seen dancing together.' Unfortunately the matron did not appear to unfreeze at this jocular opening. Perhaps she disapproved of Doc, but then she did not know him, and once you knew Doc you could not fail to love him, even if he were sometimes a little wild in his prescriptions. I used to go to his office, even if there was nothing wrong with me and have a chat, and look at the rude pictures on the walls – not drawn by him, Doc explained. Some of them dated from the time when the Germans had occupied the place. Some, however, had quite certainly been added since. Doc was always good to the ATs, and indeed I am sure that he was good to anyone who was ill. But the amount of pills issued to the female members of the unit must have far exceeded the pills consumed by the men, despite the enormous difference in numerical strength. Doc was probably well aware of their value for morale.

Later, Tony arranged the most elaborate paintings and decorations on the walls of the anteroom. I wonder what the Italians thought when they eventually took possession again. Over the bar was painted an enormous reproduction of Jon's famous 'Two Types'. We used to rush for the newspaper, the *Union Jack*, each day to see what the latest topical cartoon of the 'two types' adventure was. In our case one said to the other, 'What'll you have, the old man's drunk all the whisky?'

One day towards the end of November, when all our plans were beginning to bear fruit for decorators and so on, Tony came into the office and said, 'The CO has sent for me and told me you are to leave this office and work for Major Walsh – he needs a PA. How do you feel about it?' 'But Tony,' I protested, 'of course I don't want to go, it has taken so long to get everything shipshape here.' 'I told the CO I still needed you here,' said Tony, 'but he said it was final. You know how it is when rank comes into anything.' I was very crestfallen, for I really loved my job, and had put so much effort into it. Worse was to come – I found that as well as working for the major, who incidentally turned out to be a very decent sort of person, I was also allotted to a junior commander for part of the day. Thus I had two bosses, and was constantly falling between two stools. I was very unhappy for a time, until the CO's PA warned me that I was in bad odour, and as I was obviously not getting on well, she advised me to ask for an interview with the colonel himself and explain the situation to him. This I did and he was very understanding, and the long and the short of the whole affair was that I was removed from the jurisdiction of the junior commander and placed under that of the major – rank in that case did me a good turn. Although I was not rushed off my feet in my new job, I could devote all my time to it and perform it to best of my ability, instead of being at the beck and call of two or three people at once.

While these changes were taking place in my personal life, winter was coming hard upon us, and on the hills to the east, looking towards the famous Gran Sasso, one could see snow covering the peaks, sparkling in the sunshine. Especially in the early morning, the air was so clear that it was like looking at a particularly perfect picture postcard. Once again, Italy had to be seen to be believed.

It was getting really cold at night now, though one could still lunch out at the Pincio on a sunny day, but there were occasional dull days, and even some wet ones, when our walls dripped and water came in through the broken windows, and the paths round the camp became a morass. Electricity was a problem, for you never knew when it would fail completely. We bought some Italian candles, so as not to be caught hopelessly unprepared in an emergency, and if we went out at night, we carried torches or at least matches. Fortunately, preparations for Christmas took one's mind off the prevailing discomforts of the season. The amateur dramatics went on apace, and a show was being arranged for Boxing Day; the indents had gone in for Christmas cheer, turkeys, pork, puddings and mince pies, we hoped, though one could not count on them. There would also be an extra ration of alcohol, some port, and extra sweets; so altogether things promised to be fairly festive.

When Christmas Eve came there was an air of suppressed excitement. I had been out in the country, near Frascati with one or two of the girls, and we had managed to collect a bit of holly and a few Christmas trees. We had come upon a strangely camouflaged house in our search for the trees during what was almost a last resort, as we could not find baby firs anywhere. We drove up a drive at the end of a long winding lane, and at the top of the bend was this house, for all the world camouflaged like an airfield hangar. The inevitable *custode* and his wife came to see what we wanted, and I explained. He willingly agreed to let us have some trees, and took us through a small plantation of them, where we chose two or three of suitable sizes.

The villa, he told us, had been the headquarters of Air Marshall Kesselring, but was now unoccupied until the owners should return. One could see that the property was in a sorry state, grass growing long on the lawns, and weeds everywhere; the privet hedges were untrimmed and straggly. But the Italians were very friendly, and a few sweets comforted a small boy who followed us round with plaintive eyes. Our Welsh driver helped the countryman to heave the trees into the back of the truck, and we set off once more for Rome, through luxuriant woods, long damp grass and rich leaf mould, on to the bumpy main road.

It had been arranged that anyone who wished could attend Midnight Mass, either at St Peter's, or at the English church in the Via Babuino. I went to St Peter's with four ATS girls and several male sergeants. There were one or two others heading for St Peter's, but we were not with them. An immense crowd had gathered within the Basilica and on the great piazza in front of it. We soon became entangled in the crowd, and despite the densely packed mass of people managed to work our way up the steps and into St Peter's. The singing was of course magnificent, and the Pope himself celebrated Mass, but one was at best an onlooker, and it was extremely difficult to see anything of the actual service beyond the serried ranks of the faithful. The end

of the evening was, however, frankly unpleasant, and put me off
ever attending any sort of a festival again. Somehow or other,
just before the end, we struggled out mostly by linking hands in
a chain; but on the steps the moment came when already tired,
hot and breathless, one wondered if one would lose one's balance altogether as more and more people tried to make their
exit, and those in front were quite incapable of progressing even
a few inches further on. Somehow or other we managed to get
down these steps in the semi-darkness, lit only by the shaft of
light from the interior of the great church and the lamps round
the square. We all arrived safely back at the unit at about one
o'clock, very much the worse for wear. Fortunately no-one was
more than bruised or shaken, but I heard next day that a man in
one of the other parties had had a rib crushed in the press. I did
not know until later that one of the girls with me was subject
to fainting fits. I did not volunteer to accompany anyone to St
Peter's for any other celebration.

Decorating the anteroom was of course quite a job, but we
managed to make it look quite attractive. The troops ate their
Christmas dinner there, as it was the largest room in the building,
their canteen being too small to accommodate everyone at once.
Two or three AT officers cooked the mess breakfast on Christmas
Day, and I thoroughly enjoyed this. All the batmen came and had
tea and chatted, and the atmosphere became cheery very early in
the proceedings. After breakfast there was a fancy dress football
match, for which various articles of feminine attire were begged
and borrowed from the ATs. It was very funny, and I believe
Doc went as Julius Caesar. The dinner was a great success, and
was accompanied by the usual greetings, the band playing, and
the ever-popular sprigs of mistletoe in evidence. The officers of
course did the waiting. There was an all ranks dance that evening in the village, to which most of us repaired for a time, and
where an inordinate amount of white wine and vermouth was
consumed, and a thoroughly good time was had by all.

The officers had their dinner on Boxing Night, and afterwards
we attended a really first-class show put on by the dramatic people,

in which of course there were several good parodies of camp life, and not a few easily recognisable caricatures of camp personalities.

Tony and I planned to give a party for the ATS girls, which would be as homely as possible, and to this end we had decided to find somewhere in Rome where it could be held at reasonable expense. We hunted high and low without success, and finally, almost in despair, we asked the porter at the Eden Hotel, and he suggested the Pensione Giulia. So off we went, and I had to do the translating, for the two little old ladies who ushered us in, the Signorine Giulio, owners of the *pensione*, spoke very little English and Tony very little Italian. They received us with old-fashioned courtesy, agreed to lay on a supper for us, and showed us two rooms that we could use. We arranged the menu, and on the day itself took small presents and decorations along. The male element was composed of Tony and a few sergeants and corporals from the office staff. Altogether there were about a dozen of us. The affair was a great success, thanks largely to the Signorine who cooked us a magnificent meal, including spaghetti with tomato sauce, roast chicken and tinned Christmas pudding, the latter which we took along and showed them how to heat. They provided suitable wine, and with great charm and real kindliness made us feel welcome and at home. Afterwards various games were played, some for prizes, but the favourite among the girls seemed to be forfeits, and towards the end Postman's Knock was mooted. Fortunately it was time to depart, for their passes expired at midnight. This party was such a success that another was organised later in the winter. This time the girls made time for Postman's Knock.

We attended one or two other unit celebrations, and certain units gave parties especially for some of the Italian children, who were having rather a thin time of it that Christmas. We managed to provide Signora Pinto and Maria with quite good Christmas Boxes, with which they were overjoyed.

The next great celebration, of course, was New Year's Eve, and the New Year was ushered in according to tradition with Auld Lang Syne. There were great jollifications, for in spite of the stalemate in the Apennines and the grim winter that our fighting men were enduring, which made our discomforts very negligible, everyone felt that it would be the last Christmas of the war, and that the New Year would see the end of Hitler and the Nazis.

Just after Christmas, Jonathan came down from the Indian division to which he was attached to spend a couple of days' leave in Rome, and brought with him one of the divisional interpreters, an Italian officer, now seconded to the British forces. He was a very charming man in his thirties, I believe a film director in private life, and invited me to accompany Jonathan to dinner at his house one evening. He was a bachelor and lived with his mother in Parioli – one of the smartest parts of Rome – and here they had a comfortable house in a pleasant garden, and were well looked after for domestic service, as far as one could discover. I was most impressed with their arrangements. The other ladies of the party wore evening dress, but as usual I had to appear in uniform, not that it was a hardship. I was rather proud of it, in fact, and could never understand girls going absolutely manic about getting themselves dolled up in civvies, when half the time, if they did but know it, uniform suited them just as well, if not better.

There was a third man in the party, an elderly, distinguished friend of the family, or uncle. We were six altogether. The dinner was exquisite, and I learnt just how perfectly the Italians could do things. The waiter who served the food wore white gloves, and everything was spotlessly dainty and fresh. I have no recollection of the menu, except that everything, each course and wine, followed by coffee and liqueurs, was perfect and in keeping with the other. Afterwards, the ladies retired to the salon and I had the opportunity of getting to know Tenente Battisti's mother – a perfect Italian gentlewoman, well educated and cultured. All in all, the evening was a great success. My one regret was that, in spite of cordial invitations to visit them, with the passing of time and our isolated position outside the city, I could not keep up with such interesting and charming acquaintances.

Jacky had applied for a transfer to India, as her fiancé was stationed out there, and she hoped to join him there and get married.

She continually harried the CO to get herself transferred, and was allowed to go to AFHQ for an interview early in January. She was away for about three days and in her absence I became acting PA.

Just before Jacky went off to AFHQ, in the midst of cold spell, when we even had some snow, Jimmy and two friends turned up from Caserta. Jimmy as usual was hot on the track of antiquities, real or imagined, and insisted that I accompany him to Tarquinia. I did not know what or where it was, and felt sure that it was utterly foolish to go looking for old pots in the snow. However, they persuaded me into it, and one icy January morning found us bowling down Via Aurelia in a howling gale, with snow floating periodically into the open sides of the jeep. I had to sit in front with Jimmy, and his two friends at the back, though from the warmth point of view I would have preferred to be behind, and was not at all sorry when after Civitavecchia we picked up a pathetic and frozen-looking priest with a suitcase. It was nice that we should give this shivering padré a lift, and I was then able to climb into the back and sit between the other two, and thereby at least gain protection from the wind. Even a stop for coffee in Civitavecchia had not succeeded in defreezing us. We had found a queer little café among the ruins, with a few tables and sawdust on the floor; there we had some good coffee and chatted to the proprietor and his family. There was nothing much to be bought – just a few biscuits. But that did not worry us, as we intended to scrounge something later on in Tarquinia, if we could.

Not long after Civitavecchia we came to a hill on our right, and on its summit, perched almost in the clouds, was a small walled town. 'There you are,' said Jimmy, 'That's Tarquinia for you – we'll have some grub first and then look for the Etruscan tombs.' We drove up a narrow winding road and under an arch into the main street of Tarquinia and a sort of square, on which stood a church. We found a *ristorante* almost straight away – a completely Italian one, and my first experience of such. We had the usual spaghetti, sprinkled with Parmesan cheese, a strong-flavoured cheese that takes some getting used to. The *ristorante* seemed to be almost entirely full of men, but beyond a cursory stare we did not attract attention, although we must have been the only troops in Tarquinia – at least we saw no signs of any others.

Yet the war had not passed this ancient stronghold of the Tarquins by, and the museum next to the *ristorante*, the ancient Palazzo Vitelleschi, where we inspected some interesting Roman remains, had had a direct hit. What there could have been to bomb in Tarquinia I have no idea – perhaps the Germans had had some concealed fortifications there.

We saw the cathedral, a plain stone affair and touching in its simplicity, so different from the trappings of many Roman churches. Then we piled into the jeep, with our guide on the running board directing operations, and drove through the deserted town. All Italian towns seemed to be deserted at that time, particularly in the afternoons. We then came out on the other side and drove down a tiny country road, which ran the length of the hillbrow. Suddenly, our guide said, '*Ecco, ci siamo*'. Jimmy stopped and we stepped out into the snow. '*Venite qui*,' said the guide, and led us into a field.

We went down several steps into the snow-covered ground and entered a small room, perhaps about 12ft square, and every wall covered in what looked like painted tiles. I was quickly informed that this was a tomb of the Etruscans, whose civilisation was predominant in central Italy prior to Roman times, and whose art was famous and has influenced much art since, including Raphael. The designs were remarkable, especially the birds and animals, which struck me as being very realistic, and the colours were pure and bright as if new. Flowers and plants were rhythmically intertwined, and the whole formed beautiful artistic frescoes, of which the main impression was of airiness and grace. I was thrilled; this was much better than Jimmy had ever done before, and I felt the cold drive in the snow had been well worthwhile. We visited several such tombs, and all had been decorated in the same graceful style, with pure, delicate colouring, and various designs of birds and flowers and animals. It seemed incredible to think that the artists who had produced this work had lived more than 2,000 years ago.

We lingered quite a long time, and then transported our guide back to the town and bade him a cordial adieu. The drive back was dark and exceedingly cold, but it did not matter, for we had seen something that afternoon that we could never forget, and that certainly proved to be one of the highlights of that winter in Rome.

15

Roman Winter II

Round about this time I was also elected messing officer, and so my duties increased and I found myself really busy. Messing officer was a job that appealed to me immensely. Once a week I went into Rome to the flower, fruit and vegetable market on the Piazza Vittorio Emanuele, and bargained for spinach, cauliflowers or eggs, which I suppose were really 'black market', although in Italy there never seems to be a distinction between what is 'black' and what is 'white' market – maybe it is all 'grey'. To my astonishment, along the kerb beside the market, under a colonnade, I saw rows and rows of motor tyres, and almost every conceivable spare part neatly displayed for sale. This must have been where the vehicle parts were disposed of that disappeared daily from unattended Allied vehicles, unit parking-places, transport columns and even chained and locked cars and trucks. The strictest vigilance could not stop it, for the thieves were artists indeed. I have heard that on one occasion a jeep chained to a lamp-post was found in the early hours of the morning without any wheels, still tied to the lamp-post. Sometimes whole vehicles would disappear. I also heard that bicycle inner tubes were sent abroad in letters to soldiers, who then traded them on the black market. If that were true, you could hardly blame them for doing it, for the exchange was still officially 400 lire to the pound, whereas the real exchange, i.e., the black market, was 700 lire at least. Therefore, for each English pound of one's pay, one received just over half in lire.

The centre of the huge square was completely taken up with a mass of stalls. The flowers were up at one end, a blaze of colour, and there were stalls for meat, vegetables, eggs, fish, nuts and everything edible down one side; at the other end were clothes, underclothes, ties, materials, elastic, lace *and* silk stockings. Here you could buy everything, provided you had the money. In a side street, you could also buy every kind of NAAFI provision from tea to palm olive toilet soap or English razor blades. I used to walk all round the food stalls before making any purchase for the mess and compare prices, for my messing money was not much and had to be carefully eked out over each week, at the end of which I was provided with a fresh allowance by the captain or mess secretary. Fortunately the mess sergeant kept very accurate accounts, and so we always knew where every lira went. The sergeant was a dour Scot and I am sure greatly disapproved of me at first, but after a time we got used to each other, and I liked him immensely for his accuracy, reliability and even enthusiasm. We had long discussions on menus, small comforts that could be provided, and on all and sundry, including football, for he was a prominent member of the unit team.

I went up to the kitchen every afternoon to look round and discuss the next day's menus and what rations had come in, and to inspect them. I was only learning, and although perhaps he did not know it, Sgt Macduff was in many ways my instructor. So also was a middle-aged male cook, an old soldier, from whom I picked up a lot of hints about what to do with indents, kitchen equipment, rations and a thousand and one things that I must have learnt about at OCTU, but until then had never had to deal with. Among other things, we experimented with different methods of serving the hated 'M and V', or 'meat and veg', which can be quite palatable if curried or otherwise disguised. I introduced one or two new dishes that proved popular, and picked up as many ideas as possible from the two cooks. We were all keen to make the messing a good show, for after all food does affect morale.

Of course the officers complained – they considered grumbling a sacred rite – but I did not allow it to trouble me much, for I was convinced that the best possible was being done with the catering, and that the staff were all co-operating in making the food as enjoyable, and stretch as far, as the rations would allow. So I told a particularly vociferous grumbler on one occasion, 'It doesn't matter what you say, it'll just go in one ear and out of the other.' His reply disconcerted me for a moment, and raised a laugh at the table, 'What can you expect,' he said, 'when there is nothing in between to stop it?'

In the grey days of February, when we shivered at night, and huddled round the ante-room stove in the evenings, and slept in all our clothes, I began to have an uneasy feeling that all was not well at home. Then one night I had a most dreadful fear for my father, that he was in great danger or his life threatened. The following day I received a telegram telling me that he was dangerously ill. 'Try to come home', the wire said. It was as if I had been struck with a cosh – for a few moments my mind just did not register, and then everything in the world seemed different, strange and seen through a mist. The CO was most kind, and tried to arrange for me to have a compassionate posting home. A further telegram urged me more insistently to try for compassionate leave, but of course I knew nothing of the complaint, nor what caused it. So the CO arranged for me to journey down to our unit in Naples and have an interview with the compassionate postings branch of AFHQ to see whether anything could be done, though no-one seemed very hopeful. An application was sent in, and one cold, biting morning about two days later, I departed in a jeep with another ATS officer, Roberta, who was temporarily over from Greece before being posted home. We sat muffled up in our greatcoats, for it was bitterly cold in the jeep – although it had a roof, it lacked side screens, and the wind seemed to drive right through us. We took Route 6, now open to military traffic, and were soon in the mountains, which rose stern, aloof and snow-covered on each side of the road.

After about an hour's run we reached the approach to Cassino. There were fields on either side of the road here, and the mountains rose abruptly beyond on the left. For several miles the scars of battle stood out – burnt and stunted trees, blackened with smoke and wrecked by blast, ruined tanks, the shells of houses, useless and twisted railway lines – it was all there, the grim aftermath, but far worse than we had ever seen before. There did not appear to be a living soul about, and there was total silence, except for the purr of the jeep as she sped on through the desolation. That famous line from *La Belle Dame Sans Merci* came back and imprinted itself vividly on my mind: 'where no birds sing'. This valley of Cassino was indeed the place 'where no birds sing'.

Then we came to the rock, immortalised by the sacrifice of our men and the Poles. To our inexperienced eyes, it seemed forbidding enough, almost perpendicular, with little sign of the mass of fortifications built in and behind the monastery. One could see some ruined cloisters, and here and there a crumpled pill-box. The village was more horrifying – not a house was standing, and on each side of the road were high piles of dust and rubble. Here and there among these heaps of ground-up dwellings, small stalls, mere trestle tables, had been set up, and fruit, clothing, ironmongery and bread were for sale. It was a cold wintry day, and there was very little cheer in that comfortless place. There were shacks, where presumably the inhabitants, those left, took shelter, but on the edge of the town the foundations were already laid for what was to be the new Cassino. That magnificent resilience that had not yet appeared among the rest of the population was already apparent in Cassino, whose townspeople had suffered more than any.

Six months later I was to pass through Cassino again, and by that time the foundations had borne fruit, and solid, well-built cottages were almost completed. Perhaps by now the new Cassino is complete, and the destruction of 1944 only a memory, testified to by the blackened tree-stumps of the vale 'where no birds sing'. I hope the birds are singing there again.

After stopping for a few moments to eat some rations by the roadside, we passed through Caserta once again, now more of a hive of activity than ever, with ceaseless streams of Allied traffic proceeding to and from it. We drove through Capua, which looked no more prosperous than it had done the previous July, and reached Posillipo, on the edge of the Bay of Naples, at about three o'clock. To reach Posillipo we took a different route from the one leading to the Salerno autostrada. We threaded our way through the narrow, crowded Via Roma with its overflowing pavements, and drove along the waterfront, along past the Aquarium, and then up the hill, cutting slightly in along the coast road. Houses were built on the cliffs on each side of the road, for Posillipo stands entirely on a slope, reaching right down to the water's edge. The bay looked very different on this cold February day; there was a strong wind blowing and lashing the waves into furious breakers, which crashed on to the bastions of the Castel dell'Ovo and along the shingle of the waterfront. On the pavement fishermen were mending their nets, and small boats at anchor were tossing like mad creatures. The coastline was blurred and Capri only a vague outline in the distance. The leaves of the orange and lemon trees, which grew in every garden, shivered in the cold, and gusts of wind blew clouds of dust into the air, where they whirled and eddied feverishly. This was Naples in stormy weather – what a contrast to Naples in the sun! And yet it was magnificent, almost ferociously so, with Vesuvius glowering over everything like a malignant deity, whose wrath might have to be appeased at any minute.

I had no idea where we were going, but Roberta was billeted here and working temporarily in this branch of HQ, so she knew the ropes and I did not worry, and left everything to her. Presently we turned into a narrow drive and went down, descending gently and passing various villas on the way. Then we went down more steeply, and rounded a hairpin bend, emerging in front of a large straggling building, formerly a hotel, but now mess, office and sleeping quarters. Like many Italian buildings, it had an extra storey on the side overlooking the sea, because of the steep cliff it was founded on. I was shown my room, a tiny whitewashed closet, with a tiled floor and the ever-present shuttered windows

– '*persiane*' the Italians call these French-style shutters. Nearby was the bathroom, also with a tiled floor, but the bath was full of water, a bad sign, as it generally meant that there was a water shortage. I soon discovered that the water was turned off for certain hours of the day, which necessitated great foresight and economy in its usage.

We had afternoon tea in the small anteroom overlooking the sea. I was told that my appointment had been fixed for the next day at Caserta, and meanwhile there was nothing I could do but possess my soul in patience. I was, of course, distraught with anxiety, which rather spoilt my visit to Posillipo, or I would naturally have enjoyed it more and have observed more. Roberta was living out, billeted in an Italian flat, and so I spent the evening with her there. My only other distinct memory of Posillipo at that time is of the seas raging against the rocks on which the house stood. The dining room was below the anteroom, only one floor above sea level, and the room seemed to vibrate with the force of the water. We went out on the balcony after dinner and watched the waves and the spray shimmering in the beams of light thrown out from the open windows. Again the following afternoon, after lunch, we watched the swirling waters; they seemed to exercise a fascination so great that one just could not leave the scene.

By this time, I had had my interview at AFHQ, and kind as the people were whom I saw, they could do nothing for me. My mother and sister were both at home, and therefore my case did not warrant a compassionate posting. Compassionate leave was not allowed at that time. Of course I understood that there must be many cases far worse than mine, and more deserving, but that did not make my own anxiety and disappointment any easier to bear. Unknown to me at that time relatives of mine in London were trying every possibility at the War Office to get me home, for it was thought that my father might lose his life, and that perhaps seeing me, whom he had not seen since I left England, might at least help him at such a crucial moment. But I had volunteered for overseas service, and at that juncture overseas I had to stay, for the war was still at its height, and every available space on ship and plane was needed for the transport of war materials and key personnel. And so the following day I was once more on the road for Rome, with a heavy heart but with the consciousness that all possible had been done in the circumstances. The weeks that followed were slow to pass and depressing, for although I received news that my father had survived and was making a slow recovery, letters came erratically and were always tardy bulletins. The winter days seemed sad and heavy, but I filled in some of the evenings by coaching the AT sergeant in French, holding gramophone recitals or attending dances. Otherwise there was not much else to do, but thanks to the very regular mobile cinema shows, one could at last spend two or three evenings a week in the crowded canteen, amid a hot, smoky, cheerful crowd, watching a very good selection of films, comics and newsreels. The projector made a continuous whirr and sometimes it went too quickly, or too slowly, or films were put in upside down – usually some small accident enlivened the evening.

One bright spot was an acquaintance I struck up with a French naval officer, Captain Thiers, attached temporarily to us for liaison purposes. He seemed a very charming man and was apparently from Algeria. This gave us something in common to discuss, and I was highly flattered when one day he asked me if I would lunch with him on a given date. The day came, and I made myself as smart as possible, for we were going to the Plaza, the hotel in the Corso Umberto taken over by the Free French Forces in Italy. We had lunch in the great dining-room-cum-ballroom, with tables all round and a dance-floor. To my surprise, a large orchestra was playing and dancing was going on. We had a good lunch, cooked of course *à la française*, and drank Algerian wine, which was pleasant, but a little heady. Afterwards we danced and I became rather talkative with the unaccustomed wine at midday and the music and general atmosphere of enjoyment going on. Altogether it was a good party. I met Captain Thiers in the mess the following day, and we had a chat and I told him how much I had enjoyed my visit to the French hotel. In the course of conversation he asked me if I could possibly manage to procure for him two pairs of lisle stockings from the officers' shop '*pour ma femme, elle a si froid, la pauvre*', he explained. I said of course, that was easy, although I had never done such a thing before. But next time I went into Rome I bought the stockings. The gallant capitaine did not ask me out again as promised, and indeed it must have been an expensive party for him, as he had stinted nothing and given me a wonderful time. But the two pairs of ATS stockings must have been the dearest he had ever bought for anyone, and looking back on the affair, I wonder if his wife really needed such thick hose in Algiers with the approach of Spring. '*Honi soit qui mal y pense*'. But I enjoyed my fling notwithstanding … and it had given me the unadulterated pleasure of seeing Tony glowering at me in the anteroom when I met Captain Thiers there on the famous day and we made our exit together.

We had a visit from the ATS group commander at this time, and found her very charming and helpful. As usual every effort was made to make the ATS quarters look spick and span, and we regimentalised ourselves for the occasion, with very tidy hair, lisle stockings and a marked reduction in make-up. It was an especially cold day, and the air seemed charged with cold right from the snows of the Abbruzi Mountains to the west. I went to see Jacky after the inspection and looked at the snow-capped peaks from her window – there was no sun to brighten the scene that day. The Italian winter could indeed be bleak. No wonder tourist guides and brochures never mention it, but concentrate on the sunshine and warmth of the other three seasons. Jacky was most indignant. She was suffering badly from chilblains on her fingers, and had hoped for a little sympathy from the senior commander; instead of which the latter had taken one look at poor Jacky's red swollen fingers and remarked, 'My dear, how perfectly frightful your hands do look!'

Eileen and Jean had already left us, and now my new friend, J/Cmdr Percy, was also to leave us, posted as admin officer to the Army School of Education, which had been set up at Perugia. It must have been cold at Perugia that winter, for it stands high on an escarpment; but it is a beautiful place and there was plenty of military activity at that time, so Priscilla Percy had no objection to a little extra cold. We were really getting inured to it by that time. And yet, even in January, Cicely and I had lunched out at the Pincio on a sunny day. What an amazing country!

The School of Education was branching out at this time, and before long was running a most interesting selection of courses. As regards the ATS, these included most domestic subjects, particularly cooking, dressmaking and general housekeeping. The course lasted about a week and nearly all our girls attended it at some time or another. Quite apart from the instruction, it gave them a chance to see a different part of the country – and how beautiful Perugia is with its old cobbled streets imbued with history! By this time the girls were looking far healthier than when they arrived from Egypt. Most of them had filled out and they all had more colour and energy. The exhaustion from Cairo's sapping climate had given way to freshness and robustness. Most of them were now perfectly happy with us – only one had gone home and that was for compassionate reasons. As regards boyfriends, most of them had several.

We had girl telephonists by this time, and the telephone exchange was an excellent opportunity for admirers to get in touch with their operators. A phone had been fixed up outside the telephone exchange, where officers and sergeants could make private calls, a practice not encouraged. But many a time a certain dark-haired, copper-skinned sergeant was to be seen holding an intimate phone conversation with the object of his attachment, who was only two 2½ yards away from him inside the exchange. Entry into the exchange was, however, forbidden except by the duty officer or signals personnel on duty. Nowadays it is hard to imagine what courting couples did before the telephone was invented. We had one engagement – Sgt Entwhistle became betrothed to the ATS private who worked in the MT office, much to the detriment of all work in that place. They were married a few months later in St Peter's, as both were Roman Catholics, and the colonel gave the bride away. I was genuinely sorry to miss this ceremony – but by the time it took place the war was over, and they were able to go on leave to Venice. When they got engaged, our troops were still bitterly contesting mountain strongholds, but now spring was coming, and light and hope were dawning – and the final push was about to begin.

I had been promoted to junior commander in February 1945, which had helped to cheer me up during the cold and rather dreary winter. Meanwhile I was still very busy as messing officer, and had very little time for moping. The markets of Rome were becoming quite familiar to me, and the prices no longer caused me acute anxiety. I discovered another magnificent market place, on the Piazza Navona, where one could get olive oil, at about 350 lire for half a litre. This did not amount to much when divided among everyone in the mess. And so I did not now always go to Piazza Vittorio Emanuele, where the array of black market motor tyres, NAAFI goods, and even items of uniform was growing increasingly impressive.

The elder of the two cooks in the officers' mess had been posted elsewhere, and one of the batmen took his place. He was a young man, Welsh, very dark, handsome and desperately keen. His name was David, and he had been trying to learn as much as possible from watching the other cooks at their work. His enthusiasm was unbounded and he very soon became a passable cook, and then an excellent one. We also took on an Austrian POW – something on the lines of the Italian 'co-operators', who worked in the Posillipo mess – and he was an expert at pastry. Sometime in March the officers decided that they wanted to engage an Italian cook. Personally, I thought it was an unnecessary extravagance, but as messing officer, I was there to please the majority, who were in favour, and Peter, the other English cook, could easily be moved to the Other Ranks' cookhouse. And so I complied with as good a grace as possible, secretly dreading what the new chef might be like.

By this time we were all getting quite accustomed to spaghetti and various other Italian dishes, and as there were quite a number of Italian speakers in the mess who had known Italy and its food before the war, opinion was all for experimenting

with an Italian chef, especially as other units had them and circulated stories in praise of the delicious food they produced.
I was afraid that they would not understand the rationing system,
and prove far too extravagant – and this did in fact happen, at
least at first. However, in the meantime, the mess secretary rang
up the Civilian Labour Office in the RAAC and told him our
requirements, which were in all one cook, one dishwasher and
one waiter. Within a day or two, a small, painfully thin, half-
bald, and pathetically shabby little man arrived, and we duly
interviewed him and engaged him as cook, although to tell the
truth he looked as if six months in a convalescent home would
have done him more good. This was Renzo. A day later, the day
Renzo was due to start work, another man arrived, not nearly
so seedy looking or emaciated, and announced that he also had
been sent to us as a cook. Captain Thompson and I looked at
each other in amazement. We could not possibly have two cooks
– and what to do now? The second cook, Marcello, then produced the most panegyrical references, including one from the
American Fifth Army, with whom it appeared he had held his
previous job. He had even been at the Grand Hotel before the
war! Clearly he beat Renzo hollow, but how to make Renzo see
it? In the end the whole matter was cleared up, as it turned out
that Renzo had been sent to us as 'washer-up' and not as cook.
So everyone was happy. Meanwhile, a youth of about eighteen
was taken on as waiter – he had a roguish look in his eye and
answered to the name of Guglielmo. All these three employees
looked vastly better and healthier when they had worked with
us for a month or so, although poor Renzo lagged far behind
the other two. He was a curious character and never seemed to
get on. In the end we dismissed him as superfluous. He tried,
I imagine, to take most of his food home to his family, and perhaps he was also surreptitiously taking stores out of the camp. In
that case the penalty would be immediate dismissal. He insisted
on presenting the mess with a large bag of hazelnuts when he
arrived. I am afraid he must have been suffering very badly
from malnutrition, and I hope he recovered. There was perhaps

something of a Dickens pauper about him, and his poor tired brain could not cope with the hurly-burly of the mess kitchen and the loud-voiced, hearty soldiers.

Marcello and Guglielmo soon settled down and became good friends with David and the batmen. Marcello was without doubt a paragon amongst cooks, even if he did use nearly a week's supply of margarine and sugar at once soon after his arrival. He found the strict limitations and detailed accounting for every scrap somewhat bewildering, especially after the more liberal ways of the Americans – or more casual, one might say. Anyway we now had the famous *pastasciutta* (pronounced 'paster shooter') at least once a week, and I shall personally always be grateful to Marcello for showing me how to prepare it, and especially how to make the tomato sauce to accompany it. We even obtained a spaghetti machine for the mess, but for some reason it never worked well, and so we resumed the easier way of making '*tag-liatelle*' by hand – i.e., long, narrow strips of paste-like ribbon. How warm and satisfying Marcello's Italian dishes were on a cold day, after one had sat shivering in an office for several hours on end! He also manufactured the most delicious sweets, but these were usually very elaborate and necessitated the inclusion of a not inconsiderable quantity of alcohol, so we reserved them for special occasions.

I shall never forget, on the occasion of our first mess party after Marcello's arrival, the astonished look on the face of the barman, as he confided to me in a confidential whisper that the 'Eyetye cook had come down and asked for tots of gin, rum, sherry and vermouth, and wot's more, 'e got 'em – wouldn't go away without.' Marcello put all these intoxicating ingredients into the well-known '*Budino Inglese*', or 'English pudding', which in fact resembles anything but what its name denotes, and is quite the most sickly and succulent sweet I have ever tasted. It was Marcello's pride and joy, and each time we had a mess dinner he suggested *Budino Inglese* as the sweet course.

Guglielmo, like Marcello, became very popular with every-one in the mess. He was cheerful, happy-go-lucky and extremely patient. Often single-handed, he would wait on a room full of impatient officers, and then dash to and fro with *ancoras*, his crêpe-soled shoes squeakily covering several miles during the meal. After he had been with us for a few months he was called up – that is, after the end of the war when the Italian Army was reorganising itself. He disappeared for two or three weeks and then reappeared and offered his services again as waiter. 'But what about your military service?' the mess secretary asked him. '*Oh, non fà niente,*' replied Guglielmo cheerfully, 'they will come for me when they want me.' As far as I know, they did not come for him, and he was able to remain with the unit until it was disbanded – always helpful, conscientious and a favourite with everyone. In due course, he mastered the English language very adequately, and was usually to be seen at all unit entertainments, and especially at the cinema shows. Marcello, on the other hand, knew little English and seemed to acquire little. But no-one in the kitchen appeared to have any difficulty in understanding anyone else.

By now Heinz had been joined by two compatriots, one a major, who volunteered to work rather than do nothing behind prison bars. They were all 'good' prisoners, though of course had little liberty in comparison with the 'co-operators'. Wolfgang was a wonderful worker, diligent, polite and thorough. He always seemed to be washing up and doing the dirtiest tasks, such as scouring greasy cooking-pans or paring vegetables. I was astonished when I discovered that he was a major. There was no arrogance about him, even though he was also quite an eminent lawyer, so I heard. If he did everything else as well as he performed his domestic duties, then he must have been efficient *par excellence*. I occasionally gave the prisoners a few cigarettes, for they had a very small ration, and whatever one gave them they were profusely grateful for.

I heard from my friend David that my successor in the messing office had lost her heart to Wolfgang. It did not surprise me, only that it should be noticed. But then David was an incurable romantic, and very much in love himself – so he confided in me one day – with an ATS girl. However, she did not return his affection, and he eventually married a little Italian girl from the village down the road. I think the AT missed a nice boy, though I doubt if they were really suited.

Meanwhile, I had a problem of my own to face, also of a romantic nature. For some time Heinz had been making little pastries, in different shapes, but always with a preponderance of hearts. Beyond admiring them like everyone else, I had thought nothing of the matter, until one day he asked me if he might speak to me alone. 'Yes, of course,' I said in German, knowing that we would not be overheard, 'come into the mess.' To my astonishment, he said at once, without any introduction, 'I want to ask you to become my wife.' I was completely caught off my balance, and wondered if he were serious. But his further entreaties proved beyond a doubt that he was really proposing to me, and that I was caught in a romantic 'embarrass', as one might say. I made the usual excuse, that I had a fiancé in England whom I had promised to marry after the war (heaven forgive me for lying), but Heinz was not at all satisfied with my refusal, and after that day I felt uncomfortable each time I went into the kitchen, catching him watching me as I did the rounds. Once or twice he thrust small notes into my hand as I passed him, unobserved, I am sure, by anyone else. But the situation was awkward enough. And the number of pastry hearts increased as time went on. I knew that if things continued like this, I should have to ask for Heinz to be moved, or I should have to resign as messing officer, which I was very loath to do. But it would be complicated explaining at a mess meeting why I wanted to be rid of Heinz, for he was very popular and no-one could ever say he was a bad, or even an indifferent cook. However, fate took the decision out of my hands, and once again the die was cast without my having to make any far-reaching decision about the matter. In the meantime, Heinz assured me in his notes that he was quite certain that he would marry me one day, come what may.

Before this delicate situation had arisen, I had changed my office job. Jacky had made two or three journeys away for a short leave and to Caserta about her imminent posting to India

Command. During her absence, I had stood in for her as PA. I usually found these times very harassing, as I was not only working for the colonel while still officially the major's PA, but also keeping an eye on the mess, and sometimes paying the girls and generally looking after their affairs. At Jacky's final departure, however, the latter job was taken out of my hands, and I officially became the colonel's PA, giving up my job with the major. It was towards the end of March when Jacky went off in a whirl of good-byes and good-lucks. She was obviously delighted and more than keen to be on her way, not because she had disliked the job I was stepping into, but because she was completely single-minded at that time, with one thought in her head, to rejoin her fiancé. We heard many months later that she had succeeded, and that they had been married in Delhi during John's leave from his squadron. But she was in India some time before that happened, because leave, even to get married, was not easy to obtain in those days. I had enjoyed working for the major – in fact, I found that I enjoyed every job, and usually looked with trepidation at a new one, which eventually I got used to and liked just as much, some-times more, than its predecessor.

One incident that enlivened this period has always remained in my memory for its incongruity, and it was also my first experi-ence of the vagaries of the Italian telephone system. Major Walsh was putting through an urgent and important call on security mat-ters to a superior and exalted officer in AFHQ. I heard him say 'Hullo, sir, Walsh here', and then his tone and expression changed. From being grimly official, his face lit up, and he said, '*Buongiorno, Signora, come sta? È vero? Come mai?*' (Good day Madam, how are you? Is that so? But how come?) And the conversation then went on, 'As I was saying, sir, before we were interrupted, the fact of the matter is … *Si, va bene, Signora, ma non deve parlare con questa linea, è privata militare sa, vuole lasciare, per favore, Signora.*' (yes, all right Madam, but you shouldn't use this line, it's a circumscribed military one, please get off the line, Madam). This time his voice was not quite so caressing, and a small frown creased his smooth forehead. He went on, 'I am extremely sorry, sir, some Italian woman keeps butting in … *Ho già detto, Signora, che lei non deve parlare con questa linea, non mi interessano per niente i suoi bambini …*' (As I have already said, Madam, you must not use this line, I couldn't care less about your children …) This time his tone was menacing and he was clearly annoyed. 'I can't get rid of the damned woman, sir; she won't hang up. Just a moment, I will try the exchange before we get any further … one moment, please, sir … *Non parlavo con lei, Signora, è ridicolo, vede, sa benissimo che questo è un telefono militare, lasci subito la linea, no, non, la cognosco, lo sa bene, basta, basta, Signora, fa bene ad andarsene. Grazie a Dio.*' (I wasn't speaking to you, Madam, this is absurd; look, you know perfectly well that this is a military line, get off it right away, no I know her, you know that well, stop it, stop it! Madam, you'd better clear off. Thank God.) By this time red, perspiring and longing to let himself go, but respecting the lady, he tapped violently on the apparatus with the receiver. 'Hullo, exchange, Major Walsh here, look here I've been interrupted ten thousand times in my call to Colonel Wooton by some stupid Italian woman who keeps on chipping in. Get me another line will you, and quickly, the Colonel won't wait for me.' And then at last he got through to AFHQ and apologised once more for the interference. All this time, I was quietly filing some letters and managed to keep my face composed, although inside I could not help seeing the humour of the episode. Later, I was to learn far more about the humour, and the exasperation, of long-distance telephoning in Italy.

A distressing affair at this time was the somewhat summary dismissal of Signora Pinto. I never really did fathom the business, for though the RSM accused her of stealing firewood, and swore he saw her take some planks from the camp to the *custode*'s house, she promised me faithfully that she had never used wood, except when making a fire to burn our rubbish or to heat water for our laundry, and furthermore she would not dream of taking wood to the *custode*. She would certainly have been very noticeable, in her black dress, lugging planks through the gate, past the sentry-box, along the road and up the small path leading to the *custode*'s house, which was in full view of all our windows looking towards Rome. There must have been a misunderstanding somewhere. But the RSM was adamant and appealed to Major Walsh, and there was a somewhat heated discussion between the two men, the OH and myself, in which Major Walsh interrupted himself frequently to exclaim to the vociferate OH, '*Silenzio, Signora,*' very sternly. My passionate defence of the Signora did not help her, and despite her loyal service to the ATS she was dismissed. The major told me frankly next day that he did not like her face, and I suspected this had something to do with her dismissal, for he had a reputation for liking pretty women. The sequel to this story was rather strange. When I met Signora Pinto a year later she told me that the RSM had been angry with her and was determined to evict her from the camp, because she had rejected his romantic advances, as at the time she had had a boyfriend, a private, who was demobilised shortly before her departure. According to her, the RSM had aspired to step into the private's shoes, and when she had given him the cold shoulder, he took his revenge. This all seemed rather 'fantasmagorical', to use a word coined about that time and in frequent use in the mess. The stern RSM did not seem to have any heart at all, and it seemed ludicrous to think of him being crossed in love. The affair is still a mystery to me. Signora Pinto was given a recommendation, and was soon able to obtain another job with the occupying forces. To dismiss a civilian in those days might well be to inflict great hardship on him or her. Even more than the slender salaries, the good food and tea provided while working was of inestimable value to the civilian population in those lean times, when belts were very tightly drawn and bread itself was a luxury.

By the time I had taken over Jacky's job, and become used to it, spring in all its Mediterranean glory had dawned upon us. The sun was warm, but not unbearably hot, and the skies resumed their pure, unflecked azure. Everywhere were flowers, in the streets, in the window boxes, and on roof gardens. Of course there had been beautiful stalls of flowers around us all winter, but with the arrival of the warm sun and the exit of the icy breezes, which vanished as the snow disappeared from the mountain tops, the flowers seemed to appear fresher, more varied and numerous than ever. There were little almond and cheery trees blooming along the edge of the Via Veneto, where gardeners were carefully tending the grass borders, which had been neglected through the previous winters of poverty, starvation and Occupation. Girls were beginning to appear in gaily printed thin frocks, their long curls flowing down their backs, walking a little stiffly on the high wedge heels, still in vogue. Dressing in southern Italy is relatively simple, as you need very few winter clothes compared with a winter wardrobe in our country. Even in the mountains the cold, though it may be sharp, is short. In the north conditions are different, as the Allied armies had been finding, but in the south, especially in the plains, winter is not to be feared much. We had suffered from cold, it is true, but fortunately not for long. By March the days were appreciably warmer, and one could sit outside at midday without a battledress top and bask most comfortably in the sunshine. It was during March that it pleased RAAC to make us an allocation of fuel for the central heating, so that our building could be really warm and the very makeshift petrol-drum stoves dispensed with. We did have central heating for a week or two, but by then it was so warm that we nearly suffocated, and it was therefore abandoned. Still it was nice to know that we had not been forgotten, even if it had taken all winter and frequent visits of the administration staff down to Rome to produce the required commodity in time for Easter.

It was on one of these mild spring days that Doc and I and one or two others made an expedition to the catacombs near the Via Appia Antica. It was very interesting and Doc showed an almost morbid interest in the skeletons and loose bones. We each carried a small wax taper to light the way, but what greatly annoyed me was that the wax spilt on my best gloves and they bore the marks of the catacombs forever and a day. There is something about the catacombs, with their decaying, desiccated bones and rabbit burrow passages that makes them heavy on the spirit. I should hate to be there at night.

What interested me more was a visit paid at the same time to the notorious Ardeatine Caves, where the coffins of about 335 Italians still lay unburied. This story caused a great stir at the time. Before Rome was liberated, some Italians threw a bomb into the ranks of a German detachment marching along the Via Rasella towards the Via Veneto. Almost at once a cordon of SS was thrown round the whole area, and a whole crowd of Italian men and boys were arrested as a reprisal. Despite frantic entreaties from the municipal authorities and the crazed relatives of the victims, they and many others were shot on 24 March 1944, without even a farce of a trial, and their bodies, 335 in all, flung into the Ardeatine Caves, in front of which the execution had taken place. The caves were then sealed, and the hiding-place not discovered until after the liberation of Rome. This act of barbarism greatly incensed the Italians, and perhaps did more harm to the German reputation in Italy than any other single incident in the whole catalogue of atrocities. General von Mackensen, and Field Marshall Kesselring, C-in-C German Air Force at that time and acting Governor of Rome, were held personally responsible for the outrage, and were later tried as war criminals at Venice. They were sentenced to life imprisonment.

On the Sunday afternoon that we went to the caves there were queues of relatives visiting the coffins, most of which bore photographs of the deceased, small tinsel hearts and crosses, laurel wreaths and a profusion of flowers. There was a hush in the grotto, and a heavy atmosphere of intense sorrow. I saw several poor women brushing away tears behind their thick black veils, for most of the women wore black. There were men and children, too, in the long procession. Outside the sun shone brilliantly, almost mercilessly, and inside it was cool and fresh with the perfume of the flowers, and quiet except for the soft murmur of the mourners' voices, as they moved slowly from one bier to the next. We did not stay long, for one does not care to be a spectator to grief, and to linger would have made our brief visit an indelicate intrusion.

At one time it was rumoured that among the others an Englishman had been shot, but this was later denied. To the Romans, without a doubt, this was the wartime tragedy that touched them nearest and affected them the most deeply.

16

Posillipo

*B*ologna fell on 21 April, and on 25 April Mussolini and his mistress, Claretta Patacci, were ignominiously executed by the partisans and their bodies suspended upside down, together with the corpses of about six other leading Fascists, at a bombed garage on the Piazza Loreto in Milan. The mob threw rubbish and jeered at the mortal remains of their late leaders, and the partisans felt at least partially revenged for the torture and murder of many of their number. Milan fell to the Allies shortly afterwards.

It was at about that time that our colonel called me into his office and asked me how I would like to go with him to Naples! I had heard rumours to the effect that the CO was to be moved there, and it was common knowledge that this would be a highly unpopular move, not only with the colonel himself, but with almost the entire personnel of the camp. He was very popular and took a real interest in the work and welfare of all under his command. I knew that without his integrating, kindly encouraging personality things would not be the same for the job nor for those performing it. The one good aspect was that the war was by now clearly drawing to a close and with it the operational phase of military intelligence. Henceforth our work would be more concerned with the Occupation authorities, civil populations and liaison with the Allies.

When the colonel asked me whether I would like to go to Naples, I hesitated for a moment, and he went on to say that he was to be transferred there to the staff section that dealt with our work on Base HQ level, and wanted to take me with him to act as his PA, as before. Now for personal reasons I did *not* want to leave Rome, for as usual I had got comfortably 'dug in' there, but if the CO wanted me to accompany him, then it did not occur to me for one minute to say I would not go. In any case a refusal would probably have made no difference. He had been very good to me, and if he had expressed the wish or issued the order for me to go twenty times further, I would have acquiesced willingly, even though it did mean leaving my boyfriend of the moment. After all, as far as that was concerned, it was perhaps not a bad thing. I did not wish my heart to become seriously involved in any way, and to meet new people and breathe a fresh atmosphere was the surest way to prevent emotional entanglements from becoming too intense.

We had twenty-four hours' notice to depart, and I had to hand over both of my jobs, organise a farewell dinner for the CO and do my own packing. Most of the latter was done for me by Maria, and I should never have managed it without her. The dinner went off very well, and there was a riotous party to follow.

We left the following morning at 0900 hours and the guards gave the colonel a farewell salute. They looked magnificently smart, with spotless white gaiters and web belts, every item of uniform and equipment neatly in place, rifles and bayonets gleaming with polish. It was a moving experience, for me the only such in my life, and I felt privileged to take part in it, however insignificant my part was.

We did not have much conversation on the way down Route 7 to Naples. It was warm and as we sped over the miles south, across the Pontine Marshes, now re-drained, and along the coast with the turquoise blue sea on our right, I dozed with the fatigue resulting from our hurried departure.

This time I was billeted in Posillipo in an Italian villa, near our office-cum-mess, jutting out in a fine position right over the water's edge. The three other AT officers, Patricia, June and Betty, were also billeted there. To get to our villa, we either had to go right up to the main road and down a long, winding drive similar to that leading to the Villa Paulina where we worked and messed, or follow a path down to the water's edge and over a small bridge and then up the other side from our place.

The villa was modern and had several storeys. There were cellars underneath and a passage leading through these to the rock in front, from which it was possible to bathe whenever one liked. The ground floor was a self-contained flat and leased to an Italian family, whom we never or rarely saw. The first and second floors were occupied by the Perelli family – father, mother and three small children – and the maid, Luisa, a great character, and a Sardinian. We had three requisitioned rooms here: June and Betty shared one on the first floor, and Pat had the room next door to them. I was given a tiny room on the second floor, leading out on to a magnificent terrace with a glorious view of Capri and the coast of Posillipo in the foreground. There was a stair leading down from it to another terrace on the first floor, and sometimes three fierce boxer dogs, pets of the Perellis, would leap over the gate and into my room. I was awakened on my first morning by such an invasion, with cool damp noses snuffling all round everything. Unfortunately, the dogs were too playful and inclined to seize any piece of clothing they could find and tear round and round the terrace with it. Some of my uniform went through this ordeal, which did not improve it. I was quite alarmed by these three huge bouncing creatures, but soon found them to be friendly and harmless.

Luisa called us each morning at about eight o'clock, with the customary cup of strong sweet black coffee. At that hour she was usually wearing her curlers and looked tired and pasty-faced. She had probably been up since at least 5 a.m. She can never have had enough sleep, but like Figaro she was always cheerful.

We dressed and went over to breakfast in the mess, which was not very appetising, as the co-operators were in charge in the kitchen and allowed a very free hand. In consequence, we had execrable porridge, more like pease pudding, and spam fried in batter, or bacon and fried bread, almost every morning. The toast was burnt and rubbery. Sometimes we had a nice salad for lunch, but too often there were fried potatoes and other unsuitable greasy dishes; in the evening, doughnuts positively oozing fat were the co-operators' favourite sweet. In the end I could not face this perpetual 'fry-cooking', and Pat and I would later regale ourselves with fresh apricots and peaches, much more enjoyable, or fill up with sweets and chocolates, as much as we could procure, which was mighty little.

I shared an office with my colonel, and Pat worked in the adjoining room, with a door leading into Colonel Petrie's office. He was a full colonel, in charge of the whole section and 'overlord', as one might say, of our unit in Rome and its subsidiaries elsewhere in the Italian theatre. Another section worked in a further part of the building, and yet another was situated in the opposite corner. There was a general office where typing and duplicating was done, and down below was the admin office, the office of the GSO (General Staff Officer) Signals, and the mess.

Down below that was the Grotto, a café in a cave opening on to the beach, with a balcony in front of it where open-air dancing often took place as spring wore into summer. For the first time I saw people dancing in bathing costumes there, and cannot say it appealed to me greatly. The beach daily became more crowded, and if one was bored for a moment there was plenty to be seen from the window. But I never bathed from that crowded stretch of shingle. Pat and I invariably bathed from the villa, where there was more privacy and seclusion, and where we were not overlooked by almost every window of the Villa Paulina. Sometimes the sea was quite rough, and I had one or two narrow shaves, nearly being hurled on to the rocks. Just as you thought you were going to make a nice landing, a sort of undertow would pull you back and then suddenly throw you forward again on to the mussel-covered rocks, which were very prickly and uncomfortable. You had to catch on just at the crucial moment and leap ashore, otherwise the sharp-edged mussels would play havoc with your bare legs.

The work at the HQ was different from anything I had ever done before, and did not appeal to me at all. We seemed to deal with nothing but papers, and every morning there were piles of bumf to wade through, classify, pass to the staff colonels for reading, and then we typed letters or telegrams, made long-distance phone calls, or copied orders for lower formations. We seemed to be a glorified post- or sorting-office, and after the above-mentioned activities had taken place, there was filing and more filing, and further sifting of letters from the various units for whom we were the point of contact for AFHQ. The whole thing was on paper and completely lacked the human element.

In my previous job I had been dealing with people nearly all the time, and paper was, when necessary, incidental. At AFHQ paper seemed an end in itself, and personnel and human relationships seemed to have become mere ciphers and abstractions. However essential the central organisation was, it was not my line of country and I positively languished. In my office the filing had got out of hand, as my predecessor, Betty, departed within a day or two of my arrival without a proper handover, and I found mountains of papers and files with myriads of cross-references to be put in order, and a crowd of headings to be learnt. During the first few days I felt this just could not be endured without my going at least temporarily insane. But Pat, who worked next door, was very kind and understanding, and it did help when she came in and clarified some mystery and then said, 'Don't worry, my dear, it will sort itself out, but do have a cigarette, I've just got hold of some Senior Service.'

At about 10.30 a.m. each morning we had a cup of strong tea made with sweetened condensed milk, served in coarse shallow earthenware cups, painted green. How good that tea was! The co-operators had at least mastered the art of making a good strong brew. Sometimes, at about 12.30, or later if we were busy, Pat would say, 'Come on, let's have a cocktail.' There was no barman here, at least on permanent duty, and so we each had a little book and wrote down in it what we took in the way of drinks in the mess.

By lunch-time, the heat of the day was fully turned on, and one usually felt completely listless and lacking in all energy, and as the weather warmed up further, one was often soaked to the skin with perspiration. When we went to the office first thing in the morning, the sun was already streaming in and the beach looked inviting enough, as yet empty of its usual customers. We faced south, and with the passing hours the sun beat more incessantly and ever more strongly in at our windows, until we were obliged to close the shutters, in the hope of protecting the offices from the afternoon heat. Sometimes I would have a bath at lunch-time and change all my underclothes (what little one wore in that climate). The Perellis had two bathrooms and there was usually hot water. Sometimes I had a cold bath and sometimes a bathe at lunch-time. I would perhaps meet Signora Perelli and the children in front of the house, basking in the sun in their bathing-costumes, and the Signora was most insistent that I should try her Pizza Napolitana. This can be most delicious, a sort of glorified Welsh rarebit with fish and tomato thrown in for good measure, but the Perellis had their own particular brand, which was a kind of cheese pudding and very substantial. A helping of that and I knew it would be difficult, if not impossible, to pass the afternoon without a sleep of some sort in the prevailing intense heat. But one could not always refuse their hospitality, and once or twice I tried the pizza. Signora Perelli was very generous and gave me huge helpings each time. She then fortunately discovered that Pat and I were particularly fond of fruit, and almost every evening she would give us apricots, peaches or plums to eat when we came over after dinner. When we had been there longer, she would also give us a carafe of red wine, and in this way we learnt to appreciate good Italian wine. It was probably local red wine, Vini d'Ischia or Vino di Capri, but in any case we enjoyed it, and it was better and more satisfying than the soggy fritters that were our daily bread in the mess.

After I had been there only a week or two, I suspected that one or two things were disappearing from my kit, and we came to the conclusion that Luisa the maid was not altogether trustworthy. I had in particular a woolly monkey with a china face, which had been once broken and then very skilfully mended and repainted by Tony. This disappeared, and I asked Luisa if she had seen it. She repeatedly denied all knowledge of it, and was indignant at being questioned, but I always strongly suspected that she thought it would be a nice plaything for some small children of her acquaintance. However, after that scare all went well.

Soon afterwards Signora Perelli asked me if I would mind sharing a room with June, as Betty had gone and the Perellis were short of rooms. I agreed, though actually not bound to, but unfortunately June was not at all keen on my sharing with her. Betty had been there only temporarily and June was once more alone, which she infinitely preferred. I discovered later that she had once shared a room with a chronic snorer and was in mortal fear that everyone else might be the same. After she found out that I was no snorer, we became good friends, and I was sorry when she left for England at the end of May.

Before that happened, the war had come to an end and the exciting VE celebrations had taken place. We had expected it for some days at least, and therefore it was perhaps not such a surprise to hear over the wireless that Germany had at last capitulated and unconditional surrender had been imposed by the Allies. Hitler was supposed to have perished in Berlin, but it would appear that no-one knows even now that he really did die there, by his own hand or that of the enemy, or whether as rumoured he escaped to South America, and perhaps secretly plotted revenge and a return to Germany.

As far as the Allies were concerned, in 1945, Hitler and all that he stood for had been effectively crushed, and the great work of Occupation, de-Nazification, re-education and reconstruction was about to begin. We, in Italy, 'the land where the lemon trees bloom', were far away from the devastation of Germany, and Naples was already beginning to resume more normality. On 9 May there was great jubilation everywhere. At last the Germans would be expelled from Italy and the Italians could begin to put their house in order, without (they hoped) too much interference from outside or from the occupying authorities on the spot.

In our small unit we had no particular festivity arranged for that day, as the main celebrations, as far as the outfit were concerned, were planned to take place in Rome in a day or two, and the colonel was going up for them. And so, that evening, Pat was in her room, June was out with a boyfriend and the mess seemed deserted. As I often did, I went back to the office to continue the sorting of papers, or to write home. It was stickily hot, and I was hoping that Brunati, the batman of Italian origin, but with a cockney accent, would remember to bring me the cup of steaming hot sweet tea that I had persuaded him to provide me with every evening at about ten o'clock, when there was a 'brew-up' for the men. Brunati was a kindly cheerful soul and we always had a long and friendly conversation when he brought me the tea. I enjoyed both the drink and the chat, though the former made me perspire all over, so that I came out in beads on my forehead. But it did somehow revive me, and in those early days we had not got to know Signora Perelli very well, and our wine bibbing and fruit tasting was not organised. That came later.

Well, on VE night I decided to go along to the anteroom at about nine o'clock, just to see if there was anything doing, but it was quite empty. I was about to move disconsolately back to the office, when I met Sims, the CO's batman, who had travelled down to Naples when we took our leave from Rome. 'Oo, miss,' he said, 'do come down to the Grotto, the Colonel's down there, and Captain Trent and most of the boys. They're all celebrating VE – come and see what's going on.' 'Are you sure it's all right, Sims?' I asked somewhat anxiously, not quite sure what I was in for, but longing to go just the same. 'Well, the Colonel's there, miss, I don't see as how you can go far wrong. And Captain Trent's there too. I'll take care of you, miss,' he added, in a burst of confidence. That decided me, I would go down, escorted by Sims and at least taste the fruits of victory – it was jolly miserable being alone on such a night anyway. We went through the kitchen and down a long narrow stone passage, and came out on to the platform on the edge of the beach, where I had seen people dancing in the daytime.

The Grotto was dimly lit and there were fairy lights along the walls. The Italian owner, Signor Favini, was pouring out drinks at the bar and round it was seated a large group of men, almost everyone from our place, I figured. I would be the only girl, but no-one seemed to mind and they soon made me feel thoroughly at home, and I was almost at once provided with the usual glassful of sweet, syrupy vermouth. I must have stayed there for about an hour, and there was much jollification, drinking of toasts and singing of old favourites. I remember things getting a trifle noisy towards ten o'clock, and for some unaccountable reason Sims suddenly decided to sit on my knee. I felt as though I were nursing a rather large small boy. Soon after ten, the colonel, Captain Trent and I went up to the mess, where we met some other officers and had one or two drinks with them to toast the victory again.

Then there was a gentle tap at the door, and someone shouted, 'Come in!' A South-African, Sgt Hartz, appeared rather hesitantly at the door of the mess: 'Wondered if you were here, sir,' he stammered slightly. The colonel said, 'Come on in and have a drink, Sergeant, tonight's VE, isn't it?' 'Well, I don't want to intrude, sir,' he hesitated again, but the reply soon put him at ease 'Nonsense, man, come on in, what'll you have?' Soon Sgt Hartz was quite at home, and then someone thought of asking him to sing, and I learned then that his brother had sung in opera in the Union, and that he himself had a very fine tenor voice. I shall never forget his rendering of the 'Old Transvaal', among other African songs, that night – it was truly inspiring. It must have been about eleven o'clock when I returned to my billet, escorted by Captain Trent, who insisted that it was not safe for me to go alone, although I pointed out that I did the journey almost daily that way. On VE night it was nice to have company, even though he did talk rather loudly outside the Perelli's villa, and I was afraid they might appear at their windows at any moment fearful of revelling soldiery.

It was not much more than a week after VE Day that the colonel was demobbed. It happened quite suddenly. The first releases took place when the staff of GHQ was cut down, and he was overdue for release. I was genuinely sad when he left, for he had been such a grand CO to work for. The worst of being a PA is that you become too attached to your boss. But, all the same, I still prefer that type of work. Life seems simpler somehow when you owe allegiance first and foremost to one person in your job. I think that is why so many women like PA jobs in the services, and private secretarial posts in civilian life. As long as you hit things off with your boss, no job can be more enjoyable and worthwhile.

After my CO's departure, there was of course less for me to do, and it took me some time to adjust to the new routine. Even so, Pat and I never took whole days off, as it was always necessary for someone to be on the spot. I did a certain amount of work for a major from one of the adjoining sections, and learned a bit about a different type of intelligence work, in the course of which I met an American colonel. The major was usually in a great flap and always in a hurry. He had a high-powered sports car – a captured enemy vehicle, I believe – in which he zoomed about when he had to go on liaison to Caserta or Rome. Colonel Petrie also had a beautiful sports model, and Pat, as his PA, had the privilege of being allowed to go out in it occasionally, perhaps for an evening in Naples, if the colonel himself was not using it; but he scarcely ever went out and rarely used it except for his work. There was, however, one classic occasion when he decided that for a change he would go out somewhere on a particularly hot and sultry evening, and sent for his car. It could not be found and the news had to be broken to him that J/Cmdr Moffat had taken it. Further enquiry revealed that she had gone out to dinner at the YWCA with the sergeant from the admin office. The colonel was very gentlemanly about the matter, but on another occasion when he and the American invited Pat and me to a brigadier's party at AFHQ, and we arrived at the mess about four minutes late, he was highly displeased and the atmosphere driving along in the smart Mercedes was not a little electric. It took several stiff cocktails before he even smiled – he was more on his own level by that time. It was a lesson to us never to mix business with pleasure: remember that if you are going out with a senior officer, you are as much on duty as when you are in the office, and least of all, never arrive late for the initial rendezvous.

But Colonel Petrie was normally as unruffled as a becalmed ocean, and I never saw him except on this one occasion in anything but the most sanguine of humours. He twice took me up to Rome with him when he was driving up in a jeep to inspect the units there. The first time, we left the road to look for a cemetery where he wanted to trace the grave of a friend's relative. We found the cemetery, having followed a narrow stony lane for about a mile, with golden stubble on one side and olive trees growing in amongst it, their shadows darkening the stubble with round patches of yellow ochre; the harvest south of Rome takes place for the most part in June. It was hot and there was no sound in the cemetery except for the whispering of grasshoppers and the buzzing of flies. There were quite a few graves there – English, American and some German – but already the collecting and reassembling process of the Graves Commission had begun and we could not find the one we were seeking. So we retraced our steps to the jeep and back along the bumpy track, past the olives, to the main highway of Route 6.

It seemed strange to think of some of our men lying there so peacefully, side-by-side with some of their recent enemies, all hostility stilled by death, and the cessation it brought to bodily existence. One could not imagine a more tranquil scene than the small green field with its grassy mounds surmounted by rough white painted wooden crosses, the names haphazardly painted on in black, the German ones in Gothic script. And yet, just over a year ago, the battle for Cassino, through which we were about to pass, was raging, and that very field had possibly, even probably, been the scene of fierce fighting and death-to-death struggles. Now time had effaced all signs of strife, and only those crude little wooden crosses marked the spot where men from several races had met their ultimate end.

We went on, and I tried not to think with melancholy of the place we had just visited. A puncture fortunately took my mind off it. Now the colonel proved adept at changing tyres, and I looked on with admiration while he deftly removed the offender, having jacked it up neatly, and then rolled it aside and replaced it with the spare one. I offered to help, but realised I would be more of a hindrance than a help and mainly contented myself with admiring his handiwork.

On the second visit we paid to Rome, we had lunch in a mess in the city. The unit concerned, the Allied Screening Commission (ASC), was one newly formed and mainly consisted of officers who were ex-prisoners of war. Their function was to deal with the numerous Italians who had helped our men when they were escaping and were at large in the country, or our agents who were doing undercover work during the Occupation. In many cases these Italians had suffered grievous material loss, sometimes imprisonment and torture and even death at the hands of both Fascists and Nazis, for the penalty for shielding an ally was death, and sometimes also for the innocent family of the culprit. On this occasion I had small chance to learn much of the work being initiated by this commission, being somewhat taken up with my party manners, as I was the only girl and there were about forty men in the mess. I sat next to a very charming young major with an MC, who had a slightly Scottish accent, and met hosts of others, whose faces for the most part I forgot the same day, for there were too many of them for me to get to know personally. Their mess was a luxurious flat off the Via Flaminia. It had a round hall with ornate gilded mirrors, and the whole place seemed very well appointed. The food, though Army rations, was so exquisitely cooked that it was hardly recognisable. I wondered vaguely how the cook managed when bully beef was issued.

Altogether the visit was an enjoyable affair. As far as I was concerned there was not much work attached to these visits to Rome, although I was of course on call to do any 'stooging' that Colonel Petrie might require. But he was the most reasonable of masters, so I had nothing in the world to complain about.

17

Bella Napoli

When I had been in Posillipo about a month or more, Jimmy turned up to see me. He was on leave and was burnt a deep brown, which made him look more Spanish than ever, and I could well believe that he was descended from some sailor of the Armada, who had landed in Cornwall and settled there. We went out together once or twice, to visit the Aquarium or to the Naval Officers' Club, where we ate tomato spaghetti, and danced a little. I never knew how we gained entry to this exclusive place, but Jimmy seemed to have a way with him. The club was on the waterfront near the Castel del' Ovo, and through the open windows one could watch the changing sky as night fell over the Bay of Naples.

Another evening we went up to the famous Orange Grove, which had been taken over as a club by the Americans. It was in a truly magnificent situation on the heights above Posillipo, overlooking the complete panorama of Capri, Sorrento, the Bay, the harbour, and of course Vesuvius. It was as good as its reputation: in addition to the indoor restaurant, there was a large garden full of orange trees and palms, where an orchestra played beside a small concrete dance-floor. Tables and chairs were set amongst the trees, from which fairy lamps hung festooned round and about.

It was a romantic spot and could have a romantic atmosphere, but I decided there and then that, in spite of Hollywood,

Americans have no taste for 'romance'. The orchestra, or band, was geared to suit their very 'hot jazz' and 'swing'. Scarcely a tango or a waltz was played all the evening. The saxophone blared and drums boomed in an unending discord of syncopation. Then the 'guys' shouted, whistled, chewed gum and waggled their hips doing rumbas or what-have-you. Altogether our English idea of a quiet dinner for two, 'You and the Night and the Music', had a rude shaking up. Inside the restaurant the scene was fairly riotous and the waiters had a brisk time of it. Nevertheless I enjoyed it, but wished the Orange Grove had been a British club; at least we would have given the Italians free play with their own music, and in Naples they play such lovely things so well, such as 'Torn' a Sorrento' and other songs of the Sunny South, many of them adapted for dancing. But it was fair enough that the Americans should have a club run as they liked it. Probably they in turn found the British extremely sedate, and they had certainly picked the best spot in Naples for their off-duty relaxation. There was an ornamental pond in front of the club, and as we drove away one or two officers were fording it fully clothed. I did not discover why!

Jimmy and I got on very well and he kept on telling me it was time I thought about marriage, whether or not in connection with himself he never revealed. In any case, I argued, there was still time; for the present I was quite happy where I was, despite the daily routine of paper wading in the office. By that time I had got to know most of the personnel in the unit, and we had even managed to organise a dance in the Grotto with the stout support of Signor Favini and his attractive daughters, who were only too keen for any sort of celebration. So marriage was not figuring very largely in my thoughts just then. Anyway, Jimmy went off without making any declaration, if he had ever intended to!

The admin staff at Posillipo were a particularly pleasant crowd, and it was no small wonder that Pat chose to go out with the sergeant, who was a quiet, well-spoken and well-mannered man of over forty. As a rule ATS officers did not go out with male ORs but in this case no possible scandal could arise, as we were such a small section and the sergeant in question was a very respectable married man and a highly respected member of the unit. Pat had a sort of aversion for most of the male officers, I never discovered why, except that she seemed to have undergone some form of disenchantment in Cairo. She was wittily sarcastic and sometimes unleashed her tongue, which, though amusing, did not help towards her own popularity and actually made her enemies.

To me she was a good friend, so if she did think all men were 'beasts' (except of course *her* colonel), it did not worry me. Her main form of recreation, apart from talks with Sgt Stewart on music, was a periodic visit to the hairdresser. Colonel Petrie always said that when Pat was over-tired and had been working too hard a visit to the hairdresser was the best cure. Sometimes he ordered her to go, as apart from these regular appointments she scarcely left the office during the day, Sundays included. Even after I was there to relieve her, she took very little time off, and indeed if she did, something usually happened that required her presence. The work was not too hard, but there was always something to do – and in the prevailing heat one could not do anything at breakneck speed.

Pat's other diversion was bathing, which she liked to do at night, at about 9 p.m. That was also the hour for the fish spearing that goes on in the Bay of Naples. The fisherman swims along with his spear and a waterproof torch attached to his cap; the torch has a strong battery and illuminates the water for some way round. Pat had the habit of slipping off the top of her costume when she was bathing at night, for more freedom of movement, she explained. One night there was a shriek coming from somewhere in the bay, and it transpired that she had been illuminated by a fish-spearer in her mermaidenly attitude! She was more careful about going back to Nature after that!

About half a mile along the coast, near the naval C-in-C's villa, was a restaurant right on the water's edge. A friend came south to visit me when he was on leave from the Front, and we walked for some way up the dusty cliff road and finally turned down a narrow lane, more by instinct than by knowledge. At the bottom of this lane, where several small British naval craft were moored to a stone jetty, we came to a real open-air Neapolitan restaurant with orchestra and tables set out with a magnificent view over the bay, to the lights of Sorrento on one side, and on the other to the lights of Naples. We had dined as usual on spam and doughnuts in the mess, and so we drank some white wine and coffee and just listened to the soft, lilting music, led by a violin and accompanied by the gentle lapping of the waves on the quayside, meanwhile watching the other customers, nearly all Italian. Between this place and the Villa Paulina was, among other grandiose villas, one that belonged to King Vittorio Emanuele, and from which it was later said that he was picked up by a small motor-boat and taken to the British cruiser that bore him to his exile in Egypt after the abdication. The gardens of these villas were rich with palms, orange and lemon trees, cactuses and geraniums, and various flowering shrubs, set in beautifully laid-out flowerbeds and arbours, and most of them had their own private bathing beach, or rock. King Vittorio Emanuele certainly left Italy at one of her most beautiful stretches of coastline, although he could hardly have imagined it would be the last strip of Italian soil he would ever see.

I visited the waterside restaurant once more when I rowed a captain across the bay. We hired a small rowing-boat from Signor Favini who, as well as running the Grotto café and the beach-huts and in peace-time managing his family-owned Villa Paulina, also hired out boats, skiffs and the famous floats commonly known as *sandolini*. These are found in most Italian resorts, but were not suitable for an evening excursion, and so we took the boat and set off in the dark, the bay as usual being lit up by many lights and a thousand reflections. The officer I was transporting could not row, and he was much amused that I should be willing to take on the job. As I have always rowed after a fashion, it was no hardship, and the exercise was welcome in the slightly cooler atmosphere; during the daytime, exercise was out of the question at that time of year, even for the British. In any case, he sang rather nicely – Neapolitan songs and others – which made the task even more enjoyable. We tied up our boat among the naval dinghies and launches, and ordered fried *scampi*, a popular Italian dish consisting of some sort of prawn fried in batter and very tasty. Listening to the ever-popular music and watching the lights, occupations of which I never tired, made the excursion well worthwhile, in spite of the return journey.

But the YWCA in Naples was, however, perhaps the pleasantest place for an afternoon cup of tea or a quiet evening away from the unit. It had cool and comfortable lounges and a delightful roof garden, where we could take meals really *al fresco*, as they say in Italy. There were pots and tubs on the roof with spiky cactuses, brightly coloured trailing nasturtiums and pink geraniums. At midday it was too hot to be up on the roof, but in the evening at sundown it was delightful. The white roofs of Naples with their many terraces and balconies, nearly all sporting some greenery of plants or cactuses, were spread out below and around us. Beyond was the sea and the ever-present watchful outline of Vesuvius brooding over the scene.

It was some time around then that I awoke one night to find the room lit up by a weird flame-coloured ray and heard a thunderous though distant crash. I rushed to the window and saw Vesuvius ablaze. I immediately assumed that it must have begun to erupt again and shuddered involuntarily. There is something terrifying about the powers of nature when unleashed in all their fury, and Vesuvius always seemed just held in check, but ready at any time to belch forth fire and brimstone, endangering the homes of man and his cultivation. That night the bay and the town were bathed in an eerie pinkish light and a streak of flame was reflected right across the dark water, almost to where I stood on the balcony. I was alone and did not care to wake Pat who was sound asleep next door, so I watched for a few minutes quite dumbfounded by the horror, and yet the beauty, of the picture presented. Meanwhile the fire burned fiercely, but I realised after a few moments that it did not come from the summit itself, but from a slightly lower altitude; and then I guessed that an aircraft must have lost its way and crashed into the flank of the volcano.

I returned to my bed, and for some time watched the flames burning brightly and then gradually die down, until there was only a reddish glow on the mountain and a small streak of blood-red shimmering across the bay. Next morning, I learnt that an aeroplane had indeed foundered on Vesuvius, and saddest of all, every occupant had lost his life. The volcano was still taking her toll, even when not in eruption. A search was being organised that day for the bodies of the unfortunate victims, but I never heard that they were found.

By now we were well into June and I frequently bathed before breakfast. Sometimes the water was rather rough and I had one nasty experience, getting thrown on to our rocks, and slightly cut. It was all right as long as you swung in at just the right moment, otherwise in a swell you were pushed against the rock and pulled back again before you regained your balance. On the whole, the sea was calm, and fairly clean, although there were naturally some patches of oil from the ships. First thing in the morning most of the rubbish, consigned to the water each day from the various bathing beaches, had been carried out to sea overnight, and there was not much garbage to contend with, although orange and lemon peel was present far too often, floating on the surface and out with the tide.

The heat was gathering in intensity as the days went on, and we found that to sleep in our thick ATS pyjamas, as well as covered with a mosquito net, was a virtual impossibility. The officers' stores had no thin pyjamas for service girls, and the Italian lingerie, while being highly glamorous and most attractive, was too expensive for our purses. I was in a dilemma and meanwhile managed to sleep *au naturel*, covered by a sheet, but even that seemed like a blanket during those sultry nights, while mosquitoes zoomed around the edge of one's net. Then I heard of an Army form, perhaps 04 – it might have been any number – by virtue of which one could gain permission to export from the UK clothing not provided by the Army and unobtainable locally. I accordingly made the form out in triplicate (or was it quadruplicate?!), stating that I had no thin nightdresses, and owing to the heat could not wear the thick bed-linen provided for by the clothing scale, tropical ATS, and furthermore it was not feasible to buy local stuff. I then requested Colonel Petrie, as CO, to testify that I lacked the necessary garments and needed them from home. He took me at my word and appended his signature, without which the form could not have been despatched. I then proceeded to send off two copies to the D.H. Evans department store in London (where the third copy went is unknown to me, but it probably ended up in the 'Secret Waste' at GHQ). In due course two pretty, thin night-dresses arrived and I could at least sleep in decency for the rest of the summer. For once the Army had proved relatively human!

About that same time I had the foolishness to get sunstroke by staying out for ten minutes after lunch on a tiny balcony leading off one of the other section offices. I had had my head covered and thought all would be well, but had not reckoned with the sun of southern Italy, which of course far surpasses in heat anything like it in England. For the next four days I had the most searing pain in my head. I could neither eat nor sleep and felt spasmodi-cally giddy and dizzy, and inclined to overbalance. I managed to carry on, but only just, and I never sunbathed at midday again, at least not in Naples. The saying about 'mad dogs and Englishmen' is sometimes true, but nevertheless the beach in front of the Villa Paulina was becoming more crowded every afternoon and one could recognise many of the same people there each day. In fact we wondered how they could spare the time for so much '*dolce far niente*'. Signor Favini's two attractive daughters and their girl-friends were always present, but it was hard to distinguish anyone in the sea of brown bodies, which seemed to become daily more chocolate-coloured. The women knitted, smoked or just reclined, and children were everywhere, naked or nearly so, chasing in and out among the sunbathers, some children wearing small linen hats, but mostly bare-headed. Presumably they are used to the heat and do not need to take care as we do. If anyone from our unit was on the beach, you could at once pick them out by their fair skin. Only the South Africans seemed to resemble the Italians in the way they that were adapted to the sun, and became brown without discomfort or peeling.

As a concession to local fashions, I managed to persuade the dressmaker from Bellavista, my friend of the previous year, to make me a 'crinkly' swimsuit from an old summer dress. This she did very neatly, lining it with the remnants of an old nightdress. Thus it was that I renewed my acquaintance with her, and once again she was the means of my receiving a proposal of marriage – perhaps I should say she transmitted the proposal. This time the gentlemen was a dark and handsome young wine-merchant, whom I had met at Signora Renata's house the summer before. I remembered him as a very pleasant young man. Nevertheless, I did not feel inclined to marry then, and so I made the same excuse as before, i.e. a distant fiancé. It was received as philosophically as my other refusal had been. I made it clear that I did not object in principle to the idea of an Italian husband, but it so happened that there was someone else who engaged my affection. It was with regret that I said my last goodbye to Signora Renata and her children and their friendly home.

I had met up with some Signals friends of the year before, who now lived near Bellavista, and I sometimes went to concerts or to the opera at the San Carlo Opera House with them. I was able to hear Gigli once again, this time in Puccini's *Manon Lescaut*, but was a little disappointed – he did not seem to sing quite so brilliantly as he had done the previous November at the unofficial concert at the Grand Hotel in Rome. Once or twice I went to the Signals mess, combining it with visiting Signora Renata. The mess was a pleasant villa, just outside Portici, and it was good once more to be amongst the apricot groves and look down over the bay from the small verandah, around which roses climbed and cactuses grew in earthenware pots. The garden of this villa must have been very lovely, but now it was somewhat derelict and overgrown, trampled down by men and vehicles. Rabbits were being kept at one side, though for what I am not sure – probably for eating. The batman was in charge of them. Burglars entered the villa this summer and it could not have been difficult for them, as there were few locks on the doors of any damaged or requisitioned houses. But on this occasion they did not get much loot, as someone sounded the alarm and they took to their heels to evade capture. The great quest for loot still went on in Naples, in fact it was more the custom than ever, and the greatest care had to be taken to safeguard one's personal property and any Army property, transport in particular, of course. The Via Roma was considered to be the most dangerous spot of all, for there in the crowd a clever thief would slip the notecase from a man's pocket completely unnoticed in the throng. Sometimes, young boys, often mere children, would jump on to the back of a lorry and jump off with a case of stores, without even being detected before the lorry reached its destination. I had one such experience in Rome. I had been shopping for the mess and was sitting in the front of a PU beside the driver. We had slowed down to go under the arches of the Porta San Giovanni, when some slight sound made me turn my head and I saw two youths climbing into the back of the truck. I shrieked to the driver and shouted to them to go away. The driver at once accelerated to at least 40mph and the youths both dropped off. The second boy had fortunately not climbed in and the one who had was over the side in an instant. We lost nothing, but after that I always looked round when slowing down in an open truck in any city or town.

It was with one of the Signals friends that I visited the ruined Roman town of Herculaneum, or 'Ercolano', as it is now called. This had been destroyed, like Pompeii, by lava from Mount Vesuvius. It is smaller than Pompeii, more compact, nearer the sea and if anything more perfect. We saw the Roman baths, the shops, the streets and the temple – it was no more ruined than many bombed-out cities of our own day, but time had mellowed the scars of destruction and it seemed a whole, or at least rounded off. Grass had grown profusely, and there were wildflowers in the crevices. Oleanders had been planted along the main drive to the ruins and their perfume filled the air. All was quiet except for the occasional distant sound of an engine or, as so often, the chirping of grasshoppers. It was hot and rather dusty, and for a short time one seemed to have left modern life and yet not have entirely penetrated antiquity. One seemed to be in a sort of vacuum, so strongly was the atmosphere imbued with an indefinable, yet indisputable, aromatic sensation of the past. Our guide, a worthy man, speaking efficient English, took especial pride in displaying what he declared were ancient Roman lentils – small black beady objects. Dried beans of some sort they undoubtedly were, but surely they could not have been left by the Romans? 'But yes, Signorina, these are Roman lentils,' he assured me. I heard my companion mutter something that sounded like 'Roman, my foot!', but I had not the heart to disappoint our cheery guide by a show of scepticism.

It is perhaps most of all for its colouring that I remember Herculaneum. In the background, like the backcloth of a theatre, was the brilliant blue Mediterranean; in the foreground the creamy-grey weather-beaten stones and, contrasting against them, the rather dry green turf, relieved by the deep pink of the oleanders. Above all this was the blue sky of Italy, which must be seen to be believed. The strength of the sun was dazzling and the outlines of everything were razor-sharp. Blue, stone, pale green, bright pink and blue again, all vividly revealed by an intransigent meridian sun – that was the colour-scheme of Ercolano, bathed in a light that would have made the humblest tenement romantic – Ercolano was almost enchanted.

18

Torn' a Sorrento

*B*efore we left Naples five of us made an excursion to Sorrento and Positano. I had always longed to visit Positano again, and was not disappointed. We went by the autostrada, but turned off at Castellamare and at Sorrento we stopped the car on the crowded main piazza. There were many shops selling all sorts of souvenirs, mostly corals, cameos and other jewellery. I bought a polished wood cigarette box depicting Vesuvius and the bay. After looking at the shop we wandered down a narrow lane to the water's edge and went along a small jetty. The water was deep blue, aquamarine, and quite transparent. It was quieter than normal, for it was not yet midday and there was no-one much about. Most of the Italian population were in church or just out of it, milling round on the piazza, garbed in their Sunday best, greeting friends and acquaintances, and exchanging the day's news. One or two small fishing boats floated becalmed on the water, and on the terrace of the hotels overlooking the jetty an occasional guest wandered to the balustrade to enjoy the morning view. We did not linger long, but after admiring the rich green vegetation that abounded almost to the edge of the sea, we returned to our car, piled in and set off along the coast once more, hooting at every corner, for the road was narrow and traffic was frequent, and there were several ugly gashes in the concrete seaward walls, where vehicles had crashed (we hoped only mildly, and not to their doom) several hundred feet down on to the rocks below.

We went through Positano, wooded slopes on either side of the road, and eventually came to Amalfi, where we visited the cathedral, a very fine piece of architecture, mainly in black and white marble, commanding a magnificent view from its steps. Climbing once more into our overflowing vehicle, we ascended the road for Ravello, first up a wide curving surface and then along narrow winding lanes with high stone walls on either side, and here and there a gate set in the wall, made of thick strong timbers reinforced with iron studs. In the wall would be a bell-pull, made of iron. One could imagine the distant clanging that a tug at the rusty iron handle would produce in the hidden porter's lodge, and the grumbling that would ensue if the *custode* were disturbed during his siesta.

We were now well up above the coast road and in among the olive-covered slopes, where the trees grew on a slant, their trunks gnarled with age and often bent inward by the force of several centuries of breezes and gales. Before long we came to the former Capuchin monastery, in peacetime a hotel, but now taken over for a rest-camp. We had lunch on the terrace, shaded by vines and overlooking the sea and the small port of Amalfi. It was a little cooler up here on the terrace, and the wind rustled refreshingly in the vine-leaves, but in the sun it was as hot as ever. Inside the building the cool shuttered corridors and stone floors dispelled some of the fierce outside heat. The rooms of the hotel, former monks' cells, were small and sparsely furnished. They had distempered walls, some cream, some pink and some blue. There was an air of restfulness about the monastery, which seemed to invite one to repose far from the madding crowd of modern life. One could well imagine the monks moving softly amongst the trees and flowers, tending the vines, studying quietly on the terrace, or perhaps looking out to sea, lost in contemplation or prayer.

After an apology of a siesta, which consisted in sitting and digesting our lunch for about half an hour and then taking photographs on the terrace, we went to Ravello and saw Prince

Umberto's country house and the villa where Greta Garbo had lived. Ravello has a tiny green, surrounded by some grey stone cottages with roses climbing up their walls. There is a grey stone church there also. Round the corner from the green, if you follow the road, you come to more high stone walls, and here and there an entrance, perhaps with an armorial bearing carved in stone over the gate-posts, and pots of cactuses on either side. Through the wrought-iron gates we could see palm trees and cypresses, and the glimpse of the shuttered villa within, for of course nothing was open for visiting. It was quiet and utterly peaceful here – no wonder Greta Garbo liked it, with her reputation for loving solitude. One seemed cut off from the world, in a paradise of trees, flowers, ferns and cool stone dwellings. One of the latter had been very conveniently requisitioned for use by officers of HM services, and we had tea there in the shady garden, listening to the ringing English voices and the bantering conversations, well larded with Army slang, that went on around us. Our own conversation was just the same, but somehow it all seemed a little incongruous in that haven of exotic vegetation, semi-tropical heat and Italian architecture. But the Italians employed by the club had learned to make good English tea – an unexotic but important point.

Once again we squeezed into our car and sped down the mountainous road, past tiny scattered stone houses clinging to the hillsides and an occasional goat browsing at the road-edge, attended by a small girl with pigtails tied over her head or a little dark-haired boy, both barefoot.

We struck the coast again at Amalfi, turned back the way we had come and soon reached Positano in time for a bathe before sundown, which proved just as enjoyable an experience as the former bathe there had been. Positano had not changed, but it looked a little more prosperous and the flowers were perhaps more numerous. To me, it was just as fascinating and as romantic as ever – almost too ideal to exist.

After the bathe we had an aperitif at the pavilion on the beach, which was really not much more than a small veranda converted into a café, and then we decided to finish off the day by dining at the Katarinetta, of which I had heard but until then had never seen. It was a restaurant, open-air of course, with a small band and space for dancing. Two or three of this type had opened in the summer of 1945 in Positano, but the Katarinetta was the most famed, both for local colour and natural beauty. It was literally cut out of the rock, about 200 or 300ft above the north end of the beach, so that its stone terrace faced south-west with the panorama of all Positano spread out far below. When we arrived it was dusk and the last vestiges of a glorious afterglow tinged the grey rocks with crimson. After we had parked the car on a levelled-out piece of ground at the end of a long winding alley, we finished the journey on foot, up a steep pebbly path, emerging at last on to the aforesaid terrace, which was shaded over with arbours of vines that wreathed its parapet overlooking the sea. It was a sort of bower, where little tables covered with bright red check cloths were dotted here and there, some of them in specially designed arbours, so that a certain amount of privacy was possible for a private party. The tables in the central part were more exposed and we took one of these in order to have a good view of all the other guests when they should arrive. Although we got there at about eight o'clock, it was still early for those parts, where most of the local inhabitants did not eat their evening meal much before ten at night. In fact, the food was not even ready, so we started on a drink of some sort, and then were eventually served with huge platefuls of steaming *spaghetti al pomodoro*, i.e. tomato spaghetti, but cooked in Neapolitan fashion with plenty of oil and a rich sauce. This was almost a meal in itself, but of course it was only the beginning – I forget what followed.

By nine o'clock, more people were dribbling in. Hugh Trent, who was the leader of the party and drove our car, had been here before and had spent the time while we were waiting for the food in regaling us with stories of the distinguished Italians who patronised the place, most of them rich and high-ranking, it seemed – the aristocracy of the Sorrento peninsula. Now some of these important personages began to arrive, the women exotic, made up, décolletées, some of them in sunbathing tops and striped linen skirts, some wearing huge variegated rings that together with brilliant nail-varnish made their brown hands a blaze of colour, their varnished toenails shining through open sandals; others of them with their hair dyed copper or titian, very sophisticated and somewhat hard-boiled. The men seemed a trifle fleshy and one man looked as though he had been a local leading Fascist but had now recanted and was reaping the benefits of sums amassed during past years. I had no brief for such an opinion, but that was the impression I got of him, and of some of the other locals too – they looked smart, unscrupulous and extremely worldly-wise, 'no flies on them'. But Hugh did not stop to think of what their former politics might have been; in any case, he would probably have argued that almost everyone in Italy had been a Fascist anyway. (Strange to say, I only ever met one who admitted it!) Hugh advanced on an elegant, glamorous beauty, and we distinctly heard him say, in an exaggerated drawl, 'My *dear* Princess, how very delightful to meet you again,' and in two minutes he had swept the princess to her feet and was joggling her up and down to the tune of 'Lay that pistol down', or some such rapid foxtrot, his face simply beaming with pride and excitement. We scarcely saw him for the rest of the evening, and contented ourselves with admiring his progress with the local beauties in the distance. It seemed that the '*Caro Capitano*' was in high favour.

By now the place was full and there were also some British officers in mufti from GHQ. English was spoken on most sides and there was a Babel of voices, patterned with the quick rhythm of the band and the lilting melodies of the South, the whole atmosphere permeated by the smell of rich Neapolitan cooking and the whiff of scented cigarettes. The vine-leaves were silhouetted sharply against the deep blue of the night sky and far below one could hear the murmur of the waves on the rocks. The air was fresh and the stars twinkled brightly overhead. On the terrace lanterns gave out a warm yellow glow; far beneath us, reflections of the light shimmered on the water. What a setting!

No wonder one could feel intoxicated with its glamour and forget any misgivings one might have about those who shared it. We did not leave until after midnight, when we eventually managed to separate Hugh from his noble dancing partners, and then only when he had bade them fond farewells, with many promises of renewed acquaintance in future.

We were soon in the car, homeward bound. We had hardly travelled more than a few miles when there was a nasty hard bump at the back – a puncture. After a change of wheel, the spare wheel also punctured. 'That's our reward for using one of those captured enemy vehicles,' someone said, 'they're so ruddy unreliable!' Someone had to get out and walk to the next village to telephone for a relief truck. It must have been three in the morning when we finally reached home, quite worn out. The evening ended in a most Italian fashion, for Italian transport was at that time notorious for breaking down, and you could never travel anywhere without seeing some lorry or overloaded private car with a wheel off and its occupants squatting disconsolately at the roadside while their sweating driver struggled with jacks and spares. But as far as we were concerned, we had had a wonderful day – a puncture here and there was all part of the game.

Round about that time I became acquainted with other aspects of Italian life. To my shame I still spoke very little Italian, despite my long stay in the country, but living in an Italian household as we were, it was impossible not to absorb some of the atmosphere and observe the everyday doings of the family whose guests we were, even if superimposed ones. Two or three of the Perellis invited Pat and me to dinner, but we refused because we knew so little of the language and were afraid of getting hopelessly out of our depth. It was perhaps also because the intense heat was beginning to drag us down, and by the end of a day in the office we had no energy for anything, least of all for smartening up and being on the intellectual *qui-vive* for an exhausting Italian dinner party. As I later discovered, Italian dinner parties are very intensive, and we should doubtless have been called for our opinion of the political situation and many other complicated matters, vastly different from a simple conversation with the dressmaker or Luisa. Still our relations with the Perellis continued to be very cordial; they were extremely kind, and last thing at night we would often go into the kitchen for a chat with Luisa and sometimes with Signora Perelli. We knew their children quite well and used to take them fruit drops and other packets of sweets. Sometimes there seemed to be a current of unrest in the house and I heard rumours that things were not going quite as smoothly as they might between the Perellis. One night there was a great discussion going on in the dining-room, which was next to my bedroom and gave on to the same balcony; a sort of family conclave seemed to be in progress and there was a tension in the air. About midnight, when I was trying to sleep despite the burble of voices raised in animated discussion, there was a tap at the door – it was Signora Perelli. 'Could you let me have a few cigarettes for Signor l'Avvocato, Signorina, please, we have quite run out,' she said. 'Of course, Signora,' I replied, 'here are all I have, you are welcome,' and I gave her a packet of twenty, of which about fourteen were left. She thanked me profusely and withdrew. The men's voices droned on and on – perhaps it was a pity to have let the Signora have so many cigarettes, I thought, as they would probably now stay up until all were smoked. I could just imagine what the ashtrays must be looking like by now.

It must have been about 2 a.m. when the party finally packed up and I heard them all saying '*Buonanotte*'. I turned over with a sigh of relief, thinking it was all finished, but it only seemed an hour or two later when I heard voices again and it was obvious that the conference had resumed. I looked at my watch and saw that it was 7 a.m. Whatever was the household coming to? This was certainly quite unusual! When Luisa brought my coffee, she was bursting with importance and excitement and I wondered whether the Perellis were going to be divorced, though it hardly seemed possible in Italy. Going by the confidential expression on her face, Luisa would have liked to tell me all about it, but she remained loyal to her employers and contented herself with a knowing look.

One evening not long after this, I had strolled back from the office and was approaching the outside staircase which led to the first floor and the Perellis' flat, when loud voices from their open kitchen window rent the air. An argument was taking place, as far as I could gather, between the Perellis and Luisa, but who was siding with whom it was impossible to tell. All of a sudden a large missile shot past in front of me, missing my nose by a hair's breadth, and landed with a plop in a bed of begonias to the right of the path. I took a quick look and saw that I had narrowly missed being felled with a fair-sized alarm clock. I just walked on up the steps, pretending not to notice the occurrence, and went straight to my room, not even glancing into the kitchen, where the voices had somewhat subsided to a mere murmur. I had only been in my room for a few minutes, when without warning a shadow darkened the French window leading on to the balcony, and Signor Perelli strolled in, saying, '*Buonasera, Signorina, sta bene?*' '*Si, grazie*', I answered, rather surprised at this unwonted intrusion. '*Bene, bene*,' he answered, and without more ado passed out of my door and into the corridor, perfectly composed, and evidently much relieved that I bore no visible marks of injury.

Luisa told me a few days later in confidence that the 'Signore' himself had thrown the clock out of the kitchen window, but I always felt that she was the guilty party, because at the time she had a grievance; she desperately wanted to get home to visit her sister in Sardinia and was totally unable to afford the fare from her very small wages. Whether or not she ever got back to Sardinia I never heard, but in 1947 she was still in Naples and I sent her some part-worn civilian clothes, for which she wrote and thanked me most gratefully. While we were living in the house we occasionally gave her odds and ends, but as my wardrobe consisted almost entirely of uniform there was little enough to give. Luisa had, however, apparently summed up what was available, for shortly before the end of July, when the section was about to close down and Pat and I were due for a new posting, she asked me if I might have my scarlet zipper writing-case. 'To go with my red dress, when I go out on my day off,' she explained. 'But Luisa,' I expostulated, most unwilling to part with the case, which held all my correspondence, 'it doesn't match your dress, they clash.' 'Oh no, Signorina, they go very well together, I should so love that bag, I have nothing, and you know I can't afford one myself.' 'Very well, Luisa, I will think it over,' I said a trifle coldly, secretly cursing the day that made it possible for her to possess what must be a pretty detailed mental inventory of all my goods and chattels. In the end, I let her have it. After all, it was true that she could not afford a bag herself, and if she liked the look of my writing-case, well, she had taken good care of us and it would be a little parting gift. So I gave it to her and she was ecstatically grateful and delighted. She was such an excitable little person, one of the household in every way, not just a mere servant, but friend, confidante and housekeeper; and in the manner of domestics to the eighteenth-century English gentry or the men and maids who appear in the plays of Molière and others, she shared the joys and sorrows, ups and downs, of those she worked for in a completely personal and natural manner. She really was one of the family, and when the day came for Pat and me to depart, she helped us with our luggage, and wept when we eventually went off, embracing us as we thanked her for all she had done for us. We bade the Signora a friendly enough farewell also and kissed the three small children, who had become 'pals' by this time.

I was by now so used to this beautiful villa, to the sound of the sea, and to the homely atmosphere I had breathed in for three months, that it was with a real wrench that I left Posillipo and its orange and lemon trees. But the work had tailed off, much of the clearing up had been done, and Colonel Petrie was going home very shortly. Most of the Other Ranks had been posted and some released, and the other sections in Villa Paulina were also shortly due to close. Pat was going back to the UK, and from there would be posted to Paris. I was returning to Rome as PA to my ex-CO's successor, in the same job as before. But meanwhile, neither Pat nor I had had any leave, or even days off, for many months. Since leaving England more than a year previously, I had had no more than a day's leave here and there, and had worked on Sundays, and so we had been granted about twelve days and were travelling up north together. We were like schoolgirls in our excited anticipation, and hoped to see Florence and Venice and even go on to our unit in Austria, if transport was going that way.

Everyone was either departing, or preparing for departure at that time. We had already said goodbye to quite a number of ORs, who had gone their various ways, and there was the slightly nostalgic air of mutual farewells about the place. The Favinis were quite sorry that we were all leaving, at least the young people were. No doubt Signor Favini was already making plans for the re-opening and reorganisation of his hotel, and would not be sorry to see the back of the billetees. Captain Trent was very friendly with his dark-haired, rather voluptuous daughters, Margherita and Liliana, and it was rumoured that Margherita had set her cap in his direction, having previously been engaged to an American and then broken it off. Anyway, shortly before Pat and I were due to leave, Liliana stopped me in the lane one day, handed me an autograph book and asked me to put something in it. On looking through it afterwards I saw that it contained poems, sketches and some merely conventional greetings. Obviously my contribution must figure in the last group, and I just wrote a few words of Italian about the beauty of Naples and my regret at leaving it, wishing the family all the best. I hoped my grammar was not too appalling. Liliana had asked me to pass the album on to Pat and then to Hugh Trent. A day or so later, when I went into the latter's office on business, he said, 'What do you make of this? Will you translate it for me?' It was a letter from Margherita, showing evident regret at his imminent departure, and scarcely disguising that she was enamoured of him. I translated it and he asked me to write a reply for him. That was just the chance I had been waiting for, and I drafted forthwith a very flowery reply, in my best Italian, not quite compromising, but very nearly, and calculated to give the recipient at least a nice flutter. It ended affectionately, but not too much so. I took it down to Hugh and asked him to read it. He made it out as far as possible and then asked me if I was 'letting him in for anything'. 'Not at all,' I replied, 'That is just what she expects of you after the attention you have been paying her on the beach in the afternoons.' After a lot of discussion, I persuaded him that my reply would do very well and then he asked me to write something in the autograph book for him, which duty I also undertook most willingly, not being able to resist the temptation of trying to give the impression that he was the adoring and devoted swain, while taking care not to involve him too deeply. After all, if he would flirt with the local girls, and then ask an English girl to carry on his romantic correspondence for him, what could he expect? Anyway, I believe my literature was quite a success. What seemed to me 'pretty hot stuff' was probably like lukewarm water to Margherita and Liliana, accustomed to the vivid language and hot temperaments of the southerners, and so Hugh escaped any entanglement – at least, when I saw him later in Rome, he appeared to be fancy-free and as ready for any new adventure as ever. But sometimes I wondered what happened to Margherita and Liliana after the departure of the troops. They had dallied with the foreign soldiers, but had not found husbands among them. Could they find husbands among their own men? For to marry was indisputably the essential plank of their existence. They had no career, and marry they must. Perhaps their father went on to arrange matches for them, with handsome dowries, for they were at least comfortably off, or perhaps they did marry an 'ally' after all. One day I shall go back and find out, and probably see swarms of little berry-coloured boys and girls on the beach with Margherita and Liliana and their girl-cousins, who by that time will have exchanged their glamorous figures for the more comfortable ones of motherhood and maturity – but I am sure their eyes and smiles will be as bright and friendly as ever, and that they will know all the romantic gossip of Posillipo.

And so one hot morning, at the very end of July, Pat and I squeezed into a car with most of our baggage, a major called Alfred, who was going up to Florence on a posting, and a pet kitten I had just rescued from the mess, fearing it would starve. Having said final goodbyes all round, we drove for the last time up the winding dusty drive, waving goodbye as we went to various local acquaintances. We were soon on the road for Caserta, leaving behind us 'La Bella Napoli', her crowded streets, her oranges and lemons, her nostalgic music, her bay and the Villa Paulina. The famous song 'Tornerai' ('Je t'attendrai'), which was then so much in vogue, came to mind. I vowed to return to Naples – like so many places in Italy, it had cast its spell over me.

Soon after passing through Caserta, the kitten misbehaved very badly in the car. I had fortunately taken the precaution of putting it on an Army blanket, but we had to stop the car and take it for a walk on the sward bordering the highway, while streams of military traffic poured by in both directions.

Alfred knew Italy fairly well and insisted that we stop in Formia and have an Italian lunch, with spaghetti, which he promised us we would greatly enjoy. So we drew up at a tiny little restaurant within a stone's throw of the bluest sea I ever saw, viewed through a mass of devastated pill-boxes, tangled barbed wire and other mangled remains of the coastal defences. Contrasted against the white concrete of the fortifications, the sea looked bluer than ever. We stepped in through a bead curtain, into an almost pitch-dark interior, but brightened by clean white tablecloths, and after the glare outside it took a few moments before our eyes became accustomed to the dim light. We sat down and Alfred took charge, and before long we had before us the largest, steamiest plates of oily tomato spaghetti, with what seemed the longest and slipperiest threads of pasta I'd ever seen. It tasted excellent, but the helping was far too large. Pat always had a dainty appetite and she made no headway at all. Alfred undertook to teach us how to eat it correctly, as he could see at a glance that we had not yet really mastered the technique. I did manage with a gigantic effort to stow away about two-thirds of the massive helping, but Alfred did not seem to have the slightest difficulty in demolishing all of his in record time. A pudding followed, quite pleasant, and to wash all this down we had red wine. Needless to say, I slept for most of the remainder of the journey with the comfortable consciousness that at least with Italian food one felt really satisfied.

It was clear that one meal a day would suffice, if that meal was pasta, but I felt that it would be better to wait before embarking on any more Italian lunches in the midday heat until I was more used to the diet and had suitably fasted in advance. Pat stayed at the YW that night; Alfred and I stayed at the unit, where I dumped my luggage. We picked Pat up the following morning at 8.30 a.m. on our way up north.

19

A Journey of Discovery

*C*rossing the Tiber at the ancient Ponte Milvio, we branched right, up Route 3 for Florence, via Perugia. Our first stop was Assisi, where we left the main road to have a look at the town of St Francis. The Basilica is to me one of the wonders of the world. It consists of three churches, one above the other. The upper one is the largest and contains the magnificent Giotto mural paintings of the life of the Saint. The middle one is really the crypt and is covered in coloured frescoes, with brilliantly painted borders and patterns to each Gothic arch. One might be stepping between the pages of an illuminated manuscript of the fifteenth century.

Inside the crypt it was rather dark, but bands of sunlight shot shafts through the bright, stained-glass windows and lit up the rich reds, browns and yellows of the frescoed walls and ceiling. Then we descended a narrow, rough-hewn stone stairway and came to the tiny shrine containing the tomb of the Saint. Only the tomb itself was lit by a pinkish lamp. Everyone moved softly, almost on tiptoe, and a reverent hush pervaded the vault.

As we came up from the tomb and sallied forth into the quadrangle outside, the brilliance of the sun almost blinded us for a moment as it reflected dazzlingly from the blazing white stone of the church and the surrounding cloisters, and from the dry sandy floor of the courtyard. We decided that it was absolutely essential to find somewhere in the cool to eat our sandwiches and to 'tidy up', and so we began the search, driving slowly through narrow, deserted, shuttered streets and across an ancient square, an anti-quated stone fountain at its centre, and back again. It was about two o'clock and there was not even a dog to be seen. The place seemed almost dead.

Finally, however, we came out on to a big open piazza, where a large church confronted us, Santa Chiara, we later discovered, and to our right lay a terrace from which a glorious panorama stretched for many miles. Assisi is at the end of a ridge, so that the view, right across the plain of Umbria, is unsurpassed. It must have been almost impregnable in the Middle Ages, when it car-ried on its feuds with neighbouring towns, Perugia and Arezzo, in particular. Its rock is visible from afar, and I later heard that the British prisoners of war, interned before the Italian armistice at Poppi, about 50 miles away as the crow flies, could see the rock of St Francis gleaming golden in the sunset every evening, almost like the burning bush seen by Moses.

After we had feasted our eyes on this panorama for a few moments, we turned our thoughts to more material matters and managed to find a *ristorante* that appeared to have no customers but whose doors were slightly ajar. We went in through a room with cloth-less tables and chairs reversed on top of each other and were ushered up a few steps to emerge round the corner into the kitchen. Here the family were collected and someone was playing a piano accordion. We explained our needs and were made very welcome. They invited us to sit at the big kitchen table and eat our sandwiches there and then, and the accordion player made our meal a very cheerful affair.

Alfred, with his infectious gaiety and his easy flow of Italian, soon established very cordial relations; we were offered a glass of wine and the health of the Allies was drunk. We must have stayed there about an hour and we thoroughly enjoyed the intermezzo. But time was passing, so very regretfully we left the slumber-ing little town with its mediaeval archways, winding spiral steps and prevailing peacefulness, and set off once more for Florence, rapidly descending to the plain and leaving the olive groves for flat fields and pastures. Before long, we were rumbling through the almost deserted streets of Perugia, like Assisi a cluster of ancient grey houses and one or two towering churches on an escarpment. The only activity seemed to be that of Allied transport. We stopped for a cup of tea and a bun in a part of the town that seemed fairly busy, as far as the Army was concerned.

As we left Perugia and started another descent, we saw the gleaming water of Lake Trasimeno sparkling in the sun – it lay like a great silver shield with a small green island at its centre. We stopped for a few moments near a bower of vines and managed to purchase some grapes from a farmer's wife who was looking out from her front door on the other side of the road. Her children helped to cut the bunches down and were rewarded with the customary gift of *caramelle*.

We were soon on our way again, beginning to feel the heat a little, for it was very sticky that day. As the afternoon wore on it seemed to grow hotter, and Pat and I became very tired. The hot dust choked us and made our eyes smart. I bathed my face and hands frequently with some astringent lotion but even the soothing effect thus achieved did not last long. It must have been about six o'clock when we rounded the bend and crossed the Arno at Pontassieve, where a great many buildings were badly damaged and the bridge was a mass of rubbled arches. We crossed over a temporary bridge, leaving behind us the narrow road we had been following along the valley, with its rows and rows of small, gently waving poplars, and now we were driving into the evening sun. The sky was crimson with the sunset glow, and as we went on it turned pink like the icing on a cake, centring on a great golden ball, which gradually sank behind the trees. Then the pink faded to mauve and finally merged into the growing blue behind us – in the gamut of colour the evening star shone brightly overhead, but the valley itself was already in twilight and night soon fell. It was dark when we entered the city, but by that time I was too tired to care.

In spite of my exhaustion I was glad to see Tiny in Florence, and he took all three of us to our section, on the south bank of the Arno. But Pat and I had 'had it', as the slang goes, for that evening and the moment we got to our hotel I began to feel faint. We asked for tea and a kindly head waiter did his best to persuade me that it was far better to drink coffee if feeling faint. He had no tea, but would bring me coffee, he said, '*Lei verrà, Signorina, se ho ragione. Le farà tanto bene.*' He was as good as his word and his promise worked. Next day I felt as fit as a fiddle and spent it sightseeing with Alfred. We visited the magnificent Duomo and the Battistero, with their gleaming black-and-white marble exteriors, so characteristic of Tuscan churches and monuments. Inside the cathedral it seemed strikingly and agreeably quiet and dignified after the more crowded and ornate Roman churches. We were lucky in our guide, a fervent Florentine, and when he discovered that we both understood Italian, expressed himself loudly and volubly on art, politics and the history of his city. Probably no burghers anywhere are prouder of their city, the home of many great artists and distinguished men in all walks of life, than are the Florentines. Our guide assured us in eloquent terms that the Fascist era had been dead from the artistic point of view, as the Fascists had crushed all individualism and allowed no artist to learn his craft or develop his talent and fulfil his inspiration as he thought fit. We hoped he was inferring that with the arrival of the Allies a golden age for art had dawned, but at least he did not tell us that the Allied armies were vandals worse than either Nazis or Fascists, as he might have done. Several passers-by lingered to listen in, and I glanced a trifle apprehensively over my shoulder, half expecting a *carabiniere* to appear and take our man into custody for making a political speech in church, but no one hindered him and from the looks on the faces of those around us, I imagine they heartily endorsed everything he was saying.

Encouraged by our enthusiastic mentor, we climbed the tower of the Duomo to examine the panorama of the city and surrounding country. This was more than splendid – and revealed Florence to be unique, with her red roofs clustering cosily round the towers of the Palazzo Vecchio, the Bargello (old prison), the Church of Santa Croce and other prominent landmarks, all

The author in 1945.
(Author's Collection)

The author (third from
left) with colleagues
at Latimer House
Interrogation Centre.
(Author's Collection)

The parade ground: No. 7 ATS Training Centre, Guildford, 1942. (IWM Cat No: Art LD 1959)

British trucks entering the Piazza del Popolo, through the Arch of Titus Severus, in Rome, June 1944. (IWM Cat No: TR 1855)

British soldiers visit the Colosseum while on leave in Rome, June 1944. (IWM Cat No: TR 1960)

The author shopping in the market at Fiesole. (Author's Collection, taken by Tiny Pook)

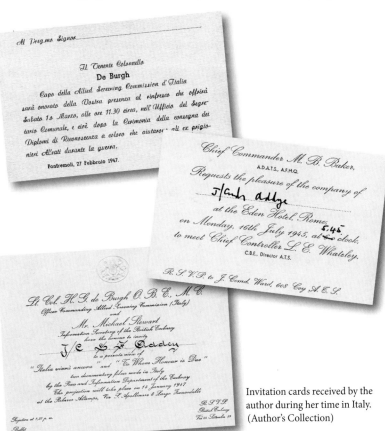

Invitation cards received by the author during her time in Italy. (Author's Collection)

The author at Padua market, Easter leave 1946. (Author's Collection)

The author in Naples. (Author's Collection)

The first Allied convoy to arrive at Naples harbour. In the foreground some of the wrecked harbour installations are visible. In the background is Mount Vesuvius. (IWM Cat No: NA 7414)

GLI ALLEATI
VI RINGRAZIANO

An award ceremony of the Allied Screening Commission for Italian partisans. The Commanding Officer is between the flags. (Author's Collection)

British aid to partisans in northern Italy, April–May 1945: on a field just outside Cuneo, Piedmont, near the French/Italian border, partisans wait for the containers carrying supplies to land. The French Alps are in the background. (IWM Cat No: NA 25393)

Demobilisation of the British Army in Italy, 1945: British servicemen catch trams outside Milan central railway station to travel to the Assembly Centre for Release Personnel at Eugenio barracks on the western outskirts of the city. (IWM Cat No: NA 26237)

A visit by the Allied Screening Commission to a mountain village. Note the Commanding Officer (saluting). Standing behind him are Major Gordon Lett and the author. (Author's Collection)

The Commanding Officer of the Allied Screening Commission (right) in a mountain village. (Author's Collection)

The author with her Commanding Officer, Venice, 1946. (Author's Collection)

The author with Signora Boldrini. She and her husband, an architect, had risked their family to mastermind the escapes of British fugitives in Tuscany, 1947. (Author's Collection)

encircled by a belt of green, sloping up gently on either side of the river, on the north past the silver olive groves up to the foothills of the Apennines. Everywhere there was greenery, from the grey-green of the olives to the dark green of yews and cypresses. One could gaze for hours at the soft refreshing colouring, so different from the more brilliant, but harsher tints of the south. And then the 'silver Arno', as it has often so aptly been called, was visible, winding in and out, and part of the landscape as far as the eye could see. The ugly destruction wrought by the retreating Germans was scarcely noticeable when the whole city was viewed in perspective. To all intents and purposes, Florence was unspoilt. There and then, I conceived an affection for this city, which with the passage of time has increased and deepened. There must be something about the quiet streets, verdant gardens and friendly, well-mannered inhabitants that appeals to the British, for Florence had a very large British colony before the war. Even then, many of them were still in the city, some having played a prominent part in anti-Nazi activities, sheltering escaped prisoners and passing on valuable information to Allied intelligence.

We regretfully descended the tower, and threading our way in and out of several narrow streets arrived at the renowned Palazzo Vecchio, a sort of fortress with a tall battlemented watchtower of the Tuscan type. This was once the palace of the Medici princes and former seat of the Republic of Florence, and so there was much of interest to be seen: paintings, beautiful ceilings and historical monuments. I cannot compete with Baedeker in describing so many marvels. Perhaps what impressed me most was the Sala dei Gigli, or Hall of the Lilies, whose ceiling has a background of deep blue, patterned by gold squares, each containing fleur de lys in gold. This is not strictly the French lily, but the Florentine one, which is slightly more elaborate and appears on many books, objets d'art and so on. It is in fact the crest of the city itself, symbolising the long connection with France, maintained by Catherine, wife of Henry II of France, and others. Now the Palazzo Vecchio is the Town Hall, and busy functionaries hurry to and fro, or work in small discreet offices, hidden from view and segregated from the display rooms. Their presence was noticed as they hurried back and forth with sheaves of files and papers, in quiet conferences with members of the public, at a window or under an arch, and in the faint but occasionally audible click-click of hidden typewriters, or the sudden ring of a telephone bell. Down in the courtyard the ubiquitous *carabinieri* scrutinised all-comers and one or two jeeps were parked near the sculptured fountain.

That day we also managed to squeeze in a visit to the massive square edifice of the Palazzo Strozzi. It was not officially on view either, now being used for offices, but we persuaded a friendly caretaker to take us round. It seemed that during the siege of Florence by our troops, the Germans moved into the Palazzo Strozzi and locked all the staff in the cellars or perhaps, as Alfred suggested, they went of their own accord, being too frightened to stay above ground. I felt some sympathy with this point of view.

We later went on to Palazzo Pitti, were there was an exhibition of French paintings. We arrived there at 6 p.m. and the palazzo was due to close at seven, and so we raced round the galleries at breakneck speed, and then decided to take a look at the famous Boboli gardens, which rise gently up behind the palace. These also seemed to be closed, but we managed to penetrate the palace through a window unobserved and found ourselves in a court-yard leading into the garden itself. As it was past closing time, all was deserted and we had the place to ourselves, a world of shimmering ponds, water lilies, carpets of thick green grass and the ever-present luxuriant foliage reminiscent of an English park. In the cool tranquillity of the sunset hour, we climbed to the top of the gardens and gazed out at the roofs and spires of Florence, framed on either side by the lush green of centuries-old chestnuts and sycamores. Beyond, the outline of the mountains was blurred slightly in the evening haze. But time was passing fast, and we had a dinner date with Tiny and Pat. Pat had of course spent the day recuperating, having her hair done, shop gazing and generally making herself spick and span for the evening's entertainment. For that, we had decided to try a place that advertised itself as a sort of glorified nightclub, but with local colour, where in a beautiful Florentine garden and mansion one could 'rest in comfortable places' and drink in the 'lemon tree bar', amongst other delights.

From the moment I saw this quaintly worded poster on the hotel noticeboard, I longed to sample the place, which would surely offer one some genuine 'atmosphere', if nothing else. The others seemed a trifle sceptical as to what it would be like, but I was resolved to enjoy it, come what may, and if it did not immediately exude 'atmosphere' would do my best to find some. The name of this magical spot was 'Bellosguardo', or 'Beautiful View', and it really did live up to its reputation. It was situated on a hill south of the river, and consisted of an old Florentine villa, or mansion, with a large rambling garden set out formally in front of the house and a broad grassy terrace overlooking the twinkling lights of the city below. There were lawns and trees everywhere, dark cypresses looming over the flowerbeds and expansive umbrella pines, throwing out a faint but clean smell of resin and pine needles. At the back of the house was a walled fruit and vegetable garden, faintly lit by small lanterns. Here two guitarists played gently, and one could wander at will along narrow paths among borders edged with small box hedges and shaded by the spreading branches of lemon and walnut trees. The air was perfumed and warm, caressed as it was by the soft notes of the guitars, playing the music of Italy's traditional melodies, which somehow seem to touch emotional chords, whose vibrations echo down the years.

Inside the house, there was dancing in the big hall, still hung with the portraits of distinguished ancestors, and where coats of armour did not seem out of place amongst the furniture. A small orchestra played at one end, and for the first time in Italy I saw people in evening dress. Needless to say, Pat and I, although dressed up to the best of our ability, were in khaki drill and almost the only English girls present. The other girls were all well dressed and looked very respectable – this was indeed quite a superior sort of place and it seemed a little sad that such a stately home should be used for such a trivial purpose. But then, a great many temporarily homeless men were passing a few hours of harmless enjoyment and relaxation there, so perhaps the purpose was not so trivial after all.

We rested on comfortable settees in the drawing room and had refreshments of excellent calibre in other equally well-furnished apartments. The house was just as it must have been when a rich and cultured family lived there, which probably they still did, and one saw solid antique furniture, a library full of good books and an air of comfortable prosperity about everything. This was probably misleading, though, because behind the facade of gentility and culture might lurk real poverty or, at best, serious financial stress. Italy's aristocracy was beginning to feel the pinch, but they were putting a brave face on it. But no such reflection spoiled our enjoyment that evening and after a final gaze at the lights below us and the faintly discernible outlines of cypresses and pines from the terrace, we betook ourselves back into town, conscious of having passed an extremely pleasant and most restful evening. There *was* indeed 'atmosphere', and it made one relax and forget the rush and tear of Army transport, cups of NAAFI tea and innumerable flies in the office. For a time we had breathed in the atmosphere of a beautiful home and the effect was strangely refreshing to the spirit.

The following day, being Sunday, I attended morning service at the English church and was surprised to see what a large English congregation there was. It seemed as though one had temporarily left Italy and returned to England, perhaps to some village church. There were the same elderly ladies, with beflowered summer hats, and respectable retired gentlemen that one would see in any parish church on a Sunday. The same hymns were sung to the same tunes and a similar sermon preached to those one had heard so many times before in the pre-war years, when one went to church in one's best hat and gloves and made a mental note before the service started of who was there, sitting where, and when they arrived, particularly if late. It was unbelievably English and only the sprinkling of military in the back pews, a variety of ranks, belied the picture of a tranquil English Sunday morning in a small parish church at home.

That afternoon we went out to Fiesole. We crossed the railway and climbed a broad, winding main road, up towards the north and presently came out into a small square set with the gayest and most attractive stalls, where all sorts of handiwork was for sale. Most notable were the intricately embroidered bags, hats, belts, handbags and mats, mostly made of raffia, string and silk by the local inhabitants. Various vendors were soon suing for our custom, cheerfully waving gaily coloured bags and the like enticingly before our eyes. Pat and I longed to linger there, but Tiny firmly told us we would have plenty of time for purchasing later and hastened us away to a small garden restaurant, from the terrace of which there was yet another magnificent view of the city, from exactly the opposite position to that of Bellosguardo. Food was still supposedly very difficult, but that day we somehow managed to achieve chicken and it was a royal feast to us. A rather shabby old man arrived and opened a box of wares, and began showing us various small objects made in coloured raffia. I could not let him go away completely disappointed, and so I bought a couple of *porta fortuna* from him. These are a local tradition and consist of a tiny man and girl made in raffia of various colours, holding hands and attached to a loop, and are supposed to be lucky charms. They cost 2s 6d each and I was very annoyed later on to see better ones for less money, but Pat and I decided to be un-regimental and each attached one to our bush shirts.

After lunch we visited the Roman amphitheatre, where with difficulty Tiny and I restrained Pat from taking a nap among the ruins. We went on to see a small Franciscan convent, with yet another delightful view of the city and tiny cool courtyards where flowers flourished, protected from excessive sunshine and drying winds. We saw everything there was to see, including the cells of monks from bygone days, still with their easels and their prie-dieux, the walls covered with drawings and sayings from the scriptures.

It was late afternoon as we descended the cobbled path from this little Franciscan convent, and once more wandered among the well-stocked stalls on the square and their cheery salespeople. This time Tiny allowed us time off for purchasing and then took us back for tea in town.

And so that day we learned that the fascination of Florence extends also to its environs, which to a nature-lover are doubtless more lovely than the city itself.

There was, however, another aspect of Florence which for the female sex held a special appeal. The shops must be among the best in Italy, and on the quaint old Ponte Vecchio, the only bridge left intact by the German engineers who carried out their demolition work with characteristic Prussian efficiency, we found shops crammed with the most entrancing trinkets, jewellery, leather, beaten silverware – everything you could think of and all very reasonable in price. I bought the most exquisite blue leather bag, with thin gold-embossed lines crossing it diamond-wise. I know for a fact that it has been shown at Mass every Sunday since its owner received it in 1945, and Florentine leather, as well as having the most attractive designs, wears well. I did just manage to restrain Pat from buying a second skirt, when she had already purchased one. I happened to be passing a dress shop with her when she suddenly exclaimed, 'That's a pretty skirt!' and dashed into the shop. I waited outside for a few moments, but seeing the assistant take the skirt out of the window and show it off with a near-triumphant look in her eye decided me. I marched inside, grasped Pat firmly by the arm, told the assistant the skirt was '*troppo caro*' and led Pat, who was too surprised to protest, determinedly out. 'You can't afford it,' I said, 'not according to the calculations we made in Naples anyway.' For we had made a joint calculation before leaving and decided just how much we could afford and for what. Pat was at first disposed to be annoyed but she admitted in the end to being quite glad still to have the cash in hand.

And so, our first three days on leave behind us, the office seemed already to have receded into another world, and we set out for Venice, our minds crammed with impressions of the City of Flowers.

It seemed strange not to have to been on duty every morning and I sometimes missed Luisa's bright '*Buongiorno, Signoree*', and the shrill voices of the young Perellis. But I already had the bee of discovery in my bonnet and I brushed away regrets and threw myself once more into the thrill of absorbing new scenes and visiting fresh places. Bologna with its burnt-sienna arcades, and its small, secretive side streets, its cobbled pavements and lopsided overhanging eaves and gables fascinated me and I longed for time to explore it. There was an air of Dickens-like respectability about the place, and yet, as in Dickens's books, you could imagine that many comedies and tragedies were enacted behind those shuttered windows.

On the way we had stopped for a brew-up at a mountain farm and the farmer's wife had boiled water for our billycan. The farmhouse was spotlessly clean and the people genuinely friendly and interested to hear that their stone-floored kitchen with its massive cross-beams was not unlike those of our own Tudor dwellings. There were frequent signs of war in these parts, bumpy roads, blown-up bridges and ruined houses, and the road into Bologna itself passed through acre upon acre of bombed buildings and riddled masonry. It was uncanny to think that only a few months earlier our men had been waging a life and death struggle in those grim mountains, often cold and hungry, cut off from base and supplies, and within sniping reach of a ruthless and desperate enemy.

We left the mountains and came to the plain of Lombardy, with its expanses of flat land, criss-crossed by dykes and punctuated by watermills and gently swaying lines of young poplars and mournful willows. Here the sun was obscured, the clouds seemed pregnant with rain, and the fertile orchards testified to a lush, well-watered countryside. The houses, painted in delicate pastels, had sloping tiled roofs, surmounted by tiled chimney pots. Shutters painted in shades which contrasted with the walls gave added colour to a scene of pleasing rusticity. But we soon came to more and more fearful signs of the recent destruction. The contemplation of the homely farmsteads and corn-stacks was interrupted, and instead one passed through towns laid low by the havoc of war, where sometimes one saw weary people grubbing hopefully amongst the dusty rubble. At Pontelagoscuro, an immense bridge lay in two truncated blocks across the vast River Po, but the waters were spanned by a magnificent pontoon bridge, a working tribute to the genius of the Sappers, and consisting of probably more than a hundred boats. I had heard that sometimes when the water was high this bridge broke and swung to either side, but always the engineers were quickly on to the job and had it right again in a matter of hours. One could not imagine Italy without Bailey bridges in those days, and even now some remain. Without them, the traffic of the country would have been paralysed, not to speak of the communications and the Army of Occupation, which could not have relied entirely on the air or sea for its many needs.

At Mestre we took on board a tommy who wanted a lift to Venice, but we were not sorry to discard him as he turned out to be rather a nuisance. We left our transport in the park and embarked with the driver in a gondola. It seemed strange to ride up to the town mayor's office in a boat, and a gondola of all things! The office was situated in a beautiful fifteenth-century *palazzo*, with the Union Jack swaying gracefully over its classical portals. A Military Police motorboat was fixed to the painted mooring stakes, to which in former times the elegant gondola of some rich merchant would have been tied with silken cords, attended by a *gondoliere* in sumptuous livery. But '*Tout passe, tout casse, tout lasse*' and we, two of the twentieth-century female soldiers of democracy, were about to spend a day or two's glorious, and what we hoped was well-earned, leave among the antique buildings of this amazing city-port.

After a wash and brush-up at our hotel, Pat suggested we should go off on our own and meet for dinner. I was slightly suspicious of her intentions, but spent a marvellous two hours, locating the great square, Piazza di San Marco, the Bridge of

Sighs, which more than comes up to expectations, and the cathedral. Here I sat for some time, drinking in the atmosphere, where Byzantine and Western art are strangely intermingled, and in marvelling at the mosaic floor, uneven in many places and much worn. The late sun shone through the open doors, lighting up the gold on pictures and altars, and casting long shadows from the Romanesque arches of the doorways. People moved about in silence, lighting the candles of devotion, or standing rapt in prayer or contemplation for a quiet moment at the end of the day.

As I went back to the hotel, tearing myself away from the most attractive shop windows (except those of Florence) that I had ever seen, I had a presentiment that Pat would have indulged in some terrible and unnecessary extravagance which we should both regret. These fears were soon justified, for she held out a hand and showed me something like an engagement ring, and asked me what I thought of it. I tried hard to appear enthusiastic; it was a pretty glass stone, cut in Venetian style, but it did not interest me much, although the setting was attractive enough. Pat herself was already tiring of it and asked if I would buy it. I soon disabused her of that hope, and she then offered it to me as a present. I told her to keep it and sell it to a profitable customer later on. She said she might as well get some wear of the ring in the meantime and placed it prominently on her hand before we went down to dinner.

When we were in the restaurant, the head AT of the Command arrived with an ATS major and her ADC. Pat became very worried, for she was far from 'properly dressed' in Army parlance: she was wearing white shoes, her sleeves were rolled up (forbidden at night), her legs were clad in the sheerest of silk stockings and her hands displayed three rings and deep crimson nail varnish. While we were sipping our coffee, Commander Turner came over to speak to us and was very charming. Pat had thrust her feet well under the table, hastily placed one ring under her plate and with the utmost sangfroid greeted the chief and offered her a liqueur. As someone remarked afterwards, had she forgotten the ring under the plate, the waiter doubtless would have taken it for a tip! Ma Turner stayed and chatted for a few minutes, probably not in the least deceived by Pat's subterfuge, and then got up to go and we were once more on our own to listen to the band and carry on interminable discussions pro and contra the unfortunate ring. That night, after saying goodnight to me in my room, she got locked out of her own and I found her wandering disconsolately about in the corridor munching a green apple and musing on the romanticism of Venice at night. 'How shall I get back to bed?' she asked. 'My door has locked itself by banging shut and my key is inside.' My key was no good and so we had to telephone the night porter to let her in.

That evening we had listened to a glorious orchestral concert on the Piazza San Marco, whose ample proportions were illumined to great effect by enormous glowing brackets of light, set at regular intervals along the edge of the colonnades which framed the square on three sides. The audience sat at tables in cafés under the arches, or congregated in a large crowd around the musicians. There was silence except for the music and the footsteps of strollers promenading up and down the square, lingering to listen. Overhead the sky was a deep indigo blue, star-spangled, and the oriental domes of the cathedral outlined dimly against it, flanked by the ornate battlements of the Doge's Palace, provided a background to the scene that seemed reminiscent of the Arabian Nights. In Italy one does not just see scenes from opera, one experiences them.

After that, in spite of fatigue, we took a short gondola trip, for we were determined to see Venice in the moonlight, and it was worthwhile to breathe in the fresh evening air and sea-breezes and see the beautiful old *palazzi*, their delicately sculpted façades illuminated by lanterns and moonbeams.

The following morning I noticed a handsome, freshly painted black gondola, propelled by a smart-looking *gondoliere* in a white suit with a red sash. In the gondola sat a beautiful girl with long fair hair, tied in a red ribbon, and classical refined features. She wore a white dress and sat with head bent, studiously engrossed in a book. She seemed to belong to a former age, perhaps to the period just over a hundred years ago, when Lord Byron lived riotously and notoriously at the Palazzo Mocenigo, and Venice society prided itself on its elegance, culture and distinction. Probably it still does, and perhaps this beautiful young Italian girl belonged to it, but we had not time to stay and find out. She belonged, we did not; we were mere birds of passage and could only glean impressions.

We managed to scrounge a lift up to our sister unit in Austria and passed through the vividly green country north of Venice, which acted on the eyes like a soothing lotion after the dazzling glare of the south. The air was much cooler and the mountains were shrouded in mist, which rather spoilt the approach to the frontier. We passed along miles and miles of flat green country, in an endless stream of traffic, mainly military, pounding north. But there were a few civilian cars and lorries, and some horses and carts too, though how their drivers had the courage to enter into the vehicle stream that almost engulfed them, we found hard to grasp. Italians seem to have nerves of steel when it comes to road safety. Every few hundred yards along the road there were enormous placards saying, 'No halting – malarial area', and so we dared not stop, for the road was well policed.

Near the frontier we halted for a few minutes while the driver looked at the engine, and a crowd of young men and girls came along the road, ostensibly from some camp. Some of them greeted us and offered help and we entered into conversation with them. They did not speak Italian, but German. I asked them if they were Austrians and they said, no, they were *heimatslose*, (literally, 'without homes'). They were Jews whom the Allied troops had freed from concentration camps and who were now making their way south in organised stages, in camps looked after by British soldiers, while the Allied governments meanwhile decided what to do with them. One nice girl, a Czech, told me she had passed through Prague on her way down, and I asked if she had seen any of her family. Oh no, she said, they had all been burnt in incinerators by the Germans. This she said in quite a matter-of-fact way, as if she was telling me that her shoes needed heeling. I suspect that if she had not been matter-of-fact about it she would have gone mad. An officer once told me that he saw a tank knock over a *camionetta* somewhere in Central Italy, soon after the end of the war. One woman, he said, lost her husband but she survived. In the moment of horror and before she fully realised the ghastly occurrence, she stooped to the ground to pick up the loaves which had fallen from her basket. That simple homely action saved her sanity. Perhaps at times of direst stress, nature temporarily blocks one's mind, so that only day-to-day matters are clearly focused, until the worst is past and the physical shock has been absorbed by the system.

Pat and I had a fierce argument as to how much the scenery altered as we sped on north. She claimed that the moment we were over the border, everything was different. I maintained that the change took place gradually. This discussion must have occupied us for an hour or two. Certainly by the time we got to Villach there was nothing Italian about the countryside, which was rich green pastureland with thick pine woods, green hedgerows, and solid two-storey houses with overhanging eaves and thick walls, which would doubtless be very cosy in winter. There were healthy-looking herds of cows about with bells attached to their necks, and the tinkling of the cowbells was almost the only sound which filled the evening air, other than the continual purr of military vehicles along the main road, a noise so familiar that one scarcely noticed it. We had passed through the mountain gorges with their glacial riverbeds and roaring torrents, and were now in the depression that holds the attractive Wörthersee, which was our ultimate destination.

When we were eventually parked at the officers' hotel that night by one of our colleagues, it was about ten o'clock and we were both very tired. It was long past the hour for a meal, though we had been given some gin-and-lemon and raw cheese in the mess. But the head waiter found some salad and the inevitable German sausage, and while waiting for this repast we enjoyed a very jolly evening, watching music and dancing taking place in the hotel. Mostly men and a few girls were present, and after a short while the party became somewhat rowdy, and we got involved to the extent that Pat was unaccountably and quite mistakenly sprayed by a soda-water siphon. This was the last straw at the end of a long tiring day; she was more than disgusted and insisted on moving to the bar to eat our meal in peace. There it was much quieter, but rather too deserted.

We had just one day in Austria, as the transport was leaving again for the return journey, and unfortunately there was a terrible thunderstorm that night. By the next morning it had cleared considerably and we were able to see something of the surrounding country, which was unbelievably green and fresh. The air was crisp and invigorating, and at the lake's edge there was a slight breeze, which whipped up the blue water to a gentle swell. We were lucky enough to stay for our second night in Marienwerth, which is a tiny village on a small promontory of the Wörthersee, consisting of one or two hotels and a few houses, all in Tyrolean style, with gables, shutters and gay window-boxes, and a small church with the traditional 'Zwiebel' or onion tower. Our hotel was at the lake's edge, with only a gravelled stretch of ground between it and the water. On this were set trestle tables and benches, so that in fine weather guests could eat and drink out of doors. Behind and around the lake rose grassy slopes, orchards and thick woods of pines, beeches and oaks. It was a scene of absolute rural tranquillity. In the village, which appeared purely residential, for we saw no shops, I met a young girl acting as governess to a party of young children, two little boys and three little girls. I asked if I might photograph them, they were such an attractive happy crowd, all ash-blonde and clean and neat. They were thrilled to be photographed, but unfortunately the result was not successful. I walked back towards the lake with them and the governess told me their history, which was tragic enough, for they were all war-orphans. Meanwhile, the children joked and chatted and when a large black dog came along, they all ran around shrieking in high-pitched voices, '*Der Wolf! Der Wolf!*'

That evening, we heard an Austrian cabaret, the highlight of which was a couple of yodellers, who took the British off

very wittily and very charmingly, especially with a song enti-
tled, 'How do you do?' All the British present of course hugely
enjoyed the jokes.

During the morning, Pat and I had been saying we did not like
Austria, it was so gloomy, wet and depressing, but now we had
had a glimpse of it in fine weather and the spell of Marienwerth
had gripped us, we were already beginning to regret our departure set for the following morning. Many people greatly preferred
being stationed in Austria to Italy. I was never there long enough
to be in a position to judge, but in spite of its charm and freshness, there was something melancholic about it. There was
an element of sadness about the dense woods and lush green
meadows, and one could observe an air of depressed lassitude
among the people. The shadow of the Occupation, and of hard
times to come, lay on Austria and there was something sombre
and almost uncanny about the atmosphere. We longed in spite of
everything to get back to the clarity and exuberance of the south.
The natural gaiety of the Italians had by no means lessened in the
period of hardship; they seemed irrepressible, and perhaps one of
their finest qualities noticeable at that time was their courage and
cheerfulness in adversity. The Austrians were rather more dour,
possibly more like the Scots, who are reputedly a silent and dour
people. Was it perhaps the case that many of our own people had
a fellow feeling for these Southern Teutons, and for that reason
preferred being stationed among them to being stationed among
the Latins? Who can tell? But we did not have much time for
reflection – we had to pack and be off before my posting to Rome.
Pat was shortly to be posted home to the UK for her first home
leave in three years, after which she hoped to get abroad again,
for once an AT had served overseas, she rarely wanted to settle
down in the service in England, unless circumstances forced the
issue on her.

Pat and I parted in Florence, as she had a few more days' leave,
and her last gesture was to hand me the famous Venetian ring
as the truck bearing me back to Rome was put into gear, ready
to start off. 'Take this,' she said dramatically. 'Certainly not,'

I replied. 'That's your souvenir and you've got to keep it!' I was sad enough to say goodbye to her. We had been constant companions for over three months, and that is quite long enough in service life to become very well acquainted with someone. And who knew when or whether we would meet up again!

20

Back in Harness, But Not For Long

*F*or a while it seemed strange to be back in Rome, at my old job again, but with a different colonel, though he was perfectly charming to me and I had no cause for complaint. I now shared the PA's office with another AT who was messing officer – until then the colonel had had a sergeant as his temporary PA, and this man had now gone on Python.* After a week or so, I had quite settled down in the mess and in my new-old job, enjoying linking up with old friends and making new ones, in particular with some Ack-Ack people, who were now stationed in the bombed cinema studio across the way, where Tony and I had 'acquired' peat the previous winter.

The beaches at Ostia and Santa Marinella had been more or less cleared for bathing this summer and recreation at Ostia was organised specially for the troops, with recreational transport regularly run there from units stationed in Rome. We sometimes

---

* Python referred to the length of overseas duty that service personnel had to perform before they would qualify for rotational 'Python' leave back to Britain. Originally this was six years, but towards the end of the war it was reduced to four years and nine months. (With grateful thanks to www.ww2talk.com for this information)

got lifts with the Ack-Ack transport and it was not long before I was invited to dine in their mess, where some of the other girls had often been most hospitably entertained.

Janet, one of our former sergeants from MEF, had returned commissioned and was a great asset to the small band of AT officers. She was very friendly with the Ack-Ack and it was with her principally that I visited their mess. When she had been a sergeant it had been more difficult to be on really friendly terms, but now that all barriers (however artificial) had been removed I found her a very good pal – where there was only a handful of women, a good girl friend was worth a great deal. Peggy, my office co-worker, was also in on these parties; she had the asset of a fine singing voice, greatly enhanced by a real brogue, for she was from Ireland.

At Ostia there was a nice little villa requisitioned for officers where one could change in privacy and then have tea after a bathe. Before going there myself, I heard that two of our people had gone down and ordered tea, but when it came it was just like dishwater. So they explained that the '*Inglesi*' liked '*una tazza di thè* molto *forte*', and the Italian attendant obligingly offered to re-brew. But when the fresh tea came, it would not pour out of the pot, except for a few drops, though they were certainly of a good strong dark colour. On removing the lid, it was discovered that the pot was full to within half an inch of the rim with tea leaves – no wonder the re-brew was strong!

21

Home, Sweet Home

I was just nicely 'dug in' once more, when through from HQ came a signal giving my name as being due for 'LIAP' or 'Leave in awaiting Python'. I was not bound to take it, but as my parents badly wanted me to get home to see them now that the war was over, I felt it was my duty to go, as well as being naturally very anxious to see my family, not having been with them since April 1944, eighteen months previously.

Of course the day for my departure *would* be just the one on which I had arranged to go on a magnificent all-day bathing party in Santa Marinella with the Ack-Ack people. But one cannot have everything, and so after two months I was sent off down to Naples once more and landed up at the ATS transit camp on the Front, a unit which had not been in Naples when I was last there. I met up once again with Charlotte, who had been on the original ATS intelligence course with me and on the journey overseas. The last time I had seen her for a few moments had been at the Katarinetta on the occasion of Hugh and the princesses. Now we had the chance of a good exchange of news and gossip, and how much there was to relate!

I have no recollection of the interior of the building housing the ATs in transit, except that it was seething with girls in khaki, a very dark and overcrowded edifice, but peopled with a joyous throng – some back from the UK, others on the way over there.

Tongues were wagging as fast as they could go on a vast range of subjects: 'What was the journey like? Did you fly?', 'What's it like in the UK now?', 'Is London still the same?', 'Did you get any tea when you arrived?', 'Do you have an FFI (Free From Infection) on the way back?', 'Are the Customs bad, or are they decent?' Questions flowed on and on, and the answers, too, were unceasing.

Next day dawned brilliantly clear, and at about half-past four in the morning our draft were piled into troop-carriers and transported to an airfield outside Naples, where planes were drawn up here and there on the green sward, which sparkled with dewdrops in the early morning sun. It was beautifully fresh and cool. The previous night we had been briefed very thoroughly as to our conduct before and during the flight, what to do if one felt sick, etc., and to be sure to go to the cloakroom before taking off – for this purpose we had had to queue up very obviously on the airfield. We were to go in RAF planes, converted bombers, though we soon discovered that there was not much converted about them, as there were no seats and you could only see out if you went into the air-gunner's turret, apart from the cockpit, of course. But we didn't mind – we were going home! There was a wait of approximately three hours on the airfield, and we seemed to be marshalled continuously hither and thither. Whenever anyone from our particular group got lost or separated from the rest, they only had to look out for Charlotte's tangerine-coloured slacks, which showed up like a beacon and were the sign, so to speak, of our party. The Italians were most intrigued by all these English girls milling round in trousers, but especially by Charlotte, who in addition spoke their own language extremely well and was quite able to give them a good laugh with some witticism that they could understand, for they knew very little English.

At last it was time to enplane and assisted by the crew about twelve of us climbed, one after the other, up a narrow little rope ladder into a Lancaster bomber and made ourselves as comfortable as possible on the floor, with greatcoats and haversacks as pillows and rugs. We were soon taking off and for most of us it was an intensely thrilling moment – becoming airborne for the first time. We had haversack rations with us, but some of the girls felt ill and could eat nothing. One had very bad earache – my ears hurt too, when we went down. It was the one thing which spoilt the flight for me, and indeed my ears and head buzzed for about a week afterwards. I went up into the turret when we were over France, taking turns with the other girls, and between huge billowing piles of white clouds I could see patches of green ground interspersed with fields neatly laid out, and here and there a house, a road or a level crossing – all so far away. It reminded me rather absurdly of *The Water Babies*, when young Tom, the chimneysweep, espied the little old lady in the red petticoat, way off from the summit of the crags.

The flight took us seven-and-a-half hours from Naples and it must have been about three o'clock when, rather tired and groggy, we touched down at Wallington, Lincolnshire and found ourselves on English soil again, in a damp, typically chilly autumn mist that contrasted forcibly with the sunshine and clear blue sky over southern Italy, which only that morning we had left behind. As I went through Customs, the excise officer asked me jocularly if I intended to set up shop, as I was carrying a grip packed full with small pieces of china – ash-trays, tiny jugs, vases, baskets and other small trinkets for presents and souvenirs – but charged me nothing. We were all given tea and nice crisp biscuits – what a joy, tea with *fresh* milk once more and really fresh biscuits! – and then we were taken somewhere to wash and tidy up. Arrangements had been made for our further routing, or for accommodation at the camp that night for those who lived too far away to begin their journey home at once. I had relatives in London and therefore decided to ring them up and see whether they could give me a bed that night. They assented at once and so I left on the London train with Charlotte that same afternoon and the two of us parted at Euston. It was about ten o'clock when I eventually reached my destination. How wonderful it felt to be in London again – and London without the blackout!

My leave was probably just like everyone else's leave from overseas – a frantic rush to see as many people as possible and fit far too many things into too short a space of time. I enjoyed myself thoroughly, but could not help sometimes wondering how things were going in Cinema City and what it would be like when I got back. How Janet, who was standing in for me, was getting on – and who had been posted to where. And sneakingly I longed to see the blue skies and the bright sun again – and hear the excited Babel of Latin voices and the roar of Allied transport through the ancient streets of Italian cities. I had grown accustomed to the life abroad and things at home seemed different; people seemed to speak a different language now. Like a lot of service men and girls, it looked as though I would find it pretty difficult to settle down to civilian life when I eventually came out of the forces. But I had no real intention of settling down at all – at least not in England. What I had seen in my limited pre-war travels abroad and what I had since seen during the war had just whetted my appetite for more – travel I must, and pay no attention to the proverb about the rolling stone to which some wise people likened me, shaking their heads.

Still it was with real regret that I again said goodbye to my parents and left our little home and the friendly village where they now lived. But our luck was in, for when we got back to Wallington, it was cold and wet, and the airfield was completely bogged. We had the eternal petrol drum stoves in our dormitories and coconut matting on the floor of the anteroom, but it was far from comfortable and extremely difficult not to bring mud into the huts. It was here that an MO gave me an 'FFI', simply by glancing at me and saying, 'You look all right.' He then signed a small chit measuring approximately one inch by one-and-a-half inches, and gave it to me. This document I preserved carefully for several years, but no one ever asked to see it.

After two or three days of the bogginess and grey lowering skies, the powers that be decided to send us all home again. I for one was more than thankful, for I was by that time in the process of developing a mild attack of influenza, and was only too glad for some extra time at home and an opportunity to shake off the germ before we really did set off. Orders came a day or two later, after my parents and I had listened to the wireless carefully several times a day, for us to report to the holding unit in Gower Street, near University College, London. This was a requisitioned student hostel, converted into a most convenient billeting place.

Here for the first time I encountered that hostility which is too frequently shown by non-overseas ATS to overseas ATS – whether subconsciously they are jealous of those who have been abroad in the service, or whether they find us cocky and showing less respect for discipline, I cannot say. I only know that there is some resentment and I have heard others remark on it too. But among those who were overseas there was undoubtedly something easier, freer, more tolerant and less stickling for minor details of regimental discipline. The essentials of discipline were what mattered first and foremost abroad, not its trappings. I am afraid that, at home, especially after the end of the war, regimentation tended to become an end in itself. As women are not by nature made to be regimented, but rather to develop as individuals in a highly personal environment, that of the family circle, they do not generally take kindly to rigidly enforced rules, regulations and regimentalism, half of it more pertaining to the male army than to the female in any case. But it is a strange fact that a few women do love military routine and even adopt masculine poses to help themselves along with it. They seem to feel that because they wear uniform it is up to them to become as mannish as possible. And so they stand with their legs apart and their hands in their skirt pockets, or they plant themselves with their backs to the fire, dangle lighted cigarettes from their mouths and laugh uproariously at the smallest whiff of a joke, sometimes clapping each other on the back like real '*bonshommes*'. If they had riding crops, they would doubtless be cracking themselves on the shins too! And their language becomes strong and spicy and they refer to the girls under them as 'chaps and fellows'. I heard tell of a WAAF mess like this, where a colonel and his second-in-command were invited to a drink, and were thumped on the back and asked what they would have. Everyone then drank double whiskies and it was the colonel and the major and not the WAAF officers who felt they had had enough first and beat a hasty retreat! I could probably come up for criticism myself on the grounds of aping men sometimes, even unconsciously; I suppose one cannot be so much with men at work and in a mess and not become somewhat toughened, but to try and be like a man always seemed so ludicrous – it's bad enough trying to be a woman!

Speaking of that, it always was a matter of conjecture and anxiety to me as to when one ceased to be a lady and became first and foremost an officer, or vice versa. Was one an officer first and a lady afterwards? 'Ladies and officers' or 'Officers and ladies'? The latter must be right, I suppose, as it is always 'Officers and gentlemen'. The troops used to call us all sorts of things: 'Madam' or 'ma'am', which is correct, or 'miss', 'lady', 'Captain', 'Lootenant', as well as other exalted ranks that I never reached. The Italians evolved their own titles for us: 'Tenentessa', 'Capitana', or 'Capitanessa' – I have been called them all. And strangely enough, in uniform, I was always 'Signora', though unmarried – that is, after I became a junior commander (captain). When I returned to Italy much later, married, it was somewhat trying to hear myself almost invariably addressed as 'Signorina'. With regard to 'officers and ladies', it does lead to complications, such as when the brigadier, being a perfect gentleman, waits for you to pass through a door in front of him, when in fact it should be the other way round. And then there is the ever-thorny problem of when the troops should salute one: some salute you because you are an officer, and others do not salute you because you wear a skirt. Men, irrespective of rank, generally seem to find it difficult to forget that we are women and to think of us as ranks, doing a job, and I suppose in all honesty we would be appalled if they really did completely forget our sex. It seems that one must adjust oneself to particular circumstances and find the happy medium, while doing one's job to the best of one's ability. It is best to forget that one belongs to the 'petticoat army' and thus not expect special privileges, but try to act like a lady and be appreciative of any privileges or special courtesies that do come one's way. The poser, 'officers or ladies', is basically just one facet of a woman's eternal problem of behaviour, but the most important thing to remember is never to let it be said, 'She throws her sex about.'

All these things and many more we ATs often chatted about among ourselves, over a hot drink or a cigarette in our rooms late at night, or over tea on a day off.

In Gower Street I met Charlotte again; she was full of beans and to my dismay insisted on our going to see *The Seven Veils*. No amount of protesting would dissuade her from taking me there, but it was a good film and one could not be depressed for long in Charlotte's company. Next morning we entrained at Victoria, Charlotte once more wearing her famous tangerine slacks. As the weather was so bad, the authorities had decided that air travel was no longer feasible and so we were travelling by the famous overland route, known as 'Medloc', across France, Switzerland and on to Italy. Once installed on the train and caught up in the hustle and bustle of the troop-train, no-one seemed very sorry to be going back.

22

Traveller's Joy

'Medloc' was the official nomenclature for the long straggling journey across France and Switzerland, and later through Germany instead of Switzerland, to Villach by troops travelling to and from their leave in the UK. It took me nearly a week to reach Rome by this method, but if long and unhurrying, the journey was not without interest. We landed at Calais after a somewhat crowded cross-channel passage, and lugged our cases off the ship and along the quay to the large and efficiently run transit camp in the dock area. Calais had had a terrible time in the last days of Dunkirk, and later suffered a second drubbing, so altogether there was very little of the town left, and the camp was almost entirely formed of Nissen huts and other recent erections. There we stayed for a few hours, but some people stayed longer and were given a NAAFI ration and an evening meal.

We entrained that night again around eleven o'clock and the train left at about midnight on its rather painful limping, jolting progress through Northern France, over newly laid rails and mended sleepers, plugging wearily along, through bombed towns and badly damaged stations. This time there was a coach full of women, some ATS and some nurses. There may also have been one or two YWCA girls with us.

As usual, we had the best accommodation possible, but even so our quarters were of necessity rather cramped. We only partially undressed in our compartment – personally, I preferred to remain more or less clothed, as you never knew when you might have to turn out. I was quite surprised at the amount of negligée some of the other girls assumed. Charlotte was caught unprepared when the train conducting officer came to see how we were soon after the start – she was removing her corsets, under her greatcoat, prior to donning pyjamas and making herself ready to doss down thoroughly. I became more than ever convinced that it was better to stay in one's clothes and not risk being taken unawares, especially as the compartment had no lock to it and theoretically (and practically) anyone could enter at any moment. After that, however, the train conducting officer gave us a wide berth until the following day. We could not sleep much, but dosed fitfully as the train joggled uncomfortably along. No one was sorry when at last we arrived at an enormous junction, where the word 'Épluches', written in outsize letters and miraculously still intact, told us that we were not far from Paris – and furthermore that we had reached our first halt and could expect a wash and a meal.

The washing facilities for the female contingent were excellent throughout the journey, and we had absolutely no cause for complaint. At each stop there was always a place set apart with a female attendant in charge, usually towards the end of a platform and suitably segregated, where we could have a good wash in really piping hot water; this was a marvellous comfort and made the long exhausting journey quite pleasant, whereas otherwise we should have arrived at our destination completely washed out. We had meals with the men, of course, and I remember the stir created by Charlotte's tangerine slacks, by then quite famous, as she marched along the platform that morning at Épluches, to the 'ablutions' and back to the dining-hall, past the queues of waiting soldiers. There were a good many catcalls, winks and whistles, but she took it all in her stride and showed not a trace of embarrassment. We soon got used to the crowd and even the tangerine slacks attracted less attention as time went on, although they could always be calculated to produce a few grins and nudges.

The food on this journey was excellent and indeed the organisation was first-class throughout – scarcely a hitch as far as one could see. We were given haversack rations at Épluches, and all that day the train dragged haltingly on through France, eventually coming to more mountainous parts near evening. There was a brew-up during the afternoon, and very welcome it was too. We knitted, chatted and gazed out of the window at town after town, ravaged or damaged by war. As we neared the south, however, the destruction became less apparent and we began to cheer up – the north under its leaden grey skies had been depressing. That night we stopped for our evening meal at Bellegarde, where we again had a good wash with hot water and ate a good warm dinner. Another hour and we were at the frontier. Strict injunctions had been issued, of course, that no one should leave the train without authority, etc. Why it was that we were allowed across neutral territory, I never quite grasped – probably only on condition that we stayed on the train throughout our travels across Switzerland. The customs officials came on board, but they did not carry out much of a search and it was more a matter of form than anything else.

All through the night we proceeded, snail-like, through Switzerland, and I saw the names Basle, Lausanne and Brig in between naps. Soon after dawn, we glimpsed the high alps and the snow-capped mountains, and then the sun rose and lit up the snow in all its morning glory, so that the grey rocks seemed coloured purple in the brightness. We had emerged from the Simplon tunnel into this scene of invigorating early morning beauty, and in the clear air one seemed to breathe in fresh energy, and acquire an appetite – most people were more than ready for breakfast with two boiled eggs. It must have been nearly nine o'clock when we finally steamed out of Domodossola, with much puffing and chugging by our hard-worked engine. It gave me quite a thrill to be on Italian soil again and to hear the Italian porters calling gaily to one another, or whistling some catchy air.

We went on, through valley after valley, some of them filled with hundreds of magnificent apple trees, where the rosy fruit glowed invitingly on the laden boughs. In other valleys, mostly pastureland, were line upon line of poplars, marking the fields, and now falling into 'the sear, the yellow leaf'. It had been raining and there was a perceptible odour of damp leaves and lush grass. What a rich harvest of leaf-mould there would be under those poplars before many months were out. Meanwhile, they swayed to and fro in the breeze, and gradually and gently shed their browning foliage on to the grassy carpet beneath. Here and there cows would be grazing, watched by a girl or boy sitting on a knoll, the girl perhaps with her knitting. Up aloft the mountain-tops were now shrouded in mist and cloud, through which the sun penetrated intermittently. There was an air of autumn about these valleys, whereas the sunshine we had seen sparkling in Domodossola was overcast – but presently we came into the bright sun again and reached the shores of Lake Maggiore, whose broad expanse of water shimmered in the light.

There was a slight haze along the shores that left the outlines of trees and houses a trifle blurred, but all the more romantic and attractive for their vagueness. We passed through Ascona, with its window boxes full of pink geraniums and its gaily painted houses, and saw in the distance the well-known outline of Isola Bella. We saw old peasant women carrying enormous cone-shaped baskets on their strong shoulders as they climbed up the mountain paths, and we saw young men and girls on bicycles along the lakeside road. Before long, we were once more passing through green fields, almost as green as English fields, for the area around the Italian Lakes is a fertile countryside. And finally we came at last to the suburbs of Milan, similar to those of any large city, and drew slowly into the great station, built by the Fascists and ornate with interior frescoes and an impressive marble exterior. The usual formalities of 'de-training' were gone through, and we were directed to the Albergo Excelsior Gallia, just outside the station on an enormous square. There, Charlotte and I were given a room on the fourth floor, from the balcony of which we could see in the distance the whole Alpine chain, including the jagged tooth of the Matterhorn, clearly outlined against the horizon.

We spent rather a cold night there, for blankets seemed to be scarce and were Army issue. In fact, the hotel had been stripped of all its trappings and the rooms looked bare and inhospitable. The dining-room at breakfast-time, however, was a blaze of sunlight and that made up for much. Next day we visited the ATS postings and movements for the second time and found that we had been allotted accommodation on a train leaving in two days' time – until then we were free. This was just the job, and we accordingly visited the magnificent cathedral, the Castello Sforzesco and the shops and hairdresser. The Castello is the ancient seat of the Sforza family, who ruled Milan as its dukes for several centuries, and is a testimony to the city's stormy past, with its moat, portcullis and heavily battlemented walls. It is a most interesting edifice to visit, but unfortunately suffered bomb damage during the war, although it had been some sort of hospital and still showed the red cross on its roofs. We saw an exhibition of modern painting there, but were far more impressed by the architecture of the castle itself and its beautifully decorated ceilings than the modern art on view.

We had heard that it was possible to visit the tower, and as our guide was very keen to take us, we agreed to brave the ascent. It began all right with reasonable stone stairs, but these developed into nothing more than a narrow spiral stairway, and eventually we were climbing wobbly iron ladders, which the guide ran up as lightly as a monkey, looking round and bidding us hold on tightly and have no fear. Each platform seemed smaller and the drop to the ground more dizzy, although of course the view was more beautiful and extensive as we climbed higher. Finally, on the last platform but one, Charlotte and I could go no further, both thoroughly unnerved by the waving ladders and their seeming insecurity. Our guide, Luigi, laughed, and said that that was nothing – he had been a sailor and he assured us that the ladders were perfectly safe. But we firmly told him that we had not been sailors, were unaccustomed to such acrobatic feats and he must excuse us. And so we contented ourselves with the view from very nearly the top, which could not have been much better.

In front of us and all round were the red roofs of the city, as well as the red turrets and battlements of the castle itself, with its green courtyards like toy lawns below. When we raised our eyes, there were the Alps, the whole Chain of Savoy in all its splendour of snow and rock, with the Matterhorn surpassing the rest in height and forcefulness. The snow glittered in the sunshine against a limpid blue sky, for that day autumn had fled and there was nothing to indicate its presence save a crisp sharpness in the air and at night a nip of frost. We lingered, drinking in the view and our guide's amusing anecdotes, but, still anxious about safety, we dreaded the coming descent. We finally made it, after much protesting, squeaking, puffing and panting on our part, and many exhortations to '*Coraggio*' and soothing words on the part of Luigi, punctuated by his frequent encouraging use of the word '*Brava*' ('good girl'). So eventually we reached terra firma again, and never was I so glad to see it! We bade our nautical friend farewell, thanking him for prevailing on us to make the ascent as high as we did, for without his help we should never have seen that wonderful view. But never again will I attempt those ladders – they were a nightmare.

The famous Scala Opera House was closed, having been damaged by a bomb, but an opera company was functioning in a small theatre in a side street and we decided that go we must; and accordingly we took seats for *Lucia di Lammermoor* (*The Bride of Lammermoor*), taken from Sir Walter Scott's novel of that title. Neither of us knew this opera and we felt the opportunity must not be missed for enlarging our opera education. When the curtain went up, the theatre was packed with troops in uniform, hushed and expectant. The hush, however, soon became perceptibly disturbed by what at first sounded like stifled giggling and guffawing, and then, more openly, gusts of semi-silent laughter swept through the audience. The reason for this mirth was that the actors were dressed, or were meant to be dressed, in Scottish traditional costume, but they strode on in plaids and kilts that looked for all the world like kitchen table-cloths, their glengarries flat as pancakes on their crowns, with feathers sticking out in front like antennae. Furthermore, the principal singer shook the ancestral walls so soundly when he made his first dramatic entry, that for several seconds it was a matter of conjecture whether they would remain standing or, like the walls of Jericho, collapse forthwith. All this was too much for the British sense of humour, and the audience was fairly bursting with the desire to break into one great roar of uncontrolled mirth. While respect for the sacred opera restrained the laughter, there were some distinct guffaws. I think the artists were genuinely surprised – doubtless they had not the slightest idea that there was anything ridiculous about their appearance. But later on, when the hero nearly dropped the sword he was brandishing and unwittingly almost brained his opposite number, even the supposedly grim laird allowed a shade of amusement to penetrate his greasepaint. The singing was not up to the usual Italian standard either, and altogether we passed a most entertaining, if not very culturally elevating, evening. We had only to see the characters acting in their Italianised Scottish costumes to enjoy a spectacle of complete incongruity. At least the Scots are used to wearing kilts, and doubtless the Italians felt ill at ease in skirts. But a good time was had by all, and there were no complaints!

It was with genuine regret on the Sunday morning that we entrained once more, and embarked on the last stage of our journey, which also proved to be the dreariest. Every Italian junction of any importance and almost every line seemed to have been damaged in some way, some with devastating thoroughness, and so our train crept along at a walking pace most of the time. Our stops were Bologna, Rimini on the Adriatic coast, and inland at Foligno. At this last stop we arrived seven hours late for our evening meal, but the staff were grand and provided us with a three-course meal and hot drinks, even though it was 2 a.m. We slept loggishly for a few hours after that, and were awakened by a violent shunting and grinding of brakes – we were at the entrance to Rome station, another badly damaged place.

I said goodbye to Charlotte, who was going to GHQ at Caserta, and hastened to the exit, but did not expect to be met, for it would have been well-nigh impossible for the unit to have known the hour, let alone the day, on which I was arriving. We had also been delayed by bad weather at first, and then the switchover from plane to rail travel had delayed us further. As it was about 6.15 a.m., I decided the best thing was to go over to the Continentale Hotel, the transit mess, opposite the station, and wait there until a reasonable hour when I could ring up our duty officer and ask for some form of transport to take me out to the unit. Accordingly I found a porter who wheeled my baggage across the road on a barrow; I then rang the bell of the Continentale, but could get no reply. After repeated ringing, a porter appeared and told me that it was too early for me to be admitted. I expostulated and became somewhat voluble and vociferous, asking him in my best Italian, accompanied by what I hoped were expressive gestures, what he thought a 'Signorina' should do in the streets of Rome at that hour, and did he want the military manager to find a young ATS officer on the doorstep, being refused admittance? While we were arguing and I noticed him weakening, I took advantage of the door being ajar to insert myself through the narrow opening and then told him I was inside, and intended to stay there. In the end he came round and even allowed me to have a room and a bath until it was time for breakfast. Afterwards I phoned for transport and a 15cwt truck came to collect me at about 9 a.m. Thus ended my leave and began my last lap in Cinema City.

23

Retrenchment

*A*lmost as soon as I got back, Peggy handed over to me and departed for Austria, where she was posted to GSI, ACA (General Services Intelligence. Allied Commission Austria) in Vienna. I also took over the messing once more and so was fairly busy, though not as much as formerly, as the unit was contracting and the work was growing less. My new CO was purely a military officer, and the nerve-centre of the 'I' work was the major, the same second-in-command as before. Thus I did in a way once again have two bosses. But this was not to be for long, as I soon discovered. Units were being cut down all over CMF and basic establishments were being rigidly reduced in order to conform with the overall retrenchment that was now in full swing. The magic phrase, 'Field Force Commitment' (FFC), appeared in nearly every circular from GHQ and new ones came out with alarming regularity. No sooner had one reduction taken place in accordance with the latest FFC than another FFC followed and more staff were to be displaced or released.

As far as this reduction of staff was concerned, I was among the next on the list. It was 13 November when I got back, and it must have been about a month later when the CO told me that he was being demobilised after Christmas and that the unit would henceforth be under a major's command, with a correspondingly smaller number of personnel. He said the second-in-command had already chosen two AT officers to remain with him, of which I was not one (this did not surprise, nor disappoint me), and that therefore as soon as the colonel went, I would become redundant. I had, unless I later chose to sign on, another six months to go before my two years' overseas service were completed. The colonel asked me if I had any particular preference about my next posting and if so he would put in a good word for me. I had a few days to think the matter over. The CO also pointed out that one option was the unit previously referred to in Rome, dealing with the compensation due to Italians for helping Allied prisoners of war. He had heard, he said, that an intelligence officer was needed there, and he knew the CO and would speak to him if I were interested. I knew all this was subject to GHQ approval, but also that it would greatly help me to have a recommendation, and I was therefore very grateful to the old man.

I discussed the matter with one or two friends. The preceding summer I had been asked if I would like to go to Greece for secretarial work of a secret nature and the idea had attracted me greatly at the time, but could not then be considered as my return to Rome had already been fixed; now, however, I began to reconsider it. The alternatives were probably GHQ at Caserta, the very thought of which sent cold shudders down my back, for Caserta was the most depressing place imaginable in winter, and I had had a taste of GHQ work the previous summer and decided I never wanted to do it again. Another option was Austria, which was quite a possibility – but again, Austria did not attract me as a country as much as did Italy or Greece, and I suspected that being employed at the big HQ in Vienna would probably be like working in Caserta. My two advisors told me that as an English girl I would probably have a thin time in Greece, as the Greek girls were so very beautiful that Englishmen there had no time for their own compatriots, which would make me lonely and possibly unhappy. Men certainly can be brutally frank at times, without even realising the full implication of their words. I agreed that life in Athens might be rather lonely, and in any case retrenchment was in full swing there and the forces might be withdrawing altogether from Greece before long. I was tempted to, but did *not*, suggest that perhaps English girls might find Greek men very interesting and handsome – such a remark would have been regarded as extremely bad taste!

After due consideration, I decided to ask the CO if he would put me forward for the job in Rome. I loved Rome and did not really want to leave it, and by working there I could keep in touch with my friends in Cinema City. As regards the work I would have to do, I had not the slightest idea what it would be like, but knew it would include shorthand and typing and that I would find my Italian useful. As long as I could be of use I was not worried. And so, one Sunday, the CO told me he had spoken to the colonel heading the commission and that I was to go for an interview a day or two later, after his own departure. As a parting gift, he presented me with a beautiful silver cigarette case, much more than I deserved, and which to my intense chagrin was later stolen from my desk in Rome by some light fingers, of which unfortunately there were far too many about. Meanwhile, we had our last Christmas as a unit, which was very jolly and included all sorts of good cheer, even if there were fewer personnel than the year before. The birds sent us for the mess consisted of one chicken, one duck and one small turkey, none overfed when alive, but by a judicious mixing of the whole lot we managed to give everyone quite a good plateful, helped out with pork, vegetables and the usual Christmas garnish. David and Marcello were reigning supreme in the kitchen now, and so we had the customary rich Italian sweets that Marcello insisted in preparing for every festive occasion, and everything was very attractively arranged. David had become a really excellent cook. We had menus typed in French, illustrated by one of our very gifted amateur artists. The Ack-Ack colonel was our guest that Christmas, and as a parting gift he was presented with an ancient blackbird which Mabel had solicitously cared for since the original RSM left on Python. We heard a week or so afterwards that the bird had arrived safely at Regimental Headquarters and was then taken over by the adjutant. Owing to a mistaken belief that it preferred gin to water, it did not long survive its new home, but breathed a rather alcoholic last breath soon after posting.

Before Christmas, as autumn wore on into winter and my fate was in the melting-pot, I took the opportunity in my free time, of which I had far more than before, of seeing something of the Roman Campagna, but from a different angle now. On Sunday afternoons I was lucky enough to be able to go for occasional drives through the countryside, some days sad in the misty, melancholic atmosphere of autumn, other days radiant in the autumn sunshine, which illuminated all the golden leaves and the scarlet berries in the hedgerows. It was often wet that year and the country had something of an English October about it, but frosts were rare before December. That winter, however, was not a hard one, and by then our heating apparatus was working efficiently and the desperate fuel shortage of the previous year had eased up a little. The anteroom had been moved into a smaller room, with a magnificent terrace facing towards Rocca di Papa. The inevitable sawdust stove had been installed, and a small bar that even had a rung for the feet, and one or two stools had been set up in a corner. There were also some easy chairs and a sofa, and so we were really well off. The troops, too, had more comfort this year, partly because there were far fewer of them. Since VE day, there had been a gradual but steady reduction in numbers in all units in the theatre of war. Our men were now all housed indoors. Some of our girls had gone already, mostly to GHQ, where all ATS ORs were eventually to be concentrated, and one or two to the company in Rome, commanded by my friend, Junior Commander Margaret Lester. By the New Year all our girls had left us, some of them with tears and misgivings. They were far sadder at leaving than they had been at arriving. Cinema City had become a real home from home.

Meanwhile, out in the Campagna, the horror of war was now fast becoming a nightmare memory and evidence of it was little-by-little becoming effaced. In the crowded villages life was still a struggle, but it had become a shade less so – people still stood about in groups, and on Sunday afternoons most of the population would congregate in the main piazza, often flanked by high piles of rubble, in their Sunday best, the men and many of the women in sombre black. This would certainly be the situation in every village one might enter, but the difference that one would notice everywhere was that the people had lost the utterly despairing look of the year before. They looked a little better fed and their beasts were not quite as emaciated and bony. In Rome the shops were filling up and the markets were hives of activity. Italy was slowly coming to life again during this long and painful convalescence, and signs of recovery were frequent and reassuring. AMG (Allied Military Government) had by now handed over all its powers of administration to the Italians, except in the Provinces of Venezia, Giulia and Udine. Our own activity was lessening. There was not much left for organisations such as ours to do now that the war was over and most civilian suspects, agents and escaped prisoners had been rounded up. Almost all the refugees had been screened and the Field Security Detachments and Military Police dealt with current matters in their own areas. There was still work for our units in Austria, but as Italian life resumed with increasing normality, the work of the Army was gradually being wound up and handed over, either to the still active Allied Commission or direct to the Italian authorities who were in the process of taking over the administration of the country from the occupying forces. Crown Prince Umberto had ascended an uneasy throne, and the question of the new constitution and the rivalry of Republicans and Monarchists was fast coming to the fore.

At the same time, life in the capital was becoming brighter and more normal almost daily. Restaurants, cafés and nightclubs were beginning to flourish again, despite the continuing food shortage and poorly administered rationing system. A chemist once confided to me that many essential medicines could not be provided, because many of the valuable substances brought in by UNRRA (United Nations Relief and Rehabilitation Administration) found their way mostly on to the black market and were used for extravagant confectionery and other rich foods, which of course only the wealthy could buy. No-one seemed to raise very strong objections to the black market, though, but for the very poor life was hard indeed.

Civilians were by now hospitably opening their homes to members of the forces, from generals to privates. A fair sprinkling of marriages were taking place between forces personnel and civilian girls. In fact 'fratting' was now in full swing, in the north as well as in the south. And the strangely mixed international population of Rome was becoming more noticeable as the domestic situation was clarified and the position of foreigners more stabilised. On one occasion I was invited to Terni, a small town in central Italy about two hours' drive from Rome. Strange to relate, a thick fog, very rare in and around the capital, blew up on the way and I was obliged to stay for the night. A Russian princess was also present – a tall, imposing and somewhat exotic figure in jodhpurs and sweater. Her uncle, an honorary colonel in the British Army, was running a riding school in Terni at that time, and was attached to the Ack-Ack unit guarding the still enormous refugee camp there. His niece worked as a secretary at Rome Area Command. To meet a Russian princess in an Ack-Ack mess may seem incongruous in retrospect, but she was perfectly at home there, much more so than I was. I felt rather ill at ease among this large crowd of men almost all unknown to me. But they were very kind, and as the fog made my journey back to Rome impossible that night, they produced soap, toothbrush and other such items for me and allotted me a small room, where a young refugee girl attended to me and smilingly brought me all the necessary articles, including a nice hot cup of tea the following morning. She spoke practically no English, but was very pleasant.

I could not help recollecting my previous visit to Terni camp, just over a year before, when I had acted as escort to two women prisoners, one of whom had been expecting a baby a few weeks later. It was a hot and dusty day in late September and the women asked me a great many questions during the journey. It was my duty to divulge nothing, and yet to keep them as 'happy' as possible. When eventually we arrived in the great Terni compound, the rage of the two ladies was unimaginable. One abused me in French and the other (pregnant) in German. In the end I had to cut them short, as no amount of assurances would pacify them – I had personally let them down and they meant me to know it and as many other people as could hear. I was personally sorry for them but it was not my duty to be sorry for suspects, even when they were about to have babies, so as firmly as possible I handed them over to the duty sergeant, and was thankful to get away over to the mess for some tea. A month or so later, I was visiting a sick AT in hospital in Rome when the sister told me she had several babies there, including a lovely pair of twins, recently born to a German lady, from Terni. She showed them to me, and asked me if I would like to see the mother. I declined, not wishing to renew our acquaintance. But it did seem a little ironic, that she should have had her confinement in a British hospital, on British soil, so to speak, when she was so passionately Nazi. And, as if that were not bad enough, her misfortune was doubled, for she had given birth to twins. In fact, she was lucky, for she had had the best treatment, as good as given to any officer's wife, and at the expense of the British government.

About the time of meeting the Russian girl in Terni, I met an Austrian in Rome. I was invited to her house, a beautiful place, not far from the Spanish Steps, and there we ate tiny cakes and drank tea – an English tea-party, where excellent English was spoken by the hosts, but where the atmosphere was utterly continental, and not really Roman. There was something strange about this family and I never fathomed the mystery surrounding them, even in my chats alone with the daughter, Daphne. Her mother was elderly and frail looking, and a complete lady. Her sister was married to an Italian nobleman, but was separated from her husband and had a keen interest in the stage. There were often artists at their house, and one would hear music and singing. Everything was refined and orderly. These émigrées were very kind to me and to many others stationed in Rome, and did their best to make us feel at home and enjoy something of the home atmosphere of which we had largely been deprived for so long.

I occasionally visited the dear little Signorine Giulia in Via Babiuno, and they allowed me to stay and strum on their piano if I had an hour to spare on a day or half-day off. I felt more truly at home with them than anywhere else, and when I moved into Rome proper, I called on them every Sunday and often drank a cup of tea with them, ate biscuits or smoked an occasional cigarette, for the old ladies were not averse to a little smoke and enjoyed English cigarettes. They also introduced me to Italian ones, which were coming back on the market again; the Nazionale were tolerable, but the other, cheaper, brands were said to be made from the thousands or millions of cigarette ends collected mainly by children in the streets, then stripped and dried off. This tobacco could be bought by the ounce (or gram) on the market, black or otherwise. It was piled high on trestle tables and sold like any other commodity – but I failed to see how it could have been at all hygienic. The other good brand was Macedonie – these or Nazionale were the ones we smoked, and the only 'respectable' types, at that time.

Another of my activities was of a somewhat different nature. Shortly before Christmas my CO (whose departure was imminent), presented me with a fine Luger pistol, at some time captured from the enemy. He explained that as I was staying on in Italy, I might need it. There was an ominous note in his voice, which seemed to hint at troubles to come, when firearms would spell safety. During this period a substantial number of people were prophesying serious civilian disturbances, particularly at the time of the referendum to decide the fate of the monarchy. But apart from any prospect of danger, never having possessed a firearm in my life or even handled one, except for shooting at moving artificial ducks at a fair, I was of course delighted to be the proud owner of such a charming little weapon, which fitted neatly into my ATS handbag and was light and handy. I received with it about fifteen cartridges. One Sunday afternoon, when all was peaceful and the local population was enjoying a well-earned siesta, I persuaded a friend to take me out to a deserted chalk-pit nearby and show me how to fire my Luger. At my first attempt I nearly shot off one of his toes, and so he quickly tried to teach me to aim and look where I was firing, which apparently I did not. Nevertheless, I greatly enjoyed the experience, though I found the noise rather worrying. But try as I would, I never convinced my escort of the necessity of my having further shooting practice. After that first day out, he was always too busy, so possibly he felt teaching me to aim was too big a risk to take, near as he was to his release date.

Finally, on 7 January 1946, I went to the commission for an interview with the second-in-command of my new unit. A day or two later I heard that I had been accepted and was to report on 14 January. I had asked for a few days' grace to pack up and hand everything over. A day or two after this interview, Hugh Trent rang up from Caserta, where he was now a staff captain with GSI (X) (General Services Intelligence), the branch that dealt with officers' postings and appointments. He understood that I spoke perfect French and explained that a vacancy for a French translator was soon to come up in the military secretary's office, and would I be interested in it? I had the disturbing impression that my name was to be put forward as a suitable candidate, and felt as if a chasm had opened up and was about to swallow me, for Caserta seemed a sort of Devil's Island, to be avoided at all costs. The thought of sitting and translating all day in an office miles from anywhere, absolutely bereft of the personal touch which interested me so much more than any form of staff work I had ever met, was appalling. Fortunately, my French was very rusty, as I had spoken it very little for several years and during my service had used mainly German and some Italian. I therefore immediately assured Hugh that while it was very nice of him to think of me, I definitely did not feel capable of doing justice to translations of a complicated and technical nature, that I had forgotten most of my French since learning Italian, and furthermore that I had just been taken on by the Screening Commission in Rome, where I would be required to utilise my knowledge of Italian.

Although he did not seem totally convinced by these arguments, the matter was left in abeyance for the time being, but a nasty shadow loomed on my horizon for some weeks to come. I was wholeheartedly determined not to go to Caserta, even if it meant promotion and not going meant demotion. If I were forced to go, I told myself savagely that I would not renew my contract to service overseas for the extra year. Instead, I would try for a posting to Germany. But of course I knew perfectly well that I was merely a cog and a pawn, and that if the powers that be decided I should go, go I would. Small as my spoke was, however, I put it in for all my worth, but during my last few days at Cinema City I was on tenterhooks. This made my departure less of a wrench; once on the strength of the commission, Caserta would, I hoped, recede into the background. All the same, it was a little sad to say a final goodbye, even though with my CO's departure my job had virtually ended.

24

A New Job – and a Fresh Angle on Italy

*I*felt a little lonely and strange when I landed up at the huge transit hotel, the Continentale, near the station, where my future ATS colleagues lived. The men of the new organisation lived in requisitioned billets. The huge dining-room of the Continentale, with its small separate tables, nearly all filled by men and more men, and the ATs who lived an independent, almost civilian life, each with her own interests, contrasted at first unfavourably with the small, friendly mess I had just left, which as it contracted had become increasingly like a family party. On my second night there, some of my friends came down to cheer me up. They were very cheerful, but after the evening was over I felt more lonely and at a loss than ever. But doubtless in time one adjusts to almost anything, and I soon found a friend in Judy, who invited me to her room for a chat and showed me the sitting-room next door. This room was actually for all the ATs to share, but we only tended to use it if we were specifically entertaining someone. Friendship with Judy developed quickly – she was the most generous soul in the world, and from that time on things looked up: the new era had begun.

I moved into the hotel on the Friday night and began work the following morning. It was strange not to go to the office on a Sunday, for previously, even when there was less work to do as latterly, we had usually paid at least a token visit to the office on

Sundays, though the Sabbath became more and more of a day off as time wore on. But the new commission, at least at its head-quarters in Rome, worked normal regular hours: eight to one, and two to five, with Saturday afternoons and Sundays off. This seemed quite like civilian life again, apart from the fact that you never knew when overtime might crop up. At first, I hardly knew what to do with myself on the free Sunday. After a while I used it as a day for getting-up late, doing chores, attending services at the English church in Via Babuino, or paying afternoon calls on my dear Signorine Giulia, chatting and strumming on their piano for an hour or so. This performance usually made me feel homesick, and probably affected the other inmates of the block of flats with a different sort of sickness, but they were tolerant and never, to my knowledge, complained.

I felt rather ill at ease that first morning in the office. The CO had at that time a male PA, a young lieutenant called Derek, who had been a POW in Italy and was engaged to an Italian girl. I was put in his office, and he went to great trouble, rigging up a desk and typewriter, for me, though as yet I had no notes to type. His fiancée frequently rang him up and they had long conversa-tions, which I tried not to overhear but could not really avoid. I had been installed in the PA's office with Derek, in place of a thin, dark lieutenant I had seen in there typing rather laboriously on the day of my interview, who had been relegated elsewhere, and it was some time before I recognised him again, or located his whereabouts. Indeed it was some time before I even found my way around the maze, almost a warren, of rooms, mostly on the first floor of a large block of offices in the Corso d'Italia, that big wide curving boulevard, tree-lined, which encircles the northern walls of Rome, taking several Roman gateways in its stride. This was the situation of our offices and from within we could hear the trams as they rattled and screeched along the Corso, with their cargoes of wedged-in human beings, the inevitable cluster of young men and boys hanging on to the back, waiting to join the scrum in the doorway at the next stop, or perhaps hanging on by one hand just for the thrill of it. The PA's office faced west and did not have the view of the trams, but looked instead over towards the Giardino Borghese and the Pincio. We were not far from the Borghese Villa, and could see the dark umbrella pines of the gardens, in the evening black against a peach sky.

I did not really know what I was supposed to do in Derek's office, but he was very gallant and bought me cakes to eat with my mid-morning tea. This greatly embarrassed me, as I preferred to pay for my own refreshments and yet I did not wish to offend him. We were not very busy at first, as the CO was then at GHQ in Caserta and did not return for two or three days. Meanwhile, the question of my transfer there boiled up again, and one or two telegrams arrived, ordering me to report down there forthwith. No-one specially told me I was to pack up and be ready to move, but a lot of long-distance telephoning went on between Derek and Hugh (in Caserta) and conferences took place between our GSO II and Derek. I shall never fathom why the powers-that-be were so keen for me to be posted to GHQ; I was just a person on paper to them, so doubtless there was a good paper reason for my going there. Whatever it was all about, a furious battle seems to have been waged over my cowed head, in which the chief of all the ATS, the colonel of GSI (X), the military secretary's department and even the C-in-C's staff colonel took part. My new CO apparently badly needed a woman PA, who would not only take over the work of his male PA (as a sort of ADC and interpreter), but would also do his own clerical work, this at present being done by a corporal typist, ATS, who was about to go on release. When the CO travelled, he wanted his PA, complete with files and typewriter, to accompany him – which is what in the end came to pass. Meanwhile, he secured me to fill an establishment vacancy on his commission, and I heaved a sigh of relief; I felt sure the new job would prove most interesting, and Caserta once more receded into the distance. The flame did flicker up again once or twice more before the scare finally died down for good and I felt really safe. Until then, I was still on probation, and was not at all certain that I would eventually be a PA. No-one had told me that I would, but I was not worried about the future now as

I was too busy learning all I could about the new job. There was a tremendous amount to learn – the more you came to understand the commission's work, the more there seemed to be to know about it, and I very much doubt if many of its personnel ever really grasped the significance of its work as a whole, distinct from their own particular role and the routine settlement of monetary claims, which, viewed from the centre of the organisation, tended to obscure its more far-reaching aims and purposes.

I was lucky in my job in having work connected with every facet of the commission's remit. I read through all the correspondence files and was shown each department, including a sort of library where dossiers on every single claimant, including those who were not actually given awards, were stored alphabetically, indexed and cross-referenced. This part of the work was done mainly by Italian civilians, some speaking excellent English, and was under the expert management of Franky, a half-Scottish Italian. All the civilian personnel had, of course, been thoroughly screened, but fortunately very little of this work was even 'Secret' and there was no 'Top Secret' material to be handled. 'Confidential' was the usual classification for anything not in general circulation.

I learnt that there were sections in the north – Florence, Milan and Verona – and that a mysterious person, who lived at Santa Margherita for most of the time, investigated claims in that area. Someone else had just been to Austria to submit a report on Austrian helpers, resulting in the recent closure of three sections by the new CO who was sweeping very clean, it seemed, and contracting the sections where possible. The closed sections were those at Turin, Treviso and Bologna. At about that time a ceremony took place in Milan for the presentation of certificates to helpers in that area – General Heidemann, Military Governor of the City, and many military and civil notabilities were present. Our colonel presided over the ceremony and gave an address explaining the purpose and function of the commission. Besides the presentation of certificates bearing the facsimile of Field Marshal Alexander's signature, payment was made as far as possible

in relation to the original disbursement of money, food and clothing, etc., in spite of an altered exchange, and sometimes clothing
was provided to help in replacing what had been lost. Help for
hospital treatment, recommendations and introductions for
jobs, visas and travel facilities, transport, assistance with property damage and considerable payments, almost a life insurance,
where one member of a family had lost his life – all these were
among the many functions of the commission. Its main purpose,
however, was to perform a 'mission of goodwill', to further the
cause of Anglo-Italian friendship, which had flowered anew
among the sacrifices and dangers shared during the German
Occupation. A further purpose, perhaps small in relation to the
whole scale of world affairs, but nonetheless important, was to
foster the spirit of fellowship and mutual well-wishing as part of
the cornerstone of future European peace and unity.

The British government allocated £1 million and the
Americans $1 million towards this financial compensation, but
even these vast sums did not nearly add up to the sums spent by
the Italians, who claimed justly on them as indemnity for loss
of life and property and other catastrophes. And unfortunately,
for at least a year, the British government postponed making a
definite statement that the money would not be paid out of War
Damages charged to the Italian government – in which case, of
course, the work of the commission would have been in vain and
nothing more than a cynical farce. Thanks to the hard work on the
part of our CO and visits by him to the Foreign Office, Treasury
and War Office when he was in England on commission business, the necessary statement at last came through: the money
was backed by British sterling and had nothing to do with Italian
war debts. From then on, the work of the commission received
a new fillip. Its personnel knew that they were not labouring in
vain, and the Italians knew that the British government, parsimo-
nious and grudging though it might appear compared with their
own generous acts of heroism and hospitality in the face of the
enemy, was at least making some attempt to face up to its obligations and fulfil its promises, as contained in the Atlantic Charter

and broadcast many times over the 'Victory V' BBC service before and during the German Occupation.

The one pity was that the work was concluded so hurriedly and that scant official recognition was accorded it by the British Army of Occupation, who consistently persisted in regarding the Allied Screening Commission (to give it its full title) a nuisance and a bunch of undisciplined cranks. Our CO, who took it over in autumn 1945, did his best to eliminate the natural hostility of the British military caste to anything out of the ordinary, but despite stupendous efforts on his part to enforce a more military discipline and keep a strict check on his somewhat unruly and individualistic personnel and heterogeneous civilian employees, the suspicion and hostility persisted, though sometimes temporarily dissipated, until the end. Probably only with more backing from London could we have achieved a more stable position, but with three masters – the Foreign Office, the Treasury and the War Office – it was not surprising that sometimes things fell between three stools? After all, London was very remote and we were a very small sideline to the people in Whitehall. Meanwhile the British Embassy in Rome was busy with many other matters and gradually setting its house in order after the war. It may be that the officials there, too, regarded the claims business as unnecessary, or perhaps thought that they should control it themselves. The commission certainly laboured against great difficulties, but despite everything, it did achieve much good work, not only in settling claims and spreading the gospel of goodwill, but also in its own running, where British (from the UK and all the Dominions), Americans, Italians, both in uniform and mufti, and other civilians of differing nationalities, all worked amicably together as a team. 'Every mickle makes a muckle', and we passionately hoped that our work would contribute towards founding that Atlantic Union, without which our Western civilisation might be shaken to its very foundations, if not completely destroyed. And the collapse of Italy, which is the cradle of so much of that civilisation and the seat of the Roman Catholic Church, would be a world-tragedy. The question of Trieste was ever-present in those days, and who knows whether Field Marshal Alexander's prompt despatch there of the New Zealand Division in the spring of 1945 may not have saved Italy at that time and made possible the creation of what is now an important bastion in the anti-Communist front? I have great faith in Italy and its new '*Risorgimento*'. It has risen from the ashes of invasion, defeat and a double Occupation with astounding speed, renewed vitality and a fervent patriotism and belief in its own destiny. Theirs is a patriotism free from histrionics and the overweening pride of the puppet Fascists, who together with their megalomaniacal Duce were the main cause of the Axis partnership and the disgraceful lick-spittling to Hitler, which culminated in the shameful invasion of Southern France in 1940 and all its terrible consequences for the Italian people.

Needless to say, the above reflections did not occur to me in the January days of 1946, when I was busy being a trial PA and quite floundering in the welter of files and information to which I had suddenly gained access. Much water had flowed under many bridges before I began to realise just what our work really was about in relation to Italy and the Italians in general. For the time being, I was learning how the business of compensation was carried out, and that in itself was complicated enough, with the preparation, checking, investigating and assessing of claims and recommendations for higher awards for bravery. The British government has unfortunately not yet seen fit to grant the issue of higher decorations to Italians, despite the promise made over the wireless which led this to be expected and even though such awards were made by the Americans as early as 1946. Perhaps in fifty years' time, when the Occupation has become almost a legend and the names of certain martyrs of the Partisan Movement are handed down as traditional heroes, their grandchildren's children will receive a summons from the British Ambassador in Rome, announcing that he has an award to make on behalf of His Majesty's Government for valour on the part of Signor So-and-so, who was tortured and finally executed by the Germans in 1944 for sheltering three British prisoners in his home in the Romagna, when it was forbidden on penalty of death to help the British. Meanwhile, some Italians are nursing a disillusionment about the good intentions of the British government, so manifest when Italian co-operation was sorely needed before and after the 1943 landings. They did not act in the hope of a decoration – their actions were spontaneous gallantry – but a decoration is worth far more than money, and not only in Italy. But in 1946 we were all still full of hope that the awards really would be allowed and given out, and there was a fund of goodwill in the country towards the Allies and towards the British in particular. I have heard of anti-British or anti-Ally demonstrations, but apart from seeing the somewhat sullen crowds in Padua a year later, I never experienced the slightest hostility from the Italian population, even though I had occasion often to be alone and in isolated places. I found them always helpful, polite, welcoming and eager to be friendly with England. They had not wanted to enter the war against us; in fact most of them had not wanted to be in the war at all. The Germans were and still are their hated enemies, and the blame for most of Italy's misfortunes is attributed to the alliance with Hitler. England could achieve much with Anglo-Italian co-operation and much has already been achieved. All lovers of Italy hope for more.

Meanwhile, I discovered that in spite of having lived for nearly two years in Italy, I really knew next to nothing of it or its people. True, I had seen Naples, Rome, Florence and Venice, but what did I know of the real Italy: the small mountain villages, where tiny overloaded donkeys trudged wearily up stony paths, where people wore sacking instead of shoes, bound round their feet with leather thongs, and where sometimes there was not even a road, only a mule-track, so that the inhabitants lived quite cut off from the modern mechanisation of the autostrada and the railway line? It was in these tiny hamlets or isolated farms, or in others less isolated, but equally remote from modernity, such as the Plain of Lombardy, that many of our men hid from the Nazis and Fascists, and it was here that dramas of life and death took place when innocent civilians were terrorised and sometimes brutally murdered merely for being suspected of sheltering an Allied soldier. For the

Nazi guards penetrated even the most out-of-the-way mountain fastnesses or inoffensive homesteads, and no-one, except perhaps in the wildest caves, was safe from the danger of denouncement, and all too often the Fascist enemy was in the midst of the patriots. I had already come to like the Italians – and indeed who could help it? – but now I began to admire them, even more than before, when I saw their patience in adversity. Here was a courage and defiance of risk and death, which we had not encountered in our much safer country. Here the choice and clash of ideals and principles had been solved simply and unquestioningly by people, some of whom could not read or write, but whose hearts were truly great. Not long after my posting to the commission, a large cake arrived for the CO. It was sent by Emilio Azzari, the pastry-cook of Rieti, who was tortured horribly by the Germans and yet never revealed the hiding-place of several English prisoners. He was finally drugged in an attempt to break his morale, but it did not break – 'I did not tell,' he said simply, 'and I never would.' The commission managed to get him some hospital treatment for his injured leg; the Germans had beaten it with a rifle-butt and then poured acid into the wound – and for a long time it was touch and go as to whether he would be able to keep it. He came to Rome occasionally for treatment, always bright and cheerful, and he never failed to bring the CO some sweets or a rich cake baked by himself.

I used to see other Italians in the corridors, but at first of course I did not know who were claimants and who employees, until one day when Iris, who was working as paying officer in the Rome Office, i.e. for the claimants in and around the city, asked me if I would do her work while she had a day off. I readily agreed, anxious to learn more, and we had the arrangement authorised. At first I was very much at sea and the recipient I was paying would often go into streams of voluble Italian, frequently in dialect, of which I only grasped a few words. Sometimes the recipients were profusely and touchingly grateful for the little I was giving them, even if it was only one or two thousand lire (then about thirteen or twenty-six shillings). At other times they were angry and disgusted at not getting more. I had to try to explain that this was for the most part a token payment, and that the British government was sincerely grateful for their sacrifices and support. If anyone became really obstreperous and occasionally this happened, then I would press the bell for the reception sergeant who always showed in the claimants, and ask him to eject them as politely as possible. As he was used to the various types by this time, he generally had no difficulty in making them see reason, and he would elbow them gently towards the door amid a stream of protests and a whirl of dramatic gestures, with myself as the stupefied one-women audience; for never before, in spite of Luisa, Marcello, Guglielmo, the OH and a few others, had I realised quite what vocal and rhetorical voices the majority of Italians seem to possess as a birthright. I set to work to become more fluent and rather more rhetorical myself, and was better able to hold my own, especially as Iris after a few weeks departed on Python and for a time I did the two jobs, secretarial and paying.

I had moved out of Derek's office, as there did not seem to be room for the two of us and anyway I wanted to be on my own. I had gone into the office opposite, which was formerly the ATS corporal's room, but which since her release a new employee, Nancy, now occupied. After Corporal Gillingham's departure, I had become for a time saddled with almost all the English secretarial work of the unit, apart from the indexing and translating and other routine admin work. All the investigators' reports and correspondence seemed to find their way to me, and sometimes about five or six people would be dictating to me, or waiting to pass on work to me, at the same time. The situation was becoming impossible, and sometimes I felt that people wrote more now that they found I could be prevailed upon to type their work. Anyway, a young civilian girl, whose father had just come out to the British Embassy, had been taken on to help me; her name was Nancy and she was sixteen. She was in many ways very young, but in others she seemed quite sophisticated, or soon became so, and sometimes I wondered if I were not the young one. As she had no mother and lived on her own at the YWCA, I felt some responsibility for her, but she seemed quite happy to look after herself and well able to do so. I soon ceased to worry, deciding that after all she had her father near, and if she were in trouble he would be the one to assist her. She was a great help in the office and on the whole we got along famously. Soon afterwards, a WAAF officer came to join us, posted out from London, and the CO told Derek in no uncertain terms that we must be given another, larger, room. I was very thankful, for our office was not much bigger than a large cupboard, and dark at that, and the room became thoroughly crowded whenever there was a rush on, and at such times pandemonium would ensue.

About mid-March, the CO called me into his office and told me he wished me to be his official PA from then on, that he considered me well enough acquainted with the work to take over completely, and that Captain Giles would be transferred to more active work. He said I was to move into the PA's office proper, and take up my duties at once. In practice, it was a few days before I was actually installed there and Derek had started new work in another part of the building, but from then on the CO kept me busy with letters, interpreting, telephoning, arranging interviews and other odd jobs. He was down in Rome for a time before undertaking any more tours of inspection round the sections.

About this time I made my first contacts through long-distance telephoning on Italian lines. The Signals Corps were not now universal, and had transferred part of their network back to the Italian civil structure, which had been repaired after the damage during the war. Thus, in order to get Verona, we would have to deal with Italians at the Central Rome Exchange, still working in conjunction with the military signals communications. But the lines were no longer secret, and therefore one was liable to get mixed up with all sorts of calls. Fortunately, we had an excellent operator in the unit, Paolo, who usually wrestled with the Central Exchange for me, but even then one could be cut off at any moment, while volumes of rapid Italian chattered away in the near, middle or far distance and one was liable at any time to find oneself talking to Genoa, Taranto, or Naples, when one was in fact trying to get GSI (b) at Caserta, or any other staff sections for that matter. Or the line would suddenly become very faint, and one had to blow out one's lungs like a bellows and roar down the mouthpiece like a bull, enunciating every word as in a phonetic lesson. Some of my calls were in Italian on behalf of the CO, not always long-distance, but the worst time was when I mistakenly got through to the Italian civilian operators at a city exchange up north. Spelling and trying the telephone alphabet in stuttering Italian, wracking my brains for words beginning with certain letters, puffing and blowing, and gazing agonisingly at the growing number of persons waiting to speak to me in the office about business with the colonel, or turning my back on them and shouting at the window, I would desperately struggle to get to where I wanted on the phone. If ever there was a trial for patience, it was the telephone system in Italy at that time. But all the same, I could not help seeing the funny side of it all, and really enjoyed it when I was not too harassed.

25

Roman Carnival

I had established a firm friend in Judy at the Hotel Continentale, and we had together made the acquaintance of the sergeant in charge of the NAAFI stores, who very obligingly supplied us when possible with anything we wanted, from cosmetics to alcohol or cigarettes. Sometimes, in the evening, he would come up to our sitting room for a chat, and used to entertain us with the gossip of the hotel. I had also got to know the maestro fairly well, who so obligingly played our requests when leading on his violin the small trio that played every evening in the dining room. And Tullio, our waiter, was a firm friend of Judy's and mine, and brought us an *ancora dolce* almost whenever we asked him for it, his calf-like eyes meltingly acceding to our entreaties – I am sure he was quite amused at the ATS officers. He always looked after our table, and even when some members of the Pay Corps tried to rob us of it, he still waited on us as we ate indignantly at a side-table; and whenever possible he kept our own places for us. We won the battle in the end and retained our corner table, from whence we surveyed the room and summed up its occupants. You could do this even if you had your back to the centre, for there were mirrors on each end wall.

Tullio had mouse-coloured wavy hair, neatly brilliantined, and was of medium height and a trifle thickset. His eyes were distinctly handsome and he had charming manners. He was very civil and we never had a cross word from him in all the time he looked after us. We rewarded him as generously as we could out of our NAAFI cigarette ration, which was still the easiest and best way of tipping. I heard about two years later from an officer who had come home, but had known him for a time in the hotel, that Tullio had a dual profession: as well as being as a waiter, he was what in polite old Italian would, I believe, be called a '*cicisbeo*' or '*cavaliere*' to a highly placed and wealthy Roman lady. He certainly had the right diplomatic manner for coping with women and sufficient charm to get away with almost anything.

Shrove Tuesday fell on 5 March that year and as it happened Jonathan was down on leave from Austria, spending a few days in Rome. He asked me to spend the evening of *Martedì Grasso* with him, and we decided to see what the Romans did on this most popular of fiestas. The previous year I had heard stories of crockery flying out of windows and of wild jubilations, so I was quite agog with excitement.

We began with the opera. The Rome Opera House was now in full swing again and although I have seen several famous opera houses, the one in Rome is to me the most attractive and beautiful of all. There is no gallery proper, just tier upon tier of boxes, and then seats as usual in the auditorium. The lights in the middle are extinguished before the commencement of an act, but all the boxes remain illuminated and look like several hundred arched windows, brilliantly lit up, into which one can gaze and survey the occupants, the men mostly in black and women in various colours, many wearing stylish hats, outlined against the walls behind them. Then the lights in the boxes go out, and the act begins amid an expectant stillness, broken only by the tapping of the maestro's baton on his music stand. In those days, any performance was preceded by the playing of the national anthems of America, Britain, France and Italy. Fortunately, not all the anthems of the Allies were played, or the performance would have been lengthened by half an hour. In the interval it was customary to promenade up and down the foyers, and many interesting faces and fashions were to be seen there.

In 1946, most of the seats were still reserved for the military, and on Shrove Tuesday Jonathan and I were in the stalls. It was *Madama Butterfly*, and the performance was superb – it made me weep, so pathetic was the final scene. On a subsequent occasion I took a small girl of nine to see *Madama Butterfly*. She intensely enjoyed it and was not at all abashed by the cruel tragedy she was witnessing. I prepared her during the intervals for the sad ending, thinking that she would in that way be less upset by a scene which is one of the most moving in all opera – Butterfly's final disillusionment, her farewell to her baby and her eventual desperate suicide. But my small companion was delighted with the story, and throughout the last act she questioned me at regular intervals in a stage whisper, shrill with anticipation, 'Is she going to die now?' or 'Has she killed herself yet?' She was not at all saddened by the story, but thoroughly entertained by the opera from start to finish.

On that occasion, I had no time for emotion, but this time I felt quite depressed at the end and was glad we had to be busy searching for a *carrozza* immediately afterwards to take us down to the Orso, but there were great crowds out that night and not a free cab to be found. A *carrozza* is an open carriage, with a turned-back hood, usually painted black, but often with red bands round the coachwork. It is drawn by one horse and in the early days of the British Occupation in Rome, when the *carrozze* again began to put in an appearance, only a few of them at first, the horses were pathetically under-nourished and meagre, with all their ribs visible and their hip-bones sticking out from their skinny flanks. But after about a year, they began to look better, as food for both humans and animals became more plentiful. In fact, by the time I eventually left Italy, they were nearly all well nurtured and glossy, drew freshly painted vehicles and had greatly increased in numbers. They were as popular a mode of travel as the taxi, and perhaps a little less expensive, and it was certainly far more pleasant to amble along unhurriedly, enjoying the balmy air and watching the changing architecture or the busy pavements. And at night, in an open *carrozza* one had the full benefit of the clear skies and the stars, as well as the neon lights illuminating the main thoroughfares or, in the quiet side streets and squares, the silhouettes of gateways, houses and churches – for all the world like any scene from Italian opera. I once drove past the Fontana dei Trevi in a *carrozza* at night. We clattered along the cobbled streets and suddenly came out on the piazza which was darkened, for it was about 11 p.m. There was scarcely a soul to be seen and the tightly shuttered houses were silent and were reflected in the motionless water of the fountain basin. The great sculptured figure of Triton was lit up by the moon, and in the moonbeams, one saw the fountain itself and the surroundings vaguely illuminated. Here and there a light glowed softly across the *persiane*, and occasionally the distant chords of a guitar broke the stillness. It was utterly peaceful and might well have been a scenario from *Rigoletto*. It hardly seemed real, and yet five minutes away lay the Via Tritone, one of the city's main streets, brilliantly lit up with all sorts of signs, far gayer than London, and with thronged pavements, transport of all kinds and *carrozze* plying up and down it.

On Martedì Grasso, however, we could not find any form of transport to take us down to the Orso, which must have been two miles away, so we walked there instead. It was very pleasant to pass through the narrow streets where people were celebrating at small cafés, with frequent bursts of music and occasionally the distant crashing of breaking pottery, of which we had been warned. On Shrove Tuesday, the Romans throw all their chipped and broken crockery out of the windows into the street below – and woe betide the unwary passer-by!

We found the Orso crowded that night and upstairs the dance-floor was so packed, chiefly with Britishers, that one could hardly move. A lot of people were wearing paper hats and there was a general air of jollity. The bar was crammed with unattached officers and every seat was taken. It was at the Orso, I had recently learned, that some members of the Rome Organisation, the parent of our commission, used to dine, with German officers eating peaceably at the next table. The Rome Organisation was formed by escaped prisoners and internees, who took refuge in the Vatican, and while there organised a vast escape network with the help of many brave and enthusiastic Italians. Many contacts had to be made and arranged with persons in the city of Rome, and so it was that the Orso, on the opposite side of the Tiber to the Vatican, but conveniently near, became a sort of trysting-place; and right under the noses of the Gestapo some of the very men they were hunting contrived to carry on their dangerous work undetected. Chatting with the barman, he told us of the breathtaking moments he had witnessed, but no-one was ever caught in the Orso and the signatures of some of the bold characters who so gaily courted disaster can still be seen in a small frame in the bar. On the parchment lampshades are scrawled names originating from half the countries of the world, and from both hemispheres.

The British-sponsored clubs normally closed at eleven, but remained open until midnight at the latest for special occasions such as Shrove Tuesday, and so in deference to the Italian fiesta, the Orso opened late on that occasion. We decided there must be more to see, that the Italians would never close down so soon, and so we wandered back on foot the way we had come, but left an hour early, as it was too crowded to dance. I had heard exciting tales of Italian soirées that went on almost all night, and a friend had told me how his hostess had once been truly offended when he had pleaded that for reasons of duty he must leave her party at 4 a.m. Italian hospitality is unbounded, and its generosity is only equalled by its gaiety and cheerfulness. But despite our conviction that the Italians would not relinquish the festivities until the early hours of the morning, it took Jonathan and me some time to find the sort of show we were looking for.

Our first port of call was the Warrant Officers' and Sergeants' Club in Via Nazionale, and here we found great celebrations in progress. How it was that we eventually found ourselves outside what seemed to be a cinema in the Via Quattro Fontane is still a mystery to me, but we heard the sounds of music, and asked the doorman what was going on. '*C'è un ballo,*' he replied, '*Volete entrare*?' We went into the hall, and saw a vast room full of people in evening dress, some of them dancing on the stage, others sitting at small tables around the edge of the room or on the balconies. We decided that this was the place for us, and we were soon dancing on the stage too. It is impossible to relate all the details of that amazing night: how there was only one other Englishman there, how friendly the Italians were and how welcome they made us, how before long we found ourselves drinking champagne with a gentleman in exquisitely cut tails and a white tie worthy of Savile Row, and how we were all toasting the Allies, '*Inghilterra and l'Italia*'. And how Anna Magnani came and sang on the stage and was greeted by a thunderous roar of applause, and was listened to with rapt attention throughout. She was not so famous then outside her own country as she later became, but I had the impression of a buoyant and vigorous personality. She wore a powder-blue evening dress, rather low-cut, and her hair was long, in accordance with the prevalent fashion.

We paired up with a young Italian and his girlfriend, one of whose fathers had treated us to the champagne, and soon we were all wearing fantastic hats and flinging streamers down people's backs, hurling small multi-coloured balls about, bagging other people's hats, blowing whistles or whirling rattles – and generally entering into the spirit of the carnival with a spontaneity of which personally I never believed myself capable. With the Italians, who are for the most part so natural, one somehow did not feel silly, shy or self-conscious; we all just behaved as we felt inclined, forgot our troubles for the time being and gave ourselves up to enjoyment free from inhibition and vulgarity. It was just complete fun, and everyone had a whale of a time. My feet began to ache and feel sore, but I still danced – we all danced and danced till we were nearly dropping. Then we revived our flagging bodies with long, thirst-quenching glasses of fresh lemonade and sat for a few minutes and chatted to some of the mamas sitting at the tables, wearing perky paper caps, guarding bags, drinks and ashtrays and exchanging discreet titbits of gossip as they watched the continuously revolving throng of dancers.

At 4 a.m. I declared it was time for me to be going home. Jonathan would doubtless have stayed on, but I had a full day ahead of me in the office and so we bade farewell to our kind friends with many thank-yous and promises to meet again, and I eventually got back to the hotel at about 5 a.m. The next morning in the office the CO dictated me about twelve letters – perhaps he thought it would be a good thing for my Lenten period to begin with a penance – but anyway he kept me extremely busy all morning. By the end of it, my head was beginning to feel not a little heavy, with all the excitement and fatigue of the night before gathering momentum, so that the shorthand ciphers positively danced feverishly over the pages, and I almost wished I had never gone to the trouble of learning such hieroglyphics that became so horribly evasive if one felt slightly below par. Somehow I got through the morning, and met Jonathan and the boy and girl of the party at the 'Flower Shop', a recently reopened Italian café. They both seemed very fresh, whereas I felt by now distinctly jaded. They said they had been at the dance until 6.30 a.m., and both much regretted that we had had to leave so early! I regretted it too, but in view of the shorthand, perhaps it was just as well we had left when we did. I saw Elisabetta once or twice after that, but with the pressure of work and our own social life I eventually lost touch with her, as with so many other kind and likeable acquaintances – but I shall never forget that evening, and probably nor will she!

By now, thanks to my greatly increased practice in Italian, I was acting both as paying officer and as interpreter for the CO, which job was becoming progressively more my own. I could get along fairly comfortably in the language, and could appreciate such an evening as that just described far more than would have been possible a year before. When Italian friends rang me up on the telephone now, I did not go alternately red and white and mentally translate one sentence, while they had galloped on ahead, which meant that my answers were already out of date when they finally paused, surprised by my inarticulateness, to enquire whether I had understood and whether I agreed with them.

I invariably agreed. By now I could think at least to some extent in Italian, and the worst and most difficult period of learning it was over, but as I am only a very amateur linguist, so much remained to learn and be perfected that I decided to try to fit in some lessons. I was recommended by the Signorine Giulia to a friend of theirs, a Sicilian professor, who by reason of his upbringing, spoke with the soft accents of Tuscany. The Professore was a kind and charming teacher, but as time was too short and there was too much to be done at the office, the lessons were few and far between. There was a great deal to do at the commission and I was very glad when a WAAF officer, named Phyl, arrived from Paris to help in my department – but as she did not yet speak Italian, anything that needed translating or interpreting still fell to me and that suited me well, as it interested me the most.

Judy was a keen horsewoman and was always trying to persuade me to go out with her to Passo Corese, a riding-school about four miles north of Rome, where one could have an enjoyable afternoon riding a horse, even if one was as inexpert as I am. I went with her once and found the occasion most entertaining. Having asked for a quiet and gentle horse and been given one which was said to be 'molto *tranquillo*', I had somewhat of a shock, for my steed, having reached an open field and seeing the leading horses break into a canter, followed suit without warning. My efforts to calm him only stimulated him to further effort, and soon we were careering in a headlong gallop past the other horses down to a small valley, while I, with both stirrups flying, was clutching for dear life to the pommel of the saddle and praying to stay on the animal's back, or rather neck. In time, however, he quietened down, and after that first outburst behaved with reasonable propriety. Unfortunately, such excursions were rare, especially when I found it necessary to utilise Saturday afternoons for putting the PA's office into order – the weeks were beginning to fill up hectically, and there was rarely enough peace for filing, indexing and other routine tasks.

Some months later, I made another equestrian excursion with Judy. By then, riding facilities had been provided for the forces at Monte Mario, just outside Rome and near the Radio Station. I decided to be on the safe side and join in the beginners' class – and it was a never-to-be-forgotten experience. Men and women had gathered there, all jumbled together, wearing all sorts of clothes, and of various ranks, types and even nationalities. I had heard that members of these classes sometimes dismounted and walked home, but I had not hitherto witnessed such a thing. We were up on the brow of the hill and had to go through a pine wood to get down to the valley again and back to the school. Several of the horses led their riders through the wood at a smart trot, and horsemen and women were coming off like ninepins, some of them re-mounting, if they could find their mounts, others just strolling gently back to the stables, and yet others leading their horses back by the bridle. No-one minded in the least what happened or what one did, and if someone had suddenly appeared riding back to front, I do not think any of the class would have registered astonishment. I managed to stay on quite successfully, but my horse unexpectedly dashed among the trees, and I missed one or two branches by a hair's breadth. The animals apparently played certain tricks quite regularly on novices and got a lot of fun out of it, but I heard one sergeant muttering as he slithered to the ground and shook the pine-needles from his battledress, 'I'm glad I've been in the Paratroops – this isn't much different!' There were one or two ditches in the wood too, which accounted for a few casualties. The instructors, Italians, were quite philosophical about all the queer goings-on, and altogether there was a haphazard, happy-go-lucky spirit about the beginners' class which made it a comic-opera sort of affair that no-one need fear to join.

For a time after Iris had gone, there was only Phoebe, the accounts officer, Judy and myself representing the ATS at our corner table. Before her departure, Iris had tried hard to persuade me to dye my hair. She said to me, quite casually, one day at lunch-time, 'Why don't you change your hair, have a different colour?' Horrified, I said, 'Surely you don't mean *dye* my hair, do you?' 'Of course,' she said simply, 'When we lived in Rome before the war, I sometimes used to dye my hair, just for one evening, and it used to be fashionable to wear one's hair the colour of one's dress for the day. There were lovely pinks and blues. You would look very nice with fair hair. You should become a blonde.' If she had told me it would have suited me to wear a ring in my nose I should scarcely have been more astonished, but I just said lamely, 'But Iris, I'm a brunette, and I don't *want* to be a blonde.' She gave me a slightly pitying look – of course I know how unenterprising British women are often considered. But her Botticelli features relaxed in a smile and she just replied, 'Oh well, of course, if you rather just remain as you are, dark hair is all right, only it is nice to have a change some days.' If she did not convince me, she did, I am sure, convince Phoebe, as not long afterwards Phoebe's fine dark hair became a coppery colour and from then on it was nearly always a dark auburn, or was it 'Titian'? Anyway it was a shade that was becoming rather fashionable just then. The worst of such 'tinting' was that it could almost always be detected. Iris did not even succeed in persuading me to have my portrait painted, although she and her husband had an artist friend who, she said, would like to paint (or practise) on me – she even murmured something about nudes. But the idea of hours in a studio with an Italian artist, about whom I knew next to nothing beyond the fact that he was a very charming young man, did not appeal to me at all. Later on, the very same artist painted me a lovely little seascape of Fregene, near Rome, but that was quite different from my acting as an impromptu model. As with many English people, my Nonconformist ancestors seem to rise up at times and disapprove. Shortly afterwards, Iris and her husband gave a farewell party and she went off home and there was no news of her for a year or more, when I suddenly heard that she had had a baby girl. That must have made her happy, for she always seemed to be hankering after something, not just enjoying life as most of us were.

I missed Iris a lot after her departure, for she had been my friend for two years and we had seen a great deal together. Fortunately, with her job added to mine, even though hers was considerably diminished and nearly finished, I had plenty to keep me occupied and fortified against homesickness or melancholy.

I did, however, often feel rather lonely after work was done for the day. I would hasten down for a cup of tea at the Catholic Women's League canteen, later transferred to the magnificent Palazzo Volpi, on the corner of Via Venti Settembre and Via Quattro Fontane, and would then explore the streets and shops of Rome. I did not have much to spend, but it was fascinating just to wander along, looking in the shop-fronts, reading the signs, studying the newspaper office windows with their photographs and captions of news, watching the people bustling to and fro or sitting at the cafés, the complicated traffic and voluble drivers, the myriads of cyclists, the young men carrying their girlfriends side-saddle on their cross-bars, a form of transport that never ceased to astonish the British. In general, I was simply drinking in the atmosphere of Rome, mostly quite unnoticed myself, an observer on the fringe of the city's flow of life, and yet temporarily part of it and bound up with it, and doubtless influenced by it. One day a woman actually asked me the way. She did not seem to be aware that I was not an Italian or even to notice my uniform, which greatly amazed me. Occasionally people asked me if I were Italian, on account mainly, I think, of my dark hair. They would comment, '*È proprio un tipo italiano, Signorina*.' I realised this was a kindly compliment.

On Sundays, often rather a lonely day, I used to squeeze into one of the trolleys outside our hotel, and whizz along in it to the Piazza di Spagna, and there alight prior to attending service in the Garrison Church, the British Church of Rome. It was still run by the military and mainly for them, as an Army chaplain was still there and the civilian clergyman had not returned, or been re-appointed. I remembered that on Armistice Day, as a great idea and an example of Allied co-operation, it had been decided to ask the Americans to allow their military band to play the music, accompanying the organ. In practice, however, the organ and the congregation accompanied the band, for they played so fast and furiously on their brass that no-one could keep up with them, and drowned most of the singers too with their enthusiastic and somewhat syncopated rendering of the hymns. Even 'God Save the King' seemed to 'swing' slightly, though not in the least disrespectfully – and as for the 'Stars and Stripes', it sounded like Gershwin at his best.

On other Sundays I would wander through the Pincio Gardens or along the banks of the River Tiber – in Rome one can never be really dull, there is such an inexhaustible variety of sights, sounds, colours and persons to hold one's interest. Meanwhile, shopping began at last to have a more practical interest for us, because around this time the rate of exchange was altered from 400 to 700 lire to the pound. For a long time the so-called 'black market' rate had stood at 700 or even higher, and every time we were paid our 400 lire, as regards purchasing power we were really being done out of 300. Perhaps the idea was to discourage the Forces from buying anything outside their own clubs or the NAAFI, but naturally everyone wanted to buy some of the lovely things now displayed in the shop windows and send them home: silk stockings especially, and coloured silk scarves, were favourite presents for mothers, sisters, wives and sweethearts. Anyway the financial authorities, perhaps the British Treasury – who knows? – at last decided that the Army had done penance long enough and deserved a break, so they gave us 700 lire to our pound. Most people immediately dashed out and bought whatever they could find, for it was certain that prices would go up before long, which of course they did – and very shortly afterwards.

From then on, the lira steadily rose – or should one say sank? – until by spring 1947 it was quoted on the black market as high as 2,500 lire. Each time there was an official devaluation, there was extra work for all admin staff, as pay had to be adjusted and all NAAFI prices went up to keep in step with the change. But the free market was always ahead of the officially fixed one, and when things began to improve, it also reflected the downward trend of the lira, though unfortunately for the Italians, this was very slight. By the early 1950s, it was more or less stable, at about 2,000 lire to the pound. The black market, or street monetary transactions, were still going on very actively in Rome in 1946, and often as I walked back from the office in the late afternoon, I would hear voices murmuring behind me, or from out of dark doorways,

'*Mees, shange stairleen*', or still, '*Mees, sell cigarette*?' Sometimes one was openly accosted with the request for '*Sterline*', and a lot of slightly shady business seemed to be going on at the top of Via Nazionale, on Piazza Esedra, and round about that area, which lay on my path back from the office to the Hotel Continentale.

Here there were small displays of British and American cigarettes and sometimes other NAAFI articles on sale every few yards along the pavement, and youths in twos and threes were always ready to make a proposition of some illegal nature. Sometimes the police swooped and caught some of the black marketeers, but their activities were too prevalent for them to be completely curtailed. Occasionally there was a scare, such as one afternoon when we noticed that all the vendors of American and British cigarettes were hastily packing up their trays and suitcases near the arches of the Porta Pinciana and shuffling rapidly away. Soon, several jeeploads of *carabinieri*, armed of course with rifles and bayonets, were driving through the arches, obviously searching for prey. One or two of the jeeps had a man in civilian clothes on board, who had apparently been made captive, but he did not appear worried about it. A few hours later, the raid over, the illegal sales would be taking place just as openly as before, the *carabinieri* having satisfied their honour and replenished their stock of cigarettes. There was also a lot of currency trafficking in those days, and although I never personally witnessed such a deal, I did hear of a case where an Italian concluded a settlement in the street (perhaps in the Arcade, a favourite meeting place of spivs and such like). After his settlement, the Italian immediately discovered that all the notes in the packet he had just received (as it happened, English pounds) were fakes, except for the one on top. He quickly shouted for the policeman to come and arrest his customer, calling him loudly, 'rogue, thief and scoundrel'. The man was arrested and his accuser was then asked to substantiate his evidence. It was then discovered that the latter had also given fake notes, Italian ones, in exchange for the sterling, so he was also arrested and the two racketeers were conducted along to the police station together. On another occasion, when the Italian government decided to make a determined effort to end the black market, there was a strike of black marketeers, and they even paraded through the city in protest. For some days it was impossible to get the precious fresh eggs previously bought, though dearly, on the Piazza Vittorio Emanuele, but it all seemed to peter out. Although much of the trade at that time was termed 'black market' many people would actually regard as 'free market', so that it was well-nigh imposs-ible to ban it without seriously imperilling the food supplies of the city. And so the black market continued and flourished, and today black and white are merged into one – but what the exact blend is only an expert could say!

Another day I accidentally became mixed up in a Communist procession, again on my way home from the office. It was coming up the hill from the Piazza Barberini and my path joined it at the beginning of the Via delle Terme, as we all crossed Via Venti Settembre. The crowd seemed very jolly and good-natured, per-haps rather untidy and some ragged, but the red scarves and the kerchiefs looked fresh and new. The procession surged along fill-ing the whole road, pavements included, and as they were going in my direction, bearing aloft flags and rough banners with such captions as, '*Fuori gli alleati*', '*Vogliamo il pane*', '*Evviva i commu-nisti*', '*A morte il Re!*' and others, I had no alternative but to walk along beside them and soon found myself swept along with the tide. We surged on, I with my Army haversack over one shoul-der, encountering one or two curious glances, but trying to look as unconcerned and detached as possible. Presently we came to the great entrance of the Grand Hotel, where several impor-tant-looking personages were rather nonchalantly watching the performance of the *sansculottes*. I caught the gaze of one or two of them momentarily alighting on me with a slight air of surprise, but by this time I almost felt part of the show, and chin well for-ward I carried on as khaki left-wing until we came out into the Piazza Esedra, and here I was able to branch off on my own. After all I did not want to be arrested by itinerant military police as a political demonstrator, thereby breaking King's Regulations and becoming liable for court martial!

Politics in Italy are indeed a matter for conjecture. One of our civilian drivers informed me one day that he was an anarchist. 'But why?' I asked him. Anarchy to me suggested Trotsky, spies, subversive activity and in fact everything that was the antithesis of the pale, thin, kind little man at the wheel. 'Because, Signorina,' he said, 'I wish everyone well and I believe everybody should help everybody else.' Noble sentiments, but why anarchy? Further questioning revealed him to be certainly democratic in outlook, but as far as the accepted meaning of anarchy goes, an anarchist only by virtue of his own words. If all anarchists were like this man, then doubtless the world would be a happier and more peaceful planet.

Politics, the black market and the existence of an enormous and heterogeneous refugee population in Italy, especially Rome – all these things produced some queer manifestations at times and one of the strangest was perhaps the case of Marcus Brewster, who was a sort of Sidney Stanley, and of the same race. At the outset of my stay in the hotel I had noticed a pretty, very smart woman of about forty, rather French and 'fluffy' looking, who was always lunching and dining with one or more British officers, usually two or three, and frequently different ones. She changed her escorts as she changed her modish hats – almost daily – although there was one captain who seemed more in favour than all others. Sometimes a large stout man in civilian clothes would be seen dining with the group, but not often, and he seemed overshadowed by the lady's gaiety and that of her other companions. She was perhaps rather skittish for her age, but attractive, vivacious and extremely smart and sophisticated.

After I had been working for some weeks with the commission I gradually became aware of the presence of a big, stout, greasy-haired serious man, who called fairly frequently and was usually closeted for an hour or so with the GSO II. He seemed a person of some influence and importance, and I learned that his visits concerned the provision of transport for civilian helpers, for whom he acted as representative, or go-between. Invariably, this individual carried a large fat briefcase. This was Marcus Brewster.

It may have been in March that some form of 'flap' developed about Marcus Brewster, and it appeared that he was in for trouble of some sort. I was not in a position to know just what was going on, but a word here and there, his rather more frequent visits to the office, some correspondence with GHQ – these all led me to put two and two together. Eventually one afternoon we heard that the said gentleman had been arrested by the Italians. It then transpired that he had sold for his own profit transport handed over to him for some monastery, and had also been involved in other disreputable transactions. Everyone was pleased that the net had closed in on him at last. But after a day or two it seemed that he had been released, having told his interrogators that he was working for *our* commission. A member of the Field Security (FS) came in great excitement to see our CO and asked why this man was working for us, as he had been wanted by both the Italian and Allied police for over a year. He had actually been handed over to the Field Security by the Italian police, to be dealt with as part of the Occupation troops! The CO remarked that it was strange that the Field Security had failed to locate Mr Brewster, since he had been living for the past few months in the officers' transit hotel. 'What?! Are you sure, sir, for some of our people live there?' the FS man spluttered. 'Check up for yourself,' replied our colonel, 'in any case some of my ATS are there, and perhaps they will identify the gentleman for you.' When our GSO II asked me if I recollected this, the whole thing suddenly connected up in my mind. Of *course* the stylishly dressed lady was Mrs Brewster, but how on *earth* could she and her important consort be living at our hotel, where no civilians were allowed even to have a meal?! The answer is not known to me, nor the ultimate fate of Mr and Mrs Brewster, though on this occasion at least his case was strong and his alibis well-constructed. But the Field Security people must have felt a trifle foolish, as some of them had eaten for some time in the same restaurant, perhaps sometimes even at the next table to the Brewster pair, without any suspicion that they were sitting cheek by jowl with the man they were hunting, and whose description had been sent by signal to London, New York and Paris.

Round about the same time I was lucky enough to see something of the Roman film world, about which so much has lately been written. It was on a Sunday afternoon, bright and sunny, when I was taking a siesta, Italian-fashion, when there was a knock on the door of my room and a Scots lady came in – it was only necessary for her to speak one word for one to realise her country of origin. She wanted to know if I could lend her a uniform temporarily, as she had been asked to take the part of an ATS officer in the film *Teheran*. She did not have a large part, but was to be the AT secretary to some top-ranking diplomat or service chief. I agreed to lend her a service dress uniform, which she tried on and found it fitted perfectly. She invited me to see her scene shot, and so on the following Saturday afternoon I found myself wedged in the back of a smart two-seater, on my way out towards Cinema City, to a different sector from the part I knew so well. This studio was near the Via Appia and the Catacombs of San Callisto. It was very interesting to see part of a film made, though how anyone can ever have sufficient patience for film work is a marvel to me. There was a magnificent set for one of the scenes, a Turkish house, complete with courtyard, balconies all round, a fountain in the middle, and cool palm trees. Pillars supported the balconies, under which ran a vaulted cloister, and everywhere the delicate fretwork, and even the characteristic minaret – the whole construction dazzling white. For a few moments we seemed to be back in the Kasbah again and then we were outside once more, among the wooden huts with corrugated iron roofs and other rather haphazardly arranged buildings, clustered together in a mushroom-like way on a muddy piece of ground, and these constituted the studio. It was not magnificent like some of the shattered buildings of Cinema City, but no doubt it was post-war and doubtless also it has played its part in putting the Italian films of today into the top rank of international cinema art.

26

Will Proceed
to Milan

*I*t was towards the end of March that I heard rumours to the effect that I was to be transferred to Milan. It was said that the CO wanted to transfer the whole of his HQ to that city, now that most of the work south of and around Rome had been completed, and also because the bulk of the help given by civilians and partisans was in the mountains north of Florence or in the Plain of Lombardy. Eventually, however, the plan for such a complete removal was abandoned, for one reason because it was necessary to keep in constant touch with the British Embassy and with various Italian government departments and the Vatican. It was also partly on account of our civilian personnel, now thoroughly trained, but unable or unwilling to move their homes up north. It would have taken far too long to train new clerks in the complicated task of claim-processing and related matters, and in the inscribing of certificates, which was done by four or five Italian girls, who wrote a really beautiful ornamental script.

Nevertheless, the important and most numerous claimants were now nearly all in the upper half of the country and so the CO decided he would spend a good half of his time there, going round the sections and investigating the possibilities of an extension into Austria and other places. Pending the removal of any other 'bodies' from the HQ, I was naturally enough Victim No. 1. I say 'victim', for as time went on it became increasingly noticeable how officers and other ranks 'kicked', some quite volubly, when ordered out of the Eternal City. Rome seemed to exert a fascination over people, rather like a vast magic labyrinth – once you were there, you never wanted to leave, whatever the consequences. And so, on this occasion, when the CO told me I must be prepared to leave for Milan at any moment, although I had not the slightest doubt that from the job point of view it would be far more interesting and fruitful to go north, I was no more desirous of a transfer than I had been a year previously, when posted to Naples. In fact, I regarded myself as 'sentenced', but realising that from now on leave might well be out of the question for me, I took the opportunity of asking for a week off, not having had any leave since my return from home four-and-a-half months before. This was not at all long by overseas standards, but I reckoned, and it proved correct, that once I really got into the swing of the job, there would be no leave unless I wanted to throw in my hand, something that I was unlikely to do unless dismissed. It was already far too interesting for me to think of applying for anything else, and well worth any loss of leave or days off.

To my surprise I was granted the leave, which I had only half hoped for, and set off on 7 April, Palm Sunday, for Florence. I was quite exhausted, having attended an ORs' dance and then having been invited to the sergeants' mess the previous evening, not to mention leaving everything in order as far as possible in the office. I did my packing during the night, and was somehow ready for the road next morning at a fairly reasonable hour. I stayed the first night at our section in Florence and thought it the most beautiful place I had yet seen – and that was saying a lot after Naples and the Sorrento Peninsula. The section was not exactly in Fiesole, but on the road ascending towards it.

It was late afternoon when we reached Florence and the air was perfumed with the scent of flowers. Huge garlands of wisteria were draped from many of the houses and balconies, and I noticed for the first time what a strong scent wisteria has. The Angelus was chiming and everyone was out in feast-day garb. We crossed the city and found the road for Fiesole, after making a few enquiries. As we drove along, I noticed the roses in bloom everywhere, masses of them, red, pink, and yellow. It was more like an English June. The driver, an Italian, was loud in patriotic enthusiasm – in fact, he was enthusiastic about everything and delighted when I also enthused about his beloved Italy.

At length we came to a rather battered stone gateway and turned up a narrow drive which led to the section, which was housed in a typical Florentine villa. This property actually belonged to an Englishman, who was extremely irate at having his home requisitioned while he was spending the war in Switzerland. He had left his butler and factotum as caretaker and to keep a watching brief on the unwelcome occupants (we were not the first allies there: Americans and Canadians had preceded us, and before the Allies, the Germans had not allowed such a beauty-spot to remain unoccupied). From all I heard about the owner and his butler-spy, they were not the sort of people to derive much joy from other people's pleasure, but I think that nearly all our men and women loved this villa and thoroughly appreciated its harmonious beauty. To me, it was really quite a fairytale place, with its cool distempered rooms, elegant furniture (what had been left), its piano, its small stone courtyard and above all its garden, with a lily-pond on the terrace in front of the dining-room window, its rambling roses of different colours, syringa and guelder roses. From the magnificent terrace, one could survey the entire city of Florence and in the immediate foreground other villas lower down, some of them wreathed in freshly blossoming creepers and shrubs; then again, its lower garden, with potting sheds and goldfish ponds, flowers, vegetables, vines and cypresses. There was quite a lot to explore, all encompassed by high stone walls. High stone walls like these, which seem to surround all Florentine villas, always mystified me, and I longed to place a small ladder against them and peep over to see what was happening on the other side. From beyond the walls, one could have hardly any idea of what was going on inside the grounds of our villa.

In April 1946, it seemed to me that everything was at its best. Olive trees clothed the slopes below us, and above us too, where the ground rose a few hundred feet more, towards Fiesole and Vincigliata, the castle from which General Carton de Wiart and five other British senior officers escaped in 1943. I remember the mystery which surrounded his escape, when it was said that the Italians allowed him to make a getaway in order to bring an offer of armistice terms on behalf of the Italian Army, who were tired of fighting with the Germans. Whether or not this is true, and in the light of more recent events it seems unlikely, no-one was supposed to know of his return to the UK. When he inspected us shortly afterwards at my unit in the UK, we were merely informed that an 'unknown general' was coming. By a sort of bush telegraph, however, his identity was quickly established and most people knew whom to expect, though his eye covering and his VC were in any case unmistakable distinguishing marks.

The castle of Vincigliata looked attractive enough from a distance, with its battlemented walls and towers – I felt it would be almost pleasant to be confined to such a spot, if imprisonment was to be one's lot. In the early morning the scene was bathed in sunlight and dewdrops. The olives seemed like silver daubs on the grey-green slopes, interspersed here and there with the black figures of watchful cypresses or the crenellated towers of the scattered villas. The roofs of Florence and the high octagonal towers of the Duomo and the Baptistery were lit up cosily by the morning sun. And on our terrace it was delightfully warm, but not too hot.

I did not on that occasion see much of the work of the section, as I arrived on Sunday evening and left on Monday morning. In any case, the staff, apart from the admin officer who was nearly always present, were mostly out paying or investigating, only returning to collect fresh lists and stock up with food and petrol. The admin officer supervised everything at the section, aided by a sergeant who helped to interview any claimants and looked after the correspondence. There was also an Italian typist, whom I did not see.

The drive up north was uneventful and I renewed my acquaintance with the delightful willow and poplar country of the Plain of Lombardy, and so on to the marshland near Venice. I spent a few days in Venice, resplendent in its 'Easter Bonnet', and visited among other places the glass-making island, Murano, reminiscent of Holland with its inland waterways, small houses with curved roofs, and be-clogged inhabitants. We passed the sea-girt cemetery, with its dazzling white walls and tombs, and drank in the pure air of the lagoons and the exhilarating sea breezes, cradled in a rocking gondola on the blue sea. I had met up with old friends in Venice, on their way home, en route for Villach, but I did not envy them. We had a jolly reunion and I wished them Godspeed and good luck for Civvy Street, but I was personally glad to be staying and to have the chance of getting to know more of Italy, which is like the inexhaustible cruse – the more you drink of it, the more you want, and yet there is no end to what it will yield to the thirsty one.

The last two days of my leave were spent at the officers' rest hotel at Cernobbio, on Lake Como, whence I had managed to scrounge a lift, and my main memory is one of masses of pink, blue and mauve hydrangeas, more wisteria, lilac, roses, of course – in fact a whole carnival of flowers – and Lake Como in spring must be one of the most charming of all places. The little white houses with their freshly painted shutters looked dainty and inviting, and soft breezes stirred the lake into small ripples.

Everything was light and airy – but I barely tasted this Eden-like atmosphere. On Whit Monday I phoned my CO, who gave me permission to remain there for the day, but I had to report for duty next morning. I had managed to get the day off for Bank Holiday, but after that work would begin again in grim earnest. I began to have a sinking feeling in the pit of my stomach, what we used to call a 'match pain' at school, and to wonder what it would be like in Milan, where I would be the only English girl at the section and would once again be planted in a strange hotel-mess, among fresh faces and have to make a completely new set of friends. I would be far more in the company of the CO than before, and would have to be continually on my toes. I began to wonder if I should live up to his known high standards, or whether I should beat an ignominious retreat, accompanied by a confidential letter to GHQ, as one or two others had already been known to have done.

But I tried to banish such qualms from my mind and enjoy the last day of my leave, during which I met several friends from Milan and we went out in a boat on the lake. Everyone was very jolly and told me not to worry, so I began to think that perhaps after all things would not be so bad, and that I should somehow manage without Judy and the sergeant at the Hotel Continentale, not to speak of the Signorine Giulia, the maestro, the telephone operator in Rome, and dear old Anna, who swept out the passages and cloakroom and was always ready for a chat, and so touchingly grateful for a few lire '*per comprari una tazza di caffè*'. Her widow's pension was 1,000 lire a month, then worth about 30s after the post-war collapse of the lira, and the tragedy of many Italians at that time was that no pensions had been raised in proportion to the rise in the cost of living and the devaluation of the lira. Anna worked very hard, cleaning our offices. Her hair was greying and wispy and her face patient and careworn; she wore a plain black calico dress, coarse black stockings and an ancient pair of black slippers. In winter, this attire was augmented by an old and rather shapeless black woollen cardigan. Her expression was one of gentle resignation, but she always had a smile and a cheerful word – '*Cosa vuole, signorina*,' she would say, when discussing the current difficulties of living, '*è la Guerra*.'

27

Milano!

*I*t was exactly at 10.30 a.m. on Tuesday 23 April 1946 that I clocked in at 2.3 Section, Allied Screening Commission, situated in Via Seprio, No. 2, in Milan. The house was tall and fairly spacious with a small garden in front, now little more than a wilderness. There was a small terrace giving on to it, overgrown with creepers and convolvulus that formed a shady arbour for sitting in on the rare occasions that one had time to relax in an arbour. There was a large office where the various officers attached to the section and the acting CO had their desks, and a small admin office. Then there was a sort of anteroom (literally) which contained a Welfare ping-pong table; a small sitting room for the officers led off this, with brown stained floorboards, not much polished, and a number of somewhat faded and dingy chairs and a sofa. Next door was a dining room with a nice oak refectory table and a good dresser and chairs, and a hatch leading into the kitchen – this was the most normal and respectable-looking room of the house. Next to that was the bedroom of Luigi, the Italian cook. The offices were on the mezzanine level (i.e. between the basement and first floor), and above them, on the first floor, were the sleeping quarters. The small flat above them was inhabited by the inevitable *custode*, and was approached by an outside stairway, which I never explored. Below the mezzanine, were the sleeping quarters and mess for drivers and one or two male civilian personnel. No women lived on the premises, though an Italian woman came each day to clean, make beds and do washing.

There was an Italian waiter and general stooge, a small nervous man called Cesare, who had been interned and sent to Germany, though I could never quite discover why. But he was innocent of any crime, unless being Italian was a crime, and perhaps to the Germans it had been regarded as such. I soon noticed him, for he was everywhere, polite, obliging and always working, invariably clad in a white waiter's jacket and bow tie. His sad eyes, sometimes red-rimmed from strain, for the prison camp ordeal had left his nerves temporarily shattered, shone with devotion to duty and enthusiasm for his task. Other staff included an Italian secretary, a countess from a fabulously wealthy family, who had determined in the teeth of severe domestic opposition that she would defy tradition and work for the Allies, come what may. She was the Italian link, together with the interpreter, for the work of the section. The interpreter, Erwin, was a German anti-Nazi, who had also been imprisoned for being a freethinking schoolmaster who refused to disguise his views, and had been liberated when Germany was defeated. These two did all the many translations, drafted letters in Italian and typed them, sometimes interviewed claimants, answered telephones, and together performed an essential and important task. The only officer constantly on the spot was the admin officer, at that time a young man from the Tank Corps, affectionately nicknamed 'Zimmy', on account of his somewhat Germanic surname. Perhaps he was originally from the Teutonic lands, for he possessed some of their qualities of character, including a scientific disposition, much given to serious speculation and experiment. His main source of inspiration during my time at the section was a large box camera, about a foot square, which he would earnestly perch on a tripod, and then burrow underneath a black velvet cloth and presumably take photographs – presumably, because in spite of his various sorties with this massive photographic apparatus, and his endless discourse on its marvellous properties and potential, no-one ever saw a photograph taken by Zimmy. When I took a snap of him with my much simpler camera, a sort of cloud seemed to emanate from his head – 'his astral body', as it was jokingly described. But Zimmy rhapsodised about his machine; it was his hobby and his child, and it kept him out of mischief and everyone else amused.

The Milan Section was a very busy one, and there was a constant stream of people, officers coming in and going out on investigating and paying trips, claimants, and others passing through or merely there temporarily or on occasional routine inspections from Rome. I was not to live, or even do most of my work, in this hive of activity, but in the hotel reserved mainly for the Allied Commission, the very beautiful Albergo 'Principe e Savoia'. Apparently it was formerly 'Principe di Savoia', but when Mussolini established his régime, it became unfashionable and even unpatriotic of hoteliers to be too royal in their choice of names, and so it became 'Principe e Savoia', so that no democratic-minded person could suspect the proprietor of royalist sympathies. The hotel itself could not have changed much. It was on a great piazza, about a quarter of a mile long, with trees and green sward on either side of the road and in front of the buildings. When I arrived, the horse chestnuts were just bursting into bloom and their white candles blossomed for some time, snowy amid the bright greenery of the foliage. Lilac and laburnum bushes were also in bud, and somehow the scene reminded me of home. When we had breakfast the windows would be wide open on to the grass and towards the piazza and the sun streamed in, cooled by a slight breeze. The air was so far deliciously fresh. I was at first obliged to take a room on the inner courtyard, as the hotel was very full, but after a week or two I managed to change and was given a small room on the north-west with a glorious view away over the plain towards the Alps, whose white shining peaks I could discern on all but a very misty day, which seldom occurred. There was a balcony, and after returning from the office I often sat out on it, writing or mending, watching the sun set slowly and the mountains gradually merge into the gloom.

I was fetched every morning, either in the CO's car, or in whatever transport was available, and had my lunch at the section.

Thus my new routine was soon established, but meanwhile, on that first morning, at 1030 hours, I felt rather nervous, and wondered how it would all work out.

I was ushered at once into the 'presence', somewhat in fear and trembling, but I was received very kindly, and after a few moments put at my ease by a gin-and-lemon, for it was nearly time for elevenses. Tea was later brought in by the waiter Cesare, who of course was still unknown to me, but I noticed his neat white jacket and faithful demeanour at once. My work began within one minute of my entering the mess, which that morning the CO was using as his office until his own was properly established. Our colonel never wasted time. I was soon given some letters to take down and various papers to read and absorb, and although I had just stepped from the truck into harness as it were, I soon seemed to have the bit between my teeth and be chugging away at it. By the time that the colonel had announced that it was time for him to go home for lunch, I was left with a sheaf of letters to transcribe, telephone calls to make and arrangements for my own passage down to Rome by air next day to collect all the GSO I's files, papers and various other documents of importance.

At lunch-time a captain came in from Verona, tall and handsome, with an MC and bar (he was later awarded yet another bar to his MC). I was informed by the Contessa, who was known to everyone as Mimi, that this awe-inspiring personage was also reporting back to Rome for briefing and that he was to be my travelling companion the next day. I had lunch with him and about three others and we ate *tagliatelle alla salsa di pomodoro*. The Italian cook soon revealed himself to be adept at camouflaging Army rations. I discovered that Mimi had an enormous platterful of pasta in her office – it did not look very patrician, but in spite of her rather la-di-da English accent (she had Irish relatives), I found very quickly that she was a good sort and moreover extremely efficient, which at once commanded my respect. We were slightly suspicious of one another at first, but after a week or two, when the corners had worn off, we were on very amicable and co-operative terms, and eventually became firm friends.

After I had put a call through to Rome and tasted the '*sistema telefonico milanese*', I checked in at the hotel, was allotted a room and did some unpacking. Later, with Mimi, I went to the Allied Commission HQ, a huge block, almost a skyscraper, in the centre of the city. We mounted many floors in a lift, then foot-slogged through what seemed miles of passageway, to interview an American officer in an office with various Italian personnel, some in uniform, some not. Finally, we were given a large movement order, with my name and the MC's upon it and various instructions relating to reporting to the airfield, the take-off and so on. The paper was headed 'MTOUSA', an acronym standing for 'Mediterranean Theatre of Operations of the United States Army'. The Americans were even better than the British at this word-formation business, though we did not do badly, with LIAP (Leave in awaiting Python), LILOP (Leave in lieu of Python) and other such artificial designations. It did, however, seem rather disrespectful and unimaginative that the Supreme Allied Commander should be known in this letter language as 'SAC'.

Next day, the two of us left Via Seprio at about nine o'clock and I was agog with excitement, for apart from the return journey to England in a bomber the previous year, this was to be my first air trip, and my very first in a civilian plane. We joined a motley crowd at the airport, mainly civilians, and had our baggage weighed. We were not weighed ourselves this time, for which I was most grateful, for with all my Army kit on I always seemed to touch the scales at some totally inelegant and best-forgotten-quickly figure. We found ourselves among some Italian businessmen, an odd priest or two and perhaps one woman with her husband. There must have been about twenty of us altogether. We climbed up a tiny ladder into the plane, and were made to fasten our safety belts before the plane took off. It must have been about 10.30 a.m. when we finally got away, and this was good, for it was a fine day. On a cloudy or misty day, one might wait several hours and then perhaps be told there would be no flying until the next morning. I once heard a man expostulating violently with one of the airport officials on a day when the planes were not flying and the official explained, clearly and patiently, that much as he regretted the personal inconvenience the client might be caused, the authorities were nevertheless not going to take risks with their passengers' lives, and that it was better to arrive a day late than not at all.

Our companions were almost all talkative and friendly. As we climbed higher it became extremely cold and I was glad of my greatcoat and a rug. After about two hours we passed over Lake Bracciano, like a great jewel below us, and were soon within sight of Rome, and then flying over the Vatican, which glowed the colour of yellow ochre in the midday sun, and looked hot and dusty. The whole of St Peter's was spread out before our eyes like a parchment map, and beyond it Rome, its streets, parks, gardens and monuments all clearly revealed as on a scroll. We crossed the entire city and finally hovered over a landing ground where there was much evidence of war damage, such as twisted hangars and burnt-out buildings, interspersed with piles of rubble, all clearly visible from the air – but one could also see the cheering signs of reconstruction going on. Soon we were bumping along the grass runway, while people came dashing towards our plane and a luggage wagon was driving up in our direction. My ears were uncomfortable and I felt stiff, tired and hungry, and so after we had descended from the plane I was sincerely glad to hear an Italian voice hailing us, '*Buongiorno, Signore Capitano, Signorina, buongiorno*', and then, '*E qui, la macchina, dove esta loro bagaglio?*' ('The car's here, where's your luggage?') It was one of the commission drivers, sent out to collect us, and soon we were out of the mutilated airport and racing through the rather untidy suburb traversed by the aqueduct, so familiar to me from my Cinema City days. This suburb, with its crowds of peanut vendors and others displaying their wares in the open, and hordes of cheery, grubby children, and windows draped with washing flapping against shell-marked walls – all this had not changed. I felt a sort of warm, comfortable feeling at being back in Rome, although I dreaded the next day and a half. But returning was like coming home.

Meanwhile, present danger claimed our attention as we were driven at alarming speed through the crowded streets of the city, past the angry batons of police on point duty, round corners – almost on two wheels – and in and out of lines of trams, lorries, bicycles and all sorts of vehicles, both military and civilian. Occasionally, another driver would hurl invectives at our man in dramatic Roman or sometimes in caustic Cockney, Irish or Scots, and he would reply volubly in equally strong terms to his own countryman, or shrug and smile if cursed by an Ally – he never seemed to know more than the world 'Sorrrry' in English. One of our drivers was wont to turn round after such verbal skirmishes and report on it to his bewildered passengers, while the steering wheel somehow kept its course; or he would lean far out of the side window, bellowing abuse at a motorist who irritated him. It was all part of the game. Melodrama is part of everyday life in Italy – and very often drama too.

I was in the office all that afternoon and all the following day – it was just one hectic rush – and in between I did all my own packing and said a few goodbyes, including one to the dear Signorine Giulia, who gave me an address of relatives in Milan to look up, with many good wishes for my new environment. I was up early the next morning and 9.30 a.m. found the MC, Patrick and myself once more on the airfield, milling around the enclosure – very like a sheep pen – where expectant passengers passed their time. We were gazing somewhat casually at our fellow travellers and wondering how much longer we should have to wait before our names were called out over the loudspeaker, and together with twenty or so other people, be emplaned, our baggage stowed and ourselves strapped down. On this occasion there was some mix-up for we were not travelling in the same plane; in fact, I nearly got left behind, not having recognised the pronunciation of my name over the megaphone, but Patrick managed to get me to my plane just in time, a small twin-engine Savoia-Marchetti, with only a few travellers. It was so tiny that there was hardly room to get in at the aperture which was in place of a door, and I felt very dubious about it all. But the flight went well, I duly chewed gum and sucked fruit drops (both of which were sup-posed to be good when flying) and I met Patrick at the other end.

That evening there was a small reception in the mess, to which the CO's wife, newly arrived from the UK, was invited, along with one or two civilians, an Italian police chief and an English girl, looking very smart in black taffeta. I was quite startled at the way this girl quipped our colonel – none of the girls working for him would have dared to do such a thing. The evening was very pleas-ant and I began to think I should enjoy life in Milan.

Next day, I was back at work with a vengeance, and was slightly disappointed when the colonel told me he had fixed up a room in his villa for me to use as an office. In practice this proved very satisfactory, as there was absolute peace and quiet and it was easy to put through the numerous telephone calls without being dis-turbed. I went back to the section, about half a mile away, each day for lunch and met whomever was there, sometimes did more work, and heard the news and gossip. In the afternoon I was back at the office again, or perhaps off to the HQ or the Consulate, or on some other errand for the CO. At about 4.30 p.m. I would be invited to have a cup of tea with his family, and was then on my very best behaviour; I found this rather a strain and was relieved when I could escape back to work afterwards. I would then usu-ally return to the section to send off my letters or hand them in to the British OR who was responsible for post, rations and other admin items. After that, I would return to my hotel to change, do the eternal chores, write letters or just chat to a new acquaintance, a SAFA girl, with whom I soon became very friendly. Through her I came to know other people in the place, and what I had thought would be a somewhat depressing period soon became quite cheerful.

Meanwhile, the work was warming up, and a few days later the CO informed me that he was going over to Verona, to visit the section there for a few hours, and expected me to accompany him. I was delighted at the prospect of seeing somewhere fresh and meeting someone new, and made the necessary arrange-ments without delay. It was now my job to order the CO's car, see that the driver was punctual and that everything was laid on when the colonel's inspections took place. This meant liaising with the officers in charge of the different sections and others, and I began to meet far more people than before. Very soon I knew at least the identity of nearly everyone in the commission, and life became progressively more varied and interesting.

28

Verona and other Peregrinations

It was on 30 April that we went over to Verona, travelling in the CO's Chevrolet, a captured enemy vehicle allotted to our commission, like the many such vehicles allotted to various other units. Who had originally possessed the 'Chev', as it was affectionately named, and how it fell into British hands, I have no idea – there were a great many of these cars about, some of them really beautiful, others much battered. The Chev had already clocked up a good many miles and had certain peculiarities, some of which manifested themselves at once on that first trip to Verona. We were not far from Brescia, when a sizzling sound came from the engine and steam seemed to be bursting geyser-like from the cap of the bonnet, where water was normally poured in. We stopped and on inspection found that the water was boiling. I had some cold water in a water bottle and this was duly consigned to the tank, and replenished several times by the inevitable small boys who seem to appear from nowhere and be only too ready to help wherever one is in Italy. There was an infuriated spluttering, and then all was quiet. After a while, however, the sizzling resumed and there was nothing for it but to stop and borrow a jug and fill up the engine as far as possible. It was then necessary to proceed at a rather gentle pace, to avoid the same incident recurring. Not long past Brescia, we came to Lake Garda and I was very impressed with its grandiose layout; and although it was a chilly

dull day, there was a magnificence about the snow-capped peaks
rising majestically behind the lake, and its waters, icy-blue with
a slight swell, tinged at the edges with long waving green reeds.

Our section in Verona was based in what had been a beautiful
modern villa, the property of a rich industrialist, but it had been
badly hit and looked rather more like a desert fort, with its high
concrete walls topped with barbed wire, piles of fallen masonry
still scattered about, and its patched windows and generally dusty
appearance. Inside, however, it was very clean and fresh – like
so many large Italian villas, it was divided into several flats, and
the offices and mess were on the first floor. There was plenty of
space for transport in the yard, which presumably had been the
beginnings of the garden. There was a nice little concrete swimming pool, but it was empty, for here as in so many places still,
water was a pressing problem and had to be used with economy.
The officers working in this section had to cover the mountainous district north of Lake Garda, such as Trento, Bolzano and
Belluno, and their work sometimes lay in the Dolomites proper.
Its scenery has since been made famous in the film, *The Glass
Mountain*, the opening theme of which echoes the many stories of our work. As in the film, so many men who came down
in planes, or worked their way north having escaped after the
Armistice, hid in the mountains and were finally shepherded over
the highest passes into Switzerland or were sometimes housed
and concealed until the end of the war. The partisans had been
well organised in the north and the assistance of Allied escaped
prisoners was one of their jobs; altogether about 2,000 of them
crossed into Switzerland, in the teeth of the Gestapo, for access to
the mountains was closely guarded and patrolled by both Fascists
and SS. Numerous certificates of thanks were issued to the peasants and others of this area, many of them sturdy mountaineers,
who had risked their lives in assisting with these escapes. And our
section at Verona dealt with them all, as well as others at Udine,
Venice, Padua and the surrounding low-lying country. Quite a
few British or American personnel had taken temporary refuge
in Venice itself, and from there and Padua, to mention only two

places, Italian men and women had been seized and imprisoned for giving shelter to an escapee of the Allied forces.

The CO had a great many matters to discuss on this brief visit: administrative problems, personnel, transport (the thorn in our flesh, for the car was always needing something, or having something stolen from it, or breaking down). The roads, although improving, were far from perfection and the out-of-the-way tracks and paths that our people often had to use were frequently so unsuitable for motorised vehicles that it was sometimes even necessary to abandon ship and go on mules or on foot. Then there were problems arising from the nature of the work itself, 'difficult' or borderline cases of helpers, special claims including the replacement of vehicles used in the escape of prisoners, dependants' claims, when perhaps the breadwinner had lost his life, and so on. I took some notes, which would later be typed, and filed any necessary information being passed on by letter or phone to the GSO II in Rome.

We were of course given lunch at the section and the head of the section produced some local red wine, frothy like champagne, and the meal passed pleasantly enough. There was always plenty to talk about regarding the condition of the country, anecdotes concerning the work, and the scenery and historic monuments, which are nearly always within easy reach in Italy. I did not join in the conversation much, being unsure of myself and a stranger to one or two of those present. But I tried not to miss anything, and to notice names, people and anything which might be of use in the future. It was fairly late when we arrived back in Milan that night, but I had thoroughly enjoyed the day. I was given a meal at the section and was then taken back to my hotel by one of the Yugoslav civilian employees, who acted mainly as driver-mechanics, but also did the few odd jobs and errands that came their way.

Next day was very busy and we worked late; the following morning the CO and I were on the move again, down to Rome by air, back to HQ. A few hectic days ensued and, finding that I was assumed to have all sorts of answers at my fingertips, I decided to give myself a mental brush-up. Things were made difficult for me, as the files were for general use and in my absence all sorts of things could happen to them, and usually did. In consequence, when the colonel demanded an important letter on policy, ten to one it was not to be found, or some unthinking person had whisked the file off to his office, perhaps to study a letter on Signor So-and-So and the Topolino, which was smashed when an Australian sergeant made a getaway in it in 1943. The filing system, as it then was, did not fulfil the expanding and developing needs of the commission, and so the CO ordered me to create a new one for his own use, mainly on policy matters, and comprehensively cross-referenced with numerous copies of each letter. This was formulated after our return to Milan a few days later, and for some months I carried most of it about with me until it became too bulky. But from then on, at least I was the only person with access to the CO's files – the disadvantage being that if a letter could not be found when a visiting brigadier was waiting in the office while I was feverishly scrabbling amid sheaves of paper next door, I was the only one responsible.

On one occasion, before the special system came into being, I went up to Rome and found the files in some confusion, and without much warning a senior officer came from the War Office to call on our CO and discuss various weighty matters with him. I was caught on the back foot, and a certain crucial letter could not be traced. My CO began to look extremely grim and my heart failed me. In a panic, I rushed over to see the admin captain on the other side of the passage, exclaiming, 'Mark, I can't go back, I can't find the beastly letter, whatever shall I do? I'm sure he'll sack me now, oh dear, oh dear, mamma mia!' etc. 'Pull yourself together, old girl', he said heartily, 'Keep calm, go in there with your chin up and let them see you don't care a fig for them, and tell them you just haven't got the ruddy letter.' I could not help laughing at this horrific lack of respect, but he cheered me up and with more such good advice, I quickly plucked up courage enough to brave the presence once more. With infinite tact, neither senior officer referred again to the missing link and I breathed a sigh of relief. But it did not prevent me from passing a perfectly miserable lunch-hour and confiding in the finance officer, Phoebe, that I was sure I would not last much longer!

The journey back to Milan after this first trip by air with the CO was uneventful, except that our names were so curiously mispronounced and distorted by the airport megaphone that we had to be called several times before we emplaned. After a tot of Kümmel, prescribed by the CO to warm me up, we took off. On arrival back in Milan, we found that there was a minor revolution going on in the Milan City Prison. Some prisoners had escaped, stolen arms and barricaded themselves in one wing of the prison, holding some of their guards as hostages. The *carabinieri* were fighting the rebels inside the prison enclosure, employing Bren carriers, and the main doors of the prison were shut to prevent intrusion from outside. Wild tales were circulating and from Via Seprio it was quite easy to hear the rat-a-tat-tat of machine-gun bullets. One or two jocular spirits in the mess told me it was not safe for English women and that I would have to return to Rome. I soon referred the matter to the colonel and told him that on no account did I want to be sent away from my job. He smiled and told me he thought it was quite safe for me at present – which it most certainly was, as everyday life, though quiet, was going on more or less as usual in the city. Milan seems to be a place of minor revolutions and uprisings, and the inhabitants take these manifestations as a matter of course. Later on, when an angry demonstration was staged outside the Excelsior Hotel, housing British officers, and all British personnel were ordered to go about armed, I was escorted to and fro for a few days in a jeep with a sergeant, a private and an Italian driver. Complete with my tommy-gun and my Luger, we sped through the almost deserted streets, but to my intense disappointment we might have been in Bayswater for all the excitement we met with, and the danger period soon passed off. This was doubtless due to the very efficient police of the city, trained after the method of the London Metropolitan Police – and incidentally keen footballers – and also to the stabilising presence of the still considerable body of Allied troops. As usual, the British were warned off the streets when trouble was brewing, and as there was no one much to pick a quarrel with, the troublemakers soon calmed down and dispersed.

As time progressed towards the middle of May, the weather became delightfully warm and at midday it was really hot by English standards. The chestnuts were in full bloom now and lilac, laburnum and other flowering shrubs made our piazza more delightful than ever. After dinner in the evening, one could sit very pleasantly out of doors, enjoying the fresh night air. I met at this time a friend now out of the Army and back with his pre-war business. He was almost a Milanese, having lived there for years, and he not only spoke the language perfectly, but also knew the city thoroughly and had completely adapted himself to its ways and the prevalent mode of life. One evening, he introduced me to a business associate and we all three visited a café in the vicinity and sat outside until nearly midnight, just sipping coffee, chatting and watching the passers-by, and enjoying the mild climate. That, Theo said, was the correct thing to do in Milan and later on, when passing the Galleria at night, I saw that the cafés were crowded and it was difficult to find a seat. In our quarter, near the station, it was quieter and the cafés were not as crowded as in the centre, of which the Galleria seemed the hub.

On 17 May that year an important ceremony, as far as the commission was concerned, was due to take place in Rome. There was to be a public presentation of Alexander Certificates to Roman helpers, similar to the ceremony held in Milan a few months before, but on a grander style and in Rome, with more important personages present. I motored down from Milan with our CO and his wife and we spent one day in Florence, as the CO wanted to inspect the workings of the section there. I stayed at the section proper, which I much preferred; in this way, I could use the office for my typing and in any spare moments could drink in the view from the terrace or wander in the magical garden.

On our way down from Milan, we had stopped for a snack in Parma and had sat at a table in the square, where there were various cafés with chairs and tables in large numbers in front of them and gaily striped parasols to ward off the midday sun, which was excessive. The CO's wife knew Italy and spoke Italian like a native – and she told me I should eat a salami sandwich. Until then, I had only heard of salami and had no idea what it was, except that it was regarded as an Italian national food. So I tried it in a roll and discovered it to be a sort of very richly flavoured sausage, with a strong admixture of garlic, whose pungent odour lingered in the mouth for some time afterwards. I did not like it much at first, but became used to it after visiting more Italian houses and encountering it on almost every occasion – sometimes in larger sausages than elsewhere, but always with the same pungent taste and odour. If I had tasted it in 1944, no doubt I would have reeled back in horror, but by now I was getting acclimatised to Italian food, and even salami was not too great a shock.

The Florence mess put on a very nice dinner party for the CO and his wife and I was made to sit next to the former. 'You know what to talk to the Old Man about,' they said (I had long since discovered that colonels, whatever their age, are all referred to as the 'Old Man'). In point of fact, I always tried to avoid sitting next to my boss, as I was sure he must have seen quite enough of me in the office, and had not the slightest interest in prolonging more than necessary our official relationship outside office hours or travelling time. However, he was always very kind to me, even if a trifle grim at times, but one expected that of a CO anyway. On this occasion, though, he was in a rather morose mood, I did not know why, and when I found myself again sitting next to him on the mess sofa after dinner, he was toying with a glass of port and talking of the way in which he was wont to deal with inefficient officers and how quickly they could be given the sack. I immediately felt a twinge of conscience and felt sure this must be a prelude to my downfall. So apparently did everyone else, for after the colonel and Mrs Colonel had left, the others came round and patted me on the shoulder and said encouragingly, 'There, there, old girl, never mind, it can happen to anyone' or, 'We'd better say goodbye now, let's have a drink on it', and other such soothing remarks. I felt very uncertain of myself for a little while to come, and concluded that I was not doing my job properly; and I thereupon took stock of the situation, decided how improvements could be achieved and set about making myself more thorough and efficient from then on. I hoped the effort succeeded, but there was plenty of room for improvement.

On our way down to Rome from Florence we had the inevitable engine trouble with the Chev. We managed to limp as far as a small village – Certaldo, I think, was its name – where the sign '*Teléfono*' seemed to provide the answer to our troubles. I was instructed to get on the line to Rome and ask the mto (Mechanical Transport Officer) to send out a vehicle to meet us, as it was very doubtful that we would make it to Rome as things were. I entered the small office and saw a dark shiny-haired Italian, with a small clipped moustache. He was behind a counter in a clean and freshly distempered room. This gentleman smiled brightly and said, '*Buongiorno, Signora*.' '*Si pùo teléfonare?*' I asked, really only querying to be polite. '*Non, Signora*,' he replied. I repeated the question, thinking I must have been misunderstood: '*Si pùo teléfonare?*' '*Mi dispiace* (I am sorry) *Signora, ma non si pùo teléfonare*.' But how ridiculous, I was thinking. '*Ma perché?*' (why?), I asked him indignantly, '*Ecco*!!' (an expressive word, adopted to a great extent by the Forces, meaning, 'there you are!') And I motioned him triumphantly to the door and pointed to the smart blue-and-white sign, 'it says, "Telephone".' But my friend had the last word: '*Si, é vero Signora, ma non ci sono le linie!*' he countered, smiling broadly (that's right, Madam, but there are no lines), as I looked at him in disgust and then said good day, shrugging my shoulders, and went back disconsolately to the car. We limped on once more, marvelling at what sometimes seemed to be the comic opera of everyday life in Italy – it was so typical to put up a smart new sign saying '*Teléfono*' before the lines had been laid – but how optimistic also!

Eventually we reached Poggibonsi, and there I went through a veritable ordeal on the public telephone, when I put through a call to Rome and had to yell so that probably the whole street heard me asking for a car to meet the CO of the Allied Screening Commission. It is perhaps necessary to explain that very few houses in these villages, even small towns, have private telephones and there are no booths as in England. Instead there is one central telephone office, where everyone goes to make their calls. This is quite a meeting place and a grand spot for the gossips, as it is almost always necessary to shout on Italian lines and thus everybody's business is clearly audible to all and sundry (and they always shout, even when it is not strictly necessary). It is all very friendly and matey, and if I had not been so harassed with responsibility when phoning about transport disasters, which was usually the case when using these places, I should have been able to derive more enjoyment from such occasions.

The Rome ceremony for the awarding of certificates was a very dignified and impressive affair; the British ambassador, the Commander of the Rome Garrison, the South African representative, Admiral Stone (Head of the Allied Commission), the American ambassador, representatives of the Italian government and the Vatican, and the Mayor of Rome, Prince Doria, were on the platform, amongst other notabilities, the complete list of which it would be too long to recall. There were a number of speeches in praise of the gallant sacrifices of those Italians who had risked so much and many of whom were now waiting to collect their certificates; and emphasising the friendship which had been cemented during the Occupation between Italians at all levels and various members of the Allied Forces. The ceremony was held in the Teatro Adriano and this great theatre was full. On the platform, behind a blaze of flowers, sat the guests of honour, behind them the British, American and Italian flags, draped artistically. At regular intervals around the theatre, the *Carabinieri* were on guard in their full dress uniform, resplendent with scarlet and silver epaulettes and cocked hats – the heritage of Napoleonic Italy. The body of the theatre was packed with Italians, many Romans, others from neighbouring or outlying towns and villages, and peasants rubbed shoulders with aristocrats. That was perhaps one of the most amazing aspects of our work – people of all classes, though possibly a majority of peasants ('*contadini*', as they are called) had unstintingly given help where it was needed, and afforded asylum to men hunted like wild beasts by Fascists and Nazis alike. Some of those who had thus been saved were among our own officers – the CO was one of them – and I think it is true to say that none had forgotten what they owed their benefactors. I am sure that of all those helped who did not write again to the men and women who assisted them, very few have forgotten, even though they may have lost the addresses in the stress of war and escape.

The Chev went out of commission for a few days after the Rome Ceremony, and the CO returned with his wife to Milan in another car. I waited for a day or two before going back by air. A short time afterwards, I received a phone call at 8.45 a.m., when I was just preparing to leave for the office after breakfast. The call was from the major then in charge of the Milan Section, and he told me I was to be ready to leave for Vienna that afternoon! A few hectic hours of getting ready followed, and we eventually left at about four o'clock and spent some hours in the Verona Section. I remember being rather tired that evening and the CO made me have a whisky – for the first and last but one time in my life. I heard him ordering three whiskies and assumed that this included myself, as there were three of us; I interjected meekly that I never drank whisky, but the only answer was a gruff, 'Well, it'll do you good!' So I drank it and perhaps it did do me good.

We left first thing next morning, on the road for Vienna, of which I had read in those happy pre-war days, but which would doubtless now be overcast with the same grey, hopeless and rather sullen atmosphere which had impressed me when I had visited Austria the year before. But tunes of Strauss waltzes hummed pleasantly through my mind and I thought, 'Surely there will be *something* left of the spirit of the city – it can't all have been destroyed by war and Occupation.' Soon we were bounding through the endless green fields, straddled with vines on posts reaching one to another in an almost human gesture, and then we were in the mountains, shut in among valleys and ravines, and crossing roaring glacial torrents over which the road passed and re-passed at frequent intervals.

When we came to the frontier, I was badly caught out – and in fact found very much wanting. The previous year things had been fairly easy there, as Italy and Austria had been under one command. Now, however, a separate Austrian command had been established – British Troops in Austria, it was called (or BTA), and of course the frontier regulations had been tightened up. The year before, no movement order had been necessary and in the haste of departure, although this trip had been mooted for some time, I had forgotten that a movement order might be required. Now, too late, I found out how stupid it was to assume that things would be the same. An MP corporal stopped the car at the frontier (the Chev once more), and asked us for a movement order. My tongue positively swelled in my mouth, as the CO looked at me and said sternly, 'Where is it?' I had to confess my failure and the corporal said, 'I'm sorry, sir, I can't let you through without a movement order – where do you come from?' But the CO was quite equal to handling the situation. His commission, though its HQ was situated in the Rome Area Command, from where a movement order would normally have been obtained for a trip of this sort, came directly from the War Office Intelligence Branch, and so he did not actually need to seek permission from Rome Command to enter Austria – he could go in his own right, though perhaps the Rome authorities would have looked on this with disapproval. Despite that, he offered to make out a movement order for the MP corporal on the spot. 'Any number of them if you like,' he said with grim humour. 'We have a typewriter in the car and you can type them now for me to sign, can't you?' he added, turning to me. 'Certainly, sir,' I replied, 'It wouldn't take a minute.' The MPs gave up and let us through, though they doubtless put a quick call through to their colleagues at the Movement HQ – but no ill came of it and we heard no more, but for subsequent journeys I was always well supplied with movement orders.

At Klagenfurt, there were various sections to be visited and staff officers to be called upon and liaised with, for it had been ascertained that a substantial number of Austrian claimants existed, though it is not generally known that a large number of our people were assisted and sheltered by anti-Nazi Austrians.

The intention had been to motor right on to Vienna, but to do so one would have had to cross the Russian zone; and at that time the Russians were beginning slowing-down tactics, placing impediments in the way of Allied traffic other than their own. We were therefore strongly advised to travel by train, and the arrangements for this were made by 'Q' movements. We had to leave that night at 10.15 p.m. for Vienna, and were due to reach the city early next morning. I was very disappointed that the journey had to be made in this way under cover of darkness, and more than a little dismayed over my baggage, which had been packed to go by car and was in far too many pieces to make train-travelling straightforward. The colonel was very sporting about it and assisted me in carrying it over the line at the almost deserted station, even hoisting a couple of haversacks on to his walking stick, which somewhat amazed me. Besides those, I had a suitcase of clothes, a typewriter and a case of papers, shorthand notebooks and other office materials.

We reached Vienna station about seven o'clock the next morning after a very uneventful journey, with no excitements provided by Russian troops as I had half expected. The CO decided it would be necessary to spend one night in Vienna, in order to pay the HQ two visits, and so we put up at the famous Sacher's Hotel, then an officers' transit mess. It was typically Austrian, and of course Viennese, with thick carpets, panelled rooms, comfortable solid furniture and double windows everywhere. The dining room was partitioned off into alcoves, rather like a Viennese coffee-house. We had some breakfast, and afterwards set out on foot for Schönbrunn Palace, then the headquarters of ACA, or Allied Commission Austria. Among other things, it was necessary to arrange berths back on the train for the following night. The appropriate officers were seen at the HQ, so that plans could henceforth be formulated for a section of our commission in Austria to deal with the large number of claims there. Both in Vienna and Klagenfurt there was plenty of concrete evidence that this was necessary, and arrangements were made with GSI to publish the announcements in the local papers that claims would be settled at a future date, after presentation, as had already been done in Italy, but much earlier. By the time the section had been established, it was reckoned, the knowledge would be propagated that helpers were to be rewarded and where possible compensated.

That evening the CO took me to have dinner at the Kinsky Palace, the Viennese home of Prince Kinsky and a magnificent baroque building, but now the usual officers' club. (The commissioned ranks did not, however, always get a palace for their clubs – the Royal Palace at Naples was the biggest and best NAAFI/ EFI ORs' Club in Italy, and the Palazzo Colonna in Rome was a very good second-best). The Kinsky Palace had a broad, winding, balustraded staircase, and upstairs a dining room and ballroom. It was all very magnificent, and I felt somewhat overawed eating under such a colossal number of opulent-looking glass and gilded chandeliers, twinkling in the lights like a forest of outsize dewdrops. The small orchestra, mostly composed of strings, was of course specialising in Viennese waltzes that evening, and I greatly enjoyed one or two with the colonel, who turned out to be a good dancer. But it was oppressively hot and sticky, especially in service dress, and I was rather disappointed when the CO said he found it too much and brought the evening to a close by saying that he wished to return to Sacher's. As I did not know anyone else present, I had of course to go home too, though it would have hardly been etiquette to stay after he had taken me there – but I was sad about the Viennese waltzes. In spite of the uniforms and the military club atmosphere, the NAAFI rations on sale halfway up the majestic stairs and all the usual trappings of organised 'welfare', the magnificence of the palace and haunting strains of the musicians seemed to recreate something of the past, which was now, I supposed, dead and gone forever. It was the past of the Empress Maria Theresa and the Emperor Franz Joseph, of the more distant past, when gallant officers danced at the Congress of Vienna, the past of Mozart, Schubert, Liszt and many other famous names in the world of politics and art – most characteristic and evocative of them all, perhaps, the name of Strauss.

Next morning I had an hour or so free to wander round the city, which appeared to be in a sorry state – there was a lot of destruction, either aerial or from bombardment or street fighting. The renowned Burgtheater had had a direct hit and was a shambles, the Church of St Stephen had also been hit, and the river area seemed to be devastated as far as the eye could see. I entered into conversation with an elderly workman, idling like me at the parapet. He told me they were desperately short of food, which was clearly evident from the appearance of the population one saw in the streets, and he said that for people living in the Russian zone of the city things were very difficult indeed. The Russians were liable, he said, to abscond with the civilians' rations, and especially with their cigarettes. Life was completely uncertain. He showed no particular bitterness, only an utter weariness and mental depression in which no spark of energy or hope seemed to light up; I suppose years of semi-starvation and the hopelessness of the present situation had taken their toll, and temporarily at least had numbed the spirit of the once gay and carefree Viennese. As in all great cities there must doubtless have always been some poverty in Vienna, but now poverty and malnutrition seemed to be the rule, rather than the exception. The workman was very friendly and very frank when he found that I could converse with him in his own language, and he gave me a most interesting first-hand account of life in the city. He was touchingly grateful for a few cigarettes. Later, I saw quite a well-dressed man stoop quickly to grab the stub of a cigarette carelessly chucked away by a passing GI. The shops were literally nothing but window-dressing, for there was next to nothing to buy. In each window of a clothes shop there might be one decent-looking article, but if you went in and asked for one like it, you would be told that it was only on display and that there were no materials available for repeating any models. I have never seen such barren shops as those in Vienna, not even in Rome in 1944, soon after liberation. As for food shops, I never saw any. In Sacher's Hotel the cooking was excellent, but the helpings were small, and there were no welcome additions to the rations like those we were now able to obtain in Italy, such as fresh salad and local cheese. Here, whatever was produced locally was essential to the civilian population, and the Army once more had to make do with its own rations, which from the vitamin point of view were excellent, but were often dull with their frequent repetition of bully beef, dehydrated eggs, tinned milk, baked beans and the usual repertoire, which with the best will in the world and the greatest skill it was not possible to vary greatly.

The colonel was very irate after breakfast that morning as an over-zealous valet, acting as batman, had apparently whitened his webbing belt, so that it was as pure as snow, whereas our CO always wore it un-whitened. As he remarked, it would now have to be continually 'blancoed' and he did not like white webbing at all. Personally, I always admired it and usually wore a white belt myself in summer, but I knew it was useless and tactless to say how nice the belt would look, and so I contented myself with remarking that the man should never have done such a thing without first enquiring whether it was desirable or not. The valet in question was a small, wizened Austrian with a friendly, ingenuous face. No doubt he had waited on archduchesses in his time – and it was impossible to be really angry with him. I was, however, detailed to inform him that everyone did not care for their belts whitened, at which he could only say he had been anxious to please the '*Herr Oberst*'. I suspected he had taken a fancy to belt-whitening as there were now no beautiful top-boots to polish till they shone like mirrors.

My main responsibility that day was to see that transport was laid on to take us to the train in the evening, and that all our papers were in order for the journey back to Klagenfurt. I had great difficulty in arranging transport to the station, for although there was a so-called 'ACA taxi service', many of them driven by ATS girls, these were much in demand and there was a considerable run on them. They had to provide all transport for duty in the city for all staff except generals, who had their own cars, and at night only a certain small number were left on to act as duty trucks, and a few for recreational transport. After much frantic phoning, I managed to obtain a share for us in a shooting-brake, which was transporting

someone else to the same train. It was to pick up its original passengers and then call for the colonel and me at Sacher's at about
a quarter to nine that evening. I had thought I was supposed to
dine with the CO, but at seven o'clock he was nowhere to be seen.
I waited half an hour and then decided that if I was to have any
food at all I had better go in to dinner alone. Wondering whatever
had happened to him, I found my way to the dining room and ate
a solitary meal, with little to see as the room was nearly empty and
tables were already being laid for breakfast. After the meal I looked
into the bar, where the previous evening the Austrian barman had
presented me with a small red rosebud, the only flower I saw in
Vienna. Tonight I knew no-one present and as there was a crowd
of men drinking there, I quickly withdrew. I had the luggage
brought down, and still there was no sign of the CO. By this time
it was 8.30 p.m. and I was beginning to get seriously worried, as
the train was due to leave at 9 p.m. Finally, at 8.45 p.m. or so, our
transport arrived in great haste to pick up its passengers and be off,
for there was little time to spare. I swore black and blue that I was
sure the CO would arrive at any moment – feeling certain that my
job depended on that transport not being allowed to go off without
us. Just as all seemed lost and the other passengers were probably
thinking that I was inventing some mythical person and deciding
to wait not an instant longer, my lost commander strode round
the corner from the direction of the Kinsky Palace in the company of a tall young guards officer, who addressed him as 'uncle'.*
Suddenly I realised that he must have been with his nephew who
was stationed in Vienna, and that my previous anxious phone calls
to locate him had of course been entirely misdirected. He seemed
very cheerful and not particularly worried about the train. We got
into the truck, waved goodbye to his nephew; the driver accelerated hard and we hurtled through the quiet streets, driving in
great style on to the railway platform, almost into the train in fact.
But the driver pulled up just in time, our baggage was unloaded,

* This was Sir Ralph Anstruther of that Ilk, son of Marguerite de
  Burgh, the CO's sister.

we climbed into the train and the whistle went. We were off – with barely 30 seconds to spare!

I had to share a sleeping berth that night with a lady from UNRRA, who said she felt extremely sick, though whether from too much celebration on account of her departure she did not disclose. She got in down the line from Vienna and promptly placed in the washbasin a bouquet of flowers given her by a crowd of friends who were seeing her off. She soon said she felt ill, but declined offers of help. Sincerely hoping she would recover quickly, I managed to snatch a few hours' sleep before she was up and dressing in preparation for leaving the train, which she did before me in the early hours of the morning, and was met by another bunch of adherents. Who she was and what she did I never really discovered, except that she originally hailed from 'Mittel-Europa' and wore bright red and white UNRRA flashes on her shoulders. Like a lot of the Occupation personnel, I was a trifle suspicious of UNRRA.

In Klagenfurt we picked up the Chev and her lance-corporal driver once more, paid a last visit to the HQ and were soon on our way back to Italy. We stopped for lunch at the club in Udine, a charming old town near the border, rather like Padua, with antique vaulted arcades along many of the narrow streets and delightful views of the Alps from all sorts of angles from its squares and alleys. The club seemed to be built on three sides of a courtyard and was clean and cool, with stone floors covered with coconut matting, plain furniture, sparse but adequate, and freshly distempered walls and white painted woodwork. The Albergo d'Italia was not so frequented by members of the Forces as the Post Hotel at Villach, which was a meeting place for so many people, going to and coming from the UK, on leave, duty and release. The Post Hotel was typically Austrian and the Italia Hotel, Italian. At the latter, one would hear the cheerful hum of Italian voices accompanying the clatter of dishes from the direction of the kitchen, and in the passages one would often meet a dark and comely Italian girl in the inevitable wedge-heeled shoes, a coloured apron protecting her knee-length dress, her hair long and flowing, humming a romantic tune as she went on her way, cleaning and polishing.

I enjoyed the visit to Austria. From the work point of view it was extremely interesting and a lot was achieved, but as an insight into conditions in the country itself it was very depressing. The people seemed despondent and hopeless, and in Vienna they looked pale and ill; certainly their prospects at that time must have been gloomy, to say the least, occupied as they were by four great powers, divided into quarters and short of all the necessities of life. Luxuries were non-existent. So much has been spoken and written about the difficulties of the Berlin population that it has been rather forgotten that the Viennese had to contend with an almost identical situation, although there was never actually a blockade imposed on the city in the same way. But out in the hinterland, in the Russian zone, conditions were the same as in Eastern Germany: removal of industrial plant and farming stock and machinery to the Soviet Union, disappearance of suspected or innocent persons, starvation of the inhabitants and a general paralysis of all community life. Perhaps by now things are better and more normal – one can only hope so, for the Austrians' sake, but their problem is still as unsolved as the German one – both are inextricably involved in the game of power politics. Meanwhile, the men and women of those areas work, suffer and wait – perhaps they also dare to hope.[*]

[*] In Vienna at that moment were also John de Burgh, then a major with the 16/5th Lancers, based at Klagenfurt; Sir Anthony Meyer, husband to LFA's best friend, Barbadee, later the MP who stood against Margaret Thatcher as party leader in 1992; Michael de Burgh, her CO's eldest son, then a captain in the 9th Lancers; and, managing a canteen for refugees, Marguerite (Madge) Anstruther of Balcaskie, her CO's sister.

29

Italian Summer

*S*hortly after our return from Vienna, towards the end of May, I was up in Rome again with the CO and this time, the work over, we left by car for Milan early one morning, setting off at 5 a.m. In order to be ready for this timely start, I asked the night porter to call me, which he did, with some strong tea made in a coffee pot. It was always a rush being ready on time; on one occasion the CO arrived early to pick me up, causing consternation to the Italian night porter and his assistant, and not least to myself, but the porter helped me to finish my packing and I was soon ready.

It is a wonderful drive in the early morning, through the deserted silent streets of the city, still cool and shadowy before sunrise. We took Route 2, the ancient Via Cassia, past the ancient city of Viterbo and later past Montefiascone, a small walled grey stone town on a hill, with a long narrow drive mounting up to it. It is said that long, long ago a bishop was making a pilgrimage to Rome and being very thirsty, stopped at what is now Montefiascone for a drink. The water was so perfect that it seemed to the bishop like wine and he christened the place Montefiascone. Later on, it also became known in Italy for its wine, though not of course like the internationally famous wines such as Orvieto, Capri or Chianti. I dozed off, to awaken as we sped swiftly along the edge of Lake Bolsena, now shimmering in the morning light, for the sun had slowly crept over the hills to the east and was bathing everything in its pinkish early morning glow. We climbed up and up, through wild and barren scenery, culminating in the Norman keep of Radicofani Castle, a forbidding reminder of the inter-state wars of the mediaeval and Renaissance periods in Italy. We then descended the winding road until we reached the olive groves again, and the softer countryside and square, red-roofed farmhouses heralded the approach of Tuscany. I went back to sleep, jolting along in the back of the Chev with the baggage, a parcel of dry sandwiches and a cold rissole on my knee. (I never understood why the Hotel Continentale always included cold rissoles in their haversack rations, but they must have been familiar to hundreds of officers, who must have found them equally unpalatable, though Italian children usually liked them!)

I awoke to the blare of trumpets, and starting up and looking out of the window saw to my utter astonishment horsemen clad in mediaeval dress, with broad-brimmed plumed hats, swirling purple cloaks, high boots and spurs, and protected by gleaming breastplates. They were blowing trumpets and horns as they galloped through the narrow grey streets of the town that we were passing through. We did not at all seem to belong to the picture, which was that of several centuries earlier, and I wondered for a moment if I were dreaming, or if I really had been here before. The virile music of the trumpets stirred the blood, and the charging horses, magnificent beasts caparisoned with almost oriental splendour, gave one a strange thrill. I gazed in admiration at the horsemen's brilliantly coloured cloaks – purple, petunia and scarlet; and then suddenly it dawned on me – it was the *Palio*, that ancient Sienese festival, a sort of tournament modelled on those of old and a custom handed down from generation to generation. It was held each year in Siena, twice – I remembered that someone in Rome had murmured that some seats had been offered to our commission – and this must have been some form of dress rehearsal. The cavaliers vanished in a cloud of dust and we emerged from the narrow street, flanked by high shuttered houses, for it was still early, and passing under an ancient gateway, came out into a broad modern road. Soon we were once more on the highway, hurrying towards Florence, through that lovely Tuscan countryside, with its cypresses, olives and chateaux on the hills – usually low grey houses, with a battlemented tower, doubtless a lookout for marauding bands in earlier centuries, and doubtless also utilised for similar lookout work during the recent war. These Tuscan farmhouses or *castelli*, somewhat after the style of the English manor house of earlier times, are nearly always on the summit of a hill or rising, and stand out as a landmark surveying the surrounding country. Sometimes an avenue of cypresses leads up to them.

We lunched at the Florence Section that day and a brief conference took place with the CO; there was always some business to be done. Then we pressed on, through the wild country of the Futa Pass, towards Bologna. Halfway between Florence and Bologna, in the midst of this rugged landscape, stand the ruins of what had once been the small village of Pianoro, nestling on the hillside. Now not one house was left erect. All except one were piles of dust, rubble and odds and ends of bricks and wood. No-one lived here anymore; the place was deserted, except perhaps for an occasional hen or a stray cat, scavenging in the rubbish. Pianoro was the name of this spot – known as the 'Cassino of the North'. Its name seemed almost symbolic, so near is Pianoro to '*piangere*' in Italian – to weep or lament. It was a place to lament about, for little could be done to rehabilitate it. Nothing could be repaired – a fresh village would be necessary. And where were the materials to come from? I never saw it reconstructed. It was always a ghastly, untended wound of war, one of the worst in all the tragic devastation of Italy's countryside. Perhaps now there is a new Pianoro, just as there is a new Cassino.

In Bologna, we stopped for a few moments before undertaking the flat run over the Plain of Lombardy, back to Milan, which we reached at about eight o'clock. On a subsequent occasion, when the CO had kindly given a lift to an Italian, the brother of the owner of the ASC's requisitioned hotel in Rome, I found it necessary to 'disappear' in Siena. But ladies' cloakrooms, except in the very modern hotels, were unheard of in Italy, and after a prolonged search I was so terrified that the CO would be fuming to get on with the journey that I finally stopped a respectable-looking woman in the street, explained my dilemma and begged for help. She kindly offered to take me to her own home, which fortunately was very near – a tiny flat, rather dark, but fresh and clean. I was extremely grateful, and presented her with a packet of ten Goldflake cigarettes to prove my gratitude, which she said would be very acceptable to her lawyer brother. When I eventually arrived back at the car, the Italian stood looking completely mystified and the CO frankly angry, but I kept a stiff upper lip and made the best of a bad job!

On that occasion we had lunch in Bologna at the famous Pappagallo Restaurant, whose charming proprietor and his family did much of the work themselves – and their food did them great justice. The *Signor Padrone* always took the orders himself and has various '*specialités de la maison*' which he recommended personally. The walls were lined with photographs of persons, well-known and otherwise, who had frequented the Pappagallo and found a real welcome there. It was my first visit, but I was to know the family better later; during a strike, when the waiters in accordance with union instructions were unable to do their work, the family took over, and cooked, served and washed up themselves.

Something went wrong with the car on the day we were transporting the Italian gentleman to Milan and we were obliged to spend two hours of an intensely hot summer afternoon in Bologna. As usual between two and four, the streets were more or less empty, and all the shops closed. I could find no better amusement than to climb the tallest of the leaning towers of the city, the Torre degli Asinelli, which measures 318ft and is 4ft out of perspective, which latter fact gives the tower a distinct lurch when seen from a distance. The other tower, the Torre Garisenda, is 7ft out of perspective! I had realised that the Torre degli Asinelli would be something of a climb, but had not at all imagined it to be as stiff as it proved, especially in the prevalent heat. Once started, however, obstinacy made me determined to get to the top, which I eventually did, puffing like a grampus and with a dreadful stitch in my chest. The view was magnificent and far below I could see two tiny figures and others around them – the CO and Signor Trivulzio, talking to one or two Italians, I presumed. I descended gently, taking my time and reached the bottom, stopping on the stairs before leaving, to powder my scarlet nose; then, still very exhausted and my tongue hanging out, I tried to make a quick exit unobserved. But the CO and his companion were outside and looked somewhat surprised at my puffy and bloated face and sticky forehead. The Italian looked more mystified than ever and I learnt afterwards that he had remarked how curious English women appeared to be! I made a beeline for the nearest café, after a mumbled excuse and ordered '*limonata fresca con ghiaccio*' (fresh lemon with ice), and had two more in the span of a few minutes, emerging a little refreshed to find the car drawing up. I was glad to relax for a bit on the way to Milan, and was very glad indeed that Signor who was sitting in the back with me did not find it necessary to make polite conversation, but proved his gallantry by immediately offering me an American cigarette.

It was about the beginning of June that I persuaded the admin captain who was CO of the section that it was time for some form of entertainment to be organised for the handful of ORs, not to speak of the small collection of civilian personnel at Via Seprio. Eventually, everyone caught on to the idea and we got a party going, hired a little inexpensive band and turned the office into a ballroom. With assistance, we collected the refreshments from the large Army Catering Corps Section in Milan, who were most kind and helpful. The party went off very well, except that Cesare set fire to something in the kitchen. I happened to look through the hatch from the dining room during the interval, when we were all having refreshments, and to my astonishment saw that everything in the kitchen was glowing brightly, as if lit up by flames. I hurried out and found that this was in fact the case, and that some fat on the stove had caught fire and there was a fine blaze right up to the ceiling. Cesare was wrestling with the conflagration, complete with best white gloves and coat, but as he seemed to be rather ineffectual except for blackening his own garment, I somewhat unceremoniously pushed in front of him. Forgetting that I was also wearing a clean drill tunic, I somehow managed to get the blaze under control. Fortunately, just as this was happening a captain arrived on the scene and finished the matter off – the kitchen was out of danger, but everything was black, I was grubby and Cesare's white rig-out had to be abandoned for the evening. That was all behind the scenes, however, and meanwhile everyone seemed to be enjoying themselves; we had made a pleasant cocktail and Mimi was resplendent in a long red evening gown, looking very smart and *distinguée*, and doing excellent work in helping to entertain the guests. We had one more such party, but after that decided not to hold any others, as it was impossible to find anyone reliable to look after the bar the whole time. Heavy losses had been made, because Italian women helpers poured out doubles and charged for singles, and made other such mistakes – doubtless quite innocently, but highly damaging to the pockets of the officers who later had to make good the deficit. The soldiers had brought girlfriends, and some 'helpers' had also been invited, so that a dual purpose was served. In this way, I met Signora Merla, the gallant little woman who sheltered a British officer in her house, and also threw a bomb at the German RTO's office in Milan Station. When she heard that she was under suspicion, she rushed out and had her hair dyed. The Gestapo did eventually catch her and she was in prison for a few months, but fortunately escaped in the end-of-war confusion. She was extremely grateful for the modest sum the commission was allowed, according to its directives, to pay her, although with the cost of living as high as it was, the money cannot have gone very far.

One hot summer afternoon, just after lunch, the alarm was given in the mess; as it happened I had been back to my hotel and was just returning to the unit for post or messages. As I ascended the short flight of stairs to the mezzanine, I realised that something was up as voices were shouting rather excitedly and downstairs a small group of civilians were standing earnestly discussing something of importance, while a police car had drawn up outside and the engines of several other vehicles appeared to be running. As I neared the top of the stairs, I was nearly bowled over by the captain and his two Yugoslavs, hastening downstairs and, as far as could be seen, armed. This impression was soon confirmed, for closely upon their heels followed Zimmy, his black beret straight and purposefully placed square over his eyes, his head down and a tommy-gun clutched in one hand. I inquired what was the matter, but received only a grim monosyllabic reply, which conveyed nothing. In the distance I could hear the captain issuing sharp commands and Tom and Bertie (the Yugoslavs) answering eagerly '*Si, Signor Capitano, subito Signor Capitano, va benissimo Signor Capitano*,' while the noise of engines being revved up rose to an angry crescendo.

I hurried into the office and was told by Mimi that the CO's Lancia, a small section car used by the CO in Milan, as it was handy and used little petrol, had been stolen in the lunch-hour in spite of the presence of a *vigile*, or Italian policeman on point duty outside the section. This was serious, for it meant that *possibly* the *vigile* might have turned a blind eye, though that seemed hardly probable in view of the well-known efficiency of the Milan police and the loyal help and co-operation they had always rendered us. More likely the *vigile* had turned in for a word with the *custode* and the practised thieves had driven off in a span of a few seconds, while his back was turned. Doubtless the coup had been carefully planned and a close watch had been kept on all movements at the section, so that the most favourable moment might be chosen, and this was certainly the quietest hour of the day, when everyone was indoors after lunch, sheltering from the intense midday heat.

As Mimi and I were discussing all this there was an appalling screeching of brakes and clutches, punctuated by shouts, which attracted us both to the window, where we were soon joined by Cesare, Tina and Aldo, all very excited. Below us, all available manpower was crowded into the several vehicles of the section, about two jeeps and two trucks and a car, and all seemed to be armed in some way. The shrill voices of several small children who were watching the goings-on with keen interest added to the noise and general excitement. Now with a protracted grinding of brakes the contingent was off, and disappeared in a whirl of hot dust, leaving a growing crowd of spectators all airing their various opinions, illustrating their points with many decisive gestures at the same time.

Mimi shrugged her shoulders, saying, 'They'll never find it – it's a wild goose chase.' Her use of English idiom was almost impeccable. But she was right; later in the afternoon, a disillusioned and thirsty group of men returned, and not a trace of the Lancia had they uncovered. Even the efforts of the Chief of Police did not clear up the situation; the vehicle had gone, literally lock, stock and barrel. When the tension was over, and the loss philosophically accepted, the necessary Court of Enquiry held and all the numerous forms filled in, there was suddenly one day a telephone call from the Vigilanza Urbana or Central Police Station. The torso of the car had been found – wheel-less and robbed of everything of any value. On the front seat was a rude caption: 'With compliments to the British'. The Lancia had been discovered abandoned on some waste ground in the suburbs of Milan. The guilty persons were never caught and brought to justice. It was just another instance of the pitting of wits sharpened by the rigours and restrictions of war and Occupation against the forces of law and order. But for us at the section it was an anti-climax: a running battle, even if it had caused the car to be pitted with tommy-gun bullets, would have been a far more delightful and interesting experience, and doubtless the Italian *Celere*, or Flying Squads, becoming very noisy and active at that time, would have been only too pleased to have joined in. It was a disappointment, but one soon healed by time and the pressure of events.

One Sunday that summer I was able to go over on a visit to Turin. We were going to see a German driver mechanic, attached to our unit, who had recently been seriously injured in a motor

crash and taken to hospital in Turin. We found him comfortable
and well cared for and then went to call on an Italian colonel,
a friend of the Allies. We stayed half an hour or so and saw a
large number of dogs, for the colonel was interested in breeding.
Later we partook of a glass of vermouth in the Salotto, whose
windows were closely shuttered to keep out the noonday sun.
Next we went on to lunch with Susan, who was working for the
American Consulate in Turin, and some other consulate girls,
mainly British. Susan had had a tough time in the war, having
been interned by the Italians and not always kindly treated. She
had escaped in the end and made her way to Vatican City, where
she joined the Rome Organisation and performed very useful
and dangerous work, organising the escapes of other people,
military and civil. She was pretty, gay and charming and it was
hard to imagine her in a grim concentration camp, or fleeing and
hiding for her life – but she had experienced just that, and risked
death in finding her way to the Vatican. The English girls she
lived with probably did not know her history, as it was through
men who had been in the Vatican with her that we had heard it
and she never mentioned her escape; indeed, despite her terrible
experiences, she seemed without a care in the world. So we had
a cheerful lunch party and sat in the sunny garden afterwards,
where creeping roses enshrined the house, and large purple
clematis peered exotically from the walls. On that occasion Turin
appeared to me to be a beautiful city – clean and spacious, embel-
lished with trees and gardens; and as a backdrop to it all the high
Alps, very near and white and sparkling, against the fresh green
of the foothills. We went back to Milan in the late afternoon,
crossing a wide and roaring torrent, grey like glacial rivers, and
I noticed the brilliant green of the trees, which by midsummer
would almost certainly have lost their pristine freshness.

I was by this time beginning to discover that Milan had its own
charm and advantages, outweighing in some ways even those of
Rome. All 'Milanesi', either born or by adoption, of course consider that their city is unsurpassed and are rightly proud of its
historic monuments, its Scala Opera House and the fine modern

parts of the city. But Milan is primarily an industrial city and therefore has similar problems to all modern industrialised areas: unemployment, shortage of housing and poor quality accommodation for many workers, lack of money and, in the days of the Occupation, often lack of food. At one time, the *sindaco* (mayor) personally went out into the country to ensure supplies for the city in order to avert civic disturbances, which were not unnatural in the dislocated state of Italian industry during the immediate post-war period. Although shortages and other difficulties tended to make Milan a fertile breeding ground for Communists at that time, the Milanesi seemed to be hard-working, honest and patriotic, with the odd exceptions, of course – but Communism is unlikely to gain much serious ground in a country as intensely and fervently patriotic as Italy. '*L'Italia*' is almost a religion for Italians, and '*pro patria mori*' no mockery, but a religious creed. They did not fight in the desert, because they were not fighting for Italy, but for their traditional enemies the Germans, and their own leaders lacked cohesion and inspiration. With the right leaders and a cause they feel to be just and patriotic, Italians are probably as brave as anyone else – the achievements of the partisans and the Committee of Liberation testify to this.

Sometimes of an evening we would go down to the rowing club, of which one of our section was an honorary member, to see what was going on. It was a great social centre, where we could boat and bathe, and at night, dance and listen to music, as well as drink some bright-green fizzy drink with a liquorice taste. The club, needless to say, was alongside the canal, as Milan has no river, and it had a terrace with tables and chairs and a large garden, where one could dance and sit among the trees, festooned with fairy lights. Occasionally we went to the other side of the canal, to a similar place, though not a club, aptly named 'Bellaria', where an excellent orchestra played. These places were not expensive, and the entertainment they provided could be enjoyed by almost anyone at least once in a while; there seemed to be far more democracy about Milan than for instance in Rome, where available pleasures tend to be mostly for those with a substantial sum of money to spend.

Meanwhile, the Scala had reopened with a special festival conducted by Toscanini, now back from America and reinstated among his fellow countrymen. It was said that he had declared that he would never conduct in the Scala again as long as the Fascists were still in power – now that they had gone, he had not delayed long in returning home and showing his enthusiasm for the new Italy. Thanks to the kind offices of the Chief of Police, who was a passionate music lover, quite a few tickets were made available to our section, and on one occasion he actually gave up his seat for me. It is hardly necessary to say that Toscanini's reception was nothing short of wildly enthusiastic. I was much amused at his rendering of *Rhapsody in Blue*, which did not prove so popular with his countrymen as his classical performances, but which people said he felt he had to play to show gratitude for the hospitality he had received while in America.

I went again, with two officers, one over from Verona and an Italian captain who was attached to ASC. I had expressed a mild desire to get Toscanini's signature, but had not really considered the matter feasible. I was therefore somewhat taken aback when my English escort suddenly appeared in the interval with an Englishman in mufti, whom he introduced by saying, 'Here is someone else who wants to get Toscanini's signature.' The man seemed very pleasant and immediately told me how he proposed to obtain the valued signature. It all sounded rather harebrained and I hesitated, but when the end of the concert came, I found my two companions only too anxious to hand me over to the stranger, and before I knew what had happened, they had said goodnight and I was being led into the purlieus of the great Opera House.

We went up a long staircase, and down a long winding corridor, and at the end was a queue. It appeared that General Mark Clark was about to be presented to the great conductor. I was horrified and told my friend that in the circumstances it was quite impossible for us to stay, but he refused to budge and seemed positive we should achieve our goal. We managed to get closer and closer, but various officials were saying that the maestro was tired, and would not see anyone else, and after the general had left, it seemed more hopeless than ever. Signora Toscanini was there, looking very stern and warding off encroachers, and certainly she had justification, for her husband *was* looking very tired. Then, just as we were beginning to despair, luckily for me Toscanini somehow spotted me and spoke a word to the man next to him. It all happened in a moment, but my companion and I were then brought forward and introduced, and I was told the maestro would be pleased to autograph my programme, if I would leave it with my address. My friend was shown the same courtesy, but I felt that because the maestro had noticed me, the only girl and the only person in uniform still present, he had not wanted to disappoint me, and had prevented my being sent away. He was so courteous and charming, no wonder I went home on air! Two days later my programme reappeared at my hotel, beautifully inscribed and with a little note from his secretary. I was more than grateful to my new acquaintance for insisting on our persevering, for on my own I could never have obtained such a prize.

Life in Milan was brightened for me by Aldo, the small, long-legged four-year-old son of the *custode*. Aldo was a regular visitor to the office, and he naturally came in for a good share of sweets and other titbits. He often came to me and asked to help and though there was not a great deal he could do, I sometimes found small jobs for him. Soon I quite missed him when he did not turn up and proffer his services, so seriously regarding me with his large, dark, solemn eyes. How grateful he was too, for the small rewards those services brought! I began to lay things aside for him and felt rather guilty if he came in and there was nothing available; a few little extras were a real treat in those days of shortages and austerity. One afternoon I was suddenly aware of a small shadow at my side as I typed. After he had stood silently and patiently beside me for some time, I asked Aldo what he wanted: '*Cosa vuoi*?' I said, without looking up from my work (what do you want?) '*Quello che ha*,' he replied simply and quite naturally (whatever you've got). On this occasion it happened to be biscuits, of which he received several with customary gratitude and offers of assistance, which mainly consisted that day in carrying letters to the post clerk for stamping and dispatch. I missed Aldo when we left – like most Italian children, he was not only helpful and affectionate, but very well-mannered and carefully brought up.

It was at the beginning of July that a public ceremony took place in Florence for the presentation of certificates to helpers in Florence and the country round about. The ceremony took place in one of the historic rooms of the Palazzo Vecchio, the ancient seat of government of the former Republic of Florence and also of the Medici dukes. The setting was perfect and the room was crowded with helpers and their relatives. The VIPs sat as usual on the platform, and included the brigadier commanding the Occupation troops in the area, the *sindaco* (mayor), Professor Pieracini, the Prefect of the Province, and others. There was a reception afterwards, and after that lunch at the section for special helpers and officials who had contributed towards organising the ceremony. There were the usual speeches, after the King's Health had been drunk and Anglo-Italian friendship toasted. Afterwards everyone congregated in groups on the terrace, chatting and discussing the day's happenings, or admiring the magnificent view of the city, pointing out the various monuments to persons like myself, only slightly acquainted with Florentine landmarks.

It must have been about four o'clock by this time and already the worst heat of the day was over and it was delightfully warm outside, even hot, but not too hot. A general invitation was extended to the CO and all members of the commission present to dinner with a distinguished *ingenière* and his wife. Eventually about six of us accepted, the rest already being bespoken and it was arranged that we should meet our hosts at a certain point in our own transport, and they would show us the way out of Florence by car to their country estate, where we would spend the evening. We duly met at about 6.30 p.m., and the sun was setting by the time we found ourselves well off the autostrada, going along a narrow road, not much more than a lane, with a burn running beside it through a wild and rocky valley, and with pastures rising fairly steeply on either side. Presently we turned a corner and came in sight of a stone-housed village, and the tower of an ancient castle rising beyond it on top of a veritable Mount of Olives. We sped through the bumpy village street, where hens scattered in our path and barefooted children smiled and waved. Then we climbed up the winding drive to the castle itself, in the wake of our hosts' car, turning round steep horseshoe bends. Soon we were at the top and dismounted and entered the lower courtyard. We ascended an antique stone stairway leading to the first floor and were greeted by a very old gentleman – we learnt later that he was ninety-three. That was the *proprietario*, grandfather of the *ingenière* and great-great-uncle of his young nephew, still at school, who was also with us.

We spent a delightful evening in this castle, kindly and hospitably entertained in true Italian fashion, with Italian food, most of it home-grown, the menu completed by home-distilled wine and liqueurs. While we were having coffee, one of our number, a squadron leader, formerly a member of the Sadlers Wells Opera Company, gave some exquisite renderings of Italian songs, such as '*Santa Lucia*', '*O sole mio*' and others, in a melodious voice. Later we danced to the gramophone, and our hostess, who was very gay and fond of company, joined her husband, also most hospitable, in pressing us to stay on, so that it was well past midnight when we finally prepared to leave this historic abode and our delightful hosts. This same castle had been the refuge of quite a bunch of our men during the fighting and even during the attack on Florence itself. They had lain hidden while German soldiers searched the whole building and the grandfather and his great-great-nephew watched, knowing that if the fugitives were discovered, they would probably all, Italians and Allies, be without more ado stood up against a wall and shot then and there. The castle was over 1,000 years old and must have witnessed many events, grave and gay, but it can have witnessed few more gallant and courageous than the heroic concealment of a large group of Allied soldiers by an old man and a boy, who held those men's lives in their hands, but preferred to risk their own.

We went back in two batches and Judy and I were in a jeep which lost the way. It then started to rain, or rather to pour, a heavy, thundery downpour, and as the jeep had no hood, we got extremely wet. So the evening finished in the early morning with somewhat of an anti-climax, but it in no way dimmed the recollection of the happy evening we had just spent; not even the acrimonious discussions as to which *was* the right way to take could do that.

Next morning an SSAFA (Soldiers', Sailors', and Airmen's Families Association) friend of mine joined me on her way to Rome on leave, and together we met the CO and his wife, and accompanied them to the opening of an exhibition of Florentine art treasure, sponsored by Professore Pieracini, the *sindaco*. The *professore* was not only a true friend of England, he was a great man, and had been imprisoned by the Fascists for daring to defy them. After the liberation of Florence, he was immediately released and reinstated as *sindaco* by the Allies. He was an enthusiast for the arts and was himself an outstanding writer, especially on the subject of the Medici family, his favourite historical theme. He had pressed our CO to attend the meeting that morning, and on our arrival he extended us a very cordial welcome and soon had the CO on the platform with all the other notables. I hoped he would not ask the CO to speak, representing the Allied Forces, as I did not at all relish the idea of having to translate a speech into Italian in front of an audience of about 200 distinguished citizens of Florence. I hoped Mrs Colonel might do it, as she spoke much more fluently than I did, and I tried to study some carved wall plaques very absorbedly and unobtrusively at one side of the room, though I feared the CO had spotted me. Fortunately he was not asked to speak, and so I escaped what would have been a nerve-racking experience. After an introduction by the *professore*, followed by a short speech by another Italian, we were all free to mingle and study the exhibits, an extremely interesting and varied collection. That afternoon we were back on the road for Milan and 4.30 p.m. found us at Bologna petrol point, where Yugoslav refugees worked in thick dust, refuelling military vehicles. Two hours later we were back in Milan itself.

Personally I was glad to be back, for I had toothache. All through June it had been getting progressively worse, and soon after the Florence ceremony it became unbearable, and long-distance telephoning was almost impossible. So the CO finally sent me, protesting somewhat, to the Army Dental Unit. When I reached it, I was told it was closed to patients until the following Monday. This was Thursday. On enquiring why, I was informed that it was in the process of being amalgamated with another dental unit, part of the retrenchment business again, and that there was a lot of reorganisation and paperwork to be done. On my pleading with the dental officer, he deigned to look in my mouth, but only to say he could find nothing wrong and that I must be imagining things. He just would not help, so I went back very disconsolately to the section.

Mimi had already recommended an Italian dentist that she knew, and I had refused to visit him, dreading treatment from an Italian, but the following day the pain was so bad that I decided that nothing could be much worse, and asked her to telephone her *professore*. My fears were certainly justified, for though the *professore* was kindness itself, it soon became clear that Italian dentists expected to inflict agony on their patients. It seemed that two teeth had to lose their nerves and after several visits and what seemed like hours of enthusiastic and excessively painful drilling, the *professore* had extracted both nerves, holding them up triumphantly for me to see, patting me on the back and telling me I was a good girl. When I complained that he was hurting me – a vast understatement – he laughed and told me jocularly that I was a fibber! Italian dentists were decidedly different from our own, both in technique and manner it appeared, but at least the visits were far from dull. The *professore* knew we were restricted for money and he never gave me a bill, but I took him plenty of good cigarettes and several bottles of Canadian whisky (every time I got a spirit ration). He seemed delighted with these, and as both had a very high value for the civilian population, who were short of such luxuries as good tobacco and spirits, doubtless they helped a great deal towards settling my obligations towards him.

He also treated one of our Yugoslavs and an Italian captain. One visit on the part of the captain was enough for him; he refused point-blank to undergo any more treatment – the drill was too much for him. Later I had infra-red treatment to ease the pain, and this followed the extraction of a wisdom tooth, which took my *professore* a quarter of an hour, struggling and heaving, employing bigger and better pincers every few moments. By this time I was on quite friendly terms with him and he would sometimes offer me a glass of vermouth or an ice at the end of my visit, which was usually the last of his day, about 6.30 p.m., when I had finished in the office. We spoke of his villa on Lake Garda, and once or twice he asked if I would like to see it. Meanwhile, I was teased unmercifully by the section, who pretended that I was infatuated with the dentist and only went to him because I liked him. I could not imagine braving the dentist's chair for any reason but dire necessity and indignantly fought off all insinuations. Finally one day I had a great shock. I was up for a few days in August after nearly two months of treatment, and the *professore* was giving me a check over. Suddenly, afterwards, as I was sipping the usual glass of vermouth, which he insisted on my accepting, he made a declaration, which righteously astonished and outraged me. He seemed very surprised at my amazement, and said he had not wished to offend. I took my departure immediately and for my last visit was accompanied by a lieutenant in uniform. Notwithstanding that, the *professore* managed to whisper in my ear that it was a shame that I did not trust him any more and various other protestations. He also begged me to use my (*my!!*) influence in assisting him to buy up a surplus Army vehicle. He greatly overestimated my importance, and though I made enquiries and did what I could, I did not achieve anything, for his case was not strong enough. At that time, only specially privileged persons had the opportunity and first choice when it came to surplus war stocks, etc., and as the *professore* had not been a 'helper' in accordance with the charter of our commission, we could not recommend him for priority. I did not see the *professore* again, which was perhaps just as well, but in spite of his ulterior motives, he was very kind and did not refuse help when it was really needed – and he gave us all many a laugh. My leg was so pulled about him and other matters that sometimes people would ask me if I had any legs left! Needless to say, about the *professore*'s 'Declaration' I said never a word. I had the last laugh that time.

30

Investigations!

*D*uring July the CO decided that he would send the Awards Officer, Judy, and me on a small investigative trip to an area near Parma, to give us some experience of that side of the work and to make some contacts for him. We were driven down by Major Girling, who was going to another town in the Plain of Lombard, and he arranged to fetch us on the way back.

We left one morning at about eleven o'clock and sped down the dry and dusty autostrada leading south. We stopped for lunch in Piacenza, a charming old-world town, its central streets crowded with traffic and pedestrians, but its side-streets quiet, dignified and with large wooden doors opening on to courtyards, and the windows shuttered to keep out the intense heat. There was a lime-green and white striped curtain in front of the restaurant door, and a small rather thirsty looking shrub in a wooden tub just beside it. Outside, sun and shade contrasted sharply like a slice cut from a large cake. Inside it was dim and cool, and there was the smell of fresh paint from some decorating work in progress.

It must have been about 3.30 p.m. when we reached Fontanellato, the village we were destined for. We turned off the main road at Fidenza, a small town on the Milan–Bologna main railway line, and proceeded inland along ever-narrower lanes with deep dykes on either side, to whose banks the knobbly roots of poplars and willows were clinging, or perhaps just a welter of long grass and weeds. There were windmill pumps here and there, and the crops seemed to be mainly Indian corn, lucerne or root crops – this was not a rice area. There were also some vines. The houses were of stone and mostly had stacks and a cattle shed or two near them.

At last we reached a tiny town, and entering the street skirted the moat of an ancient castle, which seemed to fill the centre of the town with its solid stone masonry and pointed towers, rather like those of the French châteaux. Turning up to our right, we left the castle behind and soon came to the Locale Grande, the main and only hotel in Fontanellato, which we were to make our HQ. Mine Host, we had been told, knew everyone in the village and around it, for this secluded little spot was not much more than a village built around its mediaeval fortress. We waved goodbye to Major Girling and were glad to penetrate the cool dark interior of the Locale. Soon we were chatting to the proprietor, Signor Bigi, who made one think of Figaro with his twinkling black eyes and cheerful and intelligent manner. His equally black-eyed and vivacious sister was also there, and with their help we had soon made out our programme and Signor Bigi had promised to find a pony and trap so that we could visit one or two outlying farms later on, when the cool of evening would make a drive easier and pleasanter. They showed us our rooms, on the first floor of the spotlessly clean little guest-house, and made us very welcome.

We then set off for the post office, opposite the castle, and acquired some addresses, which were ascertained by consulting the nominal roll of residents of the area. Quite a lot of information was available as to the whereabouts of the people we were seeking, as all the post office employees came to our assistance and most of them had friends or relatives of our people, or were living near them. The personal factor plays a very large part in business in Italy.

We set off in the trap at about five o'clock, and after passing a magnificent avenue of planes and sycamores, which skirted the opposite end of the town from which we had come, we proceeded along sandy lanes, still flanked by deep ditches, and sometimes also by thick thorn hedges. We were in the depths of the country and Milan and its hustle and bustle seemed a distant and almost forgotten world. There was an immense serenity about the countryside, still in the late afternoon sun, the birds chirping gently before retiring for the night and the cows plodding stolidly home to milking and rest. It seemed incongruous that in such places sorrow and privation should lurk, but so it was. One of the 'helpers' whom we had to visit was a widow whose husband had been sent to a concentration camp by the Germans for helping Allied escaped prisoners. He had never returned from the camp but had died there under the strain and brutal treatment. His widow was left with his farm to run and their two children, a boy and a girl, to bring up. Hers was a case of a 'Death Claim' and it was our job to hear her story, chat with her and elucidate some small points that were not clear in the story hitherto, after a previous investigation. Judy, in company with an Italian captain, dealt with Death Claims, and so I acted as her interpreter.

The family were all very sad and poor and hard-working. We were offered the customary glass of wine and saw the orchard outside the door, where apples were ripening and cows munching. Flies buzzed interminably and all was bathed in warm sunlight. We left feeling very quiet and serious – and then we were at our next claimant's house. He was a different proposition: a bachelor, he spoke excellent English and produced all sorts of written evidence to support his claim and had in fact worked up quite a 'case' in a very business-like manner. His small study was a typical bachelor's room, full of photographs, books, maps and papers of all sorts, with odd trinkets here and there, ashtrays, pipes, fly-whisks and a cup that had not long since contained coffee. He also had a good orchard at the back of his house. We left him after a satisfactory and friendly discussion and set off back to the village, two or three miles away.

By this time the sun was setting and we drove in past the bomb-gashed hospital which had held 600 officer prisoners of war, whose escape had evoked so much heroism and suffering for the people of Fontanellato and the surrounding country.

When the Armistice took place, the prisoners knew the great chance of escape had come and that their elaborately framed plans might at last bear fruit. The senior British officer (SBO – now our CO), had approached the Italian commandant and asked for his co-operation, in view of the changed political and military position of Italy and Marshal Badoglio's command that all Allied prisoners should be freed. The German High Command had on the other hand ordered that all prisoners should be handed over to them for transportation to the Reich. After much thought the commandant agreed to allow the British to escape, saying he would give them prior warning of the Germans' approach by ringing the prison bell. He promised to give twenty-four hours' warning, but in practice this was presumably impossible; in any case only one hour's notice was given. But one minute after the alarm had sounded, the parade ground was filled by men drawn up in the marching order of a German battalion and after one minute more the last man filed out, with the SBO bringing up the rear. The formation of a German battalion was chosen in the hope of deceiving air reconnaissance or possibly even motorcycle patrols. The ruse was successful; though some of the 600 were picked up later by the Germans on account of their uniforms (for it had been impossible to provide civilian clothes for all) or while foraging, for food was scarce, the majority got away altogether, and not one was betrayed by the inhabitants of the village of Fontanellato, who all helped and contributed food and clothing. Altogether about 300 men were fitted out in some sort of civilian garments. When all had dispersed, in companies, which would later split up, the SBO and two companions returned to the village, where the Germans were now installed and angrily engaged in ransacking the camp and selling off any stores they found there to the villages. The three Englishmen hid in the loft of Signor Bigi's hotel, in the hay and dust behind the wine jars. The hotel was searched thoroughly, but the fugitives were mercifully not discovered, perhaps due to their valiant struggle to stop themselves from sneezing in the cloud of dust.

Many stories of gallantry, some humorous, some pathetic and some tragic, could be told in consequence of that mass escape. There was the English captain who, while the Germans were combing the countryside in their anxiety to catch up with their quarry, was found reading Shakespeare aloud in a field, with practically no clothes on and his shaving kit neatly laid out beside him, complete with British Army holdall. There were the elderly Italian peasants who complained of the bad tobacco smoked by the English, sold to them by the Germans after they had taken over the camp, but which on examination was found to be tea! And there was the businessman from Milan, who owned a big house in the village where several prisoners were temporarily concealed. The Germans put him up against a wall and prepared to shoot him in full view of his whole family, whereupon he just roared with laughter, which so astonished the enemy that they let him go. But others were not so fortunate. Some of the men of the village were later deported and lost their lives. The commandant of the prison camp was arrested and later sent to Buchenwald, where he was so badly beaten up that he died a year or so after his return to Milan when the war was over. His widow was paid a considerable sum by the commission in recognition of her husband's very signal service to the Allies and the personal sacrifice he had made. He was given a military funeral, with a guard of honour and at which General Heidemann, then commanding Milan Garrison and also representing the Supreme Allied Commander, was present. This had actually taken place in January 1946, some months before our visit.

Such was the set-up of Fontanellato, where almost all members of the village community had taken part in the dramatic incident of the escape, even if they had only given old clothes or a drink of water. The nuns of the convent adjoining the hospital prison had done the prisoners' laundry and mended their linen; and after the escape they had hidden some of them in the precincts of the convent itself. Later the convent was bombed from the air and one of the sisters was killed. Some damage was done to the building and it was hard to find the money for repairs; the Vatican had to

supply funds for so many ruined and damaged churches, mon-
asteries and other shattered church properties that had suffered
during the fighting or from Allied and later German bombing.
Some of the worst damage inflicted during air raids in Italian
towns was after the Armistice, when Italian troops were actually
engaged on the side of the Allies, but the stiffened German resistance made it necessary to increase aerial warfare north of the line.

That evening, after our evening meal, various people sum-
moned by the efficient Signor Bigi, who was a tower of strength
to us, came to call on Judy and me at the Locale Grande. We
offered them a glass of wine and Signor Bigi soon offered us a
bottle on the house. The party seemed to swell, and once the
business was over became very cheerful. We had been told to
obtain and verify certain information regarding claims, and that
was not too difficult. One of our visitors was the local doctor,
who had lost his car because he had been transporting prisoners to and fro after the escape; the commission was later able to
provide him with a PU for his work. His son had been sent to a
concentration camp but had fortunately returned, though much
broken in health. But cares seemed to be cast aside for a while,
and there was much cheerful conversation and eager exchanging of reminiscences. At about ten o'clock we all went off for a
walk in the fresh night air. We went past the convent and the
famous *campo* next door, and along the spacious avenue beyond.
Everyone was in good spirits and loath to break up the party, but
Judy and I were tired with concentrating on understanding the
ceaseless flow of conversation, carried on by several people and
often simultaneously, and so we pleaded duty the next day and
bade friendly goodnights all round, before retiring to our small,
clean bedrooms for a sound sleep.

Next morning we called on the nuns, who were very welcoming. After knocking at a small postern door inside a covered
corridor, a grill opened, and first one sister appeared, and afterwards the Mother Superior herself, surrounded by her flock who
fluttered round her in their grey robes, murmuring softly to
each other, for all the world like a covey of gentle doves. We took

particulars of their claim and were told all about the damage and the poor sister who was lost, and also about many other matters not directly bearing on the purpose of our visit.

One other visit remained to be paid that morning, at another farm in the country, where we partook of cakes made of a kind of coarse oatmeal and drank some rather immature wine, while the farmer's wife chatted on cheerfully and philosophically about her family's troubles. The Italians certainly are philosophical; it seems to be inborn and unconscious in them, but it helps them to put up with things that other people would make far more fuss about.

After a very pleasant lunch, when we were visited at table and acquired some experience in receiving a meal without embarrassment (a necessary quality in Italy), we packed up and then at about 3 p.m. walked down to the castle and crossed the historic drawbridge. We were going to call on the 'Grand Old Man' of Fontanellato, the Conti Sanvitale, a great-grandson of the Empress Marie Louise, for he had also played his part at the liberation of the 'Six Hundred'. We tugged an iron bell-pull, and after a short wait the wooden gate was opened by an elderly retainer, who ushered us into a mediaeval courtyard with latticed windows in the thick stone walls of the castle, and up an external stone stairway, into a great hall with armorial bearings on the walls and numerous ancestral portraits. I especially remember the Louis XV furniture and a magnificent polished walnut table of immense proportions – it must have been nearly 12ft across. After a few moments the count came out from an inner room, old and rather frail in appearance, with thin, sensitive aristocratic-looking fingers. He was charming and courteous to us and after we had respectfully discharged our mission, he saw us to the door and bade us a kind farewell. We might have been in the Middle Ages inside that castle, with the coats of arms, the old-world courtyard, the battlements and turrets, the lantern gate and the faithful retainer (who on a later visit, when I visited the count with my CO for the presentation of his certificate of thanks, was wearing a striped livery). With a last breath drawn in that mediaeval atmosphere, we heard the iron-studded gate close behind us as we passed under the portcullis and crossed the drawbridge over the moat.

Back we went to our friendly 'Figaro', and before long Major Girling arrived to collect us. We waved goodbye to the Bigis from the open car front and had soon left the village of Fontanellato, that haven of calm and tranquillity in an atmosphere of utter detachment from the world. Before long we had also left behind us the dyke-bound lanes, and were back on the busy Bologna–Milan highway, away from the fresh green lanes and back to civilisation.

Another investigation I made, this time on my own, was a small trip up to Luino, on Lake Maggiore. We left one afternoon at about four o'clock, and I had to visit the office of the local clerk of the County Council (or his equivalent) and collect some data, and also call on a private person living in that area. I managed to get through both jobs without too much difficulty and was able to admire the magnificent scenery of the lake, the vivid greenness of the pastures and the golden stooks of corn, for it was harvest time in northern Italy. The fresh air of the lake country was like a cool drink after the hot summer dustiness of Milan – and Via Seprio was very dusty. We continued to receive a regular number of calls from claimants, some new and others re-stating their cases or enquiring when their claims would be settled. Thus, with occasional trips away from Milan and the routine work in the office, the summer was slipping quickly by, but the work did not seem to slacken.

31

Cavalcade

*D*uring August the CO had to go over to Verona and on to Venice to see the Area Commander about the petrol situation for the Verona Section, which was as usual in imminent danger of curtailment, if not cancellation. We were to carry straight on to Rome and so spent one day in Venice, staying in the transit hotel, the Albergo Danieli, a luxury place in normal times. It was built in pseudo-Gothic style, most of it nineteenth-century, but some earlier, and had a magnificent red brick exterior and interior courtyard, which had been roofed over to make a lofty lounge and ballroom. The Danieli commands a magnificent view over the lagoon towards the island of San Giorgio and also down the Grand Canal; the Bridge of Sighs, the Doge's Palace and the Piazza and Cathedral of San Marco are all within two or three minutes' walk. It was presumably these many amenities, and the still considerable comfort of the hotel, despite Army rations and other inconveniences, that caused it quickly to be earmarked after the capture of Venice for the use of Allied, mainly British, officers. In Florence, the Americans had the Excelsior, a comparable luxurious Albergo.

On this occasion Zimmy was staying at the Danieli, having a last fling for a day or two in Venice, before proceeding to Villach to take the train home on release, and that evening he dined at the CO's table. Afterwards, he prevailed upon me to go out in a gondola with him to see Venice by moonlight. It was very delightful, and now and then haunting strains of music wafted across the water to us – everywhere there were lights twinkling and reflecting in the rippling canals and the air blew in from the sea freshly, tinged with salt. Zimmy insisted on reciting passages from *Hiawatha* to me, though why he chose that particular poem, I never knew. But try as I would, I could not keep awake for any length of time, and feared that in the end he was rather hurt, for I went to sleep three times during his recitations, overcome with the fatigue of motoring in the heat most of the day and lulled by the rocking of the gondola.

Next day we were destined for the Area HQ on the Adriatic coast, at Riccione, near Rimini. It was my first visit to this part, and I noticed that the scenery was different from any other hitherto visited. The country was generally flat and there were narrow lanes, dykes and an irrigation system rather like that at Fontanellato, but here the earth was much less fertile, the trees were mainly pines, and underfoot it was often sandy and stony. Riccione itself had been badly damaged, but was beginning to pick up a little. The HQ was stationed in various requisitioned villas, most of them in large gardens where there were few flowers, but masses of azalea and rhododendron bushes, now mostly over for the season. The main road was lined with pink and white oleanders for many miles, and their rather exotic perfume hung about in the air, mingling strangely with the fumes of oil and petrol; the bright-pink oleander flowers showed up vividly against the blue sky and dusty road.

The transit hotel, the Albergo Vienna, was a simple, sparsely furnished building, but spotlessly clean and quite comfortable, on the edge of a delightfully sandy beach, where the bathing must have been magnificent. The sea was brilliantly blue, aquamarine, and many military wives and children were disporting themselves in the water or sunbathing on the hot sand.

The drive from Riccione to Rome is long and a little tiring, past the castle of Francesca da Rimini, through battered Rimini itself and then inland at Fano; next, up a high mountain pass, with a petrol point at the top in the charge of one isolated 'Tommy' (he appeared to be living with some Italian peasants); and then down to Foligno in the plain, through Spoleto with its magnificent ancient castle, down once again to Terni in the dusty plain, and up for the last time to antique Narni, with its strange arched galleries, clinging to the hillside. From then it was an almost straight run to Rome and soon the famous landmark, Monte Rotondo, came into sight, the mountain which one sees when approaching Rome from any of the northerly routes into the city.

Not long after this, we were in Austria again, accompanied by an Australian captain, Howard, who spoke fluent German and was to run the section up there. By this time, plans were well under way for starting it up. We only stayed two days, visiting the HQs at Klagenfurt and Villach, and then returned to Verona. One of my tasks prior to this trip had been tactfully to disabuse various ladies who either wanted a lift to Austria for themselves, or hoped to arrange one for their friends or retainers. The safe-conduct of a military vehicle was much coveted, but as the carrying of civilians, apart from wives and children of service personnel, was strictly forbidden to all travellers in military vehicles, appeals for assistance of this sort had to be politely refused.

On this occasion in Verona I had a morning to myself and was able to visit the house where Romeo wooed Juliet and see the balcony that he is supposed to have climbed up to. I also saw the chapel where they were married and Juliet's tomb. Like all other Italian towns, Verona has its own intrinsic atmosphere, and many interesting monuments, for beside relics of the Montagues and Capulets there is also the Roman amphitheatre, where operas and plays are performed in the open air each season, a fine statue of Dante and a number of ancient and interesting houses and churches. The river rushes through the town, at that time unfortunately under damaged bridges where reconstruction work was busily in progress; and, as at Udine, the high mountains form a splendid frame to the mass of red-brown roofs, grey spires and towers.

Shortly after this brief glimpse of Verona, a reorganisation took place in the commission. A conference was held in Milan of most of the senior officers, and there was a great pooling of views and much interesting information imparted. My job was to take everything down verbatim. The Austrian Section was now well on the way to taking definite shape, and it was also decided that a reconnaissance should be made in the Trieste area, as it was known that there were helpers in that part. Some of these, it was feared, were behind the demarcation line, where it would be scarcely practicable, let alone safe, to penetrate, owing to Tito's rigid frontier patrols. One bold spirit, however, was only too anxious to slip over into 'Jug' territory, and it was obvious that he would have to be restrained, as international incidents were to be avoided at all costs, and any hint of such a thing becoming known would have immediately brought the wrath of the gods upon the commission from Supreme HQ. Even so, the gentleman in question did manage to get into a spot of bother, despite being warned, but fortunately nothing international, and so it was smoothed over.

Meanwhile I was delighted at the prospect of a Trieste Section, as I hoped that sooner or later the CO would have to go there to start the ball rolling on an HQ level, and that I would be able to accompany him and see a part of Italy hitherto unknown to me, but where I had a relative with an infantry regiment. The conference, meanwhile, came to an end with various conclusions reached about changes of personnel and the eventual closing down of the Milan Section, tightening up of controls on the use of petrol and other stores, and other administrative matters.

Next day, I was detailed to fly down to Rome, and this journey was far from pleasant. By chance, I was travelling on my own, but met a colonel from the Allied Commission in Milan, likewise on his way south, and so I travelled with him. I was glad of a companion, for the passage proved highly disagreeable. The weather was bad and we went right out over the sea, beyond La Spezia, towards the island of Elba. We were in a storm and at moments seemed to be just skimming the water; for one awful instant it seemed we would strike it, but the plane righted itself and soared up again, to me it seemed just in the nick of time. Soon after that the weather cleared, and before long we were nearly level with Rome and out of the storm-belt. During that tense period, everyone in the plane appeared outwardly calm, although the Italian passengers could not keep up their usual incessant conversation, as the roar of the wind was deafening. I used to watch some of them gaily chatting on the airfield before take-off, and then they would continue their conversations, in spite of being given ear-plugs and even when the engines were revving up, finally raising their voices to a shrill crescendo, approaching their faces to almost touching distance as the plane took off. By this time most people had relapsed, at least temporarily, into silence, but the inveterate talkers could just be heard, though going by the exaggerated movements of their lips they were obviously bawling, yet their voices seemed no more than a murmur or a squeak. They would carry on like this until completely exhausted, and then sit back to accumulate more energy for the next bout.

That day we landed at Ciampiano, a bigger airfield than the other, and by now cleared of much of its damage, with artificially surfaced runways, over which a small black-and-yellow jeep plied between planes as they came in. Round the edges of the vast airfield, however, ruined hangars and twisted plane débris were still to be seen.

From that time on, my work was to centre more on Rome again, but I did not mind, for now I loved both north and south Italy, and felt equally at home in both. During September, there was a certificate award ceremony in the small town of Rieti, in the Abruzzi Mountains, at which many notables of the city, including the bishop, a fine cheery man with great personality, and the major of the local *carabinieri* were present. The people were universally friendly and there was an atmosphere of great cordiality at Rieti, the town where lived Azzari, the pastry cook already mentioned. He was perhaps most distinguished for his gallantry, but others of his townsfolk had also done excellent and courageous work helping our men. At the small reception, I met a professor from the local grammar school, or *ginnasio*, and also a woman teacher and curator of the town library. We talked about

English literature, and I, knowing that most people on the continent are well acquainted with the works of Lord Byron, asked them if they had any of the poetry of 'Beerronne' in the library, whereupon they both replied, a little reprovingly, that they had of course the works of 'Byronne' and we went on further to discuss him. I felt somewhat foolish at being corrected in the pronunciation of one of our own poet's names. But generally, I had found that few people abroad pronounced him rightly and thought only to make myself clear. I did not try again.

Another event that summer was a garden party held at the British Embassy, to which several of us were invited. The garden was beautiful, with tall old trees – cedars and pines in the main – a great green well-cut lawn, English fashion, and a profusion of flowers. The ambassador's wife was a charming hostess, here, there and everywhere, and friendly and welcoming to everyone. Little could anyone imagine at that cheerful party that in barely more than six months' time, a bomb would shatter half of the front of the embassy and a new home quickly have to be found for BHE (British High Embassy) staff and work.

About the same period, I attended a different type of party, a private affair, mainly it seemed, to entertain members of the Roman nobility and stray foreign aristocrats, with the gathering leavened by an admixture of oddly assorted service personnel. A German crown prince was present, a Roman prince, and other scions of nobility with varying titles. The English guests included an air vice-marshal, a beautiful girl from the British Embassy, Judy and myself, and a colonel commanding the large transit camp outside Rome. This strange gathering intrigued me, and when the Roman prince offered me a lift home in his car, I was even more intrigued. On that occasion, the only time I had a specific chance of transport back to my hotel, the commission's Italian driver made sure of coming back to fetch me. He arrived too early in the first instance, but when I told him he would not be needed, he firmly turned up after about half an hour and tooted methodically and with great determination, until eventually I decided it was best to take advantage of his willingness, though I felt rather like a child with its nanny. Some drivers would not have come back again, but perhaps he had seen me leaning out of the window with the prince, who was recounting his experiences in the desert, though I could not quite make out which side he had been on at the period he was describing, and did not like to ask. Perhaps it was this that made Enrico so determined to transport me safely home that night. As for Judy, I believe the German prince gave her a lift – anyway I left her in deep discussion with him.

That evening has always remained engraved on my memory, because it was fairly typical of Roman life at that time. The party was held by a British officer in a lovely old house looking out over the Tiber towards the Janiculum Hill. The lime trees on either side of the road running alongside the river stood in sharp outline in the light of the street lamps. Our host was a British regular Army major, with a slightly cavalry air and he was very hospitable and made everyone perfectly at home. We talked, danced, smoked and drank whisky, sherry or Frascati Spumànte, a delicious and non-intoxicating drink. Altogether it was a delightful evening – everyone was of a different nationality and profession, but thanks to the skill of our host, the ingredients fused very well. There were no contretemps, even when the daughter of a well-known Roman family arrived late, and at once demanded whisky, and drank whisky solidly for about two hours, but without showing the smallest trace of an effect. At that time in Rome, and perhaps it is always so, you might meet anyone anywhere, and it was just accepted. In that climate, the rigid differences existing in more northern lands seem to merge more easily and happily into one another when occasion demands. And so we leaned out of the windows of the small mediaeval house that evening, watching the lights reflected in the ripples of the River Tiber, and discussed art, politics, the war and other things, ex-enemy and ally together, and even the bitterness engendered by the doings of Nazi and Fascist seemed extinguished in a newly awakened understanding.

Shortly after this, General O'Connor came out to Florence to see and thank personally the Italians who had made his escape possible, and as this was within the Province of our Commission, our CO was instructed to go to Florence to meet the general. We motored up a day early, via Route 1, the Via Aurelia, and as luck would have it, the Chev again broke down, this time at a spot not far from Orbetello, the tiny town on a tongue of land jutting out on a promontory right into the sea. We had already stopped once, way back at Fiumicino; Bruno, the Italian driver the colonel had been persuaded to take on, had complained volubly that the *lazzaroni* (rogues) in the Rome garage had not serviced the car properly before we set out. Anyway, she broke down and nearly lost a wheel, as some nuts were apparently loose and had fallen off (according to Bruno). After he had hitched a lift on a passing lorry and gone in search of spare nuts, I had the none-too-pleasant task of hitchhiking on another lorry into Orbetello and ringing through to Rome on a public telephone to report the disaster. Hours were wasted, and it was finally after eight o'clock that night that the relief vehicle came and we were able to proceed to Florence. In spite of the lateness of the hour, I enjoyed the journey, especially as we had a midnight supper out of doors at a charming little roadside café on the outskirts of Siena. Here some Italian boys with a small puppy were very interested to learn that the English for it was 'dog'. They promptly proceeded to christen it 'Doggino' (little dog). But the pleasant interlude was over all too soon, and before long we were driving through the deserted and silent streets of Florence. Much went wrong on that trip, and I was genuinely glad when it was over, although General O'Connor's meeting with his helpers was a complete success. He then went on elsewhere and not long afterwards, to my delight, the CO actually decided to go up to Trieste on a short visit, and also to GHQ, which had by then moved to Padua.

32

Trieste

*I*t was sometime after the Milan conference that the CO was persuaded to take 'Bruno' as his driver. Bruno had been chauffeur to the manager of Barclays Bank in Rome and for some reason had to be discharged, as his services were no longer required. So the CO was approached and Bruno's virtues so extolled – his good and careful driving, his reliability, his polite manners, etc. – that eventually the CO, who was looking round for another driver, agreed to give Bruno a chance and take him. What we did *not* learn was that his eyesight was bad, that he was really not physically fit enough for long-distance driving, and that he nourished rather too much affection for café-cognac, an affection that revealed itself more and more as the cold weather came on.

I was always a little suspicious of Bruno, preferring a British soldier driver for the CO, and he in turn was highly suspicious of me, '*La Signorina*', from whom he took orders with evident distaste. He did not approve of women in uniform, and he was of an older generation of Italians, to whom the British way of life as it had developed in the Second World War was quite incomprehensible. His vocal chords had long ceased to function normally and his voice was wheezy and husky, but not musically so, and when annoyed he was inclined to whisper gutturally and almost inaudibly to himself. He was well turned-out in a good chauffeur's uniform and bowed politely, almost obsequiously, as he shut and opened the car doors. He was in fact probably the perfect chauffeur for town driving, but for long distances he had neither the stamina nor the experience. For one thing, he was bad at finding his way and when interrogating locals as to the right road, would invariably, to the CO's intense annoyance, say to them, 'It is that way, is it not?', at which they would of course agree with him. As his suppositions were usually off, we would go in the wrong direction and it would only be after several miles that we would be convinced of his mistake. He drove like the wind and would suddenly miss a curve in the road or a bump, and before long the CO developed the habit of watching the road the whole time Bruno was driving. Several times he saved our lives when Bruno would most certainly have been the end of us all. And so we started off to Trieste, fortunately unaware of what lay in store for us with Bruno at the helm.

It was the second week of October and already, as we drove north, the leaves were drying and falling and the stubble had turned brown and worn. The air was cooler and there was a scent of autumn about. The drive after Venice was mainly along the Gorizian coast, through Monfalcone and small villages and across flattish, rather uninspiring country until we came to the coast road proper, with its surface cut from rock, and cliffs towering above us and falling sheer beneath to the water. All of a sudden, there came into sight a magnificent Norman fortress jutting out over the sea; it must once have been almost inpregnable. It was a little disappointing to learn later that the castle was not much more than a century old. It had once been the residence of the ill-starred Maximilian who fell in Mexico, but now it housed the HQ of an armoured division. This was the Castle of Miramare, and not far past it we came to yet another magnificent fortress, the Castle of Duino, this one of genuine mediaeval origin, though much restored, where the British C-in-C had his HQ and where we were to return next day. Bruno hurried past and soon the port of Trieste came into sight, in the cusp of a large bay, the water grey-blue, not now the pure cobalt or turquoise of the southern summer. There was a slight wind blowing, but not the famous Bora, the icy local wind, said to be violent and very chilling, which fortunately we did not encounter. It was however much colder than further south and there was something of northern Europe in the air here, where Germanic and Latin influences combined with Slav produced a blend that can only be described as 'Triestino' – it had something of all three, but none predominated to destroy the others.

The CO put up at the Excelsior, the seniors officers' hotel, and I stayed in a back street at a less exalted establishment. Our main business was conducted next day, when my CO had an interview with the C-in-C, General Sir John Harding, at Duino, and I accompanied him to the castle. We were invited to lunch and this was a great ordeal for me, although Lady Harding and the brigadier's wife could not have been more charming. I sat between two ADCs at lunch at a long table lined, as it seemed, with 'brass hats'. The castle inside was in an excellent state of preservation, as it was externally too, and it was well furnished, with fine portraits on the walls. The view from the windows was unsurpassed, the breakers roaring about the bastions, so that one might almost have been on the deck of a liner. To the left, the whole port of Trieste was spread out in full view, stretching along the coast of Istria, down towards Pola.

This day turned out to be a rather sad one for our commission, as the Commander-in-Chief had irrevocably decided, in spite of pleas from our CO, to order the closing down of our section at Florence, which would of course make our work far more difficult. As a result of this interview, both Milan and Florence were to be closed down, to keep in pace with the overall retrenchment in Italy; and a new section was to be opened in Bologna to conduct ASC work over the whole area previously served by the two sections. But it was an order and 'Orders is Orders'; still it was one which would be a great disappointment to the keen officers who were trying hard to do a difficult job, often in isolated places, and a job that in winter was twice as difficult. With only bases at Rome and Bologna, their difficulties would be tremendously increased, and unfortunately the work did not seem to be decreasing to help matters out. While the fateful interview was taking place, I sat with the two ladies and afterwards we said goodbye and were soon off, getting into the car again in the mediaeval courtyard, where smart guardsmen were on sentry duty; we drove through the massive arches, several feet thick, and back to Trieste, where work had to be done in connection with forming the new section there.

Frank, the captain who was to run it, and had carried out a recce in advance, was waiting to conclude arrangements. He already knew that area on both sides of the Morgan Line, as he had been parachuted into Yugoslavia during the war and at that time collected Tom and Bertie, who were later taken on the staff of the section in Milan as civilian driver-batmen.

That evening I met my cousin in the bar of the Excelsior, also a naval officer and formerly with our unit but now on his way home.[*] I had met my cousin's wife that morning, and his little son, but she was not well and could not join us in the evening. We had a long chat and exchanged all the family news. He was by now second-in-command of his regiment and frequently recognised friends and acquaintances as we sat and sipped drinks and gossiped. It was not until about two years later that I met him and his wife again and they reminded me of that night, after which it appeared that kind persons had taken it upon themselves to inform his wife that her husband was gallivanting with an AT officer in the bar the very day she came out of hospital!

Later we went to a fish restaurant, which is apparently the thing to do in Trieste. It was on the waterfront and there was a cool breeze from the sea, and the smell of tar and seaweed permeated the air. It reminded me vaguely of my east coast home, but it did not make me homesick. Trieste was far too exciting for that, with its houses rising up on the hill behind, where it was said that Communists lurked and trouble might be brewing

[*]   Colonel John Alleyne Addey. His son Simon was also to be a soldier, later a Queen's Messenger, and attended Lucy's 90th birthday party at Richmond in 2010.

up at any moment. The city and port were quiet then, but when we got back to Rome people were surprised to hear it, as it seemed that some amazing riots had been reported in the papers. It was actually in Rome that the rioting had taken place, when the crowds of anti-monarchist demonstrations had surged up the Via Quattro Fontane, past the ASC hotel, and all round the Royal Palace of the Quirinale. Although by the referendum of the previous June a Republic had been voted for by the majority of the population, the new constitution had not yet taken effect, as for this an act of parliament was necessary. Feelings still ran high on both sides, and in Rome and the south many ardent royalists were still hoping for a return to the throne at least of Vittorio Emanuele's grandson, if not of King Umberto, his son and heir. But Umberto had not made a great impression at the time on the plebiscite: he had attempted to speak in public outside Milan Cathedral, but some ripe tomatoes were thrown at him and Cardinal Schuster, Archbishop of Milan, and they both beat a hasty retreat into the sanctuary behind; it was said that if he had stood his ground, Umberto might have won a place for himself. The Italian royal family was unfortunately too much identified, at least in the public mind, with Mussolini and all that he stood for, and in the wave of popular anger that caused Mussolini's shameful death, there was no remembrance of anything good. In Trieste, however, the royal family was a side issue compared with the international problems that occupied the day-to-day existence of the Triestini. But our visit was too short to acquire any more than a fleeting impression of the place and its unique set-up.

Next day we were back on the road for Padua, on a visit to GHQ, CMF. I did not feel very bright and at last was moved to protest as Bruno excelled himself and drove over the pitted roads at about 70mph. At length the CO ordered him to drive at a more reasonable pace and he grudgingly obeyed, grumbling to himself in wheezing and partly audible Italian, which apparently was intended to convey his disapproval of everything in a way that was just about intelligible, without being reprehensible.

33

Sacred and Profane

When we got back to Rome from Trieste, I was able to hold a long-delayed birthday party, and had persuaded the maestro of our hotel trio to come along with his two co-musicians. The party was arranged in our sitting room and we danced, drank and ate all the titbits I had managed to get from the maître d'hotel and a few more besides, such as nuts, olives and NAAFI biscuits. I always found the hotel staff very obliging and helpful when anything in the entertainment line was called for. Through the auspices of the town mayor, who had been very kind to Judy and me, I had discovered a wonderful wine distiller's out at Grottaferrata, where one could buy Frascati Spumante on the spot where it was made, at a very reasonable price, equivalent to about half-a-crown a bottle. This had proved to be the best and least alcoholic drink to offer anyone, and incidentally it seemed fairly opulent, though it was actually far cheaper than many less deluxe beverages; but champagne, even when it called itself 'Spumante', always sounded and looked good.

All in all the party, comprising between twenty and thirty people, was a success and I felt encouraged to repeat the performance a few months later, having meanwhile saved up enough lire to provide the champagne and titbits, not to speak of cigarettes for the maestro and his brood, for which they were very grateful. They played for us all evening, from ten o'clock onwards,

with the greatest goodwill and jollity – without their co-operation I could never have managed an orchestra.

On one occasion the maestro invited me to a concert at his
old school, a church school on the Aventine Hill, where he was
conducting the orchestra. It was a Sunday afternoon, and my
companion and I were shown to seats in the second row. In
front of us was a distinguished gathering of High Church dignitaries, including at least one cardinal in bright crimson robes;
these personages were probably the college principal and various
colleagues or friendly clerics. In front of such a serious-minded
audience, on a Sunday afternoon, one would have expected
mainly church music to be played, Bach and Handel, for instance.
We were astonished when the maestro at last appeared, resplendent in tails, white tie and waistcoat, and after a few bows and
some welcoming applause led the orchestra off into a hot jazz
number to which the venerable persons in front seemed almost
to be tapping their feet, and nodding in time to the rhythm.
Almost the whole programme was noticeably secular in character, but the audience, including the dignitaries, thoroughly
enjoyed the performance; and I personally thought it a far more
amusing afternoon's entertainment, especially as the playing was
excellent, than listening to what one would have expected in
Sabbath-conscious England on a Sunday afternoon. At the end of
the performance the maestro descended from the podium amid
a storm of applause, and was warmly congratulated by the ecclesiastical VIPs in the front rows, and heartily embraced by many
on both cheeks, in true continental fashion. The enthusiasm was
tremendous and there was a genuine friendliness about everyone
that made it all rather like a speech day at a public school at home.

The wine distiller's at Grottaferrata was known as the Cantina
Santovetti, and I never met the owner, only the manager and his
employees. These included a swarthy bright-eyed peasant with a
stubbly beard and a woman of about 35 who, strangely enough
for Italy, appeared to be a spinster. The first time I visited the
Cantina it was in October and we saw the immense vats pressing the grapes down in a colossal tank of fermented liquid, which

would eventually be drained and form the white Frascati wine, which was the basis of the Spumante. Red Frascati wine was also made here. The Cantina was in a sort of cave, without windows, but with electric light installed, and housing rows upon rows of bottles and enormous bottles of wine. We were always offered a drink on the spot and found the people most friendly; we established cordial relations, and I went out several times that winter and chatted with them and obtained some of the popular brew. On the road to and from Grottaferrata one could often see the peasants on their gaily painted carts, with coloured hoods, en route for Rome with huge vats of wine loaded behind – wine of the '*Castelli Romani*' or 'Roman castles', as the vintages from this area are usually called.

A rather cosmopolitan haunt which I discovered about that time was the Caffè Greco, which was the most famous café in Rome, as renowned as the Orso and almost as old an establishment. It was an old-fashioned place, somewhat on the lines of a Viennese coffee-house, situated in the Via Condotti, off the Piazza di Spagna, and near the little house in which our Keats lived and died, and which is still kept as a memorial to him and other English poets of his period. The Caffè Greco, with its plush seats, its marble-topped tables and its partitions and alcoves, has always been frequented by eminent men of letters and the arts as well as patronised by exiled or visiting royalty – Keats, Shelley, Byron, Goethe, d'Annunzio, Gounod, Gogol, Wagner and King Ludwig of Bavaria are only a few among the famous names whose signatures one can find in the massive leather-bound visitors' books, where I also inserted my humble signature, among many contemporary English and American ones.

Yet another haunt, and a vastly different one, which I made the acquaintance of that winter, was the Quirinetta nightclub, re-opened about that time. Now that one was free to visit any local spots, the officers' clubs became less well patronised, but the prohibitive prices in the civilian places of entertainment made any visits paid to them very rare occasions. They were for rich Italians (and foreigners) and probably the vast majority of Romans had never even set foot inside them, just as hardly any Parisians are to be seen at the Lido or the Folies Bergère. But the Quirinetta, whatever it may have been like pre-war, or is now, had at that time a slightly decadent vitality about it, which was entrancing and perhaps a little dangerous. You went down a thickly carpeted flight of stairs, and left hats and coats at the cloakroom halfway. The room itself was low, with tables at each end and in alcoves at one side. On the other side was a small dais for the band and in front of it, holding the centre, a small dance-floor.

The band was small, only four players, but together they formed a first-class and highly versatile dance orchestra. The music varied from Argentine and Hawaiian to Italian, German, French and English jazz, with perhaps a Negro spiritual or an Indian love song, not to speak of a Spanish *habanera*, thrown in for good measure. There was always something catching about the music, whether sad or gay, the rhythm was impeccable and one just had to dance. The violinist and leader of this orchestra was a little, quiet modest man, who had as his assistants a pianist, a saxophonist or accordionist (mostly he was the latter) and a drummer. It was the drummer who was the life and soul of the quartet; he was tall and hulky, but thin and wiry with it, and looked something like a boxer or a paratrooper – in fact immensely tough. His energy was dynamic and his facial contortions were almost mesmeric – it was said by some that he had a strange fascination for women and by others that he took drugs. Whether or not all this was true, his rhythm was faultless and he had personality. Sometimes he sang the wild sambas and rumbas, while he beat his drums to an intense crescendo, a hank of mouse-coloured hair flopping Hitler-like over one eye. At other times he would address some of the dancers as they passed him by – his penetrating gaze missed no-one. He was without doubt one of the management's greatest assets.

All sorts of people frequented the Quirinetta: Roman nobility, actresses, business people, politicians, Allied officers, embassy officials, black marketeers, tourists – there was always a motley crowd of smartly dressed people there, the women often in extravagant hats, the men in well-cut lounge units, with the cream or white silk ties that Italian men wear for informal smart occasions. The floor, like some in London, was minute and often there was scarcely room to place one foot in front of the other, so everyone jogged up and down on the spot, revolving extremely slowly, and swaying rather than dancing. It was nothing to see a tall, willowy lady, surmounted by several ostrich plumes on a model piece of millinery, curving gently over her partner, a small, dapper gentleman, as they both hopped to and fro from one foot to the other in time to the pulsating, exotic throb of a Mexican samba. The dresses were of all colours – mostly of light materials and vivid hues – nothing of the sombre black which is always considered so chic in other places. As you arrived at this place and as you left, an Italian woman clad in black calico with thick stockings and wooden-soled slippers would sell you a gardenia, or press you to buy a spray of roses, which sometimes by the early hours would be somewhat wilted. Perhaps it was the contrast in the Quirinetta to the life going on in the city as a whole that made it attractive – its unreality, which made it like a vivid dream. Some starved in Italy while others danced and made merry; it was far from the Welfare State conception, and yet there was on the whole astonishingly little bitterness at the goings on of '*i signori*'. Perhaps by now there has been a little more levelling out, but in Rome the distinctions were sharp between rich and poor – only the sunshine was available to all, and what a blessing for the poor!

The Rome Golf Club was another favourite meeting place for the well-to-do. I once saw it in the summer – it had a delightful setting, with green lawns and a swimming-pool, set near a little wood just off the Appian Way, outside the city walls. One visit sufficed, however, as there seemed to be more sunbathing and staring than golf or even swimming. It was a sort of smart country club, and had once been extensively patronised by Ciano and his circle.[*] Now that he was no longer on the scene one could not

---

[*] Galeazzo Ciano, minister and son-in-law of Mussolini.

help wondering how many of his former friends and acquaint-ances still frequented the golf club, or could afford to; this was a luxury spot and even to use the swimming pool was quite expen-sive. To me, Ostia with its sandy beach, rafts and diving boards, and its sea breezes, was preferable to the sophisticated languor of the club off the Via Appia.

An experience that winter of quite a different nature was a Beatification at the Vatican. This is a ceremony next in impor-tance to a Canonisation, and I was lucky in being able to attend it, for many people, service personnel among them, had come from all over Italy for the occasion. Immense crowds had fore-gathered at St Peter's, and the Pope played the leading role at the ceremony. We were quite astonished by the barrage of photog-raphers in the galleries and the rows of field-glasses, which were trained on the milling throng in the nave and transept from small balconies in the walls and pillars. The deportment of many people, even priests, seemed strange to us, so wild was the enthu-siasm after the Pope's entry. He was born aloft on a chair, clad all in white silk, a gold cross embroidered on his breast, and he made the sign of the Cross and blessed the people as he passed. His face was serious and careworn, but infinitely spiritual. As he moved on, there were acclamations of applause and shouts of joy, and some people rushed from spot to spot to see him better. The same occurred after the ceremony, as he went out, when some young priests even lifted up their long cassocks and, clutch-ing black umbrellas firmly in their hands, ran down St Peter's at the double, to glimpse His Holiness as he finally disappeared in the direction of the Vatican. What impressed us most was the almost hysterical devotion of the people; it was a sort of religious ecstasy, culminating in the sight of the Pope. He was acclaimed as a hero, which indeed in the spiritual sense he is, and yet he is in fact only God's representative. To us Protestants, and English at that, it was puzzling and impressive. I asked the driver, who had also been there, what he thought of it all; he had apparently found it interesting too, for his only comment was a laconic but emphatic 'smashing'.

As usual my Roman adventures, whether serious or frivolous, were curtailed by a journey up north. During the first week of November I was sent up to Milan to do a few jobs for the CO. The section was now all but closed, just a skeleton staff remaining until the 'marching-out state' had been taken and the villa handed back to its owners, and the officers' hotel had also been shut down, with just a small men's transit mess left. I was therefore obliged to stay in the YWCA, but this was no hardship as the YW was a cosy little hotel, near the Piazza della Scala and therefore very central.

Besides visiting the section, of course, I had to call on a few Italians, including one wealthy lady, whose husband was claiming for some form of vehicle to replace the one he had lost when the prisoners escaped from Fontanellato. Their flat was smart, opulent and extremely comfortable, situated in a modern block near the cathedral. I discussed the business with the Signora, her husband being at his office, and according to my instructions, was only able to offer her a 15cwt in replacement of their own civilian car, but she agreed to be content with this and afterwards gave me tea and petits-fours with her son and daughter. They were all very friendly, but the Signora could not resist observing to me that such organisations as the Women's Services would not be possible in Italy, where temperaments were hotter, and 'nice' girls would not wish to enrol, although of course there had been some of the 'other sort' working in various capacities with the soldiers. I agreed with her, saying of course that emotionally the British and Italians were totally different types (I was well aware that most Italians think the British are cold-blooded). So everyone seemed to be in agreement, and they accepted me for the weird creature I was, doubtless discussing me and my kind in detail afterwards, and professing conventional and well-bred disapproval at the existence of women in uniform and speculating as to what morals we could even profess, let alone practise.

Another visit I had to pay was to Signor Fabrizi, a young man who had guided ex-prisoners over the mountains into Switzerland and finally been obliged to flee there himself to escape the long arm of the Gestapo. He was jobless and had an aged mother to support. The CO tried hard to get him to England, where he wanted to work for a time as a pastry cook, his trade, but British labour regulations would not permit this and no relaxation was allowed, even to reward someone who had risked his life to save our own people. At that time Fabrizi's fate was still in the balance, but I had to put him in touch with an official of the consulate in Milan, who had promised to do all he could to help. After our discussion, Fabrizi insisted on taking me to see the famous 'Last Supper' of Leonardo da Vinci, for which I was very grateful, as it was not yet officially open to public inspection, having been somewhat damaged by Allied bombing. So much has been said about this most famous of pictures that there is no point in my describing it. Suffice to say that it is a masterpiece among masterpieces, and that the expressions of Christ and the apostles seem painted by an artist not only of consummate skill, but also of deep religious fervour and profound understanding.

Signor Fabrizi never got his work permit for England. When last heard of, he was veering dangerously towards Communism. He could not get work in his own trade, and after passing several months in England, staying with an ex-Army captain, he knew enough of the language to do some translations for a Communist newspaper when he returned to his own country. This appeared to be the only work he could find, and it looked as if all the pro-British sentiment he had nourished ever since he had worked for the CLN (Comitato di Liberazione Nazionale, the Italian partisan movement) during the war was being forgotten in a new-found enthusiasm for Communism, which it seemed he almost had to embrace in order to live.

Sometime during the summer the personnel of the commission had been enriched by the addition of the somewhat 'fantasmagorical' Captain L'Amour. This gentleman enjoyed a quite deserved reputation for gallantry, of both types, for he had been awarded a Military Cross for his valour behind the enemy lines, and in addition he had the reputation for being a sort of Casanova – living up to his name, in fact. His appearance helped him, for he was literally 'tall, dark and handsome', 'the answer to a maiden's prayer'. Amongst the Italian ladies of his acquaintance, he was often known, needless to say, as '*Capitano Amore*'.

The day I was due to fly back to Rome dawned dull and cloudy, though not actually very cold. At the airport, I met the above-mentioned Captain L'Amour, who was, like me, reporting back to Rome. After hanging about for an hour or two, in which there was nothing to do but drink a cup of coffee at the buffet and watch our fellow passengers, it was announced over the loudspeaker that the planes would not fly that day – presumably the visibility was too poor. So we all clambered into the omnibus which was waiting outside and trundled back to the city, to the Capodichino building, where the air offices were.

Hubert L'Amour lived up to his reputation and carried my bag back to the YW, which was fortunately not far off. On the way he told me how uncomfortable he had been during his stay in Milan, dossing down in the transit mess, which was just a small flat, and what a rough-and-ready place it was. 'I suppose,' he said, with an enchanting smile, 'you couldn't be very nice to someone and get me in at the YW, could you?' I thought for a moment. 'There are already two captains and a lieutenant colonel staying there,' I said, 'though why I don't know, but perhaps one more captain wouldn't make much difference.' In fact, I had been quite amazed to see male inhabitants of the YW – the shortage of accommodation was evidently producing strange anomalies in military life. There was an attractive blonde lady among the superintendents at the club, and I suggested Hubert might try his charm on her; but in practice it was not necessary, as I managed to put his case successfully. He did, however, persuade the blonde superintendent to change a cheque for us – on my book – as we were both almost without money and unable to obtain any. I fortunately had a cheque book, otherwise we should have been in a very difficult position. There was no longer a field cashier in Milan, which was by now off the Line of Communication, and, as our stay was unexpected, finances were becoming Problem No. 1. Anyway Hubert changed my cheque, but took charge of the cash for the time being. I believe he was afraid I would hurry out to the shops, having nothing much to do, and spend it all on stockings or cosmetics.

We had not been in the YW for more than an hour or so when an ex-colonel and his wife turned up, on holiday from London. For a few moments I thought they were going to ask me to get them put up in the YW too, but they managed to solve their accommodation problems in the end and I heaved a sigh of relief. The colonel had earlier been with our commission and I had frequently been stationed with him. He told us that his wife was longing to see something of the nightlife of Milan, and insisted on our accompanying them to a nightclub that evening, although Hubert was not very keen. And so off we went to an exotic underground place, with magenta-coloured plush chairs and sofas, dim lights, a thrumming jazz band and lots of 'ladies'. An Italian *Marchese* turned out to be an acquaintance of Hubert's and joined our party for a bit but, having bought us all flowers and champagne, he drifted off and later I saw him surrounded by a crowd of what I would have called '*grisettes*', after which he seemed to become involved in some sort of brawl. But our party was very pleasant – and the colonel's wife, on her first visit to Italy, was entranced with the atmosphere, and thoroughly enjoyed herself. I was more than a little shocked at the behaviour of our acquaintance, and suspected Hubert was too, for he went home early and refused to take me to have lunch with his friend next day, as we had been pressingly invited.

Next morning, we duly reported at Capodichino, and were driven out to the airport with the same crowd of fellow travellers as the previous day, and the same news was given us after about two hours' delay – 'no flying'. So back we went again. I was just standing in the hotel vestibule, when I heard a rich fruity foreign voice enquiring something of the hall porter, and turned round in time to catch sight of the tall, rather strapping shape of Liesel, a Dutch welfare worker, and a beaming jolly sort of person. I invited her to meet me later for coffee, as we had not met for some time. She was a great personality, and very popular with everyone in Welfare. After she had gone I suddenly realised I had only about 100 lire left, and had to ask Hubert for some money. He doled me out about 200 lire, rather grudgingly I thought, but I decided that 300 would be more than enough. I met Liesel and we each had two cups of coffee and two cakes. When it came to the bill, I did *not* have sufficient cash, for it was nearly 400 lire! I felt a fool and secretly cursed Hubert, telling myself that if this was what marriage was like, then celibacy would be preferable. So Liesel paid our bill after all, and I sent back the money to her later from Rome. She just laughed at my predicament in her comfortable Nederlander way and said, 'Ja, that does not matter, do not think of it.'

In revenge, partly, I made Hubert, by gentle persuasion and constant reference to the subject, escort me to the famous Piccolo Bar that evening, of which I had heard so much. It came up to expectations, with alcoves where one could talk undisturbed, blue-and-white striped silk upholstery, subdued lamps on the polished tables, and small roses in vases reflected in the polish. The waiter brought us dainty glasses of vermouth and saucers of nuts and olives. One could hear the distant throbbing of a small orchestra, and presumably there was a restaurant down below. We had arrived at about eight o'clock, but it was not until nearly nine that the bar started to fill up and an 'arty-crafty' set of people drifted in and talked with sophistication and *savoir-faire*. There was an array of long hair, beards, long slender cigarette holders and other hallmarks of the artistic and literary élite. There was something a little Chelsea-esque and a touch of Kensingtoniana about the habitués of the Piccolo Bar. After surveying the scene for half an hour so, we returned to the YW and I spent the rest of the evening listening to the musical trio there, who played for long periods to small and sometimes nonexistent audiences, but never flagged in their enthusiasm and were always delighted to oblige with 'request numbers'.

Next morning our plane really did take off, and we reached Rome safe and sound after an exceptionally comfortable journey. When it was heard that I had stayed at the YW with Hubert

L'Amour, there was general amusement, though I hoped it was not after this very comradely occasion that he went into the bar of the officers' mess, and passing one hand over his noble brow, was heard to remark in a blasé drawl, 'These women, how they *plague* me.' Sometimes I think he enjoyed being plagued and even invited it – at any rate he liked the Casanova legend which had grown up around him. Earlier on, during the summer, he had presented me with a portrait of himself, an almost life-size head-and-shoulders photograph, and a masterpiece of the art, as only Italian photographic art can produce. He gave me the choice of about a dozen prints, of varying sizes, but I chose the largest and most handsome and asked Hubert to inscribe it, which he did, again gallantly. It was impossible not to wonder quite how much he was tongue-in-cheek. On the occasion of our short sojourn in Milan, the Casanova aura seemed to vanish, and he was courteous, charming and perfectly natural, but the moment we were reabsorbed by the unit in Rome, Casanova reappeared at once, almost like a protective armour, and the very next day he was showing passport photographs of himself to me and the assistant PA, asking us which he should have printed and promising us copies. Of course we begged him for copies and said we *insisted* on having them, and of course he acceded to our requests, so I then had two photographs of him – but his character still remained an enigma.

34

North of the Border Once More

*E*arly one morning in December the CO rang me up at the office, where I was straightening out some files and making a few telephone calls and appointments, and said we were to leave for Austria the following morning, visiting the new section at Bologna and GHQ at Padua on the way. One of the majors travelled with us as far as Bologna. We went up Route 2 via Siena and stopped on the delightful main piazza for lunch at a small cosy-looking restaurant. In recent times the GSO II had been making great attempts to economise on various things, and officers usually took rations out on the paying and investigating trips, and sometimes exchanged these for Italian food, which might be more easily prepared on the spot. And so I, full of zeal for obeying the directive on economy, decided to try some exchanging of rations of my own, and offered the restaurant proprietor some cold cooked meat (not bully beef) in return for *pastasciutta*. While I was explaining this plan to the mystified man, my two senior officers decided that they did not approve of the marketing and ordered something from the menu; this arrived and was of course excellent. Whether anything was taken off the bill for the 'baksheesh' meat I handed to the proprietor I did not know to this day. After that, I concluded that I had obviously brought the wrong sort of rations, and as it was only very occasionally that we were eating in civilian restaurants, I thought it best to let well alone.

We stayed in Bologna that evening, but as the section was full it was necessary to put up at the Baglioni Hotel, the transit mess, a very dark and, to some, dreary hotel on the main route through the city. Personally I never found the Baglioni dreary, but rather homely with its faded chintzes, heavy curtains screening the dining room, and small basement bar, which soon became warm and smoky. But dark it most certainly was, for the electricity situation in Bologna was still acute, the lights were liable to fail at any moment and the current was usually very weak. It was advisable to have candles, lamps or torches – or all three – in constant readiness and after getting to know Bologna on an earlier visit, I had formed the habit of carrying a candle in my handbag or pocket the whole time, which was all right as long as one did not lean against a radiator or too near a fireplace.

For this trip we were travelling in the CO's new Humber Snipe and to my relief we had a lance corporal driver, while Bruno stayed in Rome with the Chev, now allotted to the GSO II. It would not in any case have been practicable to take Bruno into Austria, as he might not have been allowed over the frontier.

It was necessary to stay in Venice, as the CO had calls to pay, both there at the area HQ and also in Padua, at GHQ. I shall always remember that visit to Padua, for the riots were on, if one could call them riots. The streets were almost deserted on the outskirts of the town and most of the shops were shut. Everything was very quiet. We dropped the CO off at the financial advisor's office and, as he was going on from there to the main building on foot, the driver and I had to get the car parked. By the time we reached the city centre, the pavements were packed with men, several feet deep, and there was hardly a woman to be seen. We stopped to ask one of a group of police, both military and civil, what to do. I got out of the car and crossed to enquire, eyed by the crowd of sullen-eyed civilians who packed the pavements several deep on each side and as far as the eye could see in every direction. I had heard tales of ATS girls having their skirts torn off and I was frankly nervous, though I pretended to be quite unconcerned; but, thanks be, no unpleasantness awaited me, nor when I went to the Hotel Regina for lunch, where I was to meet the CO and one or two other people. The doorway there was all boarded up, as the glass doors had been broken with stones. There was an atmosphere slightly resembling that of a state of siege, and everyone was extremely friendly and cheerful, a little like Blitz days again. At lunch there was great talk of the riots and of who had been injured. One or two officers had been rather badly beaten up, and that evening in the Danieli Hotel in Venice we saw a full colonel with a patch over one eye; a brick had been hurled into his jeep as he was quietly driving through the streets. Next day things seemed a little calmer, and the CO suggested that we should go into a local café for a rum punch to see what things were like and, much to our surprise, we were very well received, without a trace of hostility.

On one of those evenings in Venice, I met an old friend and he took me out to a fascinating Venetian restaurant, named La Grappa d'Uva ('The Bunch of Grapes'). There was of course music – and where in Italy is there not music, even if it is only an itinerant musician with a piano accordion, who threads his way in between the tables of a restaurant or café, playing request numbers when asked and collecting on a plate afterwards? La Grappa d'Uva was different from the places I had seen before, rather more like something German or Austrian, very welcoming, almost cosy, the sort of place where you did not need to dress in anything special, but could enjoy good food and wine, pleasant music and dance, and cast all cares to the wind. But the place had its own atmosphere, which it might perhaps be too bold to call typically Venetian and yet that is how it struck me, from the variety of fish dishes to the vivid colours worn by the women guests.

From Venice the road up to Klagenfurt soon became snow-covered, and Klagenfurt itself was completely wrapped in white. Everything there was muffled and sledges drawn by horses or mules, with tinkling bells on their harness, seemed to constitute the principal form of civilian traffic. All military vehicles had chained wheels and there was much panting and blowing and stamping of heavy boots at the doors of offices, messes and canteens.

From Klagenfurt we went on to Graz, where our section was now in full swing. The road was covered with thick snow, which had been ploughed regularly and on each side was piled high and frozen hard. We managed the journey safely, in spite of a skid, when we did a complete circle round on the road. It seemed we must crash into one bank or the other, but miraculously the massive and cumbersome Humber managed to right herself again. On each side, and as far as the eye could see, were pine forests, reaching up tier upon tier into the gloom; there was absolute stillness everywhere, broken only by the incessant crackling of icicles suspended from the heavily snow-laden branches of the conifers. It was the landscape of Grimms' *Märchen*, and one could just imagine the little bearded dwarfs coming out of hollow tree-trunks as the short afternoon slid into a winter's night.

Graz seemed to be a pleasant little town, which had suffered quite a lot from Allied bombing, but not nearly so badly as Vienna. There was not a great deal in the shops, but the atmosphere was far lighter and happier than in the capital, in spite of an acute housing shortage among the civilian population, aggravated by the presence of a large Occupation force and their families. Captain Howard had everything running very smoothly with agreeable civilian personnel in his office. I had to do a certain amount of typing, translating and so on, but managed to see a little of the town and to purchase a wooden dog on wheels for the colonel's baby as a Christmas present. The transit hotel overlooked the river and the towers and spires of the town. Most houses had eaves and gables, just like a scene from Wagner's *Die Meistersinger*.

In the hotel I met 'Nanny'; that was not his real name, but I christened him that, because when we met he was in charge of somebody's baby and seemed to be perfectly at home baby-sitting. Nanny asked for a lift as far as his unit at Carno, near Pontebba, not far from the Italian side of the border, and so he joined our party for the return journey to Villach and so on. Before we left Graz, I had almost my only really severe rebuke for lateness from the CO, delivered in stern and stentorian tones in the crowded vestibule of the officers' hotel. Everyone looked up and it was with flaming cheeks that I meekly hurried through the swing door and out to the car for our departure, hoping someone else could be thought to be me, but knowing it must be well-nigh impossible. I was always in very good time after that!

On our way from Villach back to Italy, we had just crossed the frontier and were proceeding at about 30mph in the snow, when a large khaki-coloured charabanc hurtled round a corner unexpectedly, not nearly enough on its own side. Before anyone could say 'Jack Robinson', the beautiful Humber Snipe, affectionately known as the CO's 'Fire Engine', was straddling the road completely, blocking all traffic, and very much down on the port side, where the front wheel had been wrenched off, hub and all. I was too surprised even to gasp, but in a moment we were all out inspecting the damage. Fortunately, no-one was hurt, but the car was in a very bad way indeed and, worse still, traffic was already beginning to assemble on either side of her. It was obvious that in a few moments violent hooting would start up from both directions – already small, rather ominous toots were warning us, like an orchestra tuning up before the overture. Nanny and I hurried back to the frontier post, after a few expostulations, and reported the matter to the MPs, who at once telephoned for a breakdown gang. The Maltese driver of the charabanc overtook us here and entered into more rude and angry arguments, swearing that he had been travelling at only 20mph, and producing other similar fairy tales in a very aggressive manner. He kept to his stories later on, even when questioned at a Court of Enquiry, but it was obvious that if he had been telling the truth, the accident would not have occurred. It was a clear case of conscience, but as someone said afterwards, 'Well, he was an ENSA driver, so what do you expect?' Hardly fair on ENSA, but ENSA, UNRRA and all the other ancillaries of the Occupation forces were mostly regarded with some measure of suspicion, probably in the main unfair.

Meanwhile Nanny and I left the Maltese driver, still vociferously protesting his innocence and our guilt, and after we had made our report, I got on to the phone to our section in Bologna for a car to meet the CO at Udine. Nanny said he could send us on from his place as far as that. We then walked back to the Humber, to find it alongside one bank of the road and traffic able to pass it in one direction at a time. The CO and Lance Corporal Smart, having thus achieved a partial clearance of the route, were filling in time with a little shooting practice against a pine tree; and we all then had to wait some hours before the breakdown gang arrived, hauled the nose of our vehicle on to a huge crane affair and towed us along in state at an angle of about 30 degrees.

The poor old Fire Engine was never resurrected to my knowledge, but remained in the enormous Surplus and Worn Stores dump at Udine, among the mountains of scrap that cluttered various disused vehicle parks, still to be found here and there in Italy. Meanwhile the CO went back to using his Chev again, which after all had rendered more service than any – but much grief was felt over the loss of the Fire Engine. Several months' hard work had been put into extracting this splendid vehicle from an economy stricken 'Q' branch at GHQ – and then a miserable ENSA bus had hurtled round a corner in the snow and 'Goodnight, Humber Snipe'. The MTO almost went into mourning. In fact that winter was hard on transport altogether, for 'Sunny Italy' decided to show the remnants of the Allied troops what she could do by way of a really cold winter, and there was snow even in Rome, and for the towns of the north – in Bologna, for instance – there was snow for quite two months.

We reached Bologna from Udine in a 15cwt, and made the journey down to Rome via Ricione in the same way. The Futa Pass and the other pass to Florence were more or less closed on account of the snow – one could risk them, but there was no guarantee of finding them open. I was secretly rather glad that we were not going to attempt the hairpin bends with drops of several hundred feet which occurred quite often on these mountain roads – in the prevalent snow and ice it would have been quite a hazardous journey, and I felt one crash was enough for the time being. The pass over to Spoleto was high enough, but the drops in general were not as sheer as on the other two routes. All the same, I was glad enough to get back to Rome, where preparations for Christmas were in full swing.

35

Last Roman Christmas

*O*n 21 December a very large party was held for everyone in the commission – officers, sergeants, soldiers, civilian employees and their wives or other relatives. There must have been 200 to 300 people present. The mess was decorated with holly, mistletoe and flowers and looked very festive with coloured paper lanterns over the lights, bathing everything in a roseate glow. This also helped to disguise the wartime shabbiness of walls and upholstery; several years of Occupation had made redecoration priority number one for the proprietor, when at last his hotel would be de-requisitioned. But that evening no-one minded much, for there was a true Christmas spirit of friendliness prevailing. Some form of wine cup was served as the *pièce de résistance* with the usual sandwiches and some excellent fruit salad. Everyone turned out in force and the civilian band hired for the occasion did really excellent work.

At 8.30 p.m. the CO and his family appeared, and it was at that time my job to translate into Italian the speech made by the CO, welcoming the guests and wishing everyone a happy Christmas and all the best for the New Year, with some references to the aims, spirit and achievements of the commission. This was the most nerve-racking experience I had during all my time in the Service, and not being UNESCO-trained, and in any case terrified of public speaking, even as an interpreter, I did not derive any pleasure from the celebrations until this dreaded 10 minutes was over. The CO did not speak very fast, but he ran his sentences into each other, or so it seemed to me, and I was afraid of forgetting what had been said before there had been time, or a pause, for me to put it across. I had been persuaded to drink a large glass of sherry beforehand to steady my nerves, although that did not help much; but everyone seemed pleased with the speech, and my ordeal over I was free to enjoy my evening.

There was a spirit of Roman gaiety abroad that night, and frequent 'Paul Jones' helped to banish shyness and caused people to mix indiscriminately and unconventionally. The Italians were there to enjoy themselves and that they did, quite spontaneously and unaffectedly, as only Italians know how. A strange adventure befell our young soldier post clerk; he found himself dancing with a young woman in evening dress, whom he took to be an ATS officer, but who was in fact the colonel's wife. There was a certain similarity of colouring and figure, and it was only the nods and winks of his pals that put him wise to the mistake. She was very amused, but he became very hot and bothered and kept well away from the CO's office for several days after Christmas.

Another strange incident arose as a result of this slight resemblance between Mrs Colonel and Junior Commander Winnie Winter, who had joined us few months previously from Paris, complete with closely cropped black French poodle. She obstinately refused to be parted from this dog, and even obtained special permission from the area commander to live out in a civilian friend's house rather than live in the transit hotel without her pet, for dogs were taboo in the hotel. During this Christmas party, an Italian guest had approached her and after greeting her, had enquired, 'And how is your little one?' She, thinking naturally of the adored poodle, replied, 'Oh, he's very well, thank you.' 'Has he a good appetite?' was the next question, to which she answered, 'Oh, excellent, he eats everything.' 'I suppose you take him for walks in the Giardino Borghese?' her interlocutor carried on. 'Yes, he goes for a walk every day,' Winnie said, wondering a little at the tone of tender solicitude. 'And how do you take him?' 'Oh, he goes on a lead?' said Winnie, inwardly remarking to herself that Italians wanted a great many details. But her questioner's face seemed puzzled. 'You English are too savage to your children.' 'I *beg* your pardon?' returned Winnie. After more questioning and discussion, the situation was at last clarified and Junior Commander Winnie Winter was established as the owner of a pet poodle and *not* the colonel's wife, mother of a beautiful blonde baby.

I learnt that Christmas of the Italian custom of sending bunches or sprigs of mistletoe as a sentimental token at Christmas time. Our GSO II had many admirers among the women employees and he received the biggest bunch of mistletoe I ever saw, very attractively wrapped up in cellophane paper, tied with red ribbon and bearing a neat card of greeting. According to our English ideas, this seems rather an open way of showing interest in someone of the opposite sex, but in Italy it seems such things can be done and no-one thinks any the worse of one for wearing one's heart on one's sleeve.

The rest of Christmas passed off very pleasantly with the usual celebrations. Several people in the hotel threw small parties. Judy and I each invited a few friends in. I believe we had about three Christmas dinners each and it was a wonder that our digestions stood the strain. On Christmas Day we served food at the Other Ranks' dinner and had dinner in our officers' mess the same evening.

On Boxing Day I went to a wedding just outside Rome in Quadraro village. One of the drivers on my former unit was getting married to an Italian girl and I was invited together with one of our commission drivers, who like myself had previously been in the same show. We borrowed a tiny Topolino, one of our CEM cars, and tried to locate the church, the Church of Scotland, but could not find it. We finally reached Quadraro when the wedding breakfast was already in progress, and were at once, to my embarrassment, shown to seats of honour next to the bridal pair, and given vermouth or white wine to drink and cakes to eat. I had the greatest trouble in consuming these, owing to the general excitement and the fact that we were at the head of the table and I never did like people watching me eat – yet our kind hosts kept on pressing us to eat and drink more. There was of course an army of relatives present, and altogether the company must have numbered about 150, seated round three sides of a rectangular table, old and young, mothers and fathers, and children of all ages. There was much drinking of healths and shouting cheerfully from one part of the table to another, and altogether the atmosphere was thoroughly cordial and delightfully unaffected. Then suddenly there was a loud bang, the bride looked worried and one or two girls shrieked. I tried to appear completely unconcerned, even when a whole series of bangs or small explosions took place. The atmosphere became smoky and sulphur gas seemed to be filling the air, so that one coughed and spluttered and could hardly see across the tables. There was a lot of screaming and shouting and one would have thought that some form of insurrection had started, but it soon emerged that several young men, evidently thinking that the party wanted warming up, had decided to let off some squibs under the tables. So there was nothing to do but to leave the fireworks to burn themselves out and move outside; but this was no hardship, for the sun was shining and it was warmer than many days in an English April. My companion and I were both very hospitably invited to stay for lunch, so I imagined what we had just had must have been elevenses. But we declined, knowing full well that lunch would last any length of time up to about six in the evening. So we wished the bride and groom the very best of everything, said goodbye to 'Mamma' and 'Papa', and with three girls as escorts and another car full of relatives as additional escort, drove back into Rome as far as the Piazza Barberini. I drew the line at arriving at the mess with two cars full of very elated civilians – that would have been frowned on, and I should have been asked why so many of them were travelling in the car with me. One of our passengers, an olive-skinned and very attractive girl, with large dark eyes, told me her ambition was to marry an Englishman, almost any Englishman it seemed, in order to go to England and because she liked them. 'But perhaps you would not be happy in England,'

I said, 'You would miss the sunshine and dislike the fog and rain.' 'Oh no,' she replied, 'I would not mind anything, for I should be so glad to get away. Here there is nothing for me.' I never heard whether her dream was fulfilled, but certainly it was shared by many other Italian girls at that time, and for many Italians of both sexes England and America represented Utopia, to which they longed to go – and schemed diligently to reach.

When we reached the Piazza Barberini, the other car drew up behind us and I went over to say goodbye to them. There must have been seven or eight people in it, including some children, and our three passengers still had to be taken on board for the return journey. They were soon squeezed in, for where transport is concerned in Italy the seemingly impossible is invariably accomplished. Hurst and I waved them off after many handshakes and cordial farewells. I learnt much later that when the wedding pictures came out, the bridegroom said, 'Good heavens, I didn't know the junior commander and Driver Hurst were at the reception!' I asked often see the photos, but somehow never did, but the bridal pair sent me a card when on their honeymoon, which to a large extent compensated and which I thought was a charming gesture.

The afternoon after this riotous morning I attended a crazy football match, officers versus ORs, as usual at Christmas time. This was held in the magnificent Foro Mussolini, the grand new stadium which is probably the principal monument commemorating the notorious Fascist era. The match was very exciting, not least so when two persons drove a jeep down the steps at halftime, dressed exactly like Jon's 'Two Types', with the most glorious Desert Rat moustaches imaginable, made of straw, and quite 9in from tip to tip. This act went down very well with all present, and even overshadowed the bold action of an officer's wife – a singer and a countess and a dramatic sort of person withal – who became so excited at a certain tense moment in the match, that she rushed down the steps on to the edge of the pitch, and kicked the ball on to the field, all but missing a scrum – fortunately for her immaculate hair-do and high-heeled shoes.

On Boxing Evening there was a dance for the Other Ranks, and two days later a similar function in the officers' mess. On the day after Boxing Day, however, work began again and when the New Year dawned, seen in appropriately to the strains of 'Auld Lang Syne', we were hard at work again, for the commission was due to close down in 3 months' time. Much work remained to be done and no-one quite knew whether the Treasury and other departments concerned would authorise an extension or insist on closing everything down, whether or not the work was completed. We had lost a lot of personnel of all ranks, and the gradual and steady reduction of Allied forces in Italy, together with the many essential services and amenities which they provided, made our task more difficult and complicated from the administrative point of view. It necessitated more liaison with the Italians, who were by this time quite coming into their own again. Italy was beginning to stand alone. The Prestito Nazionale was meeting with a magnificent response, and the new Risorgimento (reunification) was becoming daily more of a living reality. UNRRA had done its best, and ECA (Economic Co-operation Administration) was already present in thought, if not in practice. In the changing face of things, the commission still had its work to finish, as far as humanly possible. Unfortunately the elements were not on our side and weather conditions caused delays. But much was accomplished during the closing months, despite the many difficulties.

36

Onore al Merito

*D*uring the latter part of 1946 the film *Onore al Merito* (or *To Whom Honour is Due*) was made by the Allied Screening Commission, in conjunction with the Press and Information Office of the British Embassy. Officers and other personnel of the Allied Screening Commission took part and *contadini* from the Abruzzi, the Aquila area, were trained to play Italian parts, which they did with great skill and naturalness. In those days Rossellini had not yet produced his masterpieces, such as *Open City* or *Vivere in Pace*, but the acting by the Italian peasants in *Onore al Merito* was of the same high calibre as in those great full-length films; Italians are born actors, it seems, and completely lacking in self-consciousness or awkwardness. The film was designed to show, first, the work of the partisans and other helpers who risked so much for our escaping ex-prisoners; and secondly, to show the work of the Allied Screening Commission, sponsored by the British and American governments, in seeking out, thanking and trying to recompense those who had given freely of their property, and other assistance. Several scenes were shot in our office in Rome, including one of the CO interviewing an investigating officer reporting back from a duty trip.

The story of the film was woven round one family who sheltered a prisoner, but were betrayed by a Fascist spy from their own village and thereby lost one of their members, shot by order of the Germans. The story was traced from the beginning when the escapee, after his plane was shot down, was wandering, ragged and hungry, through the countryside, sought by the German Occupation troops and Fascist police. He was taken in by the peasants, given food and drink, and lived with them for a time, until he went on his way to pass the Allied lines and join the Eighth Army in the south. The film ended with the mother, father and daughter visiting the cemetery, with its tall cypresses and elaborate white tombstones, to lay a few flowers on the grave of their son who as much as any front-line soldier lost his life in the cause of freedom.

This film was first shown at the Spanish College in Aquila in November 1946, at the time of my detention in Milan owing to bad weather. I heard that it was a great success with the local population, and that the Italian amateur actors in particular greatly relished seeing themselves on the screen. For some of them it was even their first film show. It was officially shown in Rome in January, and there were three performances, for which rather elaborate invitation cards were issued in English and Italian: one performance was for members of the Italian government and official persons, members of the Diplomatic Corps and representatives of the Vatican; the second was for members of the Allied Army of Occupation; and the third for the Press, both Allied and Italian. Unfortunately, I developed influenza and was only able to attend one performance, as along with members of the embassy, most of the officers of the commission were automatically detailed to act as ushers and hosts. Signor de Gasperi was to have attended the first show, but to everyone's general disappointment he was in America at the time. However, a great many Italian MPs were there and the film was very well received. My own chief thrill, apart from the discomfort of feeling ill, was that I had the honour of meeting Ignazio Silone, author of the famous anti-Fascist novel, *The Seed Beneath the Snow*. I had read this book in the early days of the war, being tremendously impressed by its fearless criticism of existing abuses, its vivid picture of Italian rural life and the squalid misery of the peasantry, and by its powerful literary style. The other two performances also went off well, the film was well reviewed in the Press, and was afterwards shown in various provincial cinemas in Italy; the soundtrack had been dubbed for this purpose. The film was also supposed to be shown as a documentary in England, but whether it ever reached the English public is, for me at least, a matter of conjecture. It was well received in Italy and I still have a newspaper report from Pontremoli (near Carrara), speaking glowingly of it. A very considerable amount of work was put into this film, both by the embassy staff and by the two press officers of the commission, ably assisted by Italian local authorities – and for a production almost entirely by amateurs it was a great achievement and a further example of the fruits of harmonious co-operation between the British and Italians.

37

Winter Journey

*I*mmediately after the film, the CO undertook a longish and fairly far-reaching tour of Northern Italy, the main purpose of which was to visit various important claimants, and also to pay a periodic visit to GHQ and the ASC Section at Bologna. I accompanied him to carry out my usual duties of general factotum and secretary, and more especially this time to act as interpreter, for few of the Italians we had to interview spoke English.

Our first stop was at La Spezia, a large port badly damaged by Allied bombing, where the CO interviewed several claimants and was introduced to various prominent local personalities, such as the *prefecto*, the *sindaco* and a leading journalist, to whom he gave an account of the commission's work. Much of our work everywhere depended on successful co-operation with the Italian authorities, and almost without exception they were found to be helpful, courteous and interested. A British major, who was the Press and Information Officer in La Spezia at that time and a member of the British Embassy Staff from Rome, and who had himself fought with the partisans in the mountains of the Province of Massa, made most of the arrangements for this visit. He gave a lunch party, to which he invited among others the *sindaco*, a Communist, and a violently anti-Communist count. But there was no friction, even though someone was wearing a red buttonhole, and the party was highly successful, probably due to the skill and obvious popularity of the host. As far as our commission was concerned, it was sometimes necessary to remind the Italians that we were not interested in their politics as such, but only in what they had done for Allied escapees; to them it sometimes appeared a little strange that their most ardent political enemies were received with equal cordiality by members of the commission, but impartiality was, and had to be, our watchword; to get involved in Italian internal politics would have been fatal.

From La Spezia we went on via Chiavari to Genoa. In Chiavari, the CO presented a certificate to an Italian lady whose husband had been shot for helping a prisoner. She lived in a tiny clean flat in a pleasant villa, not far from the seashore. It was all so orderly and peaceful that the tragedy underlying the purpose of the visit seemed incongruous and almost incredible – only the photograph of the deceased man, his medals and the expression of wistful resignation on the face of his widow suddenly made everything live again in that quiet room, as in a low serious voice Signora Tommaso told us the story. The visit was concluded with a small cup of black coffee and then we were outside again, breathing the fresh sea air of Chiavari, which seemed a charming place, with avenues of orange trees, pink and white villas in luxuriant gardens and a particularly sunny and sheltered position.

It was very different when we had to journey into the mountains to present a certificate to a priest, who lived so far off the beaten track that it seemed almost the back of beyond, in a minute mountain community with only one narrow road linking it to the outer world. In Genoa there were other claimants to be seen and the American consul to be visited in connection with the provision of passages and visas for deserving Italians who wished to emigrate. The commission's scope was wide, covering many fields of activity, but obtaining priority passages was no easy task, when thousands upon thousands of refugees from all parts of Europe were clamouring to emigrate, especially to the USA or Palestine.

From Genoa we went on to Turin, where there were more visits to be paid, which included one to a man and his wife who had been living in their summerhouse in Valle d'Aosta in Summer 1943, when suddenly the quiet valley was practically invaded by British, Australian and New Zealand prisoners, all hoping to cross the Alps into Switzerland. This Italian family, with others, worked tirelessly to provide food and boots for these footsore and hungry men, and to arrange for guides to pilot them over, or at least up to the pass at the head of the valley. From there, they had only to cross the wire and find their way down to freedom – but the path to freedom was perilous and not a few perished before they reached safety. Nevertheless, thanks to the very valuable help rendered in Valle d'Aosta many ex-prisoners evaded a further and probably more rigorous term of imprisonment in Germany. All this good work was carried out under the very nose of the Gestapo.

It was very strange to go from Genoa to Turin in January; it was like going from spring to winter. On the Riviera the sun was shining all day and it was warm and sunny, sufficiently so to sit out of doors quite comfortably at midday. As one climbed gradually out of Genoa, the air became colder and colder and finally, after Alessandria, there was snow on the road and it was bitingly cold. The journey from Turin to Milan was worse still, the air bitter and the road surface unpleasantly slippery. Turin itself seemed a different place from the verdant city I had seen the previous summer. A permanent fog now enveloped everything, rather like a London pea-souper and shops and houses burnt continual light. There was no view, for this dense foggy atmosphere blanketed streets and houses alike. Every house seemed to have a small pipe issuing from some window on its facade, and these pipes rose for 6ft to 10ft upwards and then stopped, capped by a small cowl. They were all emitting smoke clouds, which swelled the fog. Frozen mounds of old and beaten-down snow lined the streets, the air was icy and the fog caught at one's throat. People crowded the cafés, drinking steaming cups of coffee or rum punch with slices of lemon. The more crowded a café was, the warmer and jollier it seemed to be. Keeping warm seemed of necessity to be the prime occupation of man, woman and child.

The shops looked attractive and inviting and prices were reasonable. Food of course was dear, but there did not seem to be such a shortage now. Food probably rationed itself by its cost, for the people did not look too well-fed and one could not but suspect that there must have been quite a lot of privation and hardship, in spite of the well-filled shops and busily puffing chimneys.

Milan was much the same as Turin, but not so cosy. It seemed cold and unfamiliar in its winter garb. The people seemed cheerful enough, though, and the meeting there with a small crowd of about twenty helpers was a very cordial one. In fact, the little cocktail party held by the CO lasted until ten o'clock, when our guests eventually departed.

Padua followed Milan – and again the air, permeated by Alpine currents, was cold and cutting, and gusty blasts blew at one from alleys and arches. There were only administrative problems to be discussed here, and we were soon back on the road for Bologna to find winter more in earnest than ever. Padua had been cold and rather snowy, but Bologna was almost cut off. Huge piles of dirty and ancient snow lined the streets, but it seemed to snow regularly and at our section in Via Gandino, in the residential quarter of the city, the garden was constantly carpeted in fresh white. The section itself was housed, transport and all, in a slightly war-damaged villa that had once been a rather palatial and luxurious place and even contained a magnificent blue-marble hip bath of enormous size, as the wife of the former wealthy owner had been a particularly large lady. Now the many amenities of the place were not so obvious, as there was little fuel to burn; it was only warm in the cookhouse, which was in the basement and capacious and cosy, but some of the windows and doors were broken and electricity was scarce. Like many Italian villas, this villa seemed ideal for Italy when it was sunny, but when the snow came, well, that was just too bad and draughts and cold had to be suffered: '*Pazienza*, the sun will soon be here again' was the attitude. The sun came, even sometimes when it was snowing, but unfortunately at night all froze again, including the water in the radiators, both domestic and of cars, and even the drinking water. In spite of everything, morale was good at the section, where hot tea, sawdust and a certain amount of alcohol all contributed to ward off Jack Frost.

Mimi had managed to scrounge a complete set of battledress, even including a forage cap and ankle boots of American type – but she was so petite and dainty in it all that she was like a Tom Thumb soldier. She had moved down with the section and was billeted out on a nearby Italian family and seemed thoroughly happy, though for the first time cut off from home.

The CO inspected the section and interviewed some of the personnel. He then arranged one or two trips to claimants of importance in the Romagna area. Bruno was with us and as luck would have it, either fate or the weather seemed against us. Bruno, needless to say, was not greatly enjoying the weather and required frequent doses of his favourite beverage to keep warm and cheerful. On our first expedition the Chev developed engine trouble and we had to turn back. I did not understand mechanics, but it occurred to me that Bruno was too vague about the Chev's troubles on this occasion. On later reflection, I wondered if he had manufactured them – certainly the road north was uninvitingly icy and the whole countryside covered in deep snow. Anyway, the Chev was figuratively speaking grounded, which probably meant that Bruno was free to pass much of his time with civilian cronies in the *trattoria*, keeping warm.

Next day we set out again, this time in a jeep, and the CO drove himself while Bruno sat behind. The road surface was again glacial, but with chains and hugging the centre of the road, we made fairly good progress along the autostrada, though I felt an inward twinge of nervousness at the prospect of 20 miles or so of this skating process. But it finished sooner than expected, for all of a sudden we went off into a horrible, veering, breathtaking skid, in which we were all powerless to do anything but await the final swerve and crash. It seemed hours, but it must have been only a few seconds, before we plunged nose first into the deep ditch on the right of the road. The snow, several feet deep here, saved us. I more or less fell out of the right seat and was at once up to my hips in soft snow. The driver, seated behind, was unscathed but reeked of whisky from a broken bottle, which had been stowed away in case of accidents, for even the prospect of being snowed up was not beyond the bounds of possibility. The CO was jammed behind the driver's seat and the wheel, and had badly bruised his legs and crushed his ribs. Within two minutes, some Italian motorists had stopped and a crowd had soon collected, all sympathetic and willing to help. The CO was helped out of the car, rather a painful process for him, and he and I were taken on to the next village by some friendly motorists, where we were told we would find a doctor and a phone. There I was able to make contact with the section on the phone and report the accident. We waited a while longer for the doctor, but he did not come, and in the end we decided to make our way back to the jeep. Within half a minute of venturing out again on to the treacherous rink-like road surface, I had slipped and sprawled flat, a neither dignified nor comfortable occurrence. One had to walk most circumspectly if one did not wish to make an undignified descent into a horizontal position. The houses were all tightly shut up and there was hardly a soul to be seen – the whole world seemed to be hibernating under its mantle of white. The air was sharp and at night must have been glacial; a not too robust sunshine was now the only redeeming feature, and in spite of it the sky was a uniform greyish colour, betokening more snow to come.

The CO was very shaken, so we stopped at a wayside *trattoria*, or inn, for a glass of wine and very soon the whole family and several guests had collected round us, where we sat sipping our wine in the kitchen – all were sympathetic and interested in our plight and many had personal experiences and reminiscences to relate. Quite a party developed, and I passed round a packet of State Express cigarettes, which were much appreciated. We could not remain long with these kindly people, and soon had to leave the warmth and friendliness of the *trattoria* for the cold open road. When we at last reached the jeep, walking almost at a snail's pace, it had vanished, driver and all. The breakdown gang must have made double quick time and preceded us, but they should have come on to look for us, as the driver knew our destination. There was fortunately a considerable amount of civilian traffic on the road, and indeed the cars were almost the only signs of activity, so I stopped a motorist who gave us a lift into Reggio Emilia. The only room for me was on the running board, but this did not seem to matter; Italians are used to much stranger sights, and their transport is nearly always utilised to much more than its fullest capacity. We stopped at an inn in Reggio and I once more got on the phone and explained the situation – by this time I was beginning to be worried about the CO and did not want sole responsibility for his injuries. After this chapter of accidents, we had to stay some days in Bologna. I worked every day at the section and the CO remained in town recuperating. He could not however be persuaded to see the MO. So many COs seem to eschew anything to do with the RAMC, while of course recommending it to their juniors. But there was no persuading him, and so I concentrated on my work. Meanwhile someone else was having a nice little holiday, and that someone was Bruno.

Doubtless Bruno was secretly and possibly overjoyed about the accident, as it meant we were obliged to remain longer in Bologna, and he had not much to do. He seemed to like Bologna, but for what specific reason I never discovered. In any case, he seemed to go rather peculiar at this time. It is not on record whether he had found that café-cognac was a warming and stimulating drink for the winter weather before he joined the commission, or whether the long drives and cold of the north caused his Roman blood to shout out for central heating – suffice to say that he was now finding café-cognac a very pleasant and convenient way of producing a sense of warmth and wellbeing. On one occasion when I was champing for a car to take me up to the section, the Chev was eventually found in the middle of a street, unattended, and Bruno was located in a nearby café, the inevitable café-cognac to hand, entertaining some cronies with tales of the English and their oddities and how it was the *sindaco*'s fault that he had found it necessary to park the Chev in the middle of the road. After that episode, Bruno's days as the CO's driver were definitely numbered, but a substitute had to be found and so he was kept on sufferance for a while longer. Meanwhile, his voice seemed to get fruitier or more laryngitical daily, and his obviously increasing consumption of alcohol made him more sure of himself, less obsequious and almost truculent. His dislike of my presence became more noticeable; at the same time my distrust of him and everything to do with him increased proportionately.

As soon as the CO was better, we set off again to visit the Cervi farm at Gattatico, which had been our objective when the jeep skidded into the ditch. It was a case of third time lucky, for in spite of sunshine and a reasonably blue sky, the weather was really no better than before. There was some trepidation on my part when the Chev turned off the autostrada after Reggio Emilia and, balancing precariously on the rounded surface of a very narrow lane, advanced between deep dykes, whose exact depth and contours were hidden by piles of soft snow, while deceptive ruts, drifts and cart-tracks further complicated our progress. Even the turnings were difficult to find, and sometimes only a signpost warned one of a transversal. As we penetrated deeper into this land, where there was hardly a house for miles around and the only vegetation consisted of small dwarfed willows weighed down with snow, the roads became narrower and the dykes wider (or so it seemed to me) and we slithered along, veering first to the left and then to the right. Several times it was necessary to stop and enquire the way, but the Cervi farm at Gattatico was well-known, and we were able to follow our directions without much difficulty – although to be truthful, it is a wonder how, for in that white tablecloth country everything looked alike.

On this occasion the CO was going to pay a vast sum of lire and present certificates to the father of seven sons, each of whom had been shot by the Germans for refusing to betray the whereabouts of some British and American prisoners, concealed on their farm. The father and mother had also been arrested, but had likewise refused to give away the refugees. The mother had died of shock after the tragic and brutal execution of her family and only the father remained, with several daughters-in-law and a brood of small children, to carry on the work of the farm and keep alive the spirit and tradition of those who should have inherited it. Needless to say, this case was unique among the 100,000 dossiers of the commission.

We eventually arrived at the farmhouse, a large sprawling building, with several outhouses. Bruno drove into the yard and we got out of the Chev and went in at the main door, a solid wooden door with two halves to it, which led into a rough passage with doors leading off it on either side. Several small, ragged children immediately appeared, with bare grubby feet and cheeky elfin faces, lit up with smiles. A young woman, also poorly dressed, but sturdy and well-made, led us into what could be best described as the parlour, a small room, simply furnished with a table and wooden chairs, with photographs, presumably of the family, on the walls. Prominently displayed were the portraits of a group of fine young men. Another daughter-in-law arrived and soon the farmer himself appeared, grey-haired and rather bent, hale still, though showing naturally enough some traces of strain in his tense rugged face. In all, the company soon numbered six or seven persons, which included the CO, a young man – doubtless an apprentice or farmhand – the old farmer, three or four youngish women and myself. The children were left outside in charge of a girl. The family were all plainly and rather poorly dressed, but they were kind, courteous and hospitable, and there was a simple and spontaneous dignity about them. The certificates were presented, amid handshakes and in an atmosphere somewhat charged with emotion, and the enormous sum of lire was paid and signed for. This sum was the highest allowed by the commission's directive, and in comparison with the loss of manpower sustained by the farmer and consequent loss to the farm, it was not very much; but it would help, both in buying new implements, and in replacing livestock taken by the Germans, and also of course in buying necessities for the young growing family. Perhaps the *bambini* would soon be wearing shoes. It was, however, as always, with the certificates of merit and thanks that the Cervi family were most pleased, and each daughter-in-law collected that of her husband, except for one or two absent at that time. The CO made a short statement, similar to his usual speech of thanks, with great feeling and sincerity – and how difficult it was to express what would seem adequate appreciation in the face of such a ghastly and utter bereavement. But the little group seemed gratified, and Farmer Cervi's reply came straight from the heart, and symbolised so much of the truly heroic sacrifices made by Italians in many different parts of Italy on behalf of fleeing Allied soldiers: '*L'abbiamo fatto per umanità*', he said, '*Erà il nostro dovere da cristiano.*' ('We did it for humanity; it was our duty as Christians.') In that tiny crowded room, among those sorely tried, rather shabbily dressed peasants, a creed had been expressed that transcended war, race, colour and even religion. There was no complicated reasoning – just simple logic and one of the oldest tales of mankind: our men had been in trouble and they had been succoured. Not even the shadow of death had frightened the Cervi family into betraying those who had taken refuge with them. Hospitality was a sacred duty and Christianity imposed its obligations, willingly recognised and accepted. One day, when those little boys I saw running round barefoot on that cold January day and regaled with NAAFI fruit-drops are grown up, I hoped they would all be fit and strong and build up the farm as their fathers would have liked it, and I hoped they would prosper and carry on the traditions of their family, for they could not inherit nobler ideals.

I felt a lump in my throat as I waved goodbye to the children and their mothers, for the whole party came to see the '*Colonnello*' off. Neither the CO nor I spoke much on the way back, and I looked hard out at the snow and felt very glad that the Cervi had been paid a really considerable sum of money – it might not go far towards rebuilding all they had to re-build, but it would help, and they deserved it so very, very much.

After that, the CO was scheduled to meet the Bishop of Pontremoli, and to reach that town it was necessary to cross the mountains to the west of Bologna. It was very snowy when we started out and Bruno was most unwilling to make the attempt, and grumbled and protested until the CO told him in no uncertain terms that we were going to Pontremoli and that was that. At this, the old rascal lifted both hands dramatically from the steering-wheel, with total disregard for the snow-caked road we were travelling along, and declared with meaning, '*Sì, sì, porterò il Signor Colonnello fin' a Pontremoli anché sì devo portaro sulle mie braccie.*' ('Yes, yes, I will take the Colonel to Pontremoli, even if I have to *carry* him.') After thus letting off steam, Bruno became resigned to the inevitable and replaced his hands on the wheel, permitting himself from time to time some almost inaudible guttural grumbling, as was his wont.

The first part of the journey was not too bad, but it then became foggy and we found ourselves at the head of a small column of cars. I took turns with the CO in getting out and walking in front of the column, until the fog had cleared sufficiently to make this unnecessary. We were able to proceed a little more quickly now, and passed one or two vehicles digging themselves out of deep ruts in the road.

On reaching Berceto, we were told that it was impossible to proceed further and cross the Cisa Pass, which was at an altitude of 3,415ft. There was nothing for it but to take refuge in the tiny hotel at Berceto that night, where several other motorists were likewise marooned. Bruno soon found friends among some other drivers and while he was having his evening meal, I could hear in the distance his wheezy voice telling all sorts of tales about the terrible life he was forced to lead, his hands meanwhile gesticulating expressively and his conversation frequently interspersed with the '*Colonnello*', '*Commissione*', '*Maggiore*', '*Signorina*' and so on, which gave away the fact that he was airing his many grievances. More I could not hear, though I guessed that he was honouring me with a large slice of criticism!

Next day was sunny and the snow was melting a little, and so the CO and I set off on foot, for the pass was still not open and a snow-plough preceded us up the road towards it. It was midday when we left, after snatching a sandwich in the bar of the small inn and imbibing a tot of warming alcohol. The CO would not even allow me time to finish eating my sandwich, which was particularly delicious thick white bread, very fresh and crusty, filled with a huge portion of hot roast veal – the sort of thing my relatives at home would have envied. So we left Bruno in charge of the Chev, and amid goodbyes and murmurs of '*Come mai!*' ('Whatever next!') from the proprietress and one or two other beleaguered travellers, we left Berceto in its little cradle on the hillside, I munching hard at my veal sandwich and afraid to ask for a second one, which I badly wanted. The Italians of course did not mind in the least being marooned in the hills, cut off from everywhere, for even the telephone was not working; they would just shrug and remark, '*Pazienza,*' wait for Mother Nature to readjust herself and then cheerfully set off again, not in the least worried by the delay, be it half a day, half a week or maybe half a month. It is not in the British nature to be so philosophical, and I was heartily glad when the CO said he thought we might walk over the pass, and perhaps pick up a lift on the other side, down into Pontremoli. I had been worried, as it had been quite impossible to get through either to our HQ in Rome or to ring through to the Bishop's Palace in Pontremoli to explain the CO's delay. As it was, the hour for his interview with the bishop had already passed, but perhaps another could be arranged for the next day, or so we hoped.

In spite of its discomforts, I enjoyed that walk. Halfway up to the pass we stopped at a *casa cantoniera* or state road-keeper's house. Road-keepers were responsible for the upkeep of the roads along a specified beat, and their small, square, red-brick houses are to be seen the length and breadth of Italy. At this one, the keeper's wife kindly invited us in and gave us a drink of water and some hot coffee, for which we were most grateful, for it was already about two o'clock and the going had been heavy. It seemed the head of the pass was not far off, and that was cheering news. After a friendly farewell we took to the road once more, but soon the weather worsened and by the time we reached the top it was sleeting very unpleasantly. At this point a car passed us; it had managed to come up the other side, though it was going to find its descent difficult. The other side faced west and for this reason the thaw was more advanced here and the roads far more navigable, and we passed several cars and trucks laid up at the curb, bogged down by hard snow. The drivers were mostly huddled together rather disconsolately in the cabs of their vehicles, and one or two hailed us and enquired the time or news of conditions on the other side. They seemed to have spent the night in their vehicles, quite cut off from everything. My hair began to hang down, limp and uncomfortable in the drizzle, and I suddenly remembered with horror that I had left behind my hair curlers. The CO had told me I was only to bring one haversack, knowing my propensity for collecting luggage, and in my zeal to comply the vital curlers had been left behind. I would not see them again until Bruno saw fit to drive the Chev on to join us; in the present state of the weather that might be tomorrow, but if there was the slightest worsening, it would doubtless be too bad for Bruno.

We arrived at Montelungo as darkness was setting in, and the long hairpin bends in the road seemed endless and never-ceasing. We came to a *trattoria* with lights in the windows, and so we went in. There was an immediate hush and everyone turned round and stared, quite unashamedly. I was by then quite used to this continental custom, so after a brief stare back, I took off my soaking hat, coat, gloves and scarf and put them on a chair to dry in front of a large stove, where someone obligingly at once made room for us. There had been nothing unfriendly in the staring and before long someone entered into conversation with the CO. One or two partisans soon declared themselves. It soon transpired that they were friends of the major we had met in La Spezia, who had himself captained the partisans in this area. As soon as they discovered that the CO knew him there was quite a stir in the *trattoria*, and before long almost everyone present had joined in the discussion and much reminiscing took place and interesting information came to light. Thanks to these good-hearted people, a lorry driver offered us a lift down into Pontremoli, a distance of about 6 miles. I was more than glad, for my joints were stiff from the unaccustomed exercise and the damp and cold. The journey was finished in comfort, in the cabin of an enormous camion, in which I discovered there are even bunks, for a woman's voice suddenly emerged from a sort of shelf behind the driving seat. I then looked round and saw that there were about four bunks behind the front seat, from which voices would suddenly join in the conversation, for all the world like disembodied spirits.

The camion eventually reached Pontremoli at about 7.30 p.m. and we were obliged to stay there until the next day, at the Albergo Principe kept by a 'helper'. What a cosy stove he had in his restaurant, from which warmth and comfort radiated. The proprietor himself was a kindly, friendly little man and was delighted to have the '*Signor Colonnello*' under his roof. He already knew of the appointment with the bishop, and first thing next morning sent off to find out what had happened; in fact, he took charge of the 'staff' arrangements, for in this delightful personal way things are done – and very satisfactorily done – in Italy. Unfortunately, the bishop was not able to receive the CO that day, as he had been obliged to go out to one of his parishes on urgent business, and as Bruno actually turned up about midday with the Chev, smiling and smirking that he had come in '*macchina*' whereas his boss had walked, we felt that the best thing was to hurry on to La Spezia without further delay.

Major Watson was waiting for the CO very anxiously, as reports of the bad weather had been filtering through. Next day, we set off after a conference with the major and stopped en route at Lucca, where the nuns of the hospital, who had nursed many of our men when it had been a POW hospital, had also hidden some of their charges after the Armistice and connived at their escape. The nuns were paid a sum of money and also given a certificate of thanks, presented to the Mother Superior in the presence of a senior Sister. They were both delighted. The Mother Superior, who spoke good English, gave us coffee and chatted about old times with the CO, who had himself once been a patient under her care. She presented him to the Italian commandant of the hospital, which was now an Italian military one, and he took us round some of the wards. Everything was fresh, clean and airy.

The last port of call was Livorno (Leghorn), and here the CO visited the American Salvage Section with a view to obtaining preferential permits to purchase salvage for helpers.

After that we were soon back in Rome, where a final spurt of work was taking place at the commission's HQ, prior to the closing down of the whole organisation on 31 March. Plans were being made for some form of continuation of the work under the direct auspices of the British Embassy, but as yet nothing had been decided. Meanwhile, hundreds of outstanding claims had yet to be settled and more claims were still coming in, as it takes so long for news from the outer world to reach some distant villages where life might almost have been on a different planet, so remote did they seemed from modern Italy – and yet even in those places British soldiers and others had taken shelter. Doubtless many of them are by now legendary figures and the stories of their escape and concealment will be handed down, gradually more and more embroidered, as part of village folklore; who knows what wonderful tales will be told a hundred years or more hence, when the escape of Private Smith, who was taken in and hidden by Signora Pola and her family, has become a part of local history just as much as incidents from the inter-city wars of the Middle Ages or the Napoleonic invasion?

38

Nearly a Bad End

As far as Policy was concerned, the main work of the commission was completed; all that remained to do was to finish off outstanding claims and lay down the structure of the very small detachment that the War Office, the Treasury and the Foreign Office apparently decided (at an exalted level, of course) between them should stay on in Rome to carry on a further 6 months in order to clear up all outstanding matters – in actual fact even that time did not prove enough and as late as 1948 claims were still being made. However, according to the broadcasts over the Italian wireless and announcements in many Italian papers, notices in mayors' offices and other means of publication, all claims should at the very latest have been made by the end of 1946, and that was already an extension. But in a country where the parish priest of a Tuscan village writes to the CO of the commission, telling him that he is at last trying to arrange for the construction of a road to his village, and inviting him, together with Field Marshal Alexander and General McNarney (formerly US Supreme Commander in Italy), not to mention Mr Winston Churchill, to become honorary members of his road-construction committee, it is certainly too much to expect that claims will not come in late. But the British have a rigid sense of time and D-day for the commission proper was 1 April 1947. After that it became the 'Claims Commission'. All this was, however, still in the melting-pot in February of that year. Once the main lines of the new plan had been worked out, the CO left his second-in-command to go into the details of the organisation and himself concentrated on making more final Italian contacts, thanking the many organisations that had helped us, as well as dealing with a few remaining policy problems, such as the ever-thorny question of salvage and surplus allied transport, which was to be made rather more readily available to helpers than to the man-in-the-street.

One of the CO's trips at this time was to Affile, in the lime-growing hills of Romagna, where the majority of the people are poor and in need of almost everything. I well remember one woman who came to make out her case, saying she had not been paid enough. She was a hearty peasant in a plain long black calico dress, blouse and kerchief, her feet covered in sacking and thong shoes, her hair untidy under her black kerchief, her complexion rather tanned by the sun, but her eyes clear and the general appearance one of health and strength. She treated the CO, the *sindaco* and one or two other leading citizens to a long dramatic tirade on why she deserved more payment and made everyone laugh with her violent gestures and vigorous mode of expression. There was nothing to be done for her, as her case for a claim had already been investigated and she had not given sufficient help to warrant a larger payment (not to her discredit, she had given all that came her way). She received the explanation with great good humour and bore her disappointment like a philosopher. There was no reviling and not a sullen look. The peasants have much to bear, and on the whole they seem to be remarkably good-humoured and singularly lacking in bitterness. But those little overcrowded towns of the Romagna are in need of much – modern hygiene and sanitation, more work, less children, for there are too many mouths to feed, and on the whole better and more progressive administration. It is hardly to be wondered at that the peasants of the far south have at last taken, in some instances, the law into their hands; for resignation does not necessarily go on forever and it may become a fertile soil for

Communists to sow in. Meanwhile the small contribution made by ASC may have helped just a little, by moral encouragement if nothing else. Doubtless the Italian government and the local authorities do what they can and perhaps now that Italy has made such startling progress towards recovery it will be possible for more to be done for these depressed agrarian areas. Goodwill, enthusiasm and diligence are rarely lacking in Italy, the climate is an almost continual ally and all these combined into a spearhead for action, armed and prepared by government backing and financial aid, should produce some really worthwhile amelioration in the lot of the townsfolk and *contadini* of southern Italy.

Tivoli was another place where a small ceremony was held in the local town hall for the distribution of certificates to helpers. Here the mayor had done wonders in leading the people towards reconstruction and recovery: what had been a shambles of rubble and fallen masonry in 1944 was now a neat, clean and attractive main street, with one-storied shopfronts painted fresh pinks and blues. Most of the rubble had been cleared away and the people at the ceremony were tidy and looked well fed and neatly dressed. There was a new spirit in the air – the despair of nearly three years earlier had disappeared and there was confidence and hope on peoples' faces. Italy was rising again: the title of the documentary shown alongside our film *Onore al Merito* was *L'Italia Vivrà Ancora* ('Italy will live again'), and it was coming true. People often said to me when they heard I would soon be returning to England, '*Lei farà della propaganda per l'Italia, Signorina, quando torn' in Inghilterra?*' I always agreed heartily that I would – and as many of my friends can testify, I have kept my promise.

In Parma, in the north, where we also had to go, I again noticed the same spirit of confidence in Italy's future. The Republic was going to be a good thing and Fascism was dead, even if a few diehards were lingering on, and Italy was now one of the democratic powers and a nation to be reckoned with before many more years had passed. The CO called on the *sindaco* of Parma, who greeted him with tears in his eyes, and spoke feelingly of Anglo-Italian co-operation and his friendship for England. It was in Parma that a doctor had been shot by the Germans for treating one of our wounded prisoners in his dispensary. He left a widow and son. There had been many other helpers in this area, and it was in Parma that the seven sons of Farmer Cervi of Gattatico met their heroic end, and Farmer Cervi was later decorated at a public ceremony by the Italian Government.

In Florence there were a few more visits to be paid, among them a call on the chief of the *Carabinieri*, a brigadier general of the corps, to thank him for all the valuable assistance his men throughout Tuscany had rendered to our officers on all occasions. There was a farewell visit to the *sindaco*, Professore Pieracini, an outspoken friend of England, followed by a call on Siena's *Carabinieri* HQ too. On 1 March a ceremony took place for the distribution of certificates at Pontremoli, in Massa, where the bishop, Sismondo, made an impassioned speech. He was so frankly pro-British that I remarked on it to Captain Edgar afterwards, who was doing the liaison work on this occasion, and was told that His Eminence was famed for plain speaking and courage. Thanks to Bishop Sismondo's help during the war, Major Watson had been able to save the town of Pontremoli from destruction by the Allied Forces and had driven the Germans out before the arrival of the Allies. There was great enthusiasm at the Pontremoli presentation ceremony, where the sturdy hill-folk came in their cloaks and thick boots to collect their certificates. A large crowd milled outside the town hall before the CO arrived and again as he drove off, on his way through the mountains, after the ceremony; the celebrations must have continued for the greater part of the day. I was very impressed by the bishop, a tall, imposing figure in his robes of magenta silk, his refined aquiline face alert with good humour and intelligence, and his white hair surmounting eyes of remarkable honesty and penetration. He was indeed the Father of his Flock in that area and they looked to him still, as they had in the dark days of the Occupation, for leadership and guidance.

Another remarkable personality I encountered at this time was Professore Moschowitz of Terni, also a helper – a great

savant and believer in international friendship and understanding. Unfortunately, time was too short and distances
too considerable for all the contacts that had to be made. We
went north once more and paid a brief visit to the mountains,
to Val d'Aosta, to see helpers who had arranged the escape of
many British and Dominion prisoners into Switzerland in 1943.
I rode a mule up the valley, led by a robust *bersagliere* (rifle-
man) in an Alpine hat with trailing feathers. It was not an easy
mode of travel in a tight ATS skirt and must have afforded my
escorts some amusement, but nevertheless they seemed to be
delighted to be photographed in their dashing uniforms. The
CO was taken in a mule-drawn sledge. The air was too misty,
so that we could barely discern the line of the pass, over which
the fugitives from Nazi imprisonment had made a desperate bid
for freedom; the perilous peaks on either side were completely
hidden from view. But we did see several helpers and one of the
places in a hotel where the prisoners had hidden, even when
Gestapo agents were in the village and on the lookout for them.
What a tension there must have been in that small mountain village! Yet all had to appear normal and unconcerned.
The inhabitants had many yarns to tell to while away the long
winter evenings, as they clustered with their beer-mugs round
the porcelain stove in the inn-parlour.

On one of our last visits in the north I lived through a highly
unpleasant experience. I began to feel ill in the car between Milan
and Verona and when we came to Verona felt so bad that I was
helped, almost fainting, into an Italian restaurant by the proprietor. He rose to the occasion magnificently and produced a coffee
cup full of vinegar, which he made me both sniff and swallow,
and so restored me more or less to consciousness. But back in
the car I became worse again, and on arrival in Padua had to be
rushed to the MO in a collapsed condition. The MO examined
me and found nothing wrong beyond general fatigue from travelling. I was useless for work, so the CO spent the afternoon in
GHQ and I in the room of a girlfriend from the SSAFA, nursing
the most appalling headache imaginable.

We left for Milan again at about 5.30 p.m., but once again the attacks started, more violent now. I could hardly breathe as they came on, I was losing all the strength in my joints, and had red and blue spots in front of my eyes. To crown all this, I was now becoming delirious and the CO told me much later, rather grimly, that I had addressed the German driver in his own language and told him, '*Ich liebe dich*' ('I love you')! It is to be hoped that over the noise of the engine he heard nothing. At Gardone I felt the end had come, but the CO was very patient, and by speaking sharply to me and ordering me to pull myself together, he somehow kept me from going under. At Verona, we stopped again, and this time a waiter from the same restaurant told us he had a brother who was a porter at the hospital (thanks be to the close family ties of Italy!) and he guided us thence. After a whispered conversation with his brother, we were admitted into a small casualty department, where two doctors examined me on an operating table and prescribed various pills and an injection, which was administered in private by a medical orderly. He was aged about 70 and looked just like Hindenburg, complete with long drooping moustache.

The doctors declared I was suffering from some form of *intossicazione*, but just what they could not determine, although they wanted to ascribe it to alcohol or tobacco – but I indignantly assured them that I neither drank nor smoked to excess. They catechised me as to what I had taken during the past 24 hours, and shook their heads rather severely when I admitted to two *small* Martinis the day before, when we had been meeting an important functionary in Milan. While I was having my injection, the next patient was being attended to, a woman who had some form of cut in her head, perhaps from a motor accident, and she howled and screamed quite bloodcurdlingly – so I was glad when it was all over for me. But the doctors said I was not to travel further that night. The CO was not too pleased about the necessary change of plan, but he was very worried about me, not relishing, as may be expected, the idea of explaining to the commanding AT in Italy that I had passed out for no known reason between Milan and Padua. We therefore had to find accommodation at a small hotel, and next morning I was much better, though still rather 'nervy'.

Meanwhile the driver had discovered the cause of the trouble. The exhaust pipe was broken, he explained, and furthermore there was a hole in the boot just under the left side of the seat where I had been sitting, and carbon monoxide gas had been pouring in and up just beneath me. When he had opened the boot that morning a cloud of it nearly knocked him out, though in fact it is neither visible nor has it a smell, which is why no-one thought of it the day before. But Heinz had known a man killed by it when servicing a car and so doubtless I had been lucky; both he and the CO then admitted that they also had endured terrible headaches the previous day, and one could not but feel that if the driver had been as affected as I was, our joint fate might have been disastrous. After our return to Rome, a student friend of mine told me it would be about a year before I was really over the phenomenon and so it proved, though I still hate enclosed or stuffy atmospheres to this day. The remarkable thing about the Italian doctors was that they would not take a fee, so I sent the hospital a small sum afterwards and a letter of thanks, also explaining the real cause of the trouble. In reply I received a courteous and charming acknowledgement.

39

A Rivederci!

At the end of March, the CO had to make his final visit to Padua to make arrangements for the closing down of the commission and the launching of the new, small abbreviated unit which was to take on ASC's job and, it was hoped, finish it by the end of September 1947. The CO himself had decided to resign and leave the GSO II to carry on. Among his team, the latter was not always the best or most suitable man for the job – nearly everyone wanted to stay in Rome and there was the keenest competition – but unfortunately a few were allowed to go who would have been of greater value than some of the non-Italian speakers who remained. However, '*maleesh*' ('never mind') – whatever shortcomings there may have been in the commission, either at its inception, in its heyday or in its decline, I am sure in general it accomplished much in the cause of friendship and understanding between Italy and the Allies.

Meanwhile, some officers and men had already been released, and others were going. There were farewell parties, many handshakes, much writing down of addresses, and doubtless not a few regrets.

As for me, I was sorry to be leaving Italy, for the new unit would have no vacancies for AT officers, but I had not been home for nearly two years. Having never done purely admin work in the ATS, and having always been one of those rather suspect persons, an intelligence staff officer, it gave me an inferiority complex every time I mixed with ATS admin officers and I felt only half one of them. I therefore wanted to change over to admin and gain experience and confidence in that direction. The head AT at GHQ was both surprised and delighted when I told her I wanted to change to admin and furthermore attend a refresher course at Windsor after my disembarkation leave. Most people wanted to do the opposite. And so I signed on until 1948, and I felt that that would give me time to think things over, and also see how the service was going to turn out – for plans were afoot then for short-term commissions, and even a permanent service, which later of course materialised.

And so I was to forsake drill and go back to England, to battle-dress and the barrack square. I did not know how it would seem after three years overseas. And it was with a heavy heart that I said '*A rivederci*'* (not '*Addio*'**) to so many kind Italian friends, including Irene, the maid who looked after me at the Continentale, Pietro my cheerful room porter, the little man in the vestibule, who in spite of a lame leg was always smiling and cheerful, the dear Signorine Giulia, my little plump dressmaker in Rome who had transformed one of my service dresses so miraculously into a smart black costume trimmed with corduroy, and many other people of all sorts and kinds, in Rome and elsewhere. I suppose Italy left her mark on most of the forces who were there at some time or another, even on those who were apparently least receptive to her influence; others, like myself, have lost their hearts to that country and its people, who are so generous and gay. Even the most Philistine cannot but appreciate to some extent such a wealth of art and natural beauty, or be quite insensible to the vital life of this country and its people.

- FINIS -

* *A rivederci* (See you again!) from Italian *arrivederci* (Goodbye).
** *Addio* (Farewell, Adieu).

The Author

Lucy de Burgh, née Addey, born 1919

*H*er father, William Fielding Addey, was born in 1873 and brought up a Unitarian, one of the many Protestant sects famed for their strict morality, hard work and frugality. After being schooled at home, learning French and German, he attended Hanover University to study philosophy and also learnt to ride, fence and sing. He was an excellent pianist and would teach his daughters to play. Not until he was over 40 did he start studying medicine at University College London. There his friends included A.E. Housman and Havelock Ellis, the pioneer of sexual psychology, later a patient in Suffolk, some of whose books his daughter still has.

Addey was the son of a successful cotton merchant in Manchester who died when his only child was aged 4. The closest relatives and childhood friends from her father's family were second cousins John Addey, later to be a gunner brigadier, and his sister Catherine. John's son is a Queen's Messenger and Catherine's grandson is the 5th Lord Acton.

During the First World War Dr Addey served in the RAMC and met his future wife, Edith Wilson, in the casualty station at Liancourt, France. She was a nurse who came from a family of Aberdeenshire farmers, all of whose children became professionals. The only brother, Ronald, was a military physician, killed in a motorbike accident. There are many photographs of Ronald holidaying with the author and her sister in childhood and teenage years.

Very prominent among her photographs is a very beautiful little girl, Barbadee Knight, her closest childhood friend who would later marry Captain Sir Anthony Meyer, Bt, Scots Guards, after he recovered from serious wounds incurred in the 1944 invasion of France. Meyer later became a diplomat and Conservative MP. He earned celebrity as a critic of Margaret Thatcher, particularly when he stood against her for the leadership of the Party in 1992, precipitating her downfall.

In Ipswich, where Dr Addey went to open a private practice after the First World War, he was an unusual man. Atheist, republican and member of the Liberal Party, he stood out in the conservative and hierarchical Suffolk of the 1920s. However, this did not make him enemies, because his charm and empathy appear to have endeared him to rich and poor alike. As did many physicians in those days, he charged the rich high fees that he might serve the poor for nothing. As late as 1982 when his grandson was seeking adoption as parliamentary candidate for Suffolk Coastal, an elderly man rose from the audience to say, in Suffolk dialect, that everybody should vote for Dr Addey's grandson because the doctor was 'the most wonderful man; he would help the poor until he was exhausted and then give them money to buy soup.' As a child Lucy Addey was often taken to Ipswich Hospital, where her father was consultant and on the board, 'to cheer up the patients'.

Both daughters attended first Ipswich High School and then St Felix, Southwold, of which their most potent recollection is of playing cricket five times a day. From an early age Lucy and Elizabeth Addey were imbued with a strong sense of public service. The Addeys were unusual for those days in that both girls were expected to seek careers in which they might serve their community and their country before considering their own desires.

Lucy Addey went up to St Anne's College Oxford in 1941 to take the degree in German and French. She was fluent in both,

as her father had sent her to board with families in both countries and in Switzerland. Her best friends were Dorothy Folkes,
daughter of Nottinghamshire farmers, who married fellow student Robin Chadburn of a Lincolnshire brewing family, and
Jean Asquith, who married Tony Barber, later Chancellor of the
Exchequer. Lucy Addey was active in the Labour Club and regularly sang the Red Flag to infuriate the Tories – whose chairman
was Jean Asquith. This did not damage their friendship, which,
with many others, continued all her life. Affection also developed
between her and the daughter of refugees from Berlin. She taught
English to Berlin professor of dentistry, Dr Fritz Munz, in return
for German conversation with his family of a boy and two girls,
of which one, Hilde, has been a lifelong friend with whom she
continues to correspond in German several times a month by
email.

With England fighting an epic struggle against totalitarianism
in 1940 her parents encouraged their elder daughter to volunteer
for the Army, where her languages might come in useful; her
younger sister Elizabeth would later become a district nurse in
the new National Health Service.

She started her army work on the Atrocities File, for MI9/19,
recording the most vile activities of the Nazi troops as they
slaughtered their way around Europe. Reports came in many languages and many of those working with her were multilingual
refugees. They also included psychiatrists; the work took place in
Latimer House, Buckinghamshire, where captured German officers were interrogated and also secretly recorded talking with each
other. She has never spoken about this work – in fact her book
has no Military Intelligence detail – because she was very conscious of the Official Secrets Act.

Keen to get away from her ghoulish activities she leapt at a
foreign posting which took her first to Algeria – she has vivid
memories of the plague of locusts – and then with our invad-
ing army to Italy. There she was engaged on strategic planning
in the Royal Palace of Caserta, headquarters of Field Marshal
Alexander. She witnessed battles, including Cassino; she saw

the Occupation of Rome by Allied forces. But mostly what she remembers is the poverty and destruction around her, the awful detritus of war. Because of this, for much of her later life, no matter how difficult her own circumstances, she worked for the alleviation of suffering, in particular through Save the Children Fund.

These are some of the things she has said in recent years:

Wherever I went there were beggars, stick-thin children without shoes or shirts, crying out for anything to eat. People made fires in the ruins of their homes to try to keep their babies and their grandparents alive.

When we arrived in Rome we gave a reception for the important people of the city. They arrived in beautiful clothes sagging over emaciated bodies. They arrived with large handbags; while the Allied officers fasted and pretended not to see, the snacks we had put out were shovelled into those handbags to be taken away to feed families.

Every night outside the soldiers' barracks hundreds of women queued, from teenagers to grandmothers, selling themselves for a meal to keep their loved ones alive.

As a specialist on atrocities, Junior Commander Addey knew very well what the Head of the SS and his associates had done; yet when she was with Himmler's wife and daughter after their capture, she registered only awed pity. When asked to tell about the encounter, she said:

Mrs Himmler and her daughter were ragged. I remember most the fear and hunger in their eyes. The Tommies jeered as they made them run a gauntlet to the lavatory. Mrs Himmler was so thin and frightened and so pathetic. She was laughed at and sneered at by our soldiers; when I gave her daughter some biscuits, mother and daughter both wept.

After her move from Caserta to Rome, Addey applied to join the Allied Screening Commission, notwithstanding that this required a drop in rank. As the Allied forces took over larger areas of Italy and in particular once the German forces had surrendered, the Commission was researching the fate of Allied escapees and agents in Italy and Austria and the roles of the local population in their survival or otherwise. She thought this more interesting than remaining at HQ, and a better use for her languages, for her Italian was now quite fluent.

The Commanding Officer, Colonel (Hugo) Graham de Burgh, had himself led the largest ever break-out from a prison camp, when 600 men incarcerated at Fontanellato, near Parma, had managed to avoid the Germans entraining them to Poland by escaping to the hills and breaking up into small groups. De Burgh took the route to Switzerland, surviving a hazardous trek over the Monte Rosa.

Some of the activities of the ASC are described in the current book, and there is a more detailed account in Roger Absalom's *A Strange Alliance*. J/Cmdr Addey worked with the ASC until its disbandment in 1948 and the retirement of its CO, whom she married, on 14 April 1946 in the Orange Street Congregational Church.

Dr Addey was opposed to his daughter's desire to marry Colonel de Burgh. He did not admire the '*erste Gesellschaft*' as he jokingly referred to the nobility, but he also would say, 'They are always ready to die for us, and I admire them for that.' He himself passed away, exhausted from his immense efforts in the war, in 1947. In much reduced circumstances, his widow retired to a small house in Felixstowe and the daughters had to fend for themselves.

Mrs de Burgh, as we must now call her, had a short married life. After wounds, serious maltreatment in one prison camp and illness following his escape, her husband suffered from what would today be called Post-Traumatic Stress Disorder and was increasingly unwell. After a succession of short-term jobs, she was offered a position as a teacher in Cyprus and, once there, found a post for her husband. As she waited for him to join her, the news came that he was dead. She remained in Cyprus from 1952–55, taking her son on trips by fishing boat and local bus to Nazareth and Cana, site of Our Lord's first miracle. She returned to teach in London (at Haverstock Hill, the 'Eton of the Left') and in Oxford, where she made her home and many new friends in the refugee community, through the Munzes. In 1956 she took a job in Rome at the Parioli International School (now St Michael's School of Florence), which gave her son Hugo a free place.

As they had in England, they lived in a succession of rented rooms until she took a small flat on the Aventine Hill in 1959, next door to a German couple (formerly of the German Army Film Unit) who had hidden in Italy posing as Dutch refugees after the Nazi surrender; their two sons became Hugo's playmates. In Italy she wasted not a single free day, taking her child by bus or third-class train all over central Italy to see the beautiful buildings and art and hear the operas, delighting in Italians' friendship and reading deeply in Dante, Leopardi, Pirandello and the great literary geniuses of Italy who began to rival Goethe and Schiller for her affections.

Concerned for her child's future in an impoverished country with few opportunities for foreigners, she returned to England in 1961 where she took two jobs teaching three languages. She settled near her mother, who was by then declining rapidly, in Suffolk. With the financial help of a former student of her father's, she and her mother bought their present house in Woodbridge. Apart from three years lecturing in Oxford, she remained in Suffolk, teaching A-Level languages, tutoring at a Boys' Borstal and giving her spare time to Save the Children Fund (for which she was later awarded an MBE) until her stroke in 2003. In September that year she had gone on one of her regular visits to see her lifelong friend Iselle Simmonot at Trouville, where she suffered first a heart attack and then a stroke. After some months in hospital in France and in St Thomas' London she has lived first near her son's family in Bermondsey and since then in the Royal Star and Garter, Richmond.

In 2009 a party was held for her ninetieth birthday in the Royal Star and Garter, music provided by a band of the Coldstream

Guards. Aside from her sister's children and her son's family, present were friends – or the children and grandchildren of friends – from Ipswich, St Felix, Oxford, Cyprus and Woodbridge days.

The present book was found among many letters and papers from the war period, long forgotten during a busy subsequent life. Mary Hodge edited it down from an original manuscript of 150,000 words (now in the Imperial War Museum) and the author's son proposed it for publication, with the essential help of the appeal chairman of the MSMT, Vanni Treves, appeal chairman of the Monte San Martino Trust. The Imperial War Museum's head of publishing Elizabeth Bowers worked hard to arrange its publication and Jo de Vries of The History Press has brought it to fruition with enthusiasm and dispatch.